ISIS

A BOB DYLAN ANTHOLOGY

First edition published in 2001 by Helter Skelter Publishing
Reprinted 2002

4 Denmark Street, London WC2H 8LL

All rights reserved
Cover design by Chris Wilson
Typesetting by Caroline Walker
Printed in Great Britain by The Cromwell Press, Trowbridge

A CIP record for this book is available from the British Library

ISBN 1-900924-29-3

ISIS

A BOB DYLAN ANTHOLOGY

edited by

Derek Barker

Helter Skelter Publishing

To Tracy
"Without Your Love I'd Be Nowhere At All"

THANKS AND ACKNOWLEDGMENTS

This book is the result of sixteen years writing about Bob Dylan and as such it would be impossible to thank all those who have contributed throughout the years. However, the editor would like to make special reference to –

For their contributions to this book –
Al Aronowitz, Mark Carter, Martin Carthy, Chris Cooper, Peter Cox, John *Stringbean* Cumming, Derek Davies, Alan Davis, César Díaz, Michael Goldman, Peter Higginson, Institute of Popular Music at Liverpool University, Mickey Jones, James Joughin, Patricia Jungwirth, Dave Kelly, Paddy Ladd, C.P. Lee, Robert Levinson, Jacques Levy, Scott Marshall, Andrew Muir, Roger Pulman, C.D Smith, Peter Smith, Elizabeth Thomson, Nick Train, Dave Whitaker, Janet Woodward, Matthew Zuckerman.

Front cover illustration –
Oil painting by Brian West. This Interpretation depicts Bob Dylan performing *'Isis'* during the 1975 Rolling Thunder Revue tour. Information regarding Brian West paintings at – www.dylanart.co.uk

For past help and assistance above and beyond the call of duty –
John Baldwin, Mark Carver-Smith – 'cause he'll only complain if I don't mention him, Dave Dingle, Alan Fraser, Michael Gray, Mel Gamble, Peter Goodsell, the late John Green, Patrice Hamilton, John Hume, My Back Pages, Mr. Smith, Phil & Ali Townsend.

Works that have been consulted extensively during the completion of this book –
Dave Engel, *Dylan In Minnesota*; Clinton Heylin, *Bob Dylan – Behind The Shades: Take Two* and *A Life In Stolen Moments*; Anthony Scaduto, *Bob Dylan*; Robert Shelton, *No Direction Home*; and to the late John Bauldie for his ground-breaking work with *The Telegraph*.

Extraordinary thanks to –
Sean Body, my editor at *Helter Skelter Publishing,* and to Ian Woodward for his constant help and advice during the thousands of hours we have spent discussing Dylan. To each and every one of the ISIS Magazine readers world-wide, without whom ISIS would not exist. To Jeff Rosen at *Special Rider Music* for his patience and cooperation over many years and to the main man, Bob Dylan, whose words and music make this world gone wrong a better place in which to live. May he *keep on keepin' on.*

Photo credits –
1969 – Isle of Wight, UK © Dennis Grice
1976 – Houston Texas, USA © Watt M. Casey
1986 – New York USA © John Hume
1996 – Lollipop Fest, Sweden © Roland Hansson
1999 – Murcia, Spain © Andrea Orland
2000 – Florence, Italy © Giulio Molfese
2000 – Zurich, Switzerland © John Hume

Permissions –
The author and the publisher wish to express their sincere thanks to the copyright owners listed below for their permission to quote material written and composed by Bob Dylan. Many of the quotations contained in this book are taken from the officially printed lyrics contained in *Lyrics 1962-1985,* published by Jonathan Cape, London, 1987, and may differ from those sung by Bob Dylan.

Talkin' New York © 1962, 1965 by Duchess Music Corporation
It Ain't Me Babe © 1964 by Warner Bros. Inc. renewed 1992 by Special Rider Music
Mr Tambourine Man © 1964, 1965 by Warner Bros. Inc. renewed 1992 by Special Rider Music
The Lonesome Death of Hattie Carroll © 1964, 1966 by Warner Bros. Inc. renewed 1992 by Special Rider Music
It's Alright, Ma (I'm Only Bleeding) ©1965 by Warner Bros. Inc. renewed 1993 by Special Rider Music
Desolation Row © 1965 by Warner Bros. Inc. renewed 1993 by Special Rider Music
She Belongs To Me © 1965 by Warner Bros. Inc. renewed 1993 by Special Rider Music
Highway 61 Revisited © 1965 by Warner Bros. Inc. renewed 1993 by Special Rider Music
Fourth Time Around © 1966 by Dwarf Music
Visions of Johanna © 1966 by Dwarf Music
The Ballad Of Frankie Lee And Judas Priest © 1968 by Dwarf Music
George Jackson © 1971 by Ram's Horn Music
Tell Me Mama © 1971, 1973 by Dwarf Music
Forever Young © 1973, 1974 by Ram's Horn Music
Never Say Goodbye © 1973, 1974 by Ram's Horn Music
Idiot Wind © 1973, 1974 by Ram's Horn Music
Shelter From The Storm © 1974, 1975 by Ram's Horn Music
Hurricane (with Jacques Levy) © 1975 by Ram's Horn Music
Romance In Durango (with Jacques Levy) © 1975, 1976 by Ram's Horn Music
Black Diamond Bay (with Jacques Levy) © 1975, 1976 by Ram's Horn Music
Changing Of The Guards © 1978 by Special Rider Music
We Better Talk This Over © 1978 by Special Rider Music
Senor © 1978 by Special Rider Music
Where Are You Tonight? (Journey Through Dark Heat) © 1978 by Special Rider Music
No Time To Think © 1978 by Special Rider Music
New Pony © 1978 by Special Rider Music
Gonna Change My Way Of Thinking © 1979 by Special Rider Music
Precious Angel © 1979 by Special Rider Music
Saving Grace © 1980 by Special Rider Music

"The songs are there. They exist by themselves, just waiting for someone to write them down. If I didn't do it, someone else would."
Bob Dylan, 1962

"My real message? Keep a good head and always carry a light bulb."
Bob Dylan, 1965

"My songs are just talking to myself. Maybe that's an egotistical thing to say, but that's what it is. I have no responsibility to anybody except myself."
Bob Dylan, 1965

"I have no idea how much I make and I don't want to ever find out."
Bob Dylan, 1965

"The world don't need me. Christ, I'm only five feet ten. The world could get along fine without me. Don'cha know, everybody dies. It don't matter how important you think you are."
Bob Dylan, 1965

"God, I'm glad I'm not me."
Bob Dylan, 1965

"I don't break the rules, because I don't see any rules to break."
Bob Dylan, 1966

"I do know what my songs are about... some are about four minutes; some are about five, and some, believe it or not, are about eleven or twelve."
Bob Dylan, 1966

"I didn't create Bob Dylan. Bob Dylan has always been here, always was."
Bob Dylan, 1978

"People can learn everything about me through my songs, if they know where to look."
Bob Dylan, 1990

"My songs are different than anybody else's songs."
Bob Dylan, 1997

"To me, music either expresses ideas of liberty, or it's made under the oppression of dictatorship."
Bob Dylan, 2001

CONTENTS

EDITOR'S INTRODUCTION

"Sixteen years. Lotta water under the bridge, a lotta other stuff too."

'ISIS – A Bob Dylan Anthology,' has been compiled in the hope of satisfying the needs of both the casual fan and Dylan obsessive alike. It is a best-of selection of essays and interviews, spanning sixteen years and one hundred issues of a magazine devoted solely to the life and work of Bob Dylan. This material, together with some previously unpublished pieces – commissioned especially for the book – is arranged in chronological order. The resulting volume can be read from cover to cover as a potted biography, or more appropriately, simply dipped into and read as individual essays.

An enthusiastic music lover and an avid concertgoer, my first chance to see Bob Dylan in concert was in the spring of 1978. Dylan had last visited mainland Britain in 1966 – I would have been twelve years of age at the time – I liked his music and even owned a few of his albums. This surely would be my one and only chance to see him in concert and to tick Bob Dylan off my long list of artists seen.

Finally, the day arrived – Tuesday, June 20, 1978. The venue was Earls Court, London, and front-row seats were luckily the order of the day. We talked casually until the house lights dimmed and the big backing band – eight musicians and three female singers – came on. Following an instrumental warm-up tune, Dylan took a British stage for the first time in twelve years. The greatest lyric-smith of our time opened his set with *'Love Her With a Feeling,'* a cover version of a song by an old blues man named Tampa Red! That was my first experience with the perversity of Bob Dylan.

Within minutes of his arrival on stage, I was completely captivated. To this day, I'm uncertain how to define the word charisma, but whatever it is, Dylan had it in truckloads. To say that concert changed my life will probably sound melodramatic. Nonetheless, it's true. The man and his music have consumed much of my life since that June evening more than twenty-three years ago.

I started ISIS in September 1985, to communicate with my ever-growing circle of friends. People sent snippets of Dylan news, which I would collate and send back out by way of a newsletter. This *free* exchange of information continued for more than two years, until the sheer volume of participants and news made it impossible to continue in this vein. During those two years, the five-page newsletter had grown to more than 30 pages and by default had become a magazine. The only option left open to me was to have it professionally printed with a cover price. The rest, as they say, is history.

Why have I devoted sixteen years of my life to running ISIS, when psychiatric help is readily available? Simple: I believe that Bob Dylan is, without doubt, the most important songwriter/performer of the twentieth century. I also believe that in the future, his verse and prose, which transcend popular music, will be acknowledged as the equal of anything created by Keats or Shakespeare.

Like so many fans I have followed with great interest the numerous twists and turns of his extraordinary career. Unaffected by changing trends, he continues undaunted to plough his own unwavering furrow and I continue to follow the plough because I believe there is still much to reap.

There are many in the mainstream music press that would have us believe that Bob Dylan is a spent force creatively, a ghost from another era, and apart from the critically acclaimed album *"Time Out Of Mind"* there is some justification for this assumption.

Many of us who have witnessed Dylan's performance art over the last four decades have only recently begun to see what Dylan has always known, that he is first and foremost, a *performance artist*. When in 1965, he told one perplexed interviewer that he was just a *"song and dance man,"* it seems he wasn't kidding!

In concert, Dylan is unlike almost any other *popular* musician – outside perhaps the world of jazz – in that his performance art changes nightly. The object of his concert performances is not to faithfully reproduce his recorded works, but to continually reinvent them. Sometimes these new interpretations fall short of the mark, but if you are fortunate enough to be in attendance on a night when all the component parts come together, you will witness an unparalleled creative genius.

This book is about a living artist and *we* are most fortunate to be living at the same time as that artist. The longevity of ISIS Magazine is a testimony to the transcendency of its subject. Long may he continue to paint his masterpiece…

Derek Barker, May 5, 2001

THE ROBERT SHELTON MINNESOTA TRANSCRIPTS
INTERVIEW WITH ABE AND BEATTY ZIMMERMAN
Conducted by Robert Shelton

Introductory Note by Ian Woodward

Since Issue 86 in 1999, ISIS has been printing *"The Robert Shelton Minnesota Transcripts,"* taken from a series of interviews conducted by Shelton in preparation for his Dylan biography, *No Direction Home.* Over the years, there have been several Bob Dylan biographies but *No Direction Home* is unique in a number of ways.

First, Shelton played a significant role in the story, having been the writer of the September 1961 *New York Times* article which helped boost Dylan's career at a crucial stage. Shelton was around the Greenwich Village scene from the late fifties to the late sixties, living on Waverley Place. He was present when some of the notable events in Dylan's life took place. This gave *No Direction Home* a special insight but it came at a price. Some say that Shelton was too close, lacking the necessary detachment. This is arguable but few would dispute that, once the two Roberts had left New York City, *No Direction Home* becomes less illuminating.

Second, Dylan actively supported the Shelton project by agreeing to give interviews. As far as can be established, Shelton began work on the biography in 1965. The interview with Dylan took place quite early in the process, on March 12 and 13, 1966. It can be found – at the end of Chapter nine of *No Direction Home.* Shelton undertook other – as yet unpublished – interviews with Dylan, both before and after 1966; there was one at the Lion's Head in Greenwich Village in 1964 and another at the Henry Hudson Hotel in New York on May 13, 1971.

Third, Dylan's family and friends knew that he was supporting Shelton's project. In one case – that of English folk singer Martin Carthy and his then-wife Dorothy – a handwritten note from Dylan survives:

" Martin & Dorothy, This man is an old friend here – he is happening right now to be a reporter – unlike the people from Disk Weekly & Melody Maker etc, he is on a different assignment – be nice to him – you can freely talk about me if he asks you &

everything will be printed – there will be no editing on his story – Love, Bob."

It is possible that Dylan wrote similar notes to his Minnesotan acquaintances. In May 1966, Shelton went there to conduct the interviews, which form the basis of *"The Robert Shelton Minnesota Transcripts"* appearing in ISIS Magazine. During this visit, Shelton met Dylan's family. We know this because there is a letter, dated June 13, 1966, from Robert Shelton to *"Mr and Mrs Z. and David,"* expressing thanks for *"your hospitality"* and *"a memorable visit."* However, there is no evidence that Shelton interviewed family members at this time.

In May 1968, Shelton returned to Minnesota and did interview Dylan's parents. This is the clearest possible indication of Dylan's continuing support for the Shelton biography. The interview took place in the family home in Hibbing. What follows is based not on the actual tape recordings but on Shelton's typed transcript, which is in two parts.

The first part is twenty-six pages of double-spaced typing on foolscap paper; it is labelled *"TAPE IV"* and headed *"Side One."* After twenty pages, the tape index number *"324"* is noted and it says, *"END OF SIDE ONE"* and *"Pickup Side 2."*

The second part is a further twenty-seven pages of double-spaced typing on foolscap paper but in two different typefaces. Like the first part, it is labelled *"TAPE IV"* but there are no tape index numbers in the heading, only during the course of the text. The interview may have been longer but, if so, no more material has yet been located.

Although, as one would expect, Shelton employs a question and answer format, this is not used throughout. The text develops into a conversation. There are disjunctions in the narrative flow; the subject matter changes abruptly and without explanation. Sometimes, this is because the participants are looking at artefacts – photo albums, newspaper and magazine clippings, record collections and so on – and their comments move to something else which comes to hand. Without those artefacts before us, the conversation is less easy to follow but still fascinating.

As far as we at ISIS are aware, this is the only interview ever given by Abram Zimmerman and the only full interview given by Beatty Zimmerman. Obviously, Shelton drew on this material in *No Direction Home.* What follows, unique as it is in this format, is an edited part of the transcript. It appears with the agreement of Elizabeth Thomson, acting on behalf of Robert Shelton's sisters, and of Mike Brocken, previously with the Institute of Popular Music at the University of Liverpool. Shelton spent the last part of his career in Britain. Though many of his papers went to the Experience Music Project in the States, some were lodged at Liverpool University. There is some overlap between the two archives.

As one might expect, Dylan's parents come over as loving and proud but also a little defensive, possibly even misleading at times. Dylan was protective of his privacy and had likely instilled, in family members, his own wariness of press intrusion. Moreover, at times, Dylan was distant from his family, not just geographically but in other ways, too. For example, at the time of his July 1968 motorcycle accident, his parents contacted Shelton for news. When Dylan was on tour, their contact was through his management office. This could have continued when he stopped touring. Calls were not always returned. Also Dylan's relationship with his father, in particular, had been strained for some time. This is the background to these interview extracts. More speculatively, it is also possible that Abe Zimmerman was not well at the time of the interview – May 1968, as he died of a heart attack soon after, on June 5, 1968.

Beatty Zimmerman remarried in the early seventies, outlived her second husband and died on January 25, 2000.

Bob's Mom & Dad – Hibbing, May 1968.

R.S: I would like to know some things about your family. Where were you born? What the immediate members of your family were like? What your childhood was like? Was there anything comparable in your dreams, or aspirations to what Bob did? Let's us take them one at a time – you were born in Superior?

Dad: No, I was born in Duluth. In 1911... I went to school there. In those days, you were just required to pass, which everybody did. We were all from immigrant parents, everybody worked when they were seven years old...you sold papers or shine shoes, because that was the thing that was done, and you didn't know of anyone who wasn't doing anything like this. All your friends were doing this. Then you grew up, and tried to play ball, athletics were the big thing. You had to amuse yourself with games, because there was no television, no radio. Like any other town, we did what was common. If you were younger, you played hide and seek, and as you got older, you played baseball – sand lot – differently than you do now, because you played over the rocks and bottles.

R.S: When did your parents come from the old country?

Dad: My parents came in 1907. They came from Odessa, Russia. They came to Duluth because other people from Odessa had come to Duluth. You always settled where you knew somebody...My father did what everybody did then – he peddled.

R.S: What was his trade in Odessa?

Dad: He had the shoe factory. His name implies – the word Zimmerman – RS: He pronounced it Tsimmerman – means shoemaker but he was not a shoemaker, he had a very substantial business. Like everybody else, he fled from the Czar. The Jews were leaving fast because of the pogroms and everything. They lived in the city proper. My mother used to tell me how beautiful it was. Anyway, they came here and there were five boys and one girl in the family. My father's name was Zigman and my mother's name was Anna. He and my mother became citizens early; they didn't stop off on the east coast they came right here. My father came first and my mother came maybe six months later. My eldest brother and sister were born in Odessa[1].

There were enough in the family working at all times to bring in some money but nobody really owned anything. My dad was peddling materials – cloth goods – from farm to farm with a horse and buggy. That was a trade. When you didn't have any other business, or couldn't perform a trade, you went from house to house. All the relatives were in peddling in different areas, in rural sections, house to house. Then he finally mastered the language better and got a job in a department store as a shoe salesman. It was called The Fair Department Store.

R.S: What about your mother's family? Also from Odessa?

Dad: Yeah, her sisters also came to Minnesota, to Duluth. In 1918, one sister moved to Arizona because she was consumptive.

...We all sold papers, before school and after school. We lived right across from the high school in Duluth, right near Central High. It was also half a block from the Washington elementary school.

R.S: Was this any sort of ghetto?

Dad: – Emphatically – No.

Dad: It was all peoples. In fact, the area we lived in was predominately Scandinavian, a few Jewish families here and there, but there was no ghetto there. There was a section in Duluth, they called it 'Up On The Hill,' that was divided equally between Polish and Jewish families. They were small but this is where all the fruit peddlers would work. This was Ninth Street, a pretty street, in fact, I used to feel almost guilty sometimes not living in the area. We spoke Yiddish in the house, like everybody else. My whole family spoke Yiddish. I didn't know any Jewish home that didn't speak Yiddish.

R.S: What did your brothers do?

Dad: I have only one younger brother, the rest are older. I can't remember all the things they did, but none of them were in any profession. My older brother, in the plush days of Duluth, ran a fleet of private cabs. That was in the early twenties. During the depression years, there was maybe only one or two of us that were working, which was enough, because, at the prices, you didn't have to make too much to survive. Rents were cheap and food was practically given away. All you had to have was a few dollars and you couldn't carry home enough food for that. – R.S.: He makes the American depression sound like the greatest thing that ever happened – On Lake Avenue, which was the house across from the school, we lived in the upper storey. As I recall, it was a five-roomed house. I also recall getting our first telephone, which was quite an exciting thing because we didn't know who to call, because no-one else we knew had a 'phone. That was about 1920, when I was about eight or nine years old.

R.S: Was there any music or writing interests in your family?

Dad: I remember the coal stove for heating in the living room. You had to chop wood and bring up fuel and do chores. Like everybody else, my parents were thrilled to be in America. In America, the land of their dreams. From this house, we moved into a big nine-roomed house with two bathrooms, which, in those days, was quite a thing. They had bath tubs too, not like the other house we lived in. I was about thirteen then. Those were the days when you thought that this was how it was going to be forever – we never anticipated the depression. I've never forgot that I was going to pay my mother's way to New York to see her sister. This was the Fall of 1929. I agreed to it, I was working for Standard Oil at the time – I lied about my age to get the job. I worked for two months and I already felt I could obligate myself to pay for her trip. I was an office boy, who started off at sixteen, then I was laid off and I didn't know how to tell my mother, so she went anyway. Fortunately, they called me back to work in two weeks. My first job at Standard Oil paid $60.00 a month but, when I finally worked myself up to $100.00 a month, I got cut back to $90.00 because of the depression. It was a six day week. I stayed with the firm until we moved to Hibbing. I was with Standard Oil from 1928 or 1929 until 1946. No, I'm wrong. In 1946, I had polio, we moved here in 1947. During the war years, I had many offers for jobs, but I couldn't leave or else I would get drafted. During the polio epidemic, I only stayed one week in the hospital, because they didn't have the equipment. I'll never forget coming home, I had to crawl up the front steps like an ape. This was the house where Bobby was born but it was worth it to get home. I stayed out of work for six months. Everybody we knew was very nice and the Company was very nice. They told me to come back when I could. I came out of it, I only had one bad leg, where I have lost the muscles, the other leg is a little weak. When I got married in 1934, I was already making $100.00 a month. I didn't know anybody that was making that much money. We lived high on $100.00 a month.

R.S: How did you meet Beatty?

Dad: We met at a party down in Duluth. She came for a New Year party. That was the beginning of 1932. The reason she liked me was because I had a job. She didn't know anyone else who had a job.

Mom: That worked in those days. My father was Ben D. Stone. I had the pick of the crop. He was the lucky one. You must remember I always had a car. It was my father's but it was like mine. It was a four-door Essex. My dad said *"You learn to drive, I'll teach you."* I said *"You don't have to."* I got in the car and drove away. I just had watched him a few times. Bobby is very much like I am. You either do or you don't. Remember, we bought the piano and gave Bobby lessons. We started him and Harriet came; that was our cousin, Harriet Rutstein. He said, *"No lessons for me."* She was a music teacher, a University of Minnesota graduate, and she said I will give the boys lessons. He took one lesson and he said, *"I'm going to quit."* He said, *"I'm going to play the piano the way I want to."* Now when he plays *'Mr Jones'* by himself, he's pretty good. He has a gorgeous concert grand piano in his living room.[2]

I was born in a town twelve miles out of Hibbing called Stevenson Location, named after a man who went there to mine. My father opened one of the first stores there, 55 years ago, in Stevenson Location in 1913. I was born there two years later. In fact, all four children were born in that little town.... My brother, who will be 56, I will be 53, my other brother...My brothers' names are Lewis and Berne, who is in the Bahamas, and my sister Irene.

Dad: There is no more town there. It is an abandoned mine and the houses are all gone. It is just weeds and forest now. It is due west from here. We took Bobby up there once to show him the house, and there was no house. It was just a dead end.

Bob's Birth

Mom: The house we were in then was 519 Third Avenue East. It was a nice place. It was a double house. We had our own yard...It was a frame building and it was painted beige.

Dad: I do remember when he was going to enrol – at kindergarten – he wouldn't go with her. I do remember that I was the only man enrolling a child at the kindergarten. I left my job to come home because he wouldn't go unless I went with him. Then he was happy.

R.S: Did he talk early?

Mom: I would get his white shoes ready and he was ready. When he'd see me polishing the white shoes, he got ready to go out. He was the most gorgeous child in Duluth. It was a waste on a little boy. He must have started talking when he was two, because he would say, *"I am two in May."* People would come up and ask him how old he was and he would say *"I will be two in May,"* And people would stand back from him and look, because of the way he talked and how he dressed. He was dressed in outfits all the time. I only put outfits on him. Even when this little boy was dirty, he was clean. I'm going to find you the little white suit that he wore at my sister's wedding, at five years old. He sang *'Some Sunday Morning.'* He sang it at Irene's wedding that morning.

Dad: Before that, his song was *'Accentuate The Positive.'* He'd get so mad when people would ask him to sing it but then he would say, *"OK I'll sing it one time."* He would go through the whole song even though he never knew what the words meant. They would laugh; they really loved him. He was, I would say, a very loveable, very unusual child. People would go out of their way to handle, to talk with him, to ask about him – they just loved him. I think we were the only ones who would not agree that he was going to be a very famous person one day. Everyone said that this boy is going to be a genius, he was going to be this or that. Everyone said that, not just family. When he would sing *'Accentuate The Positive'* like other children would sing *'Mary Had a Little Lamb,'* they would say that this boy was brilliant. I didn't pay too much attention to this, because I figured any kid could learn it if he heard it often enough. He learned this from the radio: he was four years old.

RS NOTE: Beatty had just brought in the little white suit, Bobby's first Palm Beach suit, from the age of four, a handsome, collarless, three buttoned suit – which, his mother said, he wore with a white shirt and white shoes. –

Mom: My sister bought it for him at Dayton's. – RS NOTE: Made by Maurice Rothschild of Chicago – The uncles all got together at the wedding and gave him $25.00 to sing. He got stubborn, the uncles said: *"Bobby, you've got to sing."* He went to his father and asked if he should he sing.

Dad: I said, *"You should sing. All these people came."* I told him that he wouldn't have to do it any more. I said, *"Just sing it today."* We pestered him so much…

Mom: It wasn't a boy soprano voice. It was just a middle-range voice. So he sang and took the money. He took $25.00. Then he came over to me and said *"Mummy I'm going to give the money back."* And he went to the uncle, who wasn't really an uncle, but a brother-in-law on the other side, and gave him back the money and they absolutely ate him up. One thing you have to remember about Bobby, and that was true when he went off to start his career; he wanted it quiet when he would sing. *"If it's quiet, I will sing."* He said that even when he was five years old. This was in the Covenant Club, a private Jewish social club in Duluth, on Second Avenue West, at First Street.

RS NOTE: Beatty showed a wonderful photograph of Robert at the age of fifteen months, with enormous apple cheeks.

Mom: He was a gorgeous child who just exuded personality. I put ribbons in his hair up to a year old. I used to say to him *"Bobby, you should have been a girl."*

R.S: Let's see, Bob was born at St. Mary's Hospital in Duluth? How far was that from your house?

Dad: About four blocks.

Mom: I was in hospital for a few days. There was one false alarm before the birth. If it hadn't been for the best doctor in Duluth, Bobby would have been born dead, because I had a crooked bone at the end of my spine. I didn't know this. Only because I had the leading obstetrician in Duluth, the nuns told me that.[3] He did operate, and it was a forced labour. Bobby was almost a 10lb baby. – Note ed. Robert's actual weight was 7lb, 13oz, 10 grams – As you can notice, even on this picture his head was large, he was a chubby little guy. He weighed thirty pounds at one year old.

R.S: How did you choose the name Robert?

Dad: It was a good name. We used to call him Bobby Allen, or Robert Allen. We went through a list and thought Robert was a good name.

R.S: Did you make with the cigar routine around your office?

Dad: Bobby used to come down to the office, when he was two or three years old, and sing into the Dictaphone machine. They were on wax cylinders and I startled the secretaries by having this little singing voice in with this office business. Bobby would get a big kick listening to himself on the Dictaphone machine. When you look back, he really was unusual.

Mom: It was only after he got into high school that he began to dream and – scheme or sing.

Dad: He was never really detached.

Mom: No, he was never detached from family or friends, but he dreamt a lot. He would go upstairs and dream that someday he would be famous…and do something different. He was going to dream what that was going to be.

R.S: Were these day dreams or fantasies or real dreams?

Dad: He worked hard at being an entertainer.

Mom: If it was to be an architect, he was going to be the very best of architects. He was going to go to New York and build something different. It wasn't going to be the general plan, it was going to be something different. If there was going to someone going to the moon, he was going to be on that. He would tell his grandmother, *"Grandma, someday I'm going to be very famous. Grandma, you are never going to have to worry about anything."* This was when he was about ten or eleven. He would tell his grandmother that she would never have to want for anything, because he would buy it for her. He said he was going to do something different. I am going to make a lot of money and I know that I will give you anything you want. Unfortunately, she never lived to see that come true. He was very good to my mother, both of my boys were. In fact, they still call it Grandma's room. It is still Grandma's room although she has been gone seven years.

Dad: We only had two rules around here. One, don't come and ask me for anything unless you are prepared for me to say no, and two, do things for us because you like us, not because you are afraid of us. It worked pretty good.

Mom: We were more like friends. We'd tell them that they would have children of their own and they would want to be friends with them.

R.S: But there weren't many arguments?

Dad: Well, the only thing about it was Bobby might pick on David to the point where he might hurt him.

Mom: That was the only argument that we had…We would come in, David would be on the floor and this kid could lift the refrigerator, he was strong – and I was afraid that he would break a few bones.

…Like I told both of them, it was a privilege to raise them because they were never any trouble. No-one was ever calling me and telling me that they were throwing rocks in the yard, or they were touching their dog, nothing but high regard in the whole neighbourhood for them. They didn't go out of their way to be a nuisance.

…When he first went to visit Bobby Vee, he and Bobby Vee were very good friends, you know, until Bobby Vee dumped him of course.

Dad: He didn't dump him…

Mom: Well, I mean, he wasn't too nice to him.

Dad: He had his brother and his relatives in the group and he never had room for Bobby. He wrote him a letter and said if any of the boys ever quit I would like to have you. Bobby went to Fargo to play with him…From Fargo he had to go some place in South Dakota.

Mom: It had to be junior and senior years…because he was Dylan when he got to Minneapolis the first year.

R.S: But he had wanted to make a record during his high school years?

Dad: …First he wanted to make a tape. Their number one goal was to make a tape and have it played at the radio station. One of the announcers out there arranged it. …But when it came out of the radio even they knew it wasn't too good. I'd doubt if there are one or two of the boys that Bobby went to school with in town now.

Do you want to go downstairs a minute?

NOTE: There is a long, slow conversation on the telephone with David Zimmerman. Shelton notes: The room downstairs was turned into virtually a museum or shrine for their son.

Dad: Here is how Bob learned to play the guitar.

R.S: Nick Manoloff's Spanish guitar method, Book No.1 – Dad indicates he thinks he got it when he bought the guitar. Price $1.00, publisher, *M.M Cole & Company.* The latest, most modern guitar method ever published, copyright 1932.

Dad: He bought this at the music store, and took it home and started to play the guitar.

R.S: Reading a poem that Bob wrote to his father – When he was ill. The title of the poem is *'For Father's Day.'* It ends, *"Happy Father's Day. Love, Bobby."*

Mom: In *my* poem that he wrote to *me*, I read the ones that he wrote to me when he was ten, with eighteen stanzas. I read to women. That was seventeen years ago. These women are all dead and buried but I must have had twenty of then crying, crying their eyes out.

Those poems are in my drawers but I promised him that I would never give them away to anyone. One of them I held so long, that the words are already off the paper. Bobby doesn't care now about having them read. He cared in the beginning. Now I could show it to the world but he still says, *"Mother never give that away."*

Dad: He wouldn't dare have that printed – ever.

Mom: There are some things that are sacred.

Do you remember how the first poem came out?

He just said *"Mom, I have a present for you – it's a Mother's Day poem."* Then it was sketched and outlined, and there were phrasings. I remember there were twelve stanzas, not phrases. There were about five lines – then a gap you know. It was on school paper, notebook paper. To my mother and how I took care of her, and how my shining face was in the light all the time. …Everything rhymed, and how I put him to bed and how I kissed him goodnight – everything…where would I be, mother, if it were not for you? Probably six feet under stuff like that. Everything rhymed. And the last stanza said –

My dear Mother, I hope that you
Will never grow old and gray,
So that people will say:
'Hello, young lady, Happy Mother's Day.'

Everything was *"Love, Bobby."* Everything was love.

– Dad plays a tape of Bob singing, very primitive rock and roll, but the singing is intense. The title of the song is *'Rock And Roll Is Here To Stay.'*

Mom: – over tape – They'd leave the front door open and the whole neighbourhood would hear it…He would come down here and pound and pound on the piano, and always Hank Williams. Hank Williams was always there. – Over another tape, close harmony singing of *'Dream, Dream, Dream.'* He never had the time to get in trouble. The kid was in the house or mowing the lawn or taking the garbage out.

– R.S: The singing on the whole tape was very professional; it sounded like either early Everly Brothers or Buddy Holly –

Mom: Yes, Buddy Holly, he mourned him, how he mourned him when he died. In his senior year, he fell off the honour roll three times.

R.S: What do you remember about the first couple of years with Bobby at the Nettleton school?

Mom: It was just one year. He only went to the kindergarten there. He started first grade at the Alice School here. Our address was then 2323 Third Avenue. The building was just torn down.

Dad: We lived next door to the school for pretty near one year. We moved in there while we were looking for a home here.

Mom: My mother and dad lived there. We were there exactly one year, we wanted to give the people here time to move out. Their son lived in the basement.

R.S: Was this the Maddens? – they said *"yes."*

Dad: There are no children left now though. Just the old people. They are all gone. Everyone of them. Isn't that something?

R.S: Did Bob keep in touch with any of these kids?

Both Parents: Not after school.

R.S: He mentioned to me the names Larry Kegan and some girl he took to the Junior Prom?

Mom: Echo. Echo was her name…I don't know her parents' name.

Dad: A few months ago, we sent him Larry Kegan's address… Larry was the boy who broke his neck when he dived into the sand at Miami Beach. Bobby told us to look him up in Miami Beach.

Mom: He was paralysed for life. I think that must have had something to do with Bobby's career. That happened about ten years ago, when the boy was seventeen. This was a real tragedy in Bobby's life – even though dad disputes it affected Bob's career.

Dad: He – presumably Bob – got over it, like everything else.

Mom: That was the biggest tragedy.

R.S: How old was Bob then?

Dad: Maybe he was fifteen…He was really upset…that was real tragic…He was also upset when Hank Williams died. He was twelve years old then. Buddy Holly was later.

R.S: These must have been pretty rough times to have those teenage years so associated with death?

Dad: I always tried to console him. Then he started his collection…but Jimmy Dean was the worst, because he started reading all about him and getting into the literature that was coming out in those days. It was gathered in and it was repeated and repeated. He went to see *Rebel Without A Cause*. He must have seen it twelve times, because he got in for nothing. That played the Lybba. He went there continuously. That was before he died. – R.S. check these dates I think they are very wrong.[4]

Then he started collecting pictures like people collect pictures of him and the Beatles, he collected Jimmy Dean.

R.S: Did he ever talk about wanting to be like Jimmy Dean?

Dad: He would never talk about it, but you could just see that, yes, he wanted to be…all the kids wanted to live like Jimmy Dean. I got quite a kick out of one of Bob's reviews at Newport Festival, the last time, one of the Providence papers called Bob Dylan *Rebel With A Cause*. I liked that very much…He sent that to us…I'm sure Bobby said, when he read it, in the back of his mind that *"this was terrific."*

R.S: Do you remember the graduation party? [5]

Dad: Yes, he said that he didn't want to come and why all these people were coming. He said that he was graduating and didn't understand that it was customary, because this was a milestone. I said to him *"Bobby, this is a milestone. You only graduate high school once, and you graduate college once."* He said, *"Well I won't be here too long."* But I remember when he came, he stayed, and he felt good that all these people had come.

Mom: Bobby is the kind of boy that would make you think he wasn't interested but he was interested all right.

Dad: When he saw that people had come twenty-five or thirty miles, and they brought him presents…I figure that in his mind he said *"This is a celebration."*

Mom: He loved David's confirmation too. He loved David's party. He stood up and performed like Little Richard there.

Dad: Once it starts, you get over the embarrassment of these things. He didn't know half the people. He hadn't seen some of them for ten years. They all knew him but he didn't know half of them.

R.S: Did Bob know the whole Hebrew ritual. Did he study the language?

Dad: Bobby could speak. He knew 400 Hebrew words. Literally. I think he forgot everything but he was the only one. He could speak Hebrew like they do in Israel today. This Rabbi took great pride in him and took him to show him off one Friday night. The Rabbi would say the sentence in English and Bobby would say it in Hebrew...Rabbi Maier, Reuben.

Mom: Did he ever tell you the story, when he was five years old how he went with his grandma, Zimmerman, to the Mother-Son day affair, I couldn't go, David was very young. It was Mother's Day, twenty-two years ago. Bob was just going to be five, two weeks later....So he gets up...and they see this little codger get up with his tousled curly hair and he is going upon the stage too, he stamps his foot up there – she makes the sound – and he commands attention and he says, *"If everybody in this room will keep quiet I will sing for my grandmother Zimmerman. This is Mother's Day and I'm going to sing 'Some Sunday Morning'."* And he sang it and of course they tore the place apart. And then they clapped and he sang the other song...he didn't know much more. Well, our 'phone never stopped.

R.S: There's a tough question to ask you. Maybe it is the most difficult question of all. There is something that mystifies me. When someone comes from this kind of warm, appreciative environment, what does make him a rebel? Does every teenager rebel? – Mom says, *"Yes."*

Dad: He didn't really rebel...He convinced himself that he had something to *sell* different.

Mom: Yes, he convinced himself, we didn't.

Dad: He convinced himself that he had something to sell and that if he didn't do it in New York, after a reasonable time...The deal was, he said, if I don't make it in a year, then I will come home and go to school...but I can't go to school because I have to go NOW. Which meant that he knew more about the temper of the times for the music than I knew.

Mom: He sent me $1000 one day in this kind of envelope...well, that's Bobby. It was to me, you know. Now, here is his card that he sent.

Text on postcard sent from New York, April 28th, 1961.

"Dear everybody – I've finished my time at Folk City now I am at the Gaslight in New York, too. My union costs were $128.00. It came out of my pay at Folk City, I am now making $100.00 a week for five nights playing...that's not bad, considering that three months ago I was unknown. I've already played the top place in New York for folk music...I will call home on Sunday at Aunt Irene's house. I don't know if I can come home then – or when. – Mom said he meant he didn't know when he could come home – I expect to now...I am clean and I am brushing my teeth. Say hello to everybody for me. Love, Bob."

– The letter was addressed to them c/o the mysterious Uncle Vernon Stone, the gambler, who the parents were visiting in Las Vegas.

Dad: But he was keeping clean and brushing his teeth. This was the major controversy.

Mom: This was the big thing.

Dad: As long as he was gone and we couldn't do anything about that...but we told him *"keep clean and brush your teeth...remember, you only have one set."*

R.S: Now you say that the prime reason for his leaving was that there was no audience here?

Mom: Oh, there was nothing here for him...what could he do here? There was an audience in Minneapolis, yes, but that wasn't the audience he wanted. The audience he wanted was in New York. He knew it was either New York or California.

RS NOTE: Bob's mother talks so much like Bob in some of his animated moods, that the similarity is astounding. The phrasing, the cadence, the pitch, the speed, are almost identical.

Dad: He had to know if he had something

R.S: Do you have the feeling that he was leaving in anger?

Mom & Dad: – thundering disapproval – Oh, no.

Dad: It was a chance at success.

Mom: Oh, no. He kept in touch with us all the time.

R.S: I wasn't saying in anger at you, but at the town.

Mom: Oh, no, not the town, he loved the town. To this day, he says, Mother, don't sell the home...don't leave Hibbing. What do you want to leave Hibbing for. No, he never left in anger.

R.S: Do you believe that his rebellion was out of belief, that it wasn't just show business?

Dad: It was hard to tell. He didn't really know, I believe, that he was becoming this famous.

Mom: He had no idea...

Dad: In New York, he was influencing some New York kids, but when he went to this Newport thing, he reached kids who disseminated from there, and they spread the gospel of Dylan...then he was already a big, big influence.

Mom: When we saw him at Carnegie Hall and Milwaukee he was already – Dad finishes the sentence – A big man.

Mom: At Carnegie Hall, when we saw the people that turned out, we were thunderstruck. We didn't know what to think. Is it possible? Is it a dream.

Dad: I had seen him perform before, and I knew that on stage he was different, that he had mannerisms that were meant to attract attention and that were meant to identify him, and separate him from the ordinary.

Mom: I thought, oh my gosh!

Dad: At Carnegie Hall, he lopes out and commands this respect and the awe of the people there. He's just a different person.

R.S: Have you ever felt that there is anything in Bobby's attitude towards religion that he felt should be explained or challenged?

Dad: No, when I heard about this song – *'With God On Our Side'* – being sung at Newport and I mentioned it to Bob, he said, *"Dad, it's not the kind of song you think it is"'* Because I hadn't seen the words yet. I said, *"The title infers that it is a beautiful song,"* and he said, *"No, it's kind of a sarcastic song."* When I saw it in print, I could understand what he meant.

R.S: When did he start using the Dylan name?

Mom: Well, we came home from Minneapolis once and I said, somebody said to me that Bobby goes by the name of Bobby Dylan. Is that so? I said that I didn't know. The next time he came home, I asked him: *"Bobby, do you play the guitar and sing in Twin Cities?"* He never needed money! He kept saying that he never needed money, that he had plenty of money. We knew that he played for himself, but professionally, we didn't know that anyone wanted to listen to him. And I told him: *"Somebody said that you go by the name of Bobby Dylan. Is there a place there called The Purple Onion?"* He said, *"Yes, Mother there is,"* I said, *"Why didn't you tell us?"* He said, *"Oh, Mother, you wouldn't like that name."* – Dylan.

R.S: Did he like the poet Dylan Thomas?

Dad: Don't know. It was a short name and he liked the sound of it. We never asked him about it, because this was his name and the way he wanted to spell it. It was also a way to get a little discussion about the way you spell it Dylan or Dy-lan.

Mom: It was just another gimmick, and its still a gimmick today.

R.S NOTE: We talk about the censorship of John Birch song from *Columbia Records* and the Ed Sullivan show.

Dad: He told us that he wasn't all that happy with *Columbia Records*...

R.S: Do you think Bob will come back to Hibbing?

Dad: – long pause, no answer – R.S. The irony of this is that three weeks later the father died and Bob came back, reluctantly, for his funeral. There's some pictures of him as a boy scout. He wasn't in the scouts for too long. He got the uniform, I was glad he joined, but I didn't ask him if he liked it or not.

R.S: Do you think he will come back to Hibbing one day, or don't you know?

Dad: – Continues to look at picture and ignore my question. Here is a picture of him in August 1954 at the Theodore Herzel Camp, outside of Webster, Wisconsin.

R.S: How long did he go to that camp?

Dad: He went there when he was thirteen, fourteen, fifteen and I even think when he was sixteen. When he was sixteen, he took over the camp. He was the leader of the camp, the Rabbi told me. There's a picture of us on Visitors' Day with me wearing balloon knickerbockers. There's a picture of Bobby playing a bullfighter, holding a towel for a cape. He was about twelve or thirteen here. These are priceless now. There he is playing the bongos.

R.S: What do you think about some historical pictures in this book?[6]

Dad: If you get permission, I would like that very much. He has told me never to give out any of his old pictures, but in your case...Here's the medicine he used to take for his asthma. He doesn't have too much trouble with his asthma now. I've sent him some pictures already and he got a kick out of them. Some day we are going to get all the pictures together.

R.S: Here's a shot of him with his hair piled on top making him look a little like Elvis Presley. I bet you liked having the bongos round here.

Dad: Oh, they closed the doors and we didn't mind.

RS: What about his whole fascination with bad men? In Central City he was trying to buy a picture of a criminal in a gift shop. Is that right that he was very interested in outlaw types.

Dad: He was fascinated. That's true. Oh, sure, everybody was interested in those bad men, I was myself. Here's another one of him in 1958 – with a tie.

Dad: – leafing through copies of the comic, *Illustrated Classics: Cyrano, Twenty Years After, Gulliver's Travels, The Hunchback of the Notre Dame, The Corsican Brothers, The Pathfinder, The Black Arrow* – by Stevenson, *Lorna Doone, The Three Musketeers.* You see the difference from the way David did things, he organised things. *Moby Dick, Ivanhoe, Tale of Two Cities, Robinson Crusoe, Don Quixote,* I used to read these.

R.S: What would your opinion be if Bob ever would have studied music in a formal way?

Dad: No one will ever know. I just wonder if he would have become a serious composer. As to records, he had about every record ever made by Hank Williams, even those on 78. Then he had a lot of 45s of people playing hard rock, such as Little Richard, and by some groups you never heard of.

R.S: Is Sara Jewish?

Dad: Yes, her name was Novozovotsky. In fact, Bobby was tracing it out and her grandfather from Odessa, too. The name is Novozletsky.[7]

Records In The Basement:

'Baby Blue' by the Hot Rods and Gene Vincent. *'Dearest'* and *'There Ought To Be a Law'* by Mickey and Sylvia. – Label is *Vik. 'Blue Suede Shoes'* – Elvis Presley. Also Presley's *'Heartbreak Hotel.'* Also *'Tutti-Frutti'* – presumably by Little Richard…The Clovers on *Atlantic*. Little Richard on the *Speciality* label. *'Long Tall Sally'* and *'Miss Ann,' 'Slipping and Sliding'* by Buddy Holly. *'Hank Snow Sings Jimmy Rogers.'* He was a Nat – King – Cole fan. *'Flying High'* by Bobby Vee and the Shadows on the *Soma* label. On the *Minneapolis* label, which Dad says they distribute themselves. Gene Vincent on *Capital*. Of all the records that Dad looks at the one he gets most exited about is one by Freddy Gardner which has *"A gorgeous saxophone solo."* I didn't buy too many records in those days, but…a whole flock of Hank Williams titles come along. Dad says *"I bet he took a bunch of records out to play when he was home."* I heard Bob's voice on some of these small 25-cent records. He and David used to act up and we would record them. More records – The Everly brothers, Bill Hailey, I think, says dad, *"That 'Rock Around The Clock' is a real classic."* More records – the Platters, Pat Boone, Webb Pierce, *'High Noon'* by Frankie Laine. Dad says, *"Gee, all my Billy Daniels records are broken."*

R.S: Do you think he really hurt himself badly in the motorcycle accident?

Dad: No, he showed me where he tipped over. It was right on the curve, I asked him, *"How come you were on the motor cycle and the others were riding in a car.' 'Well,"* he said, *"I was taking the cycle in and I was riding it all the time."* Whenever you fell on a motor cycle this is the…you have got to get hurt even in front of your house…I didn't ask too many stories. – R.S. Ironic that he didn't say facts – I asked him if he was hurt pretty badly and he said: *"Yeah, I got cracked up pretty bad."* He said, *"I was really scared."* He got his face scratched. Every time I go round that bend there I always think of the accident. As I recall the spot was about four or five blocks from his house, it's hard to describe how narrow the road is. It's so narrow, there is room for just one car.

Notes

1 Note: Abe says that his *"eldest brother and sister were born in Odessa."* Later, however, he contradicts this by saying *"I have only one younger brother, the rest are older."*

If this second statement were correct, then three of his brothers and his sister would have been born in Odessa.

In his book *Dylan In Minnesota,* Dave Engel states that four children came from Odessa and that Abe and his younger brother Max were born in the USA. However, Howard Sounes states in his biography of Bob Dylan, *Down The Highway,* that only three children came from Odessa. Sounes' data, which was probably taken from the US Records Dept., would appear to be incorrect. The reason for this discrepancy would have occurred with the entry of the USA into World War One in 1918. At this time, all aliens in the USA had to be registered and it seems rather than listing Jake, aka Jack, as an alien, the Zimmermans took this opportunity of registering their son as being born in the USA.

2 This was Dylan's Woodstock home.

3 The obstetrician was Dr. James R. Manley MA.

4 At the time of Dean's death in 1955, Dylan would have been fourteen. Therefore, the dates would seem to fit.

5 Robert Zimmerman graduated from Hibbing High School on June 5, 1959.

6 Three pictures are published in Shelton's biography, *No Direction Home: The Life And Times Of Bob Dylan.* The pictures are captioned as being *"Courtesy of Bob Dylan."*

7 Sara's maiden name is Noznisky, not Novozovotsky. It might also be prudent here, to clear up some careless journalism, which, in the past, has not only provided Sara with two incorrectly spelt surnames but with an incorrect husband! The popular misconception was that Sara's first husband was *Playboy* executive Victor A Lownes, a mistake perpetuated by Robert Shelton in *No Direction Home.*

In fact, Shirley Noznisky was married to fashion photographer Hans Lownds and it was Hans – born Heinz Ludwig Lowenstein – who persuaded Shirley to change her name to Sara. Note that the surname is Lownds and not Lowndes.

GOD SAID TO ABRAHAM...
by Derek Barker

Although the names Edelstein – on his mother's side – and Zimmerman are of German origin, Bob Dylan's ancestral roots are in Russia.

"I don't know how they got a German name coming from Russia. Maybe they got their name coming off the boat or something."
Playboy interview with Bob Dylan, 1978.

"My so-called Jewish roots are in Egypt. They went down there with Joseph, and they came back with Moses, you know, the guy that killed the Egyptians, married an Ethiopian girl and brought the law down from the mountain. The same person who killed three thousand Hebrews for getting down, stripping off their clothes and dancing around a golden calf. These are my roots. Jacob had four wives and thirteen children, who fathered an entire people. These are my roots too... Delilah tempting Sampson, killing him softly with her song. The mighty King David was an outlaw before he was king, you know... The wonderful King Saul had a warrant out for him – a 'no knock' search warrant. They wanted to cut his head off. John the Baptist could tell you more about it."
Martin Keller interview published July 1983, *Minneapolis City Pages*.

Benjamin Harold Edelstein was born in Kovno, Lithuania, but later settled in Vilkomir, Russia, where, in 1891 he married Lybba Jaffe. The couple arrived in Superior, Michigan, USA on Christmas Eve 1902, where they stayed with relatives before moving in 1904 to Hibbing, Minnesota. Of the ten Edelstein children, four are born in Lithuania, two in Superior, and four in Hibbing. The eldest child Florence will be Dylan's grandmother.

Benjamin David Solemovitz – Ben Stone – was born to Sabse and Bessie Solemovitz in Lithuania in 1883. After five years living alone and making a new home for his family in Superior, Sabse sends for his wife and children.

Ben married Florence Sara Edelstein in 1911; their first child Vernon is born the following year. The family settle at the Stevenson steel location west of Hibbing and on June 16, 1915 the second of their four children, Beatrice, is born.

Zigman Zimmerman, originally from the Russian Black Sea port of Odessa, is now living in Duluth, Minnesota. Once Zigman has settled in Duluth he sends for his wife Anna Chana (Greestein) Zimmerman. Like many other European immigrants, Anna and her four children arrive in Duluth by way of New York's Ellis Island.

Today more than 40 percent of all living Americans can trace their roots to an ancestor who came to the USA through Ellis Island. Of the 5.4 million immigrants who arrived in the United States between 1820 and 1860, about 3.7 million entered through that gateway. During the years 1892 to 1924, America was the recipient of the largest human migration in modern history. Ellis Island processed about twelve million of those immigrants. The transatlantic steamers anchored at quarantine in the New York narrows. First- and second-class passengers were inspected aboard and along with American citizens were landed in New York. Steerage-class passengers – who paid on average thirty dollars for the passage – were loaded onto barges for Ellis Island.

Exactly how Anna Zimmerman and her children made the 1400-mile journey from New York City to Duluth is not known. Most Jewish immigrants simply settled in New York, but the Zimmermans already had family in Duluth, which was a small but busy fishing port not unlike Odessa. The first child born to the reunited couple on US soil is Abraham H. Zimmerman – October 19, 1911.

Beatrice and Abraham are introduced to each other at a New Year's Eve party, but with Beatty living in Hibbing and Abe in Duluth, the 1932 northern winter snows keep them apart. However, with spring comes a blossoming romance and by June a wedding. The date of the wedding, June 10, 1934 is set to coincide with a visiting rabbi. The Zimmermans' honeymooned in Chicago and on their return to Duluth, they move in with Abe's mother at 402 East Fifth Street. Anna and Zigman are now separated.

By 1938 Anna, Beatty, Abe and two of Abe's brothers, Paul and Max, move a couple of doors down the road to Apartment A, 308 East Fifth Street. Beatty and Abe eventually find a place of their own, Apartment 201, 503 East Third Street, but with their first child on the way, the Zimmermans soon move up to 519 Third Avenue East, where they rent the upstairs duplex of wooden frame house owned by the Overmans.

At 21.05 local time, on Saturday, May 24, 1941 at St. Mary's Hospital, in Duluth, Minnesota, the first child of Abe and Beatrice Zimmerman is born. Dr. James R. Manley MA, records the baby boy at 7lb,13oz,10 grams and 20½". The name of the child is Robert Allen; the Certificate of Birth, No. 54389-838 was filed on May 28, 1941. The child is described in Dave Engel's wonderfully descriptive book *Dylan in Minnesota – Just Like Bob Zimmerman's Blues,* as being *"about as big as a good-sized lake trout."*

Young But Daily Growin'

May 12, 1946 – Twelve days before his fifth birthday, young Robert gives his first *public* performance. Along with other guests, Robert gets up to perform in front of a large gathering at a Mother's Day celebration. He sings *'Some Sunday Morning,'* a current favourite by Forrest and Haymes, and Johnny Mercer's *'Accentuate The Positive.'*

June 9, 1946 – A month after his début, Robert, now five, performs at his Aunt Irene's wedding reception at the Covenant Club in Duluth. The exact nature of the repertoire is not certain, but the turn is likely to be a repeat of the Mother's Day performance.

1947 – The Zimmermans – Abe, Beatty, Robert and baby brother David Benjamin – born the previous year, David is named after Beatty's father Benjamin David – leave Duluth for Hibbing. Due in the main to an acute shortage of housing in Hibbing, the family move in with Beatty's mother Florence at her apartment at 2323 Third Avenue East.

1948 – The Zimmerman family move to their own house, 2425 Seventh Avenue East, formally owned by the recently widowed Exhilda M. Madden.

May 13, 1951 – Beatty is presented with the gift of a poem on Mother's Day from her nine-year old son Robert.

1953 – Robert spends the first of four summers at Camp Harzl. The Hebrew summer camp is near Webster, Wisconsin and is attended mainly by boys and girls from Duluth and the Twin Cities. While there, Robert meets Judy Rubin, an early girlfriend, Louis Kemp, organizer of the 1975/6 Rolling Thunder Revue tour and Larry Kegan. Kegan, who later becomes permanently wheelchair bound after injuring his spine in a diving accident, will remain a lifelong friend.

1952-1954 – 'The Drunkard's Son'

First published in Issue 44 of ISIS Magazine, this previously unseen poem/lyric signed *'Robert Zimmerman'* purports to be an original hand-written poem by the youngster. The item, which, I believed to be genuine, probably dates from circa 1952/1954 and if so, is the earliest example of his written work. The lyrics appear to be based on, or to be more precise, *borrowed* from, a Hank Snow song of the same name. Credited to Clarence E. Snow *'The Drunkard's Son'* was released by Hank Snow in Canada in the early forties and was first released as a single in the USA in 1950 – RCA 21-0303. Young Master Zimmerman's words differ only slightly from those in the Snow song and whether these differences are due to adaptation, or merely poor transcription, are open to debate. Snow's recording may have been based on a Jimmie Rodgers song, *'A Drunkard's Child'* released in 1930 (BVE 56618-3), both pieces share the same sentiments and opening line. It has been suggested that the Zimmerman poem could have been motivated by stories of an abused child found the previous year in the Hibbing Memorial Building on Twenty-Fourth Street and Fourth Avenue, a couple of blocks from the Zimmerman home.

May 22 1954 – Two days before his thirteenth birthday, Rabbi Reuben Maier conducts Robert Allen's bar mitzvah. Robert is already taking instruction in Hebrew from Rabbi Maier above the L&B Café on Howard Street.

1955-56 – Bobby Zimmerman has joined The Gutter Boys, a local tenpin bowling team. The team are winners of the Teen-Age Bowling League competition for the 1955-56 season.

According to Howard Sounes in his biography *Down the Highway,* Dylan's first group is an a cappella outfit called the Jokers. Bobby and two friends from summer camp, Larry Kegan and Howard Rutman, form the group together with other friends from St Paul. This group is believed to have appeared on a television talent show broadcast on Channel 9 in the Twin Cities. In the summer of 1956, Bobby, Kegan and Rutman pay five dollars to cut a 78 rpm record. One of the songs included on the disc is *'Earth Angel.'*

Toward the end of 1956, Bobby Zimmerman and three school friends form their first *proper* group – with instruments – the Shadow Blasters. The group consists of Larry Fabbro, guitar, Bill Marinac, string bass, Chuck Nara, snare drum and cymbal, and Bobby on piano. The drum and bass are on loan from school.

April 5, 1957 – The Shadow Blasters perform their first major concert in front of nearly 2,000 people in the auditorium at Hibbing High. The occasion is the Junior High Student Council variety show. Three songs are performed including two Little Richard tunes, *'Jenny Jenny'* and *'True Fine Mama.'* The set is repeated, more or less, at the Junior *College Capers.*

1957 – Bobby puts together his new band, The Golden Chords, featuring Monte Edwardson (lead guitar), LeRoy Hoikkala (drums), and Bobby on piano, vocal and later some rhythm guitar.

February 6, 1958 – The coronation of homecoming queen Shelby Clevenstine provides the perfect opportunity for Bobby and The Chords to play their first major gig. The Golden Chords play an afternoon concert in front of 1,800 students in the auditorium in Hibbing High. With an array of amplifiers and his piano miked, Bobby proceeds to break a pedal off the High School's 1922 Steinway Grand. The Chords also perform in front of nearly 2,000 people at the evening concert.

1958 – The Golden Chords continue to play at venues in and around Hibbing, at PTA gatherings, Moose Lodge meetings and anywhere else that will have them. They remain together until late spring 1958 playing *'Peggy Sue,'* Little Richard covers, and even write a few songs of their own, including a number called *'Big Black Train.'* The song, which, probably started life as an instrumental, has been credited both to Zimmerman and to Monte Edwardson by subsequent biographers. More likely still, the song was contributed to by both boys and may well have remained unfinished for some time as it seems that Edwardson continued to work on the song after he and LeRoy Hoikkala left the Chords to form a rival group, the Rockets.

"Well big black train, coming down the line,
Well big black train, coming down the line,
Well you got my woman, you bring her back to me,
Well that cute little chick, is the girl that I want to see." [1]

Bobby is now playing more guitar and quickly progresses from an old acoustic to a turquoise Silvertone electric. However, the $22.00 Silvertone is soon replaced by a $95.00 gold sunburst Ozark Supro Stratocaster copy. Bobby and John Bucklen buy one each and it is believed the resulting *bulk purchase* enables the boys to get the guitars for about $60.00 each. After the demise of the Golden Chords, Bobby puts together the short-lived but reasonably successful Satintones. The group comprises Bobby's cousin from Duluth, Bill Cohen (drums), Marsh Shamblott (piano) and Dennis Nylen (string bass) – Bobby is again the vocalist. If there is a piano at a venue, Bobby will play it if not, he plays guitar.

The Rockets soon become a big name on the Iron Range and after the departure for college of their rhythm guitar/vocalist Ron Taddei, Bobby asks to join the group. They reluctantly agree to the request, but wild Bobby Zimmerman doesn't fit in and his stay in the band is a short one.

Spring 1959 – Bobby gives his final performance at the High School Jacket Jamboree. *'As Time Goes By'* and *'Swing, Dad, Swing'* are performed with John Bucklen on guitar, Bill Marinac string bass, and Fran Matosich, Kathy Dasovic and Mary Defonso providing backing vocals. The name of this new combo seems to have been lost in the mists of time. However, according to Dylan, the next and probably the last of his Hibbing/Duluth bands is the short-lived Elston Gunn and the Rock Boppers. Elston Gunn – at first with three *n's* seems to have been Bobby Zimmerman's first alias.

June 5, 1959 – Robert Zimmerman graduates from Hibbing High School. His ambition, according to the school yearbook is *"To join Little Richard."*

Summer, 1959 – It has been rumoured that after Bobby's graduation from Hibbing High, the Zimmermans *might* have paid for their son to attend Deveraux reform school in Pennsylvania! If indeed Bobby did attend this school for difficult adolescents, his stay there must have been a short one. While a stay at Deveraux could have been the inspiration for Dylan's 1963 composition *'Walls Of Redwing'* – about the strict Redwing State Reformatory – the song is more likely to have been based on the experiences of Jim Beron, a friend of a friend from Duluth who had served time at Redwing in 1959.

According to John Bucklen, Bobby appears on a local TV station around this time. The station is Channel 11 out of Minneapolis and Bucklen is certain that the drummer was Bobby's cousin, which would indicate the band was the Satintones. The group play one song. Around this time, Bobby and his band record a brief session for Duluth radio.

Bobby gets a summer job in Fargo, North Dakota, working as a busboy at the Red Apple Café. He plays a few gigs with a local group called the Poor Boys, but by August has *conned* his way into Bobby Vee's group the Shadows by telling them he has played piano with Conway Twitty. He informs Vee that his *stage name* is Elston Gunnn. In his book *Dylan in Minnesota,* Dave Engel states that around this time Elston dropped one of the superfluous n's from his name. However, in an interview recently published on Bobby Vee's official web-site, Vee says – *"Bill made arrangements to audition him at the KFGO studio and said he was a funny little wiry kind of guy and he rocked pretty good. ...He told Bill his name was Elston Gunnn – with 3 n's). Kind of weird but let's try him out."* [2]

"His first dance with us was in Gwinner, ND. All I remember is an old crusty piano that hadn't been tuned...ever! In the middle of 'Lotta Lovin'' I heard the piano from hell go silent. The next thing I heard was the Gene Vincent handclaps, bap bap...bap...BAP BAP...BAP and heavy breathing next to my ear and I looked over to find Elston Gunnn dancing next to me as he broke into a background vocal part. Obviously, he had also come to the conclusion that the piano wasn't working out. The next night was more of the same. He was good spirited about the fact that none of us had the money to secure a piano for him and there were no hard feelings on the part of anyone as he made his exit for the University of Minnesota." [2]

1 *Lost and Found #5.*
2 www.bobbyvee.net

The above text owes much to *Just Like Bob Zimmerman's Blues – Dylan In Minnesota.* Written by Dave Engel, published 1997 by Amherst Press. ISBN: 0-942495-61-6

Commissioned for inclusion in *ISIS: A Bob Dylan Anthology.*

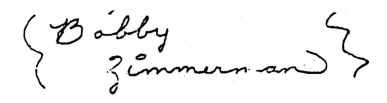

My Name It Is Nothing
by Derek Barker

"I didn't create Bob Dylan. Bob Dylan has always been here...always was. When I was a child, there was Bob Dylan. And before I was born there was Bob Dylan."

On August 9, 1962, at the Supreme Court building in downtown Manhattan, New York City, Robert Allen Zimmerman legally changed his name to Bob Dylan. However, several questions remained unanswered. How and when did he first adopt his new identity and was the name originally spelt Dylan or Dillon?

When

"Throughout the time Echo (Helstrom) *was his girl friend, Bob was seriously trying to come up with a name to use professionally; 'I can't use my real name,'* he told a few friends. *'I need a good stage name.'* Echo remembers – *'It was the summer before our senior year. Bob and John Buckland... drove over, and Bob was kind of excited. 'I found a name,' he said. 'I decided the name I'm going to use when I'm a singer. It's going to be Bob Dylan...' Echo says she didn't ask him whether it was inspired by Dylan Thomas because she just assumed that's where the name came from."*[1]

Echo again – *"Bob came over to my house one day and told me he'd finally decided on his stage name. Yes, it was Dylan after the poet, I think."*[2]

Despite Echo Helstrom's recollection of events, none of Dylan's Minneapolis fraternity brothers remember Zimmerman using the name Dillon/Dylan when he arrived at college in the fall of 1959 and it is highly possible that Helstrom has confused the name Dylan with an earlier stage name, that of Elston Gunnn.

Helstrom says Bobby came up with the name Dylan in the summer of 1958. However, that would have been around the time he formed the group Elston Gunnn and the Rock Boppers, in which, assumedly, Bobby was Elston Gunnn.

After graduating from Hibbing High and before commencing college in Minneapolis, Bobby Zimmerman spent some time travelling and working at odd jobs. During a stay in Fargo – summer 1959 – he played a few gigs with Bobby Vee's band, The Shadows, and Vee has stated in interviews that Dylan wanted to be known by his stage name, Elston Gunnn. In a separate interview Vee's sax player, Bobby Keys, told Robert Greenfield that he remembered *"a kid called Eldon Gunn"* (sic) being rejected by Vee. Therefore, I must concur with Dylan biographer Clinton Heylin when he says that Helstrom's memory must be *faulty* with regard to Bob's pseudonym. The new name that the excited young singer came running to her with, must surely have been Elston Gunnn and not Dylan.

While Dylan himself is not to be trusted with either fact or memory, he has on every occasion, steadfastly denied that he conceived of his stage name in Hibbing. Scaduto says that Bob would not discuss the origin of the name with him. However, he did say he first used the name on the spur of the moment, without having thought of it before and that it *"did not happen in Hibbing,"* but about a year later.[1]

Presumably, Dylan is referring here, to the Ten O'clock Scholar story. [David Lee]: *"Lee remembers Bob as a 'clean-cut kid,' very intense and determined. 'Do you mind if I play?' Bob asked when he wandered into The Scholar sometime in October, 1959. 'I want to be a folk singer'."*[1]

After learning that the kid had some experience, Lee informed him that he could play but that he would not be paid. He asked the kid's name, to which Bobby replied, *"Bob Dylan."*'

Dylan said in 1971, that when by David Lee asked what his name was, he simply replied, *"Dylan."* He said it just came to him as he was standing in the Scholar.

The way in which Zimmerman plucked his new pseudonym spontaneously out of thin air may seem a little fanciful; the time nonetheless seems right. Sometime in late 1959, and October at The Ten O'clock Scholar, remains the best candidate for the debut of Bob Dylan, or was it Dillon?

Dylan or Dillon

Shelton states in *No Direction Home* – *"Only after he had achieved some early recognition in New York did Minneapolis friends learn that Bob was spelling his name Dylan."* I assume that Shelton is referring here to a conversation that he had in 1966 with Harvey Abrams. Unfortunately, though, even these Minneapolis acquaintances cannot agree as to the correct spelling.

Harvey Abrams, part-owner of The Bastille, Minneapolis – *"Bob began to play at The Bastille at weekends* (circa 1960). *He always went as Bob Dillon, not Dylan. The only time we saw it with the Dylan Thomas spelling was in your New York Times article* (September 1961). *At school, he was registered as Bob Zimmerman but all his music billings here were spelled as Dillon."*[3]

Some of Bob's Minneapolis friends were told that Dillon was his mother's maiden name, while others had heard that Dillon was a town somewhere in Oklahoma. If indeed Bob had told people in Minneapolis that his alias was taken from one of these sources, it would surely follow that the spelling at that time must have been Dillon.

Unfortunately, another close friend disagrees with Abrams. Hugh Brown who lived with Bobby on Fifteenth Avenue Southeast, Minneapolis and was closer to him than most told Robert Shelton, *"I don't know why Harvey Abrams says he spelled his name Dillon then, because as I recall, he spelled it Dylan here."*[3]

There is no doubt that by the time Dylan reached Greenwich Village he was spelling his name with a 'y'. Therefore, if the name did undergo a change in spelling, it must have occurred between late 1959 and January 1961.

Origin

In the sixties, Dylan always vigorously denied taking his name from the Welsh poet. Mikki Issacson – *"I remember the first time I asked him how to spell Dylan –' like in*

Dylan Thomas?' and he said 'No, like in Bob Dylan'."[1]

When asked at a Sydney Airport press gathering in April 1966, why he changed his name to Dylan, he said that it was not because of the Welsh poet; *"I don't care for Dylan Thomas."* However, Dylan has mellowed a little with time. When asked the same question nearly twenty years later on a WNEW *Rockline* 'phone-in show, Dylan replied, *"Well, I think I've heard that story* (laughter)*, and I knew who Dylan Thomas was but, I'm not sure if I was familiar with his poetry or not."*

During the early sixties Dylan even concocted a long-running story about an uncle named Dillon, a professional gambler in Vegas. When questioned on this subject by Toby Thompson, Beatty Zimmerman had this to say – *"Bob took it from the poet Dylan Thomas, didn't he? Of course, there was never any uncle by that name, and my maiden name is Stone. Bob changed his name for show business reasons, and made it legal only because he had to carry two cards around to get in to clubs. I remember the night he called home to ask his father about it; he said, 'Do you mind?' and his father had said, 'Bobby, of course not, what's in a name? It's the person that counts."*[2]

Christopher Ricks – *"Well, there's only one famous person called Dylan, and that's Dylan Thomas. And it must therefore be that Bob Dylan took the name from there, whatever he says."* Ricks, however, went on to say, *"I think it's a fluke really."*
Radio Wales interview with Prof. Christopher Ricks, 1981

In 1968 Bob Dylan asked his semi-official biographer Robert Shelton – *"Straighten out in your book that I did not take my name from Dylan Thomas."*

Villon

Although cited by all, as having an influence on Dylan's work – Dylan told Robert Shelton that he converted the *"drama"* of Hattie Carroll into a song with a structure from François Villon – none of the major biographers mention the French medieval poet as being a possible candidate for the source of Dylan's name. However, a recent conversation with one of Dylan's close friends from Minneapolis has revealed that a number of Bob's early confidants thought he derived the name from the poet, simply substituting 'V' for 'D' and that he later changed the spelling purely for reasons of visual appearance.

We know that Dylan had an appreciation of Villon's work and that his discovery of the poet was around the time he adopted the Dylan/Dillon alias.

Bob Dylan – *"I didn't start writing poetry until I was out of high school. I was eighteen or so when I discovered Ginsberg, Gary Snyder, Phillip Whalen, Frank O'Hara and those guys. Then I went back and started reading the French guys, Rimbaud and François Villon."*[4]

Villon was considered by many scholars as France's outstanding *"lyric"* poet; a young Bobby Zimmerman would also have been attracted to the poet by his outlaw lifestyle.

During his *first* four years of banishment from Paris – for killing a priest in a street brawl and for his involvement in the theft of 500 crowns – Villon wandered around France, later earning himself the name *"The Vagabond Poet."* Later still, by order of the Bishop of Orleans, Villon was arrested and imprisoned. Returning to Paris after a pardon, he soon found himself in yet more serious trouble; he was re-arrested and condemned to death. A year later, his sentence was again commuted to banishment from Paris and thereafter there are no records of his activities.

Matt Dillon

According to Robert Shelton, the Zimmermans were the first family in Hibbing to acquire a television set, a fact that is not too surprising when you consider Bob's father was a partner in the town's electrical appliance store. The new set was installed in 1952 and both the Zimmerman boys were, *"glued to this fantastic new gadget for hours on end."* At first, as with any new toy, they watched almost anything and everything. Bobby, however, generally preferred music, variety shows and western adventures, featuring the likes of Daniel Boone and Wyatt Earp. The television series *Gunsmoke*, featuring a fictional character named Matt Dillon, was premiered on *CBS-TV* on September 10, 1955; at the time schoolboy Robert Zimmerman was almost fourteen-and-a-half and had just formed his first high school band. Could US Marshall Matt Dillon have been the inspiration for the name?

Dylan's personal guitar/amp tech, band member and occasional confidant, César Díaz, informed me that while they were on tour together in the early nineties he asked Dylan where he got his name. The answer, which was instant and seemed completely genuine, was Matt Dillon.

It should also be noted that the name Dillon was quite common in Hibbing. James Dillon was one of the originators of the town of Hibbing. During the fifties local boy Bobby Dillon – yes, Bobby Dillon – was a Green Bay Packers star. Merritt Dillon owned Dillon's farm on Dillon Road by Maple Hill, which is where Bob's girlfriend Echo Helstrom lived.

Dylan On Dylan

I took the name *'Dylan'* because I have an uncle named Dillon (sic). I changed the spelling but only because it looked better. I've read some of Dylan Thomas's stuff, and it's not the same as mine. We're different.

Chicago, November, 1965. Taken from *Bob Dylan in His Own Words* Miles.

Q: *Do you say Dylan or Die-lan?*

A: *Oh, I say Dylan, Die-lan, I say anything that you say really.*

Q: Did you take it from the Welsh poet?

A: *No, no, that's uh, I would say, a rumour, made up by people who like to simplify things. It's a name in my family, but uh, it's from my uncle's family. It's not my first father's name, it's the name of my mother's, my mother's side of the family and it's uh, spelled D-I-L-L-O-N, and I uh, changed it from there.*

Marlin Bronstein interview, February 20, 1968.

"Get it straight, I didn't change my name in honour of Dylan Thomas. That's just a story. I've done more for Dylan Thomas than he's ever done for me. Look at how many kids are probably reading his poetry now because they heard that story."

Jules Siegal interview, published July30, 1988.

Q: Why did you change your name from Zimmerman to Dylan?

A: *Why do people change their towns, nationalities, lives? I didn't possess this name, it just fell off my tongue...(it) rained on me and I kept it.*

Q: Is there any link with Dylan Thomas?

A: *No, none at all.*

L'Expresse interview, July 1978.

Q: You changed your name from Robert Zimmerman to Bob Dylan: was it because of Dylan Thomas?

A: *I haven't read that much of Dylan Thomas. It's a common thing to change your name. It isn't that incredible. Many do it...I wouldn't pick a name unless I thought I was that person. Sometimes you are held back by your name. Sometimes there are advantages to having a certain name...I just chose that name and it stuck. That name changed me...I didn't sit around and think about it too much, that's who I felt I was...But getting back to Dylan Thomas, it wasn't that I was inspired by reading some of his poetry and going 'Aha!' and changing my name to Dylan. If I thought he was that great, I would have sung his poems...*

Malibu, January 1988, and *Playboy* interview, March 1978.

Q: What's your real name?

A: *William-double-yew-Kasonavarich.*

Q: Why did you change it?

A: *Wouldn't you change yours if you had a name like William-double-yew-Kasonavarich? I couldn't get any girlfriends.*

Sydney Airport interview, April 1988.

The above retort is similar to the answer Dylan had given a reporter in Los Angeles a few months earlier – December 1965 – *"My real name was Knezelvitz and I changed it to avoid obvious relatives that come up to you in different parts of the country and want tickets to concerts and stuff like that."* As Miles.

Q: What possessed you, Bob, to change your name from Robert Zimmerman to Bob Dylan?

A: *Hmm, that's an interesting question. I really can't say, it's been so long. I think I was just playing somewhere one night and the club owner asked me my name, and that was the name that came into my mind. I don't think there was really anything profound about it.*

WNEW *Rockline* radio prog, June 17, 1985.

Meaning

Regardless of the origin of the name Dylan, the noun's meaning remains the same and is *Sea* or *Ocean*. Dylan Thomas's father, an ex-school teacher and an authority on Welsh folklore and myth, named his son after the Welsh god Dylan, *"Son of the Wave," "Divine Fish-Child."* The tale of *Math the Son of Mathonwy* is to be found in the *Mabinogion,* one of a collection of *romances* compiled by Lady Charlotte Guest (1848). The story is recounted by Robert Graves in his book *The White Goddess – A Historical Grammar of Poetic Myth.*

The tale is a complex one and depending on the version read, Dylan, Llew Llaw Gyffes and Gwyn are either brothers – with the possibility of Dylan and Llew being twins – or they are as one, a type of trinity. Llew would start the year as Dylan, *'Divine Fish-Child'* (January to Spring); after the summer solstice his name would change to Llew, *'the Lion with the Steady Hand.'* In autumn he would become Gwyn, *'White Rider on the White Horse,'* and in mid-winter the *'Eagle of Nant y Llew.'* It seems to me, however, that Llew was probably Dylan's *'twin'* and *'other self'* reincarnate. This of course fits with the essence of the White Goddess, Life-in-Death and Death-in-Life.

Interestingly, according to Graves, in primitive European belief only kings, chieftains, magicians and *poets* were privileged to be reborn.

Though Graves does not cite the circumstance of Dylan's demise, it would seem from Lewis Spence's *The Minor Traditions Of British Mythology'* that, *"Dylan was slain with a spear by his uncle Govannan,"* and that *" the waves of Britain, Ireland, Scotland and the Isle of Man wept for him. The sound of the sea rushing up the river Conway is still known as Dylan's death groan."*

While it is *extremely* unlikely that Dylan would have read Graves' *White Goddess* by the time he chose his new identity, he certainly became aware of the tale later and used elements from the book in the film *Renaldo and Clara*.

Mel Howard – *"There were all these themes running through it (Renaldo and Clara). Sara is very much into Robert Graves and his notion of the muse... So there was this scene in Niagara Falls where Sara played this kind of witch goddess creature."*

Summary

The first pseudonym that the young Bob Zimmerman came up with was almost certainly that of Elston Gunn, and not Bob Dylan as suggested by Echo Helstrom.

Bob first used the name Dillon or Dylan in Minneapolis sometime late in 1959 and October at The Ten O'clock Scholar remains by far the best candidate for the debut of Bob Dylan, or was it Dillon?

Dillon vs Dylan would seem to be down to Harvey Abrams vs Hugh Brown. Result, a draw. Without any documentary evidence such as a handbill, etc., we may never know for sure. What we do know for certain, is by the time of his arrival in New York City, January 1961, it *was* Bob Dylan.

How did the name originate? Christopher Ricks says – *"...there's only one famous person called Dylan, and that is Dylan Thomas."* Personally, I don't believe that Bob took his new name directly from Dylan Thomas and if it was originally spelled Dillon then this could not have been the case.

His first stage name was almost certainly taken from Peter Gunn, a television drama about a hip detective. The show was first aired in the summer of 1958, at exactly the same time that Bobby told Helstrom about his new name. He assumedly added the third 'n' for effect.

Therefore, my guess would be that the answer he gave Díaz in 1991 about taking the name Dylan from Matt Dillon is correct. It would seem reasonable to me that just over a year after taking the name Gunn from a contemporary television hero and changing the spelling so that it looked better, that he could have taken the name Dillon from another contemporary television hero and again change the spelling for reasons of appearance. If so, the name would have come from Matt Dillon, with the spelling change coming from Dylan Thomas. Maybe for once we should believe Bob when he said; *"I changed spelling, but only because it looked better."*

Regardless of whether Dylan took his name from Dylan Thomas or not, the meaning of the noun remains the same, *'sea'* or *'ocean.'* However, the name has now taken on a new meaning and I will leave the final word on the subject to Greil Marcus – *"The weight of Dylan's legend has now virtually changed his name into a noun, producing all kinds of words – 'Dylanesque', 'Dylanology' and so on – that Dylan now literally means just that: Dylan."*

Rolling Stone Magazine, December 13, 1969.

Sources used in the preparation of this text

1 Anthony Scaduto, *Bob Dylan An intimate Biography,* Signet edition 1973
2 Toby Thompson, *.Positively Main Street..* New English Library edition 1972
3 Robert Shelton, *No Direction Home* New English Library 1986
4 Clinton Heylin, *Behind The Shades – Take Two* Viking 2000

Minor Sources Used

Interview by author with – anon – associate of Dylan's from his time at college in Minneapolis. *The Minor Traditions Of British Mythology* by Lewis Spence. *Behind The Shades* by Clinton Heylin. *Bob Dylan – Or What's In a Name* by Richard David Wissolik, from the book *Bob Dylan's Words by* Wissolik/McGrath. Patrick J. Webster *"The Nine Billion Names Of Bob" The Telegraph* #21 autumn 1985. *Bob Dylan In His Own Words,* compiled by Miles, Omnibus Press 1979. Robert Graves *The White Goddess* Faber and Faber 1966, amended and enlarged edition.

Published in issue #64 January 1996

Alternatives To College
Incorporating a Chat With Dave Whitaker
by Derek Barker

An eighteen-year-old Bobby Zimmerman arrived in Minneapolis in September 1959. He was there to attend the University of Minnesota on a state scholarship and as such, on September 29, he moved into the Jewish fraternity house Sigma Alpha Mu, at 925 University Avenue Southeast. Bobby was unable to settle there and soon gave up his room at the frat house for a crash pad that he shared with Harry Weber and *"Spider"* John Koerner. Koerner later described the apartment as *"A horrible place, a sort of three-man slum."*[1]

The stay at 42 Seventh Street Southeast was a short one; Weber had problems coping with Dylan's demeanour, but in reality, it was their finances that dictated their actions. None of the three could come up with the money to pay the rent and after only a few short weeks they vanished before the landlady caught up with them.

Bobby then found a tatty, partially-furnished green painted room over Gray's Drugstore. The room on the corner of Fourth Street and Fourteenth Avenue was just half a block from his favourite haunt, the Ten O'clock Scholar, and although he kept the room for some time – a couple of months – it was nonetheless just one of the many places that he found to lay his head during his fifteen months' stay in Minneapolis.

Another such place was 714 Fifteenth Avenue Southeast, where he lived first with Dave Morton and Harvey Abrams and then a string of others including Max Uhler and Hugh Brown. As Brown later informed Robert Shelton, *"Living arrangements changed week to week."*[1]

Brown also told Shelton a wonderful tale of how Dylan had given him and his new wife a wedding present of a toaster and an iron, both of which had previously belonged to Brown when he had lived at the Fifteenth Avenue apartment.

Although his appearances at college were becoming increasingly irregular at this time, Bobby was still managing to attend some classes. Official records at the University of Minnesota show that Robert Allen Zimmerman attended classes for three semesters from September 1959, to the fall of 1960. In reality, he stopped going to classes almost completely after the first six months.

After leaving the fraternity house and discontinuing classes at the university, Bobby seemed to disassociate himself from most of the student body, the bulk of whom were working diligently toward more conventional professional goals. A close friend from the Zionist summer camp, Camp Hertzl, was now also in Minneapolis at the University of Minnesota Hospital. Larry Kegan was being treated for damage to his spine, sustained in a diving accident while on holiday with his parents in Florida. During his stay in Minneapolis Bobby spent a great deal of time at his friend's bedside, often playing songs for him at the hospital piano.[2]

Another such friend from summer camp was honey-blonde Judy Rubin whom Bobby had known and had dated off and on since the age of twelve. After discovering that she was now living at Sigma Delta Tau – situated just across the way from his own frat house – Bobby continued to pursue Judy. However, any relationship between the two was strongly discouraged by Rubin's parents and they soon drifted apart.

Dylan changed girlfriends almost as frequently as he changed address and on occasion, the two events would coincide. One such episode took place after he met Ellen Baker at the Whitakers place on Fourteenth Avenue.

Ellen Baker – *"We talked and he said he was from Hibbing, but I didn't find out his name was Zimmerman until later... I said my father had some old seventy-eights, of Woody, Cisco and others. And like a total collection of bound issues of every issue of Sing Out! He hardly ever seemed to have a place to live... He came over a couple of days later for dinner... and said 'Gee, can I stay here if I have no place to go?' ...He ended up staying over that night and on several other occasions, too."*[3]

Another girlfriend and probably his first real muse and the true *'Girl of the North Country'* was Bonnie Jean Beecher. When the two met in Minneapolis Dylan was beginning to learn to play the harmonica and Beecher apparently bought him his first trademark harmonica holder.[4]

David Whitaker – *"Wavy Gravy is married to Bonnie Beecher, Dylan's first girlfriend in Minneapolis. She goes by the name of Jahaunra now. Dylan, Wavy and I go back a long way. My daughters are counsellors at a summer camp; camp WinaRainbow for the children of the rock 'n' roll stars. Jahaunra runs the camp and Wavy is the head clown."*

Sometime in late January or early February 1960, Bob met Gretel Hoffman. Gretel, a slight local girl with long hair and radical left-wing views, had just dropped out of Bennington College. The two hung out together throughout February, meeting most evenings at the Scholar coffeehouse. Bobby was already using the name Dylan when he and Gretel met.

Gretel Hoffman – *"He said that it was his mother's name. There were a hundred stories about his background. Then it dawned on us that they were all stories."*[3]

When Bob wasn't playing and singing at the Scholar, he and Gretel would without fail attend the nightly parties, thus giving Bob a captive audience on which to try out his newly learned songs. Bob Spitz states that it was on one such evening in mid-March that Gretel took Bobby to a party at the home of an old school friend and it was during this rather dull party that Bob and Gretel were introduced to, *"A wiry dynamo"* that would change both of their lives. Enter David Whitaker.[3]

David, however, informed me that it was he and Gretel that met at the party and that his first meeting with Bob was at the Ten O'clock Scholar.

David Whitaker – *"Things get turned around. As I remember it, I think there might have been a party later, but it was at the Ten O'clock Scholar coffee house that I first met Bob. Though that was kinda like a party, it was where everybody hung out. I met*

Gretel at a party, but then there was always a party, life was a party in those days for sure. We were just learning to live, smoking dope, drinking beer, hanging out, and hanging in."

David, originally from Minneapolis, had been away on his travels for a number of years. The son of progressive ex-Socialist Party members, he dropped out of school in 1957 and by March 1960 this free-spirit had already ridden Woody Guthrie's freight trains, worked on a carnival and lived in San Francisco, where he hung out with Jack Kerouac, Neal Cassady and Bob Kaufman. He then spent more than a year on a Kibbutz in Israel, returning home to Minneapolis in February 1960 via Paris and London. Gretel says of David – *"He lived on the edge long before it became fashionable."*

David Whitaker – *"...I'd already been out and about before I met Bob. I'd been with the Beats, Kerouac, Cassady, all the guys and the girls in North Beach, San Francisco in 1957. And then I travelled around, I was in the Beat Hotel, I was in London during the skiffle era in Soho. I visited London on the way out from the States and on the way back. So, I got back to my parents' home in Minneapolis and my sister said they had just started this beat coffee house down in Dinkytown so of course I'm there. I'm there the very next day and here's this kid playing the guitar and it's Bob Dylan. So, I met Bob as soon as I got back to Minneapolis. When I met him, he had just shed the name Zimmerman. We all knew that he was really Bobby Zimmerman, though."*

Gretel Hoffman – *"I wasn't really Bobby's girlfriend, in any sense. But I was considered to be his girl, I guess. Then I started going with David."*[3]

Bob did not see much of Gretel toward the end of April and the beginning of May and then one evening shortly before his nineteenth birthday, he and Gretel bumped into each other on Fourth Avenue, near The Scholar. Dylan asked Gretel where she had been, and Gretel informed him that she had just got married to David Whitaker. Dylan walked off and then called back over his shoulder *"Let me know when you get divorced."*[4]

It seems, however, that Dylan was not too hurt by the situation and Gretel, David and Bob were soon seen around as a threesome and for a short while Dylan even moved in with the newlyweds.

Dylan told Anthony Scaduto that David Whitaker was responsible for an enormous change in him. Dylan – *"I saw Whitaker and it was like that"* – motioning with his hand as in a karate chop – *"Just over and out. I was on this side and suddenly I was on that side."*[3]

Without doubt, David Whitaker had a major part to play in shaping the course of young Bobby Dylan's early life. Whitaker turned Dylan on to Woody Guthrie by persuading him to read Guthrie's book *Bound For Glory.* Dylan immediately fell in love with the Guthrie persona and carried the book around for weeks, insisting everyone should read it.

David Whitaker – *"After reading* Bound For Glory, *Bob would play Guthrie's 'Tom Joad' all day long. That half-hour song, all day, day after day."*

While it seems certain that Dylan would have moved on to New York sooner or later, the timing of the move was unquestionably influenced by his reading of that book. Before he left, Dylan also borrowed much from Whitaker's past, including carnivals, freight trains, and the Beats.

David Whitaker – *"Yeah, I was in a carnival and I used to tell him all those stories, but more than that, I don't know. But, riding freight trains and all that stuff, yeah I did all that, but I don't want to, you know, say that he took all of that stuff from my past. But he definitely invented himself to be what he wanted to be and that's amazing... Because he got a lot of slings and arrows, as any person who's a square peg in a round hole did in those days. He was a natural nonconformist and if you were a nonconformist in those days they shit on you for sure in every possible way."*

Bobby Dylan was developing fast and how much his trip to New York tied in with his wish to visit Woody Guthrie, who lay dying with Huntington's chorea in Greystone Hospital near Morristown, New Jersey, is unclear.

Dylan left Minneapolis for Chicago around Christmas 1960, hung around for a while and then decided to head back north, hitchhiking as far as Madison. For the moment, he seemed to have given up the notion of visiting Guthrie and wrote to the Whitakers, notifying them of his change of plan. However, while in Madison Dylan met Fred Underhill who was planning a trip to New York City. Dylan decided to tag along as relief driver and history was back on course.

On his arrived in New York City he soon got work playing in the many clubs and bars in Greenwich Village but, according to Bob and Sidsel Gleason he also took a job with the NYC sanitation department clearing snow!

David Whitaker – *"That was his first job before he started playing around, but that was way early, when he first got there. I don't know if he did a day, or half a day, but he did it for sure.*

He came back up to Minneapolis a few times and he sent postcards. I saw him too, when I went to New York. He was living on Fourth Street. I was there after the March on Washington and all that. I went to the party for the entertainers and Dylan was at the party. I saw him in New York a few times. At that party he asked me to come and stay with him, so later I went to New York to spend time with him. At that time he was living in this empty place – almost empty. I think Suze had just left...

I think Bob misses the old days in Minneapolis and those early times in New York... Did you see that piece in The New Yorker about the sixties? There was this quote where Dylan said that back then it was like being a member of a secret society and now he thinks maybe he's the only one left. I thought that was pretty good. I know exactly what he's talking about. It can feel like that.

I love his new album "Time Out Of Mind." It's simply great. He's talkin' about what it's like to be Bob Dylan TODAY, you know. 'It's not dark yet, but it's getting there.' What's he doin?' 'He's standing in the doorway crrrryin'.' I really like 'Highlands.' You know, being older myself, I mean I'm a little older than him – though younger in some ways – I can see exactly where he's coming from. I can feel what it must be like to be totally isolated from the world and why he would write that thing in The New Yorker. I mean that was a little unusual. He was speaking from the heart there. He wonders what happened to everybody and I think that was an important message and it was contemporary with the album... The man seems to be in total isolation. Everyone that I know who has been close to him gives the impression that he's now totally isolated and that the man has no friends at all. I saw Victor Maymudes, I don't know when, not too long ago, and he doesn't see Bob any more! I knew Victor from way back, and he and Bob had been friends for, you know... I guess he's still friends with Larry Kegan though... I invited Bob up to the Rainbow Gathering, but instead Kegan came up in his super van, with his right hand man and a few other people; it was in Minnesota. I had seen Kegan with Bob in LaCrosse at the concert there – June 12 1990. I never imagined that we would get to talk because there were too many people around and you just can't get to Bob. He was coming through, his face was hidden, so I just gave out a shout: 'Dylan, Bob Dylan, it's Dave Whitaker.' He just held up his hand and the crowd, which was surrounding him just opened up – the hand of Bob, you know. The waters parted and I walked straight on through.

We stood by the banks of the Mississippi and talked. It was our first conversation in many years. We just talked about poetry. I did a couple of my poems, which he liked and we talked about our kids. Dylan and I have a few between us. I mean I have nine children, seven are bi-racial...Bob gave my eldest son Ubie Doobie his first guitar, a Fender Stratocaster...We were giving kids funny names back then, like Wavy's first kid was Howie Dudey. Anyway, that is when I invited him to the Rainbow Gathering. He'd heard about the gatherings and was very interested, but instead of coming himself, he sent Larry Kegan! The Gathering was camped at the end of a trail so we – not me but some of the younger guys – picked Kegan up and carried him in his wheelchair down the trail to where the gathering was held. He videotaped the whole thing. I assume what he does is that Dylan then watches the videotapes because he feels that he could not come himself. Could not expose himself to all those unknown people.

I don't think that he feels free to do anything, poor guy. He just seems to be so alone, and that's what "Time Out Of Mind" is all about. He sees all these people doin' this stuff and all the kids out there; the young boys and the pretty girls and he'd give what? $10,000 to be one of them again. Maybe not money, but you know, instead of being with those young people he's 'Standing in the doorway crrrryin.' He's 'Got nothin' to go back to now.' 'Got no place left to turn.' 'All the laughter is just makin' him sad.' It's the New Yorker thing again, the secret society and him thinking that he's the only one left from the fifties and sixties. It's all there on that album; what does he say? 'I feel like talkin' to somebody, but I don't know who.' I really must get in touch with him.

My girlfriend paid $75 to take me to a show recently! She really wanted to meet him and like a lot of people she thought that somehow I could, you know – but $75 for a show! And I'm right at the back. It was this spring when he was touring with Paul Simon. I did send a note in because she insisted that I do. And she said that he said something cryptic, which was referring to me, but I don't know. To me it was like a cover band though. It seemed like a cover band but there was Bob Dylan! So they said. I guess it must have been. It should have been for $75!"

1 Robert Shelton, *No Direction Home*
2 Howard Sounes, *Down the Highway – The Life of Bob Dylan*
3 Anthony Scaduto, *Bob Dylan*
4 Bob Spitz, *Dylan a Biography*

Note – All quotes by David Whitaker in the above text are from an interview with David Whitaker conducted by Derek Barker on October 13, 1999, exclusively for ISIS Magazine. Published in issue #88, December 1999.

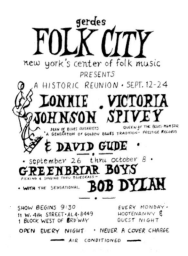

Dylan's Village
by Derek Barker and Robert Levinson

Greenwich Village occupies a small patch of land near the southern tip of Manhattan Island and a sizable slice of emotional space for Dylan fans everywhere, as it is the spot where he launched his spectacular career during the stormy winter of 1961.

The Village, as everyone calls it, holds a mysterious, almost forbidden aura for outsiders, whether they're from nearby Brooklyn, or from the far, frozen, mined-out regions of barren Minnesota. Greenwich Village has always been informal and very different from the rest of the metropolis, ever since its beginnings. It is hard to believe now, but in colonial times this section of Lower Manhattan was a distinct village called Greenwich, which became a neighbourhood of conservative Georgian brick houses with white trim over the doors and carriage barns in back-alley mews. A few of these houses remain, but conservative the Village isn't.

In the 1960s, strolling through Washington Square Park, the heart of the Village, on a pleasant afternoon, you'd find a hundred different groups of people doing a hundred different things. Intimidating, silent combatants played fierce games of speed-chess while ancient Sicilian men played loud vocals game of bocce just a few meters away. The benches were filled with people reading *Village Voice* while scores of would-be musicians squatted on the grass, playing for small, appreciative audiences as well as just for themselves. Children squealed jubilantly beneath the cold-water sprinklers, dogs bounded in and out of the fountain, co-ed teams played friendly games of volleyball and kites, along with the strong pungent smell of marijuana, filled the air. It was a carefree, creative and energy-filled place that was overflowing with some of the country's finest young artists, musicians and writers.

Cheap lodgings, inexpensive places to eat and numerous speakeasies have made Greenwich Village a destination and haven for artists and bohemians since the mid-nineteenth century. The Village remains an art, music and literary colony today, filled with a life and vitality second to none in a very vibrant city.

Today the students of New York University on Washington Square who still keep the Village cafés, bars, bookstores and record shops in business maintain the lack of orthodoxy. Artists are a little harder to find now, though every year at the Washington Square Outdoor Art Exhibit – a summertime tradition since 1931 – hundreds of painters, sculptors and photographers display their works.

The limits of Greenwich Village run north-south from Fourteenth Street to Houston Street and east-west from Broadway to the Hudson River. However, from Sixth Avenue to the Hudson is a more sedate West Village, an area of brick houses and tree-lined streets.

Accompanied by his friend Fred Underhill, Bob Dylan arrived in New York City on or around January 24, 1961. They had arrived by car, a four-door Pontiac, and had been deposited in uptown Manhattan – somewhere around Sixty-second Street – by the expedition's main driver Dave Berger.

Dylan's trip to New York had been anything but direct. He left Minneapolis arriving in Chicago just before Christmas 1960, but then changed his mind and turned back north to Minneapolis, stopping off in Madison, before changing his mind again. This time the trip to New York was made in one continuous drive, stopping only to change drivers.

Dylan was greeted by the coldest New York winter since 1933. A week before his arrival, the city had endured a foot of snow and drifts were now piled high. Dylan decided to take what he would later refer to in *'Talkin' New York'* as *"a rockin', reelin', rollin' ride,"* down to the West Village by subway.

Tuesday night was hootenanny night at the Café Wha? and after finding his way to the centre of the Village and wandering up and down MacDougal and Bleecker, taking in the sights and checking out the clubs and coffee houses, the Wha? is where he ended up.

Dylan quickly approached the owner, Manny Roth and was allowed to play a very short set of mostly Guthrie songs. Dylan would later claim that the club patrons *"flipped"* when they heard him play. *"I played there and they flipped...They really did."*[1]

Waitress Maddy Bloom, however, remembers the Wha? as being half empty that night. Nevertheless, Roth must have noticed him, because Dylan was soon playing at the Wha? most afternoons.

Nearby Washington Square had been a *venue* for a plethora of musical expressions, including folk music, throughout the fifties. However, by the middle of the decade, the folk singers were beginning to come indoors, invading the Greenwich Village Jazz clubs and by the turn of the decade folk music was flourishing in the Village, especially at the many coffee houses on and around MacDougal Street and Bleecker. Coffee houses with compelling names such as The Limelight, Kettle Of Fish, Café Au Go Go and The Fat Black Pussycat, all encouraged folk musicians to play, not only because the musicians brought in more customers, but also because the musicians were often prepared to play for no payment.

The clubs where the artists' only form of payment was from audience tips, were known as *"basket houses,"* so named after the practice of passing a wicker basket through the audience to collect money that would be shared by the entertainers at the end of the evening. Among the first basket houses were the Commons, Café Wha?, Gaslight and Figaro.

To begin with, the basket house circuit was Dylan's only opportunity to be heard. The Café Wha?, Café Bizarre, Commons, Figaro, Caravan Café, Thirdside and Gaslight, were just some of the places Dylan played. He could be seen around the Village most nights wearing his trademark black button-down corduroy cap and an extremely ill fitting jacket that cost him seventy-five cents from a Village thrift shop.

It seemed that anyone could open a coffeehouse simply by renting a storefront and putting in a coffee machine. Moreover, it was not only the musicians that worked for no payment, most of the waitresses also worked only for tips. Another added bonus for the club owners was that the clubs did not require a music licence in order to operate. Cabaret licences were only necessary if amplification or drums were used. In addition, the local bars were required by law to close by two am but, because most of the Village coffee houses chose not to serve liquor, they were able to remain open longer, with some venues remaining open and providing entertainment until four or even six a.m. Some of the smaller joints could only be described as dives. Tom Pasle said of the Café Raffio – probably the dingiest in the Village – *"I don't have to do this for a living. I could starve."*[2]

Between 1963 and 1968 it seemed every third storefront along Bleecker and MacDougal was a club or coffeehouse. At any one time there could be as many as forty coffee houses operating in the Village. The streets became so crowded at weekends that wooden barriers were erected between Bleecker and West Third on MacDougal to prevent traffic from entering the area. As more tourists flooded into the Village – often staying until the early hours – bad feeling started to rise within the local community, which resulted in residents' groups like the *Village Board* and the *Minetta Street Organization* applying pressure to the authorities to close down any unlicensed clubs.

At the time of Dylan's arrival on the scene – early 1961 – a campaign of harassment had already begun and for a time the Gaslight and other clubs on MacDougal and Bleecker were being raided nightly.

The Village Gaslight – or Gaslight Café as it was better known – and Gerdes Folk City were probably the two clubs most responsible for giving Dylan his early breaks. The Gaslight was a favourite haunt of manager Albert Grossman and it was while playing a weeklong residency there in July 1961 that Dylan was first introduced to Grossman. It would be some time before *The Bear* became Dylan's manager, but the inevitable union would create the biggest force ever to hit folk music and in the same way that Elvis Presley and Colonel Tom Parker, and the Beatles and Brian Epstein became as one, so the names Dylan/Grossman became synonymous.

The most celebrated of all the Greenwich Village folk clubs was Gerdes Folk City. In 1952, William Gerdes sold his restaurant to three Italian immigrants, Mike Porco, his brother John, and their cousin Joe Bastone. The new owners retained the name Gerdes, made a few improvements and the restaurant began to prosper. However, after four years they were forced to relocate from their West Third Street building – which was to be demolished to make way for a couple of high-rises – to a six-story brownstone building at 11 West Fourth Street.

The new Gerdes restaurant was located in an industrial area and had itself once been a spray-gun factory. During the day the place sold inexpensive Italian food to the local factory workers, but after the demolition of most of the surrounding factories, Gerdes became in danger of closing. Mike Proco brought in a piano player and then a trio, but business didn't pick up enough so, in January 1960, Porco allowed Izzy Young and Tom Prendergast to begin promoting folk music there. Israel *"Izzy"* Young who ran the Folklore Center around the corner at 110, MacDougal Street, was well liked in the Village. The centre, a narrow two-room shop that sold books, folk records and other musical paraphernalia, was also the meeting place for the Village folk musicians.

Young and Prendergast operated their club as the Fifth Peg – a name derived from the tuning *peg* that adjusts the short fifth string found half way along the neck of a banjo. This new venue was exactly what the Village folk scene needed. Gerdes was bigger than most of the clubs, it had licence to sell liquor, and promoter Izzy Young was paying his musicians! The Fifth Peg officially opened on January 26, 1960 with Brother John Sellars, Ed McCurdy and Bruce Langhorn being paid $150 for the weeklong engagement. The venture got off to a good start but some nights were much better than others. Izzy noted in his journal that on Sunday March 13, Brownie McGhee and Sonny Terry played to just two paying customers. In April, Porco stopped the folk club for a week and whatever momentum it had was lost. Any money that Young and Prendergast made went on advertising and paying musicians. However, Porco's bar receipts were up and he knew he was on to a good thing. Just three months after they had started their venture at Gerdes, Porco squeezed Young and Prendergast out and the venue was again closed. Porco brought in a manager, Charlie Rothschild, and on June 1, 1960 the club was reopened as *Gerdes Folk City*.

Although the club was successful, Monday nights were slow. Therefore, Porco took-up the suggestion of Charlie Rothschild to introduce an amateur night on Mondays, which at the suggestion of Robert Shelton became known as the Monday Hootenanny.

Most of the Village clubs were free to patrons but, even with its dollar-fifty admission fee, Gerdes Folk City was always filled to its official capacity of 175, with as many, or more, waiting outside to get in. This success soon prompted The Bitter End and Gaslight to began hoot nights of their own.

Dylan quickly graduated from the Monday hoots to playing paying gigs at Gerdes. Porco paid Dylan just over ninety dollars a week plus some food, drinks, and a few old clothes. His first major break came when Porco booked him to play a two-week residency supporting John Lee Hooker. The booking ran from the 11th to the 23rd April 1961 – excluding the 17th.

Five months later, Bob Shelton would review the opening night of another two-week residency at Gerdes. This time Dylan was supporting The Greenbriar Boys and the headline of the resulting review, published in *The New York Times* on Friday September 29, 1961, read: *"Bob Dylan: A Distinctive Stylist."* The piece, which gushed with praise for Dylan, closed with the abiding lines – *"Mr Dylan is vague about his antecedents and birthplace, but it matters less where he has been than where he is going and that would seem to be straight up."*

1 Billy James interview 1961
2 Robert Shelton *No Direction Home*

Adapted extract from an article published in issue #95 March 2001.

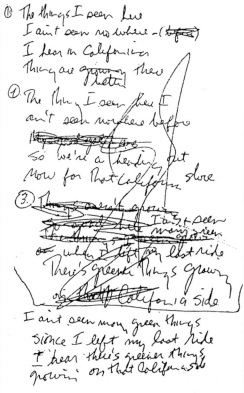

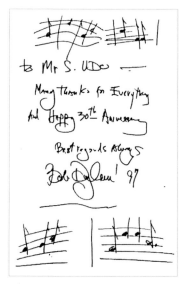

The Troubadour

🎵🎵🎵🎵🎵🎵🎵🎵🎵🎵🎵🎵🎵🎵🎵🎵🎵🎵🎵🎵

LONDON'S OLDEST FOLK CLUB IS

✂ 10 YEARS OLD IN MARCH ✂

265, OLD BROMPTON ROAD, LONDON, S.W.5.

TUES: 9.30   WED: 8.30   SAT: 10.30   SUN: 8.30.

One Time in London
by Derek Barker

The following piece is an attempt to *fine-tune* the chronology of Dylan's visit to London in the winter of 1962-63. For those of you that may be unfamiliar with this period I will attempt to give a brief description of Dylan's stay, while at the same time – for the more completist Dylan enthusiasts – focusing on, and attempting to clear up some of the misconceptions that have been attached to this visit. Clearly, thirty-seven years after the event we will *never* be in a position to substantiate *all* of the rumoured dates and venues. I hope, however, that this piece will help to clear up at least some of the anomalies appertaining to Dylan's first UK visit.

December 1962

18 Tue. Arrives Heathrow Airport, London. Checks in at Mayfair Hotel, Stratton Street.
18 Plays Troubadour 265, Old Brompton Road, London, SW5.
19 Wed. BBC Television Studios, Shepherds Bush. First reading for *Madhouse On Castle Street.*
22 Sat. Plays Singers Club, at The Pindar of Wakefield (pub) Gray's Inn Road, WC1
23 Sun. Plays King and Queen (pub) Foley Street, W1.
28 Fri. Visits *Melody Maker* offices – lunchtime – in the hope of talking with Max Jones.
29 Sat. Ballads and Blues, Partisan Coffee Shop.
29 Plays Troubadour 265, Old Brompton Road, London, SW5.
30 Sun. BBC Television Studios, Shepherds Bush. Partly aborted recording of *Madhouse on Castle Street.*
30 Singers Club, at The Pindar of Wakefield (pub) Gray's Inn Road, WC1
31 Mon. Plays King and Queen (pub) Foley Street, W1.
Late Dec. Possibly plays at Bunjie's Folk Cellar and Coffee House on Lichfield Street.

January 1963

1 Tue. Plays King and Queen (pub) Foley Street, W1.
Early January. Visits poet Robert Graves, *possibly* accompanied by Rory McEwen.
2 or 3 Interviewed for issue #17 of *Scene* Magazine – around midday – in his hotel room

at the Cumberland.

4 Fri. BBC Television Studios, Shepherds Bush, London. Second and final recording of *Madhouse On Castle Street.*

5 Sat. Flies to Rome to meet Grossman, who is on tour with Odetta.

10 Thurs. Arrives back in London from Rome, late afternoon/early evening.

10 Attends sound check and Odetta concert at Prince Charles Theatre, Leicester Square.

12 Sat. Plays Troubadour 265, Old Brompton Road, SW5.

14 Mon. records Dobell's Jazz Shop, 77 Charing Cross Road, WC2. Probably went over to Bunjie's after recording.

15 Tue. Records at Dobell's Jazz Shop, 77 Charing Cross Road, WC2.

15 Plays Troubadour 265, Old Brompton Road, SW5, after recording at Dobell's

16 Wed. Flies home to New York from London's Heathrow Airport.

The importance of this first visit to London cannot be overstressed. Whilst Dylan was developing at an incredible pace during his formative period – 1961-'64 – only his three-week trip across America by station wagon, in February 1964, would produce so vast a change in so short a time.

During his four-weeks in London and shortly after his return to New York, a near metamorphosis appears to have occurred. From inspiration gathered from this visit Dylan wrote, *'Girl Of The North Country,' 'Boots Of Spanish Leather'* – both written during a short vacation in Rome and both borrowing their melodies from Martin Carthy's arrangement of *'Scarborough Fair'* – *'Bob Dylan's Dream,' 'Liverpool Gal,' 'Farewell,' 'Only a Hobo,' 'With God On Our Side'* and possibly *'Masters Of War.'*

Although *'Masters Of War'* is widely believed to have been written during his stay in England, the exact date of its composition has always been something of a mystery to me.

As Heylin states in *Behind The Shades – Take Two* – *"The song was singularly absent from the Witmark demos* – that – *Dylan cut a couple of days before his trip to England."* Conversely, both Martin Carthy and Anthea Joseph have stated that Dylan played *'Masters Of War'* within a couple of days of arriving in England. In any event, it was not the amount of songs written, but a change in his approach toward song writing that made his time in London so significant. On his return to New York, Dylan told Robert Shelton – *"I'm goin' through changes. I need some more finger-pointin' songs... 'cause that's where my head's at right now."*[1]

This change in direction was confirmed in a conversation recounted by Richard Fariña – *"Take Joanie, man, she's still singin' about Mary Hamilton. I mean where's that at? She's walked around on picket lines, she's got all kinds of feelings, so why ain't she steppin' out?"*[1]

Dylan again – *"I went to England in '62... and when I went back to the States it had already began to happen. I wrote a lot of things which hadn't been done before, just all these different influences"*[1]

And – *"I ran into some people in England who really knew those* – traditional English – *songs. Martin Carthy, another guy named Nigel Davenport* (sic) (Dylan is referring here either to Bob Davenport or Nigel Denver). *Martin Carthy's incredible. I learned a lot of stuff from Martin."*[2]

Martin Carthy – *"I've read a lot of books about him and not one of them talks in any detail about his time in England. As far as I can hear, by listening to his records, his time in England was actually crucial to his development. If you listen to "Freewheelin'," most of which was made before he came to England, and you listen to the next album after that, which is "Times They Are a-Changin'," there's an enormous difference in the way he's singing, in the sort of tunes he's singing, the way he's putting words together."*

Producer Philip Saville had brought Dylan to London to appear in the BBC television play *Madhouse On Castle Street.*

Philip Saville – *"In 1960, I was in New York, doing a television production with Alan Lomax... We were working on* Dark Of The Moon, *an American play* [by Howard Richardson and William Berney]. *I'd seen Dylan playing down in Pastor's Place in Greenwich Village... Back in London, I was preparing a theatrical piece, Evan Jones's* Madhouse on Castle Street, *and suddenly had the idea that it would be exciting to cast this young American poet in the role of an anarchistic young man. I approached him and discovered that there was this bogeyman, Al Grossman, to deal with.... We struck a deal. Al Grossman said that Dylan was coming to Hamburg to do his first European concert* (sic?) There was no such concert. *...He said he'd pay for the trip back if I'd organise the outward fare.*

It was an extraordinary move for the BBC at that time. I was there as an independent, working on contract; they literally didn't know who Bob Dylan was. I brought him over, at enormous cost, relatively speaking.

...At the Mayfair Hotel, where I went to see him, it was obvious he was very excited about the 'new' England. I said to my assistant, 'You've got to keep tabs on him: tomorrow is the first reading of the play.' Dylan said 'Don't worry, I'll be there.' He wasn't, so we went to get him and eventually he arrived half an hour late.

We had a difficult time on the days of the camera rehearsal – This implies more than one rehearsal *– because he would go missing. He liked his smoke and he usually had a fair amount on him. One time, I literally found him under a car two streets away from where I lived. He wasn't irresponsible, just very involved with the present. He had this wonderful way of living in the now...*

Anyway, we began to realise that Dylan wasn't able to deal with the dialogue at all. He was quite honest with me – he did find learning the lines genuinely difficult... he asked whether he could write his own part... 'Do I have to act – why can't I just be a singer?'

He loved London. It was his first visit. I took him around the various parties... At the end of filming, we went off to a Greek restaurant – they were something different in those days."

Originally, Grossman had asked Saville for a fee of $2,000 – at the time around £500 – plus Dylan's air fair to England. However, with the prospect of a delay in the recording of *Madhouse,* due to a technicians' dispute, Grossman *"wrung another fee"* out of the BBC – assumedly a further $2,000 – plus Grossman asked for and got, the price of Dylan's plane ticket home.

Saville told Robert Shelton in 1971 – *"This became undoubtedly the most expensive money ever paid for a singer to do the opening and closing music for a play and to deliver only one spoken line."*[1]

According to Shelton, Dylan's visit to London became a rich source of anecdotes:

"He told me about various surreal parties, with fat Americans, an adolescent English girl who looked French, and a crippled old lady who took ten minutes to hobble from the door to the middle of a room. At another party, while the piercing English winter was penetrating his bones, everyone else walked about in short sleeved shirts. At a party of 'England's top hippies,' Bob positioned himself so close to the gas fire, his trousers nearly caught fire. They danced to Everly Brothers records. 'The English could do the twist by moving only one leg!' He sang for them, but their looks matched the rooms chill."[1]

Make Me a Pallet On The Floor

Some confusion exists over exactly where Dylan stayed while in London. He was booked into The Mayfair Hotel on Stratton Street by the BBC for the duration of his contract with them. However, Dylan took an instant dislike to the hotel.

Bob Dylan – *"The Mayfair had these hooded little guards outside that look you over. They looked like George Washington all dressed up. They come and take your baggage in to the hotel. Then you get inside the door and somebody else comes to meet you there, and you tip the guard from outside for having taken your baggage inside. Then your baggage goes from inside to the elevator; someone else hits you for a tip to take your baggage to the elevator. Then you tip him and the elevator chap puts your baggage in and you have to tip him when you get out of the elevator. Then someone else takes the baggage out of the elevator and he opens the door to your room and puts the baggage at the end of the bed. Man, you end up tipping about ten guys."*[1]

Having now reached his room, Dylan concludes that the Mayfair is not for him and decides that he will have to find somewhere else to stay. It has been rumoured that Dylan checked out of the Mayfair immediately. However, as the BBC is footing the bill for the hotel it is likely that he remained there until other accommodation could be found. Saville's comment about going to see Dylan at the Mayfair seems to indicate that Dylan must have stayed there for a time, or at least used it as a base.

Dylan had been told by Pete Seeger that he should look up Anthea Joseph while in London, and he appears to have done so on his first night in town. Dylan went to the Troubadour in search of Joseph, who was the organiser of the Folk Club there on Tuesday nights.

Anthea Joseph – *"There I was – on the door at the Troubadour – and these feet came down the stairs – with cowboy boots, which in those days were rather unusual, and jeans, which were also fairly unusual. Then the jacket. Then the face. Then the hat... He trundled up to my cubbyhole and started shoving money at me and said, 'I'm looking for Anthea. Can I come in please?' And I said, 'Well, I'm Anthea' – and the penny dropped – and I said, 'You're Bob Dylan, aren't you?' And he said 'yes.' I said, 'Right, well you can have your money back provided you sing for us'."*[1]

Not wishing to return to the Mayfair, Dylan asked Joseph if she knew where he could stay that night. Anthea asked around and after singing he eventually went off with somebody he met at the club.

It is believed – though far from certain – that the next day, December 19, Dylan attended the first reading for *Madhouse* at the BBC studios. It was possibly after this reading, though more probably after a second reading, that Dylan spent two nights at Philip Saville's home.

Philip Saville – *"...As I got to know Bob quite well, I asked if he'd like to stay at my home – I had a house in Hampstead. He was complaining about the Mayfair Hotel being worried about his appearance, his not wearing a tie, his playing a guitar in the foyer, staying up all night and dragging in groupie girls off the streets. So he came to my place for two days."*

After departing the Mayfair, Dylan moved to the more homely Cumberland. Dylan's room at the Cumberland – again paid for by the BBC – ran out with the end of his BBC contract. His last night at the hotel was therefore January 4. With his commitments now out of the way and Odetta scheduled to play in Rome, Dylan decides to take a short break there himself, leaving on January 5. It seems Dylan might have played a couple of impromptu performances while in Rome. The story that Dylan told biographer Anthony Scaduto about going to Italy to look for his girlfriend Suze Rotolo, seems dubious, as by that time Rotolo was back in New York.

After returning from Rome on January 10, Dylan spent time with Eric von Schmidt, Richard Fariña and friends who were now occupying two rooms at the Hotel de France in South Kensington. Before their move to the somewhat shabby looking baroque hotel,

Fariña and von Schmidt had been staying at a rather opulent townhouse in Tregunter Road. The house was the family home of Alex and Rory McEwen, who at the time, were holidaying in Scotland. While staying at the McEwens' Dylan had visited Fariña and von Schmidt, spending the night. At around that time, Dylan attended a party at the home of folk singer Susan May and an all night party at a flat belonging to singer John Shear.

Contrary to popular myth, at no time on this visit did Dylan stay at the home of Martin and Dorothy Carthy. Dylan and Carthy became friends, spending a great deal of time together, playing and visiting numerous London folk clubs. Dylan visited Carthy several times at his Haverstock Hill home, but did not stay there.

The Dust of Rumour

There has been a long-standing rumour that during this visit to London Dylan appeared at the Surbiton and Kingston Folk Club, held at that time on Wednesday evenings at the Surbiton Assembly Rooms. Due to the Christmas recess, the Surbiton folk club only met three times during Dylan's London stay. The only realistic date for a visit by Dylan to the club would seem to be January 2. On that night, the featured act at Surbiton was The Strawberry Hill Boys – later to become The Strawbs. I have spoken with Dave Cousins of The Strawbs who had already briefly met Dylan a fortnight before at the Troubadour, and he is certain that Dylan was *not* at Surbiton that evening.

Club organiser Derek Sarjeant has stated on a number of occasions that Dylan did perform at Surbiton during his first visit to England and even claimed to have photographic evidence. However, on production of a photograph to ISIS subscriber Chris Cooper, the harmonica accompaniment provided during a Carolyn Hester set, turned out not to be Bob Dylan, but Richard Fariña. If further evidence was needed, Carolyn Hester was not in the UK at the time of Dylan's visit. One interesting aside is that at one such performance at Surbiton, the harmonica playing Fariña introduced himself as Blind Boy Grunt, and this may well have helped attribute to the confusion.

Another club that Dylan is believed to have performed at during his stay is Bunjie's Folk Cellar and Coffee House on Lichfield Street. Dylan almost certainly went there after recording at Dobell's on Monday, January 14 – Bunjie's Folk Cellar operated just across the road from Doug Dobell's Jazz Records shop.

All the major biographers including Howard Sounes and David Hajdu in their recent books, erroneously credit a stoned performance by Dylan, Ethan Signer, Martin Carthy, Richard Fariña and Eric von Schmidt at the Troubadour to January 14, 1963. The performance, which took place after Dylan and co had ousted Jewish folksinger Judy Silver from the stage, contained goodies such as *'Cocaine,' 'The London Waltz'* and *'Overseas Stomp'* performed by the ensemble, and *'Don't Think Twice, It's All Right'* and *'Blowin' In The Wind'* by Dylan performing solo. This impromptu performance allegedly took place after the first night of recording at Dobell's. This mistake, which seems to have been duplicated from one publication to the next, has to be incorrect simply because the Troubadour did not open on Monday nights. I have flyers for the Troubadour, contemporary with this period, which state the club was open on Tuesday, Wednesday, Saturday and Sunday. Anthea Joseph, who ran the Tuesday night folk sessions, confirmed to me that the club did not operate on a Monday and she was on the door for the Tuesday night session when the episode took place.

The rumoured appearance by Dylan on December 25 at the King and Queen is almost certainly incorrect, as is the rumour that Dylan visited Les Cousins Folk Club on Greek Street. Evidence has now emerged, which strongly suggests that Cousins' was not open at that time. We are also informed in the Shelton biography that Dylan played at the Establishment Club at least once during his stay in London, and thanks to some detective work by ISIS collaborator John Cumming – who has discovered what must be the earliest published review of a performance by Bob Dylan in this country – we can now confirm Shelton's statement.

John takes up the story...

The author of the review, Anthony Smith, lives in Bristol and in the early sixties, he was a young reporter working for the *Western Daily Press*. He was responsible for the paper's Arts Section and in late December/early January 1963 he was in London to write a report on the burgeoning popularity of the Establishment club in Soho.

The Establishment was, of course, the stamping ground of the young satirical writers and performers like Peter Cook and Willie Rushton. The club was also a focus for visiting performers from America like Lenny Bruce.

Anthony says that Bobby Dylan appeared in the break between the two sets of the resident satirical cabaret. The residents did not impress him on that evening but the appearance of Bobby Dylan has remained in the memory and as he says now with some relief, *"Thank God I said he was good."*

Anthony cannot be precise about the date that he reviewed Dylan at the Establishment but it is likely to have been either Friday December 28 or Friday January 4. What we do have for certain is hard evidence of one of Bob's earliest performances in Britain and, despite being pushed into a slot in the middle of the *main turn*, it is clear from Anthony's review that the highlight of the evening was Dylan's performance, which earned five reprises from a London audience not renowned for showing its enthusiasm readily.

"...Certainly, on the night I went it wasn't the satire that earned five reprises but the English debut (sic) *of a young American folk singer whose face is called Bobby Dillon* (sic) *and whose fortune looks good.*

Strikingly resembling Updike – striking for those who know what Updike looks like anyway – he sang some ballads straight and some with an irony dry as manzanilla; the whole accompanied on a guitar fired from the hip or thrust shoulder-high, and a mouth-organ strapped to his collar-bones. One particularly relished the understatement, arguably America's chief contribution to demotic English."

Extract from Western Daily Press January 7, 1963 by Anthony Smith.

What ballads and songs of irony dryly sung that evening we can only speculate, but Anthony's description of *"a guitar fired from the hip or thrust shoulder-high"* comes running down the years like a lightning strike in its accuracy. I think we can, with all justification, describe Anthony Smith as a critic prophesying with his pen who kept his eyes wide open.

John *Stringbean* Cumming

1 Robert Shelton, *No Direction Home.*
2 Kurt Loder, Rolling Stone interview, March 1984, published June 21, 1984
All quotes by Philip Saville are taken from *The Dylan Companion,* edited by Elizabeth Thomson and David Gutman, Macmillan 1990. Due to be reprinted 2001
Also used in the preparation of this text were *Steppin' Out* Lawlan,
A Life in Stolen Moments, Heylin.
Thanks also to Ian Woodward and Chris Cooper for their invaluable help.

Published in issue #85, July 1999.

A Chat With Martin Carthy
Interview by Matthew Zuckerman

Martin Dominic Forbes Carthy is one of the most important and influential singers in the English folk revival; a fact recognized officially in 1998 when he was awarded the MBE. Like so many singers of his generation, he started in a skiffle band, but soon began to specialize in traditional British – and generally English – music. After stints in the Thameside Four and the Three City Four, he made his first solo recording in 1965, the eponymous *"Martin Carthy."*

Through the next three and a half decades, Carthy has made a series of tremendous albums many of which feature fiddle maestro Dave Swarbrick, and some are credited jointly to the two musicians. Carthy has also worked with such bands as Steeleye Span, the Albion Band and The Watersons. In 1996, Carthy appeared on his wife's first solo release, *"Norma Waterson."* In recent years, Martin, Norma and daughter Eliza have toured and recorded together as Waterson/Carthy, and the two albums they have released – *"Waterson: Carthy"* (1994) and *"Common Tongue"* (1997) – have been every bit as good as one would expect them to be. No, even better.

Other notable projects he has worked on include Peter Bellamy's folk opera *"The Transports"* and John Kirkpatrick's excellent album of Morris tunes, *"Plain Capers."* Carthy and Kirkpatrick are also members of Brass Monkey, an amazing band that features the unusual instrumentation of guitar, accordion, trumpet, saxophone and trombone.

I met Martin before the sound check for a Waterson/Carthy performance at Bristol's excellent club, The Fiddler, and he talked enthusiastically until the tape ran out!

MZ: You first met Dylan in 1962 and at that time only his first album was out.

MC: Yes, as far as I could gather, just from talking to him at the time, he was in the process of recording *"Freewheelin'."* Because one of the things he said was *"Oh, you don't want to listen to that album – 'Bob Dylan' – That's rubbish. Wait till my new album comes out."* The implication was: *"I'm just doing it."* He was – over here – doing this play, *Madhouse on Castle Street,* with a director called Philip Saville...David Warner actually took the part that Bob Dylan was originally slated to do; they had to write an extra part in for Bob. He was just this guy who sat on the stairs and played the guitar.

MZ: Is that because he wasn't much of an actor?

MC: It was because he looked at the part and said: *"I can't do this!"* As far as I understand it, he just didn't have a clue...Philip Saville never told him what he wanted him for. He didn't tell him he had a part. So they basically had him sitting on the stair singing all these weird songs about a swan on the river going riding.

MZ: That was *'Ballad Of The Gliding Swan.'* Was that a traditional song?

MC: Naw, I don't know but I've a feeling there were a few songs written into it for him to sing. And he was given these things and he tore them apart, and then glued them back together. The verse I remember from *'The Swan On The River'* went *"Lady Margaret's belly is wet with tears / Nobody's been on it for twenty-seven years / And the swan on the river went gliding by."* (Laughter) There were other songs, which were equally weird. And of course he sang *'Blowin' In The Wind'* on the stairs.

MZ: Was that the first time you'd heard it?

MC: No, no, he sang it a few times at the Troubadour. He turned up at the King & Queen in Foley Street, where I used to sing with a group I was in called the Thameside Four. We called them groups in those days, not bands. We were a *group.* I knew his manager, Albert (Grossman) because whomever he was with, he would always bring his charge down to whatever folk club was going.

MZ: And were you aware of him before you met him?

MC: Well, I knew who he was, and I saw him and I recognized him because his photo had been on the front of *Sing Out!* In fact, I think it was the current copy *of Sing Out!* So I went up to him and asked him if he fancied singing. And he said: *"Ask me in the second half."* So I got up and sang a couple of songs, then I looked at him and said: *"Do you fancy singing?"* and he just nodded. So I introduced him and he got up and sang. He probably sang *'Blowin'In The Wind'* first time he was up. He sang *'Honey, Allow Me One More Chance'* or...I don't remember if it was that one but it was one of those raggy things. And he sang a talking blues. I think it was *'John Birch Society.'* He did three songs and the place just fell at his feet. It was fabulous.

MZ: Was it immediately apparent what a striking song *'Blowin' In The Wind'* was?

MC: Well, I suppose so, yeah. It was eloquent. People used to try to write songs in those days and one or two people wrote decent songs. I suppose it was apparent. It was a nice song. We just thought of it as a nice song.

MZ: In a recent interview – in *Folk Roots* – you mentioned that so many of the young writers nowadays seem to have lost the ability to know what a song is. Do you think that's because many of them just haven't played enough traditional songs?

MC: Oh, no, I don't think that's it, because there's a whole tradition of songwriting in America that has nothing to do with traditional music. People have gone off at a tangent, and I also said in that article that I think the person who's responsible for it is probably one of the finest songwriters alive, but only she can do what she does, and that's Joni Mitchell. She's fabulous, and she writes in these free forms. But she has a stupendous sense of melody and a brilliant way with words...and I'm sorry, Alanis Morissette doesn't cut it. She's an offshoot of Joni Mitchell but without any of the imagination. I think that one of the things that's happened is that people are not thinking of melody, and they're not thinking of form. It's me, me, me songs. And they're not dreadfully interesting. You don't actually learn anything from them. They're not crafted. I think some people are starting to craft songs now. I think Jarvis Cocker (Pulp) is a songwriter, and Noel Gallagher (Oasis) can write, and the fellow out of Blur, Damon Albarn. There's some good writers about now, but there's that whole stream of writers who do that stream-of-consciousness type of stuff over a repetitive chord sequence, and it doesn't reach me. I think Bob could be said to be partly responsible. He didn't do anybody any favours when he wrote *'It's Alright Ma.'* That opened the door for all sorts of banana-brains. And a lot of banana-brains have gone down that route. For him, it was a form. For them, it's a cop-out.

MZ: A lot of Dylan's songs are very self-involved, very personal, yet they often don't come out that way. They're much more universal. How do you think his songs escape that self-indulgence?

MC: Well, that's the kind of person he is. Like when he writes a song like *'Gates Of Eden.'* That's an astonishing song. And some of that stuff on *"Blood On The Tracks"* like *'Tangled Up In Blue'* or *'Idiot Wind.'* Oh, I mean, what a song! Even the stuff where he gets personal, like *'Positively Fourth Street.'* I seriously think he's only written one truly rotten song...

MZ: Let me guess. I'd say *'Ballad In Plain D.'*

MC: Absolutely. *'Ballad In Plain D'* is a piece of junk..

MZ: He thinks so as well.

MC: So I gather. I remember seeing that in an interview. It's a piece of junk and he knows it's a piece of junk. I think he knew it fairly soon afterwards. He must've done. He said to her: *"I'm gonna get you. I'm gonna get you in a song."* And he didn't. He missed by a fucking mile. It's nice he's acknowledged it. We've all done stupid things in our lives, and probably the first rule is to acknowledge it.

MZ: Getting back to that first visit, did he sing mainly his own stuff or...

MC: He sang all his own stuff. Well, he sang *'Pretty Peggy-O.'* He used to improvise *'Pretty Peggy-O.'* I heard him do it three or four times, and eventually he added another verse. Basically, he was going through all the ranks in the army. *"The captain he is gone, he's long gone / He's riding down to Texas with the rodeo."* His last verse, which is not on the record, went: *"The sergeant – or whatever it was – he is gone, he's long gone / He's fighting with the wild man down in Borneo."* He sang that because he was in the studio, and one guy kept saying to him – *"If you're a folk singer, sing a folk song."* *"I'm a folk singer,"* he said. *"Of course I'm a folk singer."* 'Cos he was always taking the piss about being a folk singer. So, the man said: *"Why don't you sing a folk song?"* *"What do you call a folk song?"* Bob asked and the man said *'Pretty Peggy-O.'* *"Of course I know 'Pretty Peggy-O',"* he said, and he went and sang: *"The sergeant he is gone, he's long gone / He's fighting with the wild man down in Borneo."* He used to crease the audience up when he sang it. He's a very funny man, wicked.

MZ: When was the last time you met him?

MC: In 1978, I saw him at Blackbushe. He was still the same, still very funny. He's a very kind man, very sweet, and very ordinary.

MZ: That description of him is a little at odds with many accounts.

MC: But he met people all the time who were trying to turn him into something that he wasn't. You know, he said he was going to be bigger than Elvis and all that stuff. (Laughter) It's a hoot, and the irony is that he *did*. It's hilarious in that sense, in that he did go on to become bigger than Elvis. But it's the sort of crack that he would make when somebody was trying to pin him down. You know the whole thing about America and ambition and being a winner. He's one of a minority of American people I've met to whom the notion of winning and losing is utterly meaningless. It doesn't mean a fucking thing to him. So when he's asked questions about his ambition, of course he's going to say his ambition is to be bigger than Elvis, because he takes the piss. That's the nature of the man. He's an extraordinary man in that sense, and that sense only. He also happens to be a wonderful writer. But he won't be pinned down on his writing. Once it's gone from him, it's currency. You make of it what you want to make of it. You do some work. Don't ask me to tell you. I've done my work. I've written the bloody thing. Now *you* do some work. How does it affect *you?* Don't be an audience. Be involved. That's the nature of our work as well. We can't abide it if people just sit there and are an audience. We require involvement. It's the music. Spread it as wide as you like. People's music requires involvement, not spectators. Bob doesn't want spectators! He wants involvement. So, you must do the work. Don't ask stupid questions. *"What's the song about?"* I've seen it in interviews. *"You tell ME what the song's about."*

MZ: Back in 1962 Dylan met Ewan MacColl; I hear they didn't get on.

MC: I don't think they talked very much, quite frankly. Bob went to the Singers Club, which at that time I think was at The Pindar of Wakefield in Gray's Inn Road, and he sang there. He did three songs and the audience liked him, but Ewan and Peggy Seeger, MacColl's wife, didn't like him and Bert Lloyd didn't like him. They didn't like him because he wasn't direct enough. Ewan and Peggy, all through their writing lives, were the kind of people who name names. I accuse *you*. It wouldn't just be *"You masters of war,"* it would be Richard Nixon or whoever was President at the time. It was Kennedy then, wasn't it? Kennedy, Johnson, whoever, you name the names. But Bob didn't do that, which is why he would say he's not a political singer or a protest writer. They didn't like songs like *'Oxford Town'* because they thought it should have named names. It shouldn't allude to anything; it should confront it directly.

MZ: And do you think the naming name songs stand the test of time?

MC: Well, *'Hattie Carroll'* is a classic. It's an absolutely wonderful song, written, I'm quite sure, in a rage, but also with a great sense of form. Whatever he did, and whatever he does, there's always form there.

MZ: And those marvellous plays on words: *"maid/made in the kitchen," "slain by a cane/Cain."*

MC: Yes, he always was a layered writer, with all sorts of allusions, and most of them are intuitive. It's not deliberate in that sense. And that's the great strength of traditional songs. I keep discovering new things in traditional songs, songs I've been singing for years and years. And I'm sure that anybody singing any one of his songs – I wouldn't be surprised if when, singing a song thirty years later, he would find things in there they hadn't thought of before. But then, he's a proper writer, and he knows how much of this is chance, and harnessing chance and making it work for you. That's what a good writer is.

MZ: When he went back to the US in January 1963, I think there were four more songs that he wrote and then recorded for *"Freewheelin':" 'Bob Dylan's Dream'* which was from *'Lord Franklin,' 'Girl From The North Country'* which was from *'Scarborough Fair,' 'Masters Of War'...*

MC: No, *'Masters Of War'* he'd sung before. He sang *'Masters Of War'* at the Troubadour.

MZ: It says here – referring to a sessionography – that he recorded *'Masters Of War'* in April 1963.

MC: Well, but he'd written *'Masters Of War'* already...I remember him singing it and me thinking: *"Oh, that's 'Nottamun Town'."* He would have learnt that from Jean Ritchie. That's Jean Ritchie's song. He might have heard other people sing it, but Jean Ritchie's responsible for people in America singing it widely. No, he certainly sang it, and he also sang *'A Hard Rain's A-Gonna Fall.'* I remember him singing *'Hard Rain...'* at the Troubadour. And that was another world. In that sense, *'Blowin' In The Wind'* was just another song and I don't mean that in a disparaging sense. But it followed the rules. It did what a song does: three verses, and it did its business. But with *'Hard Rain,'* you're in different territory.

Funnily enough, given that *'Masters Of War'* is based on *'Nottamun Town,'* which is one of the great songs of lies, when you get to *'A Hard Rain's A-Gonna Fall,'* he's writing his own song of lies. The connection between *'Hard Rain'* and *'Nottamun Town'* is much stronger emotionally than the connections with *'Masters Of War.'*

MZ: A line like *"ten thousand died that never were born"* could have come right out of *'Hard Rain.'*

MC: That's right. That's because he knows his traditional song. And he also has the imagination to play around with that. So he plays games in his songs. He plays games with himself. He plays games with chance. That's what makes him so good. He does take chances.

MZ: Which songs did he specifically learn from you?

MC: From me, he always asked for *'Lord Franklin'* and he always asked for *'Scarborough Fair.'* And he heard Louis Killen sing, and he learned *'The Leaving Of Liverpool.'* That came out as...is it *'Farewell Farewell'*? He learned *'The Patriot Game'* from the Clancys, which became *'With God On Our Side.'* Nigel Denver was around a lot, and he always asked Nigel to sing a song called *'Kishmuil's Galley.'* It's a Hebridian song, so it's originally in the Gaelic and it's translated into English, but also its tune has been stretched out a little bit...Nigel Denver used to sing that a lot and Bob would always ask him to do it. And he heard Bob Davenport sing songs. I don't know what he got from Bob. But I wasn't the only one. He got songs from all sorts of people. And he got ideas, because he was a piece of blotting paper. He'd walk into a club and just sit there, and he'd look very straight-faced, and he'd just sit there and listen all evening. It was all going in. He was wide-open to influences *all* the time. It's a fabulous way to be. Then go home and write. And write and write and write and write. And change things around. He was very imaginative.

MZ: I hear that the winter of 1962 was a particularly cold one.

MC: That's right, it was. I had a samurai sword and an old piano that was no good, and we chopped it up for firewood.

MZ: Was Bob there?

MC: Yes, he was. He helped!

MZ: Was he staying with you at the time?

MC: No, no, he never stayed with me. He was staying in a hotel. It's a myth that he stayed with me. But the piano story is true. I've still got the sword. It's in good nick. Haven't got the piano, of course.

MZ: Bob came over the next time in 1964. Did you see him at the Royal Festival Hall?

MC: Yes, we spoke on the 'phone and then he came round. And he sang...There's another one that was a complete mind-blower because it was so different. He sang *'Mr Tambourine Man'* and it was...*"Where is this man going?"* It was absolutely extraordinary. And then we saw him at the Festival Hall. As I remember, actually, it was a Sunday afternoon concert. I'm almost certain of coming out into the sunshine. The place was full. The ushers at the Festival Hall couldn't believe it. *"Who is this man? Never 'eard of 'im."* He came on stage, sang a few songs and started to chat and just warmed to his task. He was just fantastic...He told the story about this film. They'd decided to make a film, because the folk boom was on and there were all these hootenannies everywhere. They actually made a film called *Hootenanny* and they had all these muscle men on the beach and all these lasses running around in bikinis, with their navels carefully inked out. And he told the plotline of *Hootenanny,* and the place was absolutely rolling...

I don't actually remember the set list, but he could go from a rollicking good time to the real horny stuff like. Like from *'All I Really Want To Do'* to *'Hattie Carroll'*. I don't remember him giving an introduction to *'Hattie Carroll.'* He just started to sing it and it was just like the place caught fire. A fucking roar at the end of it you wouldn't have believed. It's a long song too. These days, you can sing long songs because people are used to it, but in those days, three minutes were a long time. But the roar when he came to the end of it! I'll never forget it. When he got to that *"...bury the rag MOST DEEP in your face."* Most deep! *"NOW is the time for your tears."* I just knew I'd heard something quite extraordinary. And I didn't care that he'd taken the idea from Brecht. Hooray that he knows who Bertold Brecht is. Aren't you pleased? Jesus Christ! It's only an idea. He's an intelligent man. He's not an island. He has the sort of love for humanity and love for people's music that deserves better, but he's always been the easy target. I'm in despair sometimes. People don't slag Paul Simon off to the extent they do Dylan. I really do think he's the bravest of the lot, and he really doesn't mind risking everything. He'd risk the fucking lot for music. No one can accuse him ever of selling out. To stand up and do a week of concerts at the Warfield in San Francisco and sing hymns to an audience who wants to hear *'Like a Rolling Stone'*... Please tell me, who is he selling out to?

I'm so full of admiration. I mean, one day he's a Christian, and then he's a Jew for Jesus. Who gives a fuck? He can do what he wants. Especially since it's guaranteed in his constitution. People have no right to slag him off. If he starts feeding off people, the way bloody Paul Simon does, then they have a right!

MZ: In 1965, did you meet Dylan again then?

MC: Yeah, I did. That was the last time I saw him until I met him again in 1978. He was at the Albert Hall. That was fabulous. I was there at his meeting with Donovan, which is *not* the meeting that's on the film *Don't Look Back.*

MZ: Is this the one where everybody was wearing masks?

MC: Yes, they'd all been to this club – I can't remember what it was called, but it was a really cool club for stars to go to at the time...a name like Incognito – and they had all these masks. Someone said Donovan was downstairs and Bob said, *"Come on, let's put on the masks."* So everyone sat there with masks on. Donovan came up, and he was very cool. Everybody had masks on, but he just sat there chatting, and everybody got really embarrassed and took them off, except for Bob who forgot he'd got his on. He was sat there talking away animatedly with a Dick Turpin mask on. You have to admire Donovan's nerve. 'Cos he was at that concert at the Festival Hall, and he said: *"Oh, you sang 'Mr Tambourine Man' and I couldn't quite hear it, and I went home trying to remember it, and I ended up writing a song of my own about it. Do you want to hear it?"* Bob said OK, and he sang this song called *'Hey, Golden Tangerine Eyes.'* Well, whatever else he lacked, he certainly didn't lack bloody nerve. It was all right. It was obviously a pastiche of *'Mr Tambourine Man.'*

MZ: What about *Don't Look Back* from 1965? That's an amazing film in the way he got people performing in front of the camera. Nothing like that had been done before so people weren't thinking about it being shown in a movie theatre. Like with Albert Grossman and Tito Burns...

MC: Oh, that's a brilliant one. Tito Burns obviously couldn't resist playing to the camera and Albert just made a mug of him. God, he made such a fool of Tito Burns...It's an extraordinary moment. I just sat there and watched it and just thought: *"Albert, you bastard, you rotten sod."* He knew what he was doing. You could always see with Albert. He was always laughing in his eyes the whole time when he was doing something like that. He knew he was doing a number on Tito. He's a very clever man and a brilliant manager. Apparently he was talking with Odetta – and this is all apocryphal – when she'd come to the end of his contract with her, and she said she was thinking of leaving. And he said: *"OK, you leave, and that's fine. If you leave me, I reckon you'll make half a million dollars next year"*...or whatever the figure was...*"and your agent will take twenty-five percent. I guarantee that you'll get half a million dollars when I work for you, clear."* And so she signed with him again. He used to take fifty percent and people said it was outrageous, but he worked hard. He got fabulous jobs with fabulous money, and he wouldn't take anything other than the best. He wouldn't allow his artists to be fucked around.

MZ: So he did earn it?

MC: Yeah. When he was doing *Madhouse on Castle Street* the first time he came over, there was a strike in the studio, and they actually couldn't finish the filming first time round...It was an argument about overtime...The BBC said Bob would just have to come back later and finish it. And Albert said no, if he came back again, they'd have to pay him again. *"Oh, we can't do that!"* they said. *"Well, then, you don't have a play. I'll take my boy away."* But they'd already done so much work; he had them over a barrel. So they had to pay him the same wage all over again. Bob went away to...Italy and in the time he was away, that's when I think he wrote *'Girl From The North Country.'* 'Cos he came back, and he said: *"I've got a song to play you."* It was at the Troubadour, and he started to play, and he had that little guitar thing that I play in *'Scarborough Fair.'* He was singing the song and he went into this figure, and he just burst out laughing, and he said: *"Oh, I can't do that!"* and he wouldn't do the rest of it. He went all red. And that was *'Girl From The North Country.'* Actually, I think *'Scarborough Fair'* spawned two songs, and one of them is *'Girl From The North Country,'* and the other is *'Boots Of Spanish Leather.'*

MZ: Then you met him in 1978? That was at Blackbushe?

MC: Yes, that was at Blackbushe. Apparently he wanted me to be on it. So he told Harvey Goldsmith, and Harvey tried a little bit to get hold of me. Not very hard. (Laughter) I think he actually did ring up when it was too late to do anything about it. But I got the invitation to come down...It took me four hours to get backstage. And I finally got there by a stroke of luck. A guy I know was working on the crew and he was getting everybody's autograph. He saw me outside, and he said: *"Why don't you sign this as well?"* I signed it and gave it back to him, and then he went to get Clapton to sign it and he looked at it and said: *"Is that guy here? Bob would really like to see him."* So a man came out and found me and said: *"He wants to see you. Put this on."* And he gave me the pass and we walked through all the levels. There were at least three levels of security, and then his caravan. And he had no idea. So I went in and he said: *"Oh, how are you?"* and then he said: *"How's Anthea?"* (Joseph) And I said: *"She's fine. She's out in hospitality."* And he said: *"Why doesn't she come and see me?"* I looked at him and said: *"Do you have any idea what the security is like here?"* *"What are you talking about?"* he said, and he turned to one of the blokes and said: *"Can you go and find Anthea Joseph? She's in hospitality."* They came back in five minutes and there she was, festooned in all the passes. You know, there's a level of innocence about him that's really endearing. He didn't have a clue...As far as he's concerned he's the same bloke. Which he is. Fundamentally, he's the bloke who came to England in 1962.

MZ: What did you think of the two recent acoustic albums?

MC: I loved them. I thought they were great. I don't think he deserved the flak he got in some quarters about the credits and such. I felt that *"Good As I Been To You"* was a bit of an old fashioned album really. You know, a while back, when you learnt a song, you pretty much did the arrangement you'd learnt, so there was a lot of other people in it. There was just one song there they called traditional, the tune of which wasn't – *'Jim*

Jones,' traditional words with a tune by Mick Slocum – and that was a bit of an oversight.

MZ: I think Slocum contacted *Columbia* about that, and he gets a credit now.

MC: That's good. And some people felt he should have given Nic Jones a mention – for *'Canadee-i-o.'* I think that's why he made sure he mentioned the sources on the next one, *"World Gone Wrong."*

MZ: What did you think of those notes?

MC: I loved them. They were great.

MZ: He really went off on a tangent with some of them.

MC: I think that's how he hears them. That's the great thing about traditional songs. There's so much to find in them.

Matthew Zuckerman conducted the above interview with Martin Carthy in January 1999, for ISIS Magazine.

Published in issue #83. February 1999.

"Al's wife claimed I can't be happy as the New Jersey night ran backwards an' vanished behind our rollin' ear."

'11 Outlined Epitaphs' Bob Dylan 1964

The Invisible Man – Al Aronowitz and the Hipper-Than-Thou Gang by Derek Barker

"Al's wife claimed I can't be happy
as the New Jersey night ran backwards
an' vanished behind our rollin' ear."

'11 Outlined Epitaphs' Bob Dylan 1964

During the mid 1960s and early 1970s, Al Aronowitz was the invisible link, the man responsible for getting everybody who was anybody in the pop world acquainted with one another. Art Garfunkel, for instance, once put an arm around Aronowitz's shoulder on a cross-country flight full of rock superstars and announced, *"This is everybody's Uncle Al, the man who introduces everybody to everybody."*[1]

Bob Dylan once told Aronowitz –
"You oughtta open up an office and just introduce people to people."[1]

Alfred G. Aronowitz was born in Bordentown, New Jersey, May 20, 1928. During the late 1940s he spent, *"four delicious years at the Rutgers College campus in New Brunswick, New Jersey."*[1]

After graduating from college in 1950, he started work as the editor of the *Lakewood Daily Times, "a weekly that came out every day."* By the late fifties Aronowitz had started working for the *New York Post* and by 1969, he was writing their *Pop Scene* column.

Aronowitz was soon on familiar enough terms with Albert Grossman and Brian Epstein to believe that he had what it took to become a music manager himself. He teamed up songwriters Carole King and Gerry Goffin and began managing a rock act called the Myddle Class and, on the assumption that he was going to make a million, he let his contract lapse with the *Saturday Evening Post.* The project bombed and Aronowitz lost his house in suburban Berkeley Heights, New Jersey. He later rejoined the *Post*, writing their *Music Scene* column but, after an argument with the editor about a conflict of interest, Aronowitz was sacked and effectively banished from print in 1972. He lost his wife that same year and his life went into a downward spiral. He became known as The Blacklisted Journalist, a name he now writes under on the Internet.

Al Aronowitz – *"I think I first met Bob Dylan in mid 1963. The Saturday Evening Post assigned me to interview him. We met in Chumley's, NYC, ex-speakeasy. It was a famous place and a favourite hangout of famous literary lushes... That interview was never published. I fell in love with him. I fell under his spell. l found it more important to hang out with the man I considered the Shakespeare of our times than to write about him."*[1]

"To me, Bob was The Cat's Meow, The End, The Ultimate. No other artist had ever come along with such wit, perception, insight, charm, cleverness and charisma. To me, Bob was doing more to change the English language than anybody since Shakespeare. I decided for certain that, in Dylan, I was witnessing the greatest ever. For me, nobody could beat Bob, nobody past or present."[2]

"Bob could string words together with God-like power and he also could charm the rattles off a snake's ass. Often seeming to speak in parables a lot like the liner notes he wrote for his early albums and a lot like the lyrics of his songs, he was always incredibly stimulating. But at the same time he could be moody and mysterious and unpredictable and cranky and nasty."[2]

"I consider Bob one of the greatest artists ever born, but he's not the kind of guy I would trust with my wife. Unfortunately, I already once did."[2]

Al Aronowitz was accepted into Bob Dylan's inner circle of friends· at a time when Dylan refused even to talk to most journalists, unless of course to put them down. Just to be called a *"journalist"* by Dylan was a put-down. It was a word that he used to describe people that he felt were not real writers. He told Phil Ochs – *"You're not a folk singer, you're just a journalist, you shouldn't try to write."*[3]

While it is true Dylan was on good terms with Ralph Gleason, Nat Nentoff and closer still to Robert Shelton, it was Aronowitz alone that won his close trust, remaining a confidant for more than a decade.

Al Aronowitz – *"I have no idea why Bob accepted me into his inner circle... but I thought hanging out was cool... I knew that to be a good music journalist I would have to be part of the scene. Dylan doesn't talk to me any more, not since the mid 1980s. Then there was Bobby Neuwirth who didn't want to talk to me then because I wasn't hip enough and who now still won't talk to me because I'm not sober enough... A lot of these people don't talk to me any more, it's like I'm invisible."*[1]

"Bob Dylan once told me, 'You know, Al, you're invisible. Sometimes you can be seen smoking a cigarette, but you're invisible. You're the invisible man'."[2]

Dylan of course meant this as a slight. To be on the receiving end of these frequent jibes was the price each member of his inner circle had to pay for the privilege of hanging out with Dylan. Aronowitz says that he took this particular comment as a compliment; after all, he had gained his standing in the music world by being the invisible link. Moreover, to be able to move freely in the midst of Dylan's inner circle and yet apparently remain invisible was surely a journalistic attribute to die for.

In order to escape being on the receiving end of one of those mental hammerings, there were many times when those who frequented Dylan's inner circle, including Aronowitz, would have wished that they were invisible

Dylan's first lieutenant in this *game* was Bobby Neuwirth. Dylan and Neuwirth had met in 1961 at the Indian Neck Festival and Neuwirth had now become an *"appendage"* of Bob Dylan. He would later be replaced as first lieutenant by Robbie Roberson but for now Neuwirth was *"champion hardballer on Bob's all-star team of Hipper-Than-Thou players."*[1]

Al Aronowitz – *"In those days... Hipper-Than-Thou was the favourite head game of the Dylan crowd and Bobby (Neuwirth) was maybe the game's most vicious hardballer, one of those razor-tongued originals who put the dis into disrespect. When he got finished putting you down, you could crawl out the door through the keyhole. He also could slit your throat and you'd never even bleed... He was about as charming as a mugger."*[2]

Dylan and his *gang* were not unique in playing these head games. The sport was popular with many musicians on both sides of the Atlantic. John Lennon was fast becoming a first class player but even he was no match for the king of hip. Lennon desperately wanted to meet Dylan but, he kept telling their go-between Aronowitz, that any such meeting would have to wait until he was Dylan's *"ego equal."*

The nightly sadistic put-downs soon spilled over into the lyrics of songs, *'Like a Rolling Stone,' 'Positively Fourth Street'* and *'Can You Please Crawl Out Your Window'* to name but three. *'Fourth Street'* in particular had the patrons at the Kettle of Fish and other Village haunts dancing on hot coals, speculating as to who the venom-filled single was written about.

Dylan spent a great deal of time in Al's company and many nights at Aronowitz's house in Berkeley Heights where Dylan wrote several songs including *'Mr Tambourine Man.'*

Al Aronowitz – *"Bob musta stayed up past dawn, rapping away at the keys in his cigarette fog. He had just broken up with... Suze... For him, it was a long step farther into loneliness... I found a wastebasket full of crumpled false starts. I took it out the side door to empty it into the trashcan when a whispering emotion caught me... I took the crumpled sheets, smoothed them out, read the crazy leaping lines, smiled to myself at the leaps that never landed and then put the sheets into a file folder. I still have them somewhere."*[3]

Dylan even coerced Aronowitz to help the writing of the surreal account, *A Night with Bob Dylan,* which was first published in the *New York Herald Tribune* on Sunday December 12, 1965.

The basic text, which was supplemented by a six-page photo spread by Daniel Kramer, was written by Aronowitz and then reworked by Dylan. Aronowitz surreptitiously set the piece as taking place in Grossman's fashionable Gramercy Park apartment where, according to Dylan, it was acceptable to *"write on the walls... and nobody calls you a poet."* After listening to the Temptations on the record player, the surreal tale takes us to visit a pinball arcade, a fortune-teller, a disco and a cathedral, before the whole insane episode – based largely on reality – finally made it back to Grossman's pad.

Dylan had quickly learnt that he could manipulate the press – especially in New York – to his advantage. That same year, *Village Voice* had run the text for a fictional press conference, the *script* of which was written by Dylan himself. The piece concluded with the question, *"Who do you think can save the world?"* To which Bob replied, *"Al Aronowitz."*

One evening, while getting ready for a night in the village, Dylan repeated a phase that Aronowitz had heard him say a number of times before, *"You've got to be psychically armed!"*[2]

Al Aronowitz – *"The wounds left by verbal shootouts are psychic and, obviously, not quite so lethal as gunshots. Still, the sixties superstars all sported super-egos and walked with the swagger of gunslingers."*[2]

Aronowitz saw these games, these psychic shoot outs, as nothing more than competitiveness.

Al Aronowitz – *"Competitiveness reigns in pop music just as it does in sports. Or just as it did in the quick-on-the-draw of the Wild West."*[2]

The ferocity of these attacks was something to behold, but then Dylan wasn't forcing anyone to hang around with him. If you couldn't take the heat...

During the sixties, and to a lesser extent through to today, Bob Dylan has used these psychic mind games to defend himself against the ludicrous questions frequently put to him by the world's media. Some of the finest examples of this *art* can be found in *Don't Look Back,* the film of Bob Dylan's 1965 UK tour.

Other examples litter his interviews and press conferences. When asked, *"What are your songs about,"* Dylan answered, *"Some are about eleven minutes, others are five or six."* On another occasion, a well-meaning reporter asked if he had a good quote for the press, to which Dylan quickly replied, *"If I had a good quote I'd be wearing it."* Much to his chagrin, the world would constantly look to Bob Dylan for answers, but the only advice they got was to *"Keep a good head, and always carry a light-bulb."*

1 Interview with Al Aronowitz for ISIS Magazine, conducted by Derek Barker, September 1998.
2 From the Al Aronowitz web site *The Blacklisted Journalist* www.bigmagic.com
3 Robert Shelton, *No Direction Home*

NEWPORT FOLK FESTIVAL 64

THURSDAY · FRIDAY · SATURDAY · S

JULY 23-24-25-26

Freebody Park · NEWPORT,

Four evening concerts will
augmented by daytime par
workshops and hootenannies

Tickets $2, $3, $4, $5.
Special group rates can be arrang
advance now. For information and t
write: Newport Folk Festival, Newpor
or: 176 Federal Street, Boston Mass.
Telephone: HU 2-1827
or: Folklore Center, 110 McDouga
New York City, Telephone: GR

DIRECTORS
Theodore Bikel
Clarence Cooper
Ronnie Gilbert
Alan Lomax
Jean Ritchie
Mike Seeger
Peter Yarrow
George Wein
Chairman

THE FOLKLORE CENT
Presents
BOB DYLA
IN HIS FIRST NEW YORK CONC

SAT. NOV. 4, 1961

EGIE CHAPTER HALL
th STREET · NEW YORK

All seats $2.00

le at: The Folklore Cente
110 MacDougal St
New York City 12.

KONSERTHUSET
Fredag 29 april kl. 20
OBS. Endast en konsert!

BOB DYLAN

Biljetter fr. kr. 15:—
på vanliga ställen.
Arr.: Karusell & SBA

K. B. HALLEN
Søndag d. 1. maj kl. 20
SBA præsenterer

BOB DYLAN

LEVON & THE HAWKS
ENESTE KONCERT

Billetter à kr. 15 - 20 - 25 - 30
- 35 - 40 - 50 i K. B. Hallens
billetkontor, tlf. 71 14 18, og i
City Billetbureau, PAlæ 45 31,
fra i dag kl. 11

Bob Dylan

SAT. FEB. 26 / 8:30 P.M
LONG ISLAND
At Island Garden, West Hempstead
500 Hempstead Turnpike
$4.50   3.50   2.50
Sale: Box Office
Mail Orders: Concerts, 330 E. 48th St.
New York, N. Y. 10017
Enc. stamped, self-addressed envelope

Will you be in the Isle of Wight on August 31st?

Bob Dylan will

Order your tickets now from
Fiery Creations, Ltd., Tavistock House, Ward Road,
Tatland Bay, Isle of Wight.
Saturday 30th August — 25/-
Sunday 31st August — £2
2 Day Ticket £2.10-0

Bob Dylan records exclusively for CBS

CBS Records 28/30 Theobalds Road London WC1

THE SOUND OF DYLAN

CBS RECORDS 1

Bob Dylan
NEW SINGLE
RELEASED ToDay

'THE TIMES THEY ARE A CHANGIN'
c/w 'Honey, just allow me one more chance'
201751

C.B.S RECORDS · 104 NEW BOND ST · LONDON W1

BOB DYLAN

Only New York Concert Appearance

PHILHARMONIC HALL

SAT. EVE., OCT. 31

$4.50 · $4.00 · $3.50 · $2.75

SALE & MAIL ORDERS

Philharmonic Hall Box Office
Lincoln Center, N. Y. C.
Inc. stamped self-addressed envelope

Bob Dylan

CARNEGIE HALL
FRI., OCT. 1, 8:30 P.M.
4.75 4.25 3.75 2.75
Sale & Mail Orders Box Office

SYMPHONY HALL
(MOSQUE THEATER—
NEWARK)
SAT. OCT. 2, 8:30 P.M.
4.50 4.00 3.50 2.75
SALE: All Bamberger Stores, Park Records
—Newark Village Records—So. Orange
MAIL ORDERS: CONCERTS, 330 E. 48th St.
New York 17, N.Y.
Encl. stamped, self-addressed envelope

From You To Me
by Derek Barker

The Beatles *"were doing things nobody was doing. Their chords were outrageous, just outrageous, and their harmonies made it all valid."*
  Bob Dylan to Anthony Scaduto 1971
  Al Aronowitz *finally* introduced Bob Dylan and The Beatles to each other on August 28, 1964 at the Delmonico Hotel on Manhattan's Park Avenue. I am sure we are all aware by now of the tale of how Dylan, with help from Aronowitz, turned The Beatles on to pot at that meeting. If not, then I suggest you read ISIS #81. In this essay, I would now like to consider the influence that the two parties might have had on one another *musically*.
  Paul McCartney – *"Dylan was a big hero. We admired him a lot. We all liked his early talkin' blues and he was entering; the mid-sixties was a very poetic period. We liked him because he was a poet, far out, a friend of Ginsberg, on the same road as Jack Kerouac."*
  "...Dylan's Woody Guthrie period was very nice and I liked him then, but then he had a second wave of popularity when he became more psychedelic and more associated with drugs and at that time John particularly became very enamoured of him because of his poetry. All those songs were great lyrically. Masses of clutter lyrics like John had written in his books... it hit a chord in John, it was as if John felt, that should have been me."
  We were kind of proud to have been introduced to pot by Dylan; that was rather a coup. It was like being introduced to meditation and given your mantra by Maharishi. There was a certain status to it."[1]
  "'Got To Get You Into My Life' was one I wrote when I had first been introduced to pot. ...Actually it's an ode to pot. ...It was a U-turn in the Beatles attitude toward life."[1]
  Although the above confirms a liking and respect of Dylan's early work, there is little or no evidence from this, or from any other of the myriad of interviews given by Sir Paul over the years that Dylan had any *real* influence on McCartney's own song-writing. In fact, while we can be sure that all four members of The Beatles admired Dylan's music, his influence is only audible in the work of John Lennon.
  From the outset, because of their joint recording credits, it was believed that Lennon and McCartney were a song-writing partnership. The inaugural edition of *The Penguin Stereo Record Guide* even stated – *"music principally by Paul McCartney; words principally by John Lennon."* This was of course a piece of pure – and utterly incorrect

– speculation based mainly on the fact that before the early 1960s song-writing *teams* almost always worked to the convention of one music writer and one lyricist with no crossovers between those two tasks.

With the passing of time, however, it has become clear that for the most part Lennon and McCartney worked in total independence of each other. In reality, they were both too individualistic, each with his own positive ideas and strong temperament, which did not allow for much of a workable coexistence between them as songwriters. Certainly, at the onset of writing, virtually *every* Beatles song would be the exclusive property of one or other of the group's two main writers. Further into the writing process, however, it was quite common for the other party to pitch in and help with a song.

In retrospect, the differences in song-writing styles between Lennon and McCartney were from the beginning quite distinct, and over the years it has become increasing clear as to which of the so called *'partnership'* wrote which of the songs.

Although wholly untutored, McCartney seemed drawn to the more formal aspects of his art and was able to produce work, instinctively and consistently, that was technically *finished*.

On the other hand, Lennon never cared much for the constraints of formal techniques and had a complete disregard for the rules, which he would almost obsessively go out of his way to break. While this method of writing often resulted in less *polished* work, it had a strength and spirit of honesty against which much of McCartney's work appears shallow.

Extended listenings reveal a very differing style with which Lennon and McCartney approached their song-writing. Some years ago, a theory was constructed that whichever Beatle took the lead vocal was, by association the composer. Although this theory is somewhat simplistic, as a rule-of-thumb it is actually not too far from the mark. Certainly *all* of Harrison's compositions feature him on lead vocal and of the songs that are definitely known to have been written by either Lennon or McCartney the composer does seem to take the lead vocal.

After identifying which Beatle wrote which song, we can then look at the songs that are more obviously influenced by Dylan, and in virtually every case we find the Dylan-influenced songs are Lennon compositions.

The Beatles first became enamoured with Dylan after George Harrison picked up a copy of *"The Freewheelin' Bob Dylan"* while in Paris in January 1964.

George Harrison – *"The day Bob Dylan really turned us on was the day we heard his album, "The Freewheelin' Bob Dylan." Right from that moment we recognised some vital energy, a voice crying out somewhere, toiling in the darkness. When we actually met him in '64 it had a certain effect on us, but I think the seed was already sown by the album."* Harrison is quoted here by The Beatles press officer, Derek Taylor.[2]

Melody Maker foretold the collision of these two organisms in spring 1964 in an article headed – *"The Beatles Dig Dylan."*

Transfixed by Dylan's *"untamed quality,"* Harrison urged John Lennon to take a listen and Lennon passed the summer of 1964 doing just that. That same year Lennon said, *"Anyone who is the best in his field – as Dylan is – is bound to influence people. I wouldn't be surprised if we influenced him in some way."*

A few months after their introduction to *"Freewheelin'..."* The Beatles met Bob Dylan in person at the Delmonico Hotel in New York.

John Lennon – *"After Dylan introduced us to pot we dropped drink, simple as that."*

Only six weeks after being introduced to marijuana by Dylan and Aronowitz, Lennon and McCartney inserted the words *"turns me on"* into the song *'She's a Woman.'* Lennon also confessed that by early 1965 while filming *Help!* The Beatles were *"smoking pot for breakfast."*

John Lennon – *"I remember the early meetings with Dylan. He was always saying, 'Listen to the words, man,' and I said, 'I can't be bothered. I listen to the sound of it, the overall sound'."*

It was not long, however, before Lennon took Dylan's advice, and by the end of 1964 he was beginning to employ a different approach to his song-writing. *"We've got a lot to thank him for,"* Lennon later acknowledged. Lennon also admitted that he tried writing in a *"Dylanish"* manner. *'I'm a Loser,'* written around the time of that initial August meeting, was Lennon's first nod toward Dylan. The lack of a middle-eight usually found in a *pop* tune was a recognition of the simpler customs of folk balladry, and although the song has a country-and-western, rather than a folk feel, the tone of the song, the harmonica and strummed acoustic guitar, are an unmistakably acknowledgement of Bob Dylan.

John Lennon – *"That's my Dylan period, you know. The word 'clown' is in it. I always objected to the word clown, or even the clown image that Bowie used because it was artsy fartsy. But Dylan had used it so I thought it was all right..."*

Although *'I'm a Loser'* is the song acknowledged by music historians as being the *"Dylanish"* song from *"Beatles For Sale,"* one has to wonder if *'Baby's In Black'* could have existed without Bob Dylan. At any rate, *"Beatles For Sale"* – released December 1964 – and the single *'I Feel Fine'* c/w *'She's a Woman'* marked the beginning of what Lennon would later refer to as, *"My Dylan period."* The follow-up single *'Ticket To Ride'* broke major new ground for the Beatles and was said by the British pop press to be an *"uncommercial"* departure from their previous work. *'Ticket To Ride'* certainly was not the obvious choice for the Beatles' next single and it is rumoured to have caused some disagreement within the group.

The first Beatles song to break the three-minute barrier, this Lennon composition is an amalgam of influences from the record's opening *sound*, a *Tamla Motown* derivative, to the *heavy* electric sounds and weighty R&B rhythms being explored at the time by The Who, The Animals and The Rolling Stones. Lennon's approach to lyric writing was undergoing a massive rethink and there would seem to be little doubt that this change in approach was due in the main to his exposure to Dylan and his work.

While in London for his 1965 tour Dylan was invited by Lennon to dine with John and Cynthia at their Weybridge home.

John Lennon – *"We played a few records and talked... We swapped addresses and said we'd exchange ideas for songs, but it never happened. He said he sent me things, but he got the address wrong and it never arrived. Maybe that's why we get on well – we're both pretty disorganized blokes."*[3]

Dylan says that during that visit he and Lennon wrote a song together:

Bob Dylan – *"I don't remember what it was, though. We played some stuff into a tape recorder but I don't know what happened to it. I can remember playing it and the recorder was on. I don't remember anything about the song."*[4]

Bob Dylan – *"I dug his situation where he lived. It was a twenty-two-room house. Do you know what I did when I got back from England, man? I brought me a thirty-one-room house, can you imagine that?"*[3]

The release of the *"Help!"* album brought further proof that Lennon was attempting to emulate Dylan's style. *'You've Got To Hide Your Love Away'* with its Dylansque major chord pattern was the Beatles' first all acoustic number and was clearly written under the influence of *"Another Side Of Bob Dylan."*

A close listen to *"Help!"* will also reveal a slight shift in the Beatles instrumentation;

the group's chord patterns were now beginning to adhere a little more to recognised formulas. This trend for simpler, more straightforward tunes continued on to their next album *"Rubber Soul."*

"Rubber Soul" – Released December 1965 – was without doubt the Beatles first *real* album. More than just a collection of catchy tunes, this was the group's first cohesive record and the final step toward their greatest achievement, *"Revolver."*

"Revolver" was also the closest that the Beatles came to emulating Dylan. The lyrics contained on the album were clever, on occasions humorous, but also thought provoking. All this was achieved while maintaining the sing-along *pop* tunes, catchy hooks and harmonies for which the Beatles were so well loved. A closer listen would also reveal that those *"outrageous chords"* that Dylan had liked so much while driving through Colorado in February 1964 had now all but gone in favour of simple and often more *logical* chord progressions. *'Taxman'* and *'Tomorrow Never Knows'* were written around a couple of chords; *'Here, There And Everywhere'* was written around a very basic chord structure, as was the single of that time, *'Paperback Writer.'*

I rarely find myself agreeing with Bob Spitz but this passage from *Dylan: a Biography* sums up Lennon's fast growing attitude toward Dylan rather nicely – *"Lennon became fascinated by the Dylan sound – gritty, gutsy, smart-alecky edge that gave fire to each song. He admired Bob's rebelliousness, too, the attitude in his music that seemed to say, "fuck you!" It was something he'd probably have liked to say himself, but the Beatles' image wouldn't permit it. Ironically, this gave John an inferiority complex..."*[5]

However, while John Lennon was taking on board influences from *"Freewheelin',"* *"Times..."* and *"Another Side of Bob Dylan"* he may have failed to notice that the ever-changing Mr Dylan had already taken off in a completely new direction, that of the Beatles?

Certainly, by late 1965 early 1966, Bob Dylan had taken what was for him, the unprecedented step of being part of a *group*. OK, it was Bob Dylan and *his* backing band, but Dylan had previously maintained that he did not want to have any other musicians to have to worry about. To what extent then did the Beatles' success influence Dylan's move away from folk?

Bob Dylan – *"I had heard the Beatles in New York when they first hit. Then, when we were driving through Colorado we had the radio on and eight of the Top Ten songs were Beatles songs. In Colorado! ... They were doing things nobody was doing. Their chords were outrageous, just outrageous, and their harmonies made it all valid. You could only do that with other musicians. Even if you're playing your own chords you have to have other people playing with you. That was obvious. And it started me thinking about other people.*

Everybody else thought they were for teenyboppers, that they were gonna pass right away. But it was obvious to me that they had staying power. I knew they were pointing the direction of where music had to go. I was not about to put up with other musicians, but in my head the Beatles were it. In Colorado, I started thinking it was so far out that I couldn't deal with it – eight in the Top Ten. It seemed to me a definite line was being drawn. This was something that never happened before. It was outrageous, and I kept it in my mind. You see, there was a lot of hypocrisy all around, people saying it had to be either folk or rock. But I knew it didn't have to be like that."[6]

In reality of course, the decision to employ backing musicians, play *rock 'n' roll'* and make singles was not really such a big deal: it was after all Dylan's heritage. Only a few years before the young Bobby Zimmerman had found music mainly through the black sounds being played by Little Rock disc jockey Gatemouth Page. The sounds of Howlin'

Wolf, Muddy Waters, Jimmy Reed and B.B. King were the staple diet of young Bobby Zimmerman and as a schoolboy he had already played in a number of rock 'n' roll' groups.

The Beatles' success was probably pivotal to the change in Dylan's direction, but as Patrick Humphries states, the decision was almost certainly reinforced by other factors.

Patrick Humphries – *"The public change came about largely due to Dylan's appreciation of what The Beatles were achieving within the pop format, but another indication of where he could go came with the success of The Animals' second single 'House Of The Rising Sun,' which gave them a British and American number one single during the summer of 1964"*[7]

Once Dylan had decided that he wanted a hit single it, didn't take him long do so. *'Subterranean Homesick Blues'* was released in March 1965 and although the record only just managed to break into the US top 40, it made it to number nine in the UK chart.

Four months later the follow-up single *'Like a Rolling Stone'* went to number four in the UK, and in at least one instance toppled The Beatles *'Help!'* off the top spot of *one* of the US charts. Ironically, a month before *'...Stone'* peaked at number two on the US Billboard chart, the Byrds' one-verse *pop* version of Dylan's *'Mr Tambourine Man'* had already hit the number one spot.

By the close of 1966, The Beatles had become obsessed with studio trickery and the experiments on *'Strawberry Fields...'* would soon give way to the total immersion that was *"Sgt Pepper..."* So, while The Beatles indulged themselves with everything from tapes running backwards, tape loops and multi-tracking, to the four of them playing comb-and-paper on *'Lovely Rita,'* Bob Dylan was again heading full speed in a totally different direction.

In this period of musical exploration and studio wizardry, Dylan came out with a dramatic change in style that flew in the face of the Beatles and *"Sgt Pepper..."*

Bob Dylan – *"I didn't know how to record the way other people were recording and I didn't want to. The Beatles had just recorded, "Sgt Pepper..." I thought it was a very indulgent album... I didn't think all that production was necessary."*[8]

Dylan's next change in style, a possible reply to *"Pepper,"* came in the guise of his 1968 album release *"John Wesley Harding."* Is it possible then, that without *"Sgt Pepper..."* there would not have been *"John Wesley Harding"*? Even the minimalist monochrome cover to *"Harding"* appeared to be in direct response to the flamboyant *"Pepper"* gatefold cover, which of course featured amongst others, Bob Dylan. The same *freaks* that said Paul McCartney was dead were now seeing the Beatles in the tree bark of the *"Harding"* sleeve.

Dylan's constant changes in direction seemed to totally confuse Lennon and helped to fuel his love-hate relationship with Dylan and his music. Recalling his mood at the time of writing, *'I Am The Walrus,'* Lennon remarked – *"Dylan got away with murder. I thought, I can write this crap, too."*

Dylan's direct influence on the Beatles' music is well documented: the introduction to *'Yesterday,'* the way in which Dylan's *'Desolation Row'* and the Beatles' *'A Day In The Life'* can be likened to T.S. Eliot's *The Waste Land* and the opening bars to *'A Hard Day's Night,'* a song Lennon admitted was influenced by Dylan but said *"We Beatle-fied it before we recorded it."*

One song not mentioned thus far is the perfect example of a *From Me To You* analogy. Lennon was uneasy about trespassing on Dylan's territory with *'Norwegian Wood.'* According to Alan Price, Lennon told him that before the recording of the song other Beatles were *"taking the mickey out of him"* for copying Dylan.

Lennon's worst fears were about to be realised; *"Rubber Soul,"* the album containing

'Norwegian Wood' was released in December 1965, and by February 14 Dylan had written and recorded his first take of *'Fourth Time Around.'*

In *'Fourth Time Around,'* Dylan seemed to be saying to Lennon: *"Look, I know you're copying my style, so let's not be so coy about it!"* *'Fourth Time Around'* was, of course, anything but coy; Dylan was quite blatant with the virtual wholesale lifting of Lennon's tune, which he then set his own words to.

When Lennon heard *'Fourth Time Around,'* he instantly became even more paranoid than before. At first, Lennon stated publicly that he didn't like the song, but later described it as *"great."* What should he do now? Was this Dylan's way of telling Lennon to lay off? Moreover, what did Dylan mean by the song's closing line: *"I never asked for your crutch / now don't ask for mine."*

After the break-up of The Beatles, Lennon's solo work stood in marked contrast to that of Paul McCartney. While McCartney's output remained constant, melodic, with pretty pop lyrics, Lennon's work was to say the least erratic, and more often than not would feature hard edged and bitter lyrics reminiscent of *'Positively Fourth Street,'* and *'Can You Please, Crawl Out Your Window.'*

John Lennon – *"I was always so paranoid. He said he wanted me to be in this film – Eat The Document – and he did just want me to be in the film, but I thought: Why, what, he's just gonna put me down."*

At times Lennon's paranoia became extreme and, whilst for the most part he treated Dylan as a god, he became upset when Dylan failed to live up to his lofty expectations of him.

John Lennon – *"I've grown up enough to communicate with him... Both of us were always uptight, you know, and of course I wouldn't know whether he was uptight because I was so uptight, and then when he wasn't uptight, I was – all that bit. But we just sat it out because we just liked being together."*[4]

However, the situation began to worsen in the seventies, and Lennon became incensed when he discovered Dylan's real name was Zimmerman! His anger was made public in the song *'God (I Don't Believe In Zimmerman),'* which was featured on the *"John Lennon/ Plastic Ono Band"* album from 1970.

Lennon later wrote numerous Dylan parodies, most of which were never recorded. *'Stuck Inside Of Lexicon With The Roget's Thesaurus Blues Again,'* was a dig at Dylan's wordiness, while *'Serve Yourself'* was written in response to Dylan finding Jesus. The song was eventually released in 1998 on *"The John Lennon Anthology."*

Due to the actions of one Mark Chapman, we will never know how this off-on relationship would have developed. Was it mere coincidence that by March 11, 1981, just thirteen weeks after John Lennon had been fatally shot by the deranged Beatles *fan,* that Dylan is in the studio trying out some songs for his next album, one of which will become the title track of that album – *'Shot Of Love.'*

Shortly before the end of his all-too-short life, John Winston Lennon seemed at last to be coming to terms with himself. His final album *"Double Fantasy"* featured songs of contentment and hope such as *'Beautiful Boy,'* written for his son Sean, and *'Just Like Starting Over.'* The album also contained the song *'Watching The Wheels,'* in which Lennon sings the words: *"I'm Just sitting here, watching the wheels go round and round."* Was this yet another reflection of the words Bob Dylan had sung almost a decade earlier: *"I just sit here so contentedly, and watch the river flow?"* I will leave the final words to a friend of both men:

Al Aronowitz – *"To me, Bob and John were brothers born of the same creative clay. To me, they were both towering bastions of individuality. They certainly were both so different from everybody else as to make people pick up and notice. To me, John Lennon was Dylan's English reflection through the looking glass and across the sea in the land of left-hand drive."*[9]

Main publications used in the preparation of this text:

1 Barry Miles, *Paul McCartney: Many Years From Now*
2 *It Was Twenty Years Ago Today* Bantam Books, 1987.
3 Robert Shelton, *No Direction Home*
4 *"Biograph"* notes
5 Bob Spitz *Dylan a Biography*
6 Anthony Scaduto *Bob Dylan: An Intimate Biography*
7 Humphires/Bauldie *Oh No! Not Another Bob Dylan Book*
8 Clinton Heylin *The Recording Sessions 1960-1994*
9 ISIS issue #81 Al Aronowitz.

Other publications used in the preparation of this text:

Ian MacDonald *Revolution in The Head*
Mark Hertsgaard *A Day in The Life*
Charlie Gillett *Rock File 2 Panther* edited
Terry Hounsome *RockBase Plus* V2
The Penguin Encyclopaedia of Popular Music

Published in issue #82. January 1999.

Walking Like Rimbaud
by C.P. Lee

"I was almost disappointed that there was no trouble at the LA concert."
Dylan to Robert Shelton.

Like crazed palaeontologists – well, we dig rock don't we? – the unearthing of an ancient artefact can send our little world into a tizzy. And that's exactly what I'm in now, sitting here listening to a brand new old recording of Bob Dylan live at the Hollywood Bowl in 1965. Where the hell did this thing come from? Who has had it stashed away all these years? What can it mean to us thirty-three years on?

Adopting the archaeological metaphor once again, it represents a missing link, another piece of the jigsaw that helps us build up our knowledge of the working practices of Bob Dylan approaching arguably his most creative point. It's a live recording from the early part of his quest for that *"thin, wild, mercury sound,"* a quest that took him on a musical odyssey that over the next few months would bring us the beautiful *"Blonde On Blonde,"* all the way through to the manic intensity of Manchester and *"Live 1966."*

Discounting Newport, which was experimental, the Hollywood Bowl was only the second *proper* concert for the new style Dylan, first half acoustic, second set electric, the format he was to use for the next nine months. The musicians he had backing him were the unit that had been assembled for Forest Hills, Robbie Robertson and Levon Helm from The Hawks, Harvey Brooks and Al Kooper, both of whom had worked in the studio with Dylan and were featured on the newly released *"Highway 61 Revisited"* album. This album was released barely a week before the Bowl concert, but already Dylan was beginning the monumental task of preparing *"Blonde On Blonde."* Truly, this was a man whose head was exploding with ideas.

Listening to the recording you can sense a pulling, a dichotomy, a difference already, even before the sounds that had just come on the market had time to coalesce. And herein lies the problem with the Hollywood Bowl tape, and the problem is the musicians. After reviewing what we have on tape I will discuss this in more detail.

The Gig

It took place on a warm summer evening on September 3, 1965. The venue was the prestigious Hollywood Bowl, a huge semi-circular arena that had been built to lend a kind of artistic credence to the supposed vacuity of Hollywood's film industry. Here was where *serious* artistic events took place. In the thirties Max Reinhardt had staged his Expressionist version of Shakespeare's *A Midsummer's Night Dream* starring Mickey Rooney as Puck and, would you believe, James Cagney as Bottom. It played host to the Hollywood Symphony Orchestra, as well as a plethora of fund-raising charity events. In the sixties it was increasingly used for concerts by *Pop* musicians; The Beatles and Bob Dylan were amongst the first to break through the confines of its super trendy, arts background.

The Scene

Apart from his growing legion of young fans, Dylan was appearing that night in front a kind of who's who of the hip glitteratti that represented the Hollywood scene. These weren't just movie stars and moguls such as Gregory Peck, Dean Martin, Tuesday Weld and James Coburn, but also the new breed of music makers and shakers in the Pop industry. People like Sonny and Cher, The Byrds, Brian Wilson and The Beach Boys. Interviewed at the time, Wilson said that Dylan, *"Was great with words but might destroy music,"* whatever that might mean. In Wilson's autobiography, he states that he went to the Hollywood Bowl because he needed to keep up with people such as Dylan and The Beatles. In terms of song-writing and the monumental changes it was going through at that period in history, he was certainly doing his homework that night; Dylan was about to unleash the full-scale assault on the musical parameters of Pop that he'd been working on since Newport. But this wasn't the East Coast with its army of Folk purists; this was Tinseltown, home of the Cool. At that time, in an interview with Nora Ephron and Susan Edmiston, Dylan had been singing the praises of LA and California:

"Where did you get that shirt?"

"California. Do you like it?... You can't get clothes like that here – New York – *There are lots of things out there we haven't got here... It's uptight here compared to there. Hollywood I mean. It's not really breathable here. It's like there's air out there... The people there look different, they look more like... you want to kiss them."*

Wow! The Summer of Love is still a dream away, but Bob's there already!

This might explain the chant of *"You're so groovy!"* that emanates from a group of girls in the audience during the first half. Dylan can only laugh in response to this accolade, but you know he just really digs it, man. There's a legend that abounds, but it may be more applicable to Berkeley in December, that when asked what did he get high on Dylan replied: *"Rolled up copies of* Newsweek. *"*

The Set

As far as I can gather from the various tapes and CDs there's no discernible announcement bringing Dylan onto the stage, though this would seem most unusual, for then as well as now. What we do get from the recorded evidence is a vital acoustic strumming as Dylan walks up to the microphone. This is yet another example of his *hitting the ground running* technique of opening up a performance. It works well.

'She Belongs To Me'

This opening number would have been familiar to the crowd, having been around since *"Bringing It All Back Home"* hit the record racks earlier that year. Once again, Dylan shifts the lyrical dynamic by the inclusion of the word *"red"* in describing the Egyptian ring that his lover wears. Maybe he added it for scanning purposes after it was originally recorded? Whatever, it still remains an item of heated discussion on the Internet to this day. The tune itself is taken at quite a lick, as is most of the rest of the acoustic set. As Mickey Jones has suggested, this can be construed as Dylan being eager to get it over with and the electric band brought on. Alternatively, it is simply, a man who is excited, both at the vibrancy of his offerings and the immediacy of his message – for want of a better word – or as somebody who is genuinely nervous about the outcome of the gig. Remember, only a few days before, at Forest Hills, his experiments into *"mathematical"* music had gone hideously pear-shaped in terms of audience response. Here was an artist with his act firmly on the line.

The guitar playing is hard and spare. The harmonica fills are fast, sharp and ardent in their complexity. Some degrees removed, and then some, from the delicate original recording, this version of *'She Belongs To Me'* is a great opener.

'To Ramona'

The sultry LA air plays havoc with Dylan's tuning, and an electronic horn blares its appreciation of Dylan's set.

"Aah... Y'know how it is sometimes"... says Bob as he struggles to tune his unruly guitar, and then, after finally mastering it, moves into *'Ramona.'* Lust, love, and the shimmering sidewalk streets of New York, East Harlem and the whiff of forbidden fruit. Magnificent!

Before the next song gets underway the honking klaxon brays out its stalwart hosannas from the crowd. Bob is bewildered as to the significance of it.

"What is that thing out there, man? – What are you trying to say?"

'Gates Of Eden'

As Dylan kicks off his surrealist anthem, the crowd greets it with a round of applause and whistles. His audience know what they expect and maybe even what they want, and here, now, Dylan is the Man, delivering the goods, standing alone, armed only with his mouth and guitar and harp. As always an essential song, perfect for the times and perfect forever.

'It's All Over Now, Baby Blue'

Already a concert stalwart, *'...Baby Blue'* would remain in the set list throughout the next eight months, but pace Michael Gray, I still feel that here at the Hollywood Bowl, Dylan's performance, while not quite perfunctory, is at the least, a little lacklustre. Going with Mickey Jones again, Dylan couldn't wait to get through the acoustic sets and strap his Fender across his shoulder. Bob was ready to do Rock 'n' Roll battle armed with his vision and his voice. The acoustic sets are an intrusion on his assault upon the battlements of normalcy in Pop. The cat just can't wait to plug in.

"I'm sorry – I can't hear you... – Tuning – ...This is called:"

'Desolation Row.' Popular song as comedy routine.

Dylan kicks off this newly released anthem at breakneck speed. Is this another indication of eagerness to get the electric set started, or, perhaps, a little too much medicine? When members of the audience start laughing at various lines in this song we have to remember where we are. Essentially this is the hippest place on the planet. When Dylan sings about *"sniffing drainpipes, "nurses," "leather cups"* and *"cyanide holes,"* we have to remember that there is a distinct possibility that a small, but significant, portion of the crowd pay large amounts of money to indulge in such decadence. Here in LA, the word *"hippest"* means those who can afford to do anything their wildest fantasies desire. Also bear in mind that La La Land is not that far from Desolation Row and that the elite who are gathered there that evening to listen to Dylan could be banished to Desolation Row at a moment's notice should the public or their movie-mogul masters so dictate.

'Love Minus Zero/ No Limit'

Just before starting his next song Dylan is rendered speechless by an interjection from the crowd. What sounds like two girls call out in unison:
"You're so groovy!"
Dylan, nonplussed, giggles like a bashful bridegroom and then starts off on his hymn to beauty, love and mysticism.
If he was rushing before, for whatever reason, on this number he's articulate, precise and caring. Perhaps it's because Dylan realises that this is LA and that here is the epicentre of the media universe, or it could be that he's settling into the set having overcome his nerves.

'Mr Tambourine Man'

At the end of *'...Zero'* Dylan's hippy chicks start shouting again and he does the only thing a gentleman can do under the circumstances and blasts his way into the opening chords of *'Mr Tambourine Man.'* The delivery that night in California is worth the price of admission alone. It soars and it swings with feeling of pure delight. The harmonica playing reminds us now of what a virtuoso performer Dylan was on the instrument. At that point in England during the sixties harmonica playing was dominated by freaks like The Morton Fraser Harmonica gang when Cedric the midget used to buffoon around on a gigantic, well at least for him, bass chromatic Hohner, playing numbers such as *'The Sabre Dance.'* Here at last, we are reminded of how sepulchral the instrument can sound in the mouth of a truly great musician.
And so to the intermission –
We can only imagine what went on in the dressing room between sets. Dylan no doubt gave the guys in the band a pep talk, probably similar to the ones he'd given at Newport and Forest Hills – Just go on there and play. No matter what the audience do, go for it. Music is our sword and truth is our shield kind of thing. Al Kooper stated that whatever was going on, he knew that this was Hollywood and the people out there were just too cool to boo. There is no way that they'd allow themselves to appear unhip.
Albert Grossman would be stalking around smoking through his fist, checking that Bob was all right and that everything was in place. He'd personally spent several hours at Forest Hills checking the PA and the stage gear, stomping round in the gusts of rain and the howling wind, armed only with his magnificence – pace Michael Gray – and a walkie-talkie. At least here in LA the weather was as it should be and the open-air crowd were in a carnival mood. Like Kooper intimated, they were there and they were hip to trip. The second set commenced.

'Tombstone Blues'

Is Dylan singing about the place or the thing? I don't think anybody's pursued that theme before. Gunfighters went to Tombstone, or at least they did in films. Wasn't it near

Abilene? Who knows? Who cares? Dylan makes the place his own in this song that has as many directions as a man might want to follow – to use the vernacular of the times.

To us, at the time, and probably even now, this song was a cornucopia of delights – Math-books, Galileo, chickens, Ma Rainey, jungles, Cecil B De Mille, the sun, geometry, flesh, oh my gawd! There's just so much in this song that wants to be sung, and here for the first time in our lives is a man who's singing about them! Dismiss the Now and go back to Then; imagine you're a sixteen-year-old kid and here is some skinny guy from wherever, encapsulating your thoughts into a track on an album that you've just bought. Impossible to imagine maybe, but that's how it was back then, and that's why *'Tombstone Blues'* is so important.

In Hollywood that night the song is almost an Atlantic/Stax workout. Robertson cuts a rug and you find yourself almost waiting for a brass section to kick in. Dylan wails the last line of each verse over the drum beat... Magical.

'I Don't Believe You'

By June 1965 the term *'Folk-Rock'* had entered the public consciousness. The Byrds' version of *'Mr Tambourine Man'* was riding high in the charts. Barry Macguire's version of PF Sloane's *'Eve Of Destruction'* was about to enter the Top Twenty. A fad-hungry America was about to slake its drought on the next greatest thing, which was their hybrid, ersatz new musical genre – Folk Rock.

'Just Like Tom Thumb's Blues'

Destined to be another mainstay of the electric set, *'Tom Thumb,'* is sung at the Hollywood Bowl with a wonderfully wailing Dylan cadence, the lyrics float and roll effortlessly, but overall the magnificence of the 1966 tour's saturation bombing sound is missing. Here it sounds more like saturation trilling. Kooper plays his electric piano like a little Welsh harp, frills and fills, no body to it at all. Robertson's liquid-lead struggles manfully to put some balls into it, but Brooks' pedestrian bass keeps it firmly rooted to the spot and only during the lead solo do things start to move along a little.

'From A Buick 6'

This is a chugging rockerama that, on record, is underpinned by Mike Bloomfield's lead guitar playing. Robertson here has to fight hard to make it his own number and succeeds brilliantly with two searing lead breaks punctuating Dylan's impassioned singing. Dylan even substitutes French Symbolist poet Rimbaud for Bo Diddley, possibly the first and only time that a nineteenth century wordsmith has ever been saluted in the lyrics of a Rock 'n' Roll song!

'Maggie's Farm'

Dylan's second electric single and, with hindsight, he's already far beyond this kind of twelve bar Rock 'n' Roll pastiche and into the realms of *"mathematical music."* Kooper underpins it all with a boogie pattern Hammond, but somehow it just doesn't have the chops. Robertson once again rides to the rescue with a Memphis/Fender shoot out, but the pace is too frenetic for the ensemble to hold it all together in the way it should.

'It Ain't Me Babe'

Kooper plays it Pop! This sounds like an embryonic electric version of '...Babe,' and, I would be willing to bet, a Robertson arrangement. For comparison we only have to listen to 'Long Distance Operator,' recorded in December of 1965 in Berkeley to hear how it would eventually pan out. Guitar-wise Robertson dominates, but the song is nearly put to bed by Kooper's insistence on filling any spare space with the kind of Pop piano fills you'd normally associate with mid-60s bands like The Left Banque or The Association.

'Ballad Of A Thin Man'

Dylan, on what sounds like a cross between a honky-tonk piano and a harpsichord, smears the riff across the tune. Kooper meanders unconvincingly on the Hammond. Hudson waits in the wings. This is a strum along rather than the precisely plotted and skank-like version it will grow into during 1966. Just for one moment imagine it in reggae time. Come on, it's easy; 'Knockin' On Heaven's Door' has been done that way. Now imagine '...Thin Man' on the off beat. Hmm, Dylan under heavy manners. Whatever – The crowd loves it.

'Like A Rolling Stone'

After a few moments' tuning Dylan asks the audience: *"Does anyone have a C harmonica?"*

From out of the crowd the klaxon blares. Dylan quickly replies: *"No. Not that one."* This is in the days when people would take an harmonica to a Dylan gig in case he asked for one. There's a moment of hilarity within the horror that was Newport when Dylan has returned to do a couple of acoustic numbers after playing for the first time with electric backing. He needs a harp for *'Mr Tambourine Man'* and asks the crowd if anyone has one. As if by magic, a hail of harmonicas showers down on the stage threatening to knock Dylan out. Even he laughs.

Once equipped with the donated organ Dylan and the band strike up *'Like a Rolling Stone,'* his hot new single currently racing up the Billboard chart.

Once again, this is a number that hasn't found its feet yet, but it is only the third time it has been played live. The organ, which is so dominant on the recorded version, hangs around in Hollywood sounding like it's playing the theme from Fireball XL5 or some other Gerry Anderson puppet show. Helm is confident and assertive, but somehow it lacks bite and conviction.

The number finishes and Dylan warmly thanks the audience. There is no evidence that an encore was played as has been thought for some time.

Overview

This is the second and last gig for this particular Dylan backing band. Kooper stated that he was – despite their reception at the Hollywood Bowl – frightened of the reaction that was emanating from the crowds and a trip to Dallas, deep in the heart of redneck Texas was definitely not his cup of tea. It's rumoured that his departure would have happened anyway, whether he'd resigned or not. Same thing for Harvey Brooks. Whilst both these musicians were skilled and capable in the studio, neither of them seems particularly suited for the experimental laboratory that Dylan preferred on stage. There's also an element of conspiracy going on in the background. It is not unlikely to speculate that Helm and Robertson would be suggesting to Dylan that the best team to back him would be The Hawks. And they were right. It was the perfect alchemical wedding. Possibly because, if it's true like they claimed, they had very little idea of who Bob Dylan was. With such an attitude they could bring their own influences independently into the musical mix.

Even with its flaws in the electric half, I regard this recording as an essential item. Dylan, as usual, is very good and the electric half does have its moments. The problems lie in the choice of musicians, and that is soon to be rectified. The Hollywood Bowl concert however, is a unique glimpse into the past and the transition between acoustic and electric Dylan.

Published in issue #80 September 1998

Tito Burns presents

DYLAN '66

in
Dublin
Belfast
Bristol
Cardiff
Birmingham
Liverpool
Leicester
Sheffield
Manchester
Glasgow
Edinburgh
Newcastle
London

The Geography of Innocence
by CP Lee

"I accept chaos – I'm not sure if it accepts me"
Bob Dylan, 1965

In 1990 the factual record of Bob Dylan's 1966 world tour was tantalising and fragmentary; a recording here, a memory there; a handful of photos and a few feet of hardly viewed film. Now, in the new millennium, we have books, videos, and interviews with the participants, stacks of unofficial CDs, and one official album release. What these artefacts have done is allowed us an intimate glimpse into the past, not just at the work of Dylan, but into the minds of us, his public. Here's how…

A Minstrel With His Hands On Fire

Dylan had first dabbled with electricity way back in 1962 – Robert Zimmerman had done it earlier, but that's another story – cutting four known tracks at the *"Freewheelin'"* sessions with a backing group of session men. These tracks remain a mysterious hiccup in his early career, but it does demonstrate that the idea or desire was there all the way from the very beginning. We can only surmise that it was a frustration at the limitations imposed by a strictly acoustic performance that led Dylan into experimenting with the genre again two years later.

And what an experiment – Though *"Bringing It All Back Home"* could be described as a fifty/fifty album, with its mixture of semi-acoustic and hard edged Rock 'n' Roll, it was too much for many to take. Warning shots had already been fired over his previous album, *"Another Side of Bob Dylan,"* which, while being strictly acoustic, had been perceived by certain critics to be veering away from *their* expectations of Dylan. Editor of *Sing Out!* Irwin Silber had gone so far as to publish a so-called *open letter* to Dylan shortly after the album came out:

"Dear Bob,…I'm writing this letter now because some of what has happened is troubling me. And not me alone. Many other good friends of yours as well…As with anyone who ventures down uncharted paths, you've aroused a growing number of petty critics…Some don't like the way you wear your hair or your clothes. Some don't like the

way you sing. Some don't like the fact that you've chosen your name and recast your past. But all of that, in the long run, is trivial... But – and this is the reason for this letter Bob – I think that the times they are a' changing. You seem to be in a different kind of bag now Bob...Your new songs seem to be all inner-directed now, inner-probing, self-conscious – maybe even a little maudlin, or a little cruel on occasions..."

If that's what Silber, a so-called *friend* thought, we could begin to imagine the reaction of those guardians of the Faith – the Traditionalists.

Come All My Young Lads Who Follow The Plough

The fifties *Folk Revival* in America and the UK had much in common. Both had, in a sense, originated within a Leftist framework, in a general spirit of *preserving* the tradition of working class music that was seen to be in danger of disappearing, buried under an avalanche of mass-produced pap pop. Both also shared some of the same instigators, principally Alan Lomax, that tireless collector and propagator of indigenous music. Alan had travelled with his father John, also an avid field recorder at the behest of the Library of Congress, since the thirties. His task as a folklorist and musicologist was to document as much as possible of the various strands of American Folk music that existed throughout the vast reaches of the country. As well as *discovering* such performers as Almeda Riddle and Leadbelly, the Lomaxes, and after his father's death, Alan on his own, would spread the message of purity and authenticity to anybody they could reach.

Amongst those interested in what Lomax had to say were such luminaries of the nascent Folk scene as Pete Seeger in America, and Ewan MacColl in England. I will look at Lomax and MacColl's relationship later. In the meantime let's concentrate on the American revival as it was upon Dylan's arrival in New York in 1961.

A growing disenchantment with the failure of Rock 'n' Roll to live up to its early promise had left many young people high and dry. Elvis had gone like a sheep into the army, Buddy Holly was dead, and what had once seemed so exciting was now being made vapid and bland by the leprous touch of *artists* such as Pat Boone and Rosemary Clooney. In a situation very similar to the one that exists today, the major record companies manufactured groups and solo artists to satisfy the perceived demands of the teenage market. However, an awful lot of those youngsters were fed up with being force-fed the sugar coated platters of second-rate performers, and they began to look elsewhere.

One of the directions that attracted them was what we would nowadays call *Roots* or *Folk* music.

The seeds had been sown in the early fifties with the release of Harry Smith's astonishing *"Anthology of American Folk Music"* box set. The *"Anthology"* and other seminal releases on a variety of small, independent record labels ensured that a new generation were introduced to a world of music so far removed from their conceptual reality that its new audience were totally captivated. The tunes from what seemed like a bygone era were pored over, practised, and assimilated by a growing number of musicians and listeners.

Like many of the most influential genres of popular music in the latter half of the twentieth century, Punk, Northern Soul, etc, the Folk scene developed very much under its own steam without the intervention of major agencies. Interested parties, sometimes musicians, and sometimes enthusiastic promoters, opened up venues for the music. At first, in America at least, the revival began to happen in coffee houses and dingy bars, more often than not, situated in major conurbations or campus towns. It was different, it was unusual, but it was principally an alternative. Unlikely chart success also helped the popularity of the music to spread.

In America that chart success came in 1958 in the form of a young band called The Kingston Trio, who regrooved an Appalachian ballad called *'Hang Down Your Head, Tom Dooley.'* In the UK it's arguable that the process had started a couple of years before with the success of Skiffle music. Skiffle was a kind of Country, Folk, Blues hybrid, popularised by Lonnie Donegan and other, which had led many young people on this side of the Atlantic to investigate the sources of the sound they liked so much. More importantly, it showed that you didn't need much more than enthusiasm, an acoustic guitar and three chords in order to become a performer. The problem in the UK with the revival, was Ewan MacColl.

Such a Parcel O' Rogues in a Nation

In 1952 the Communist Party of Great Britain had published a research document called *"The American Threat To British Culture."* This pamphlet argued that British cinema screens, bookshops and Pop charts were being overrun by crass American mass-produced culture. One of the ways of overcoming this problem was to *re-educate* the people into their own forms of music, preferably Folk. And so it was that a small band of CPGB'rs undertook the task. Alan Lomax visited stalwart Party member Ewan MacColl, husband of Pete Seeger's half-sister, Peggy, father of Kirsty and writer of the classic song *'Dirty Old Town,'* and played him some field recordings –

"When Alan Lomax came along with this music that had proved so popular to generations and generations, I thought, 'This is what we should be exploring!' The Folk revival had a lot of things in it at its conception, and one was to make songs of struggle in an idiom that would be immediately acceptable to lots of young people."   Ewan MacColl, 1987

Along with another CPGB member, Bert Lloyd, the three of them began a series of programmes for BBC radio entitled *Ballads & Blues* that showed the links between British and American Folk music. Shortly afterwards they opened the first *Ballads & Blues* club at the Princess Of Louise pub in London. Mixing a variety of genres, Jazz, Calypso, Traditional and Blues, the club was a success. By 1957 the highly successful enterprise was renamed *The Singers Club* and a kind of licence was issued permitting other venues to use the name. Unfortunately, the permissions were accompanied by a host of draconian orders that were known as *"the policy rules."*

Firstly, MacColl, who at one time had thought nothing of singing Black Alabama prison songs with the Ken Collyer Jazz Band and who had even sung Skiffle with Lonnie Donegan, became dismayed at the latter's chart success –

"I became concerned that we had a whole generation who were becoming quasi-Americans, and I felt this was absolutely monstrous! I was convinced that we had a music that was just as vigorous as anything that America had produced, and we should be pursuing some kind of national identity, not just becoming an arm of American cultural imperialism. That's the way I saw it as a political thinker at the time, and that's the way I still see it."   MacColl, 1987

Hammered out in heated debate with fellow comrades, the policy rules stipulated that a singer could only sing songs from the geographical area they were born in. This was quickly changed to, *"or lived in."* This proved to be a boon for MacColl who was born in Scotland and christened James Miller, but was brought up from the age of three in Salford in the north of England. He changed his name to MacColl during the Second World War in order to avoid military service, and now, through the policy rules, could sing in whatever dialect he chose. Woe betide anybody else, though, who tried to cross the theoretical boundaries and mix songs of different ethnic groupings. This ridiculous ruling even reared its ugly head in American Folk circles as Dylan told Cameron Crowe in the liner notes for his *"Biograph"* album –

"There was just a clique, you know. Folk music was a strict and rigid establishment. If you sang Southern Mountain Blues, you didn't sing Southern Mountain Ballads and you didn't sing City Blues. If you sang Texas Cowboy songs you didn't play English Ballads. It was really pathetic."

Whatever the rigidity of the Stalinistic policy rules, by 1960 it's estimated that there were 1500 Singers Clubs around Britain, with an estimated membership of over 11,000. It's a considerable number of people whichever way you slice the apple. In three years' time there would be many more.

Across The Great Divide

There's a wonderful photograph taken in London on a miserable Sunday night in late December 1962. It was taken at The Pindar of Wakefield pub, home then to the Singers Club. It's a panoramic view of the room upstairs where the singing took place. A very young Bob Dylan wearing his trademark cap and suede jacket is standing, eyes closed in mid-song, in the middle of the floor. On a raised dais behind him sits Bert Lloyd, looking for all the world like a king on a throne. Around Dylan a group of attentive looking young people are listening intently. On the right of the picture two people are not so amused. One is Ewan MacColl, whose frosty stare could chill a bottle of white wine. Next to him is his wife Peggy Seeger. It is the first time they and Dylan have met. However, in later years, MacColl would claim to have met Dylan for the first time at a festival in Minneapolis:

" – He was – an inoffensive little fellow, a student with striped trousers and a black jacket. He looked for all the world like a very respectable law student. He had a nice haircut and a nice manner – he called me, 'sir'."

MacColl was either mistaken or being economical with the truth. Bill Leader who was there that night at the Singers Club maintains it was the first time that MacColl and Dylan had ever met. Anthea Joseph who brought Dylan to the Pindar also stated that she introduced the two musicians, and that MacColl's reaction was to sit *"in stony silence."* The question we have to ask is, why? What possible reason for disliking Dylan so much could MacColl have had? Dylan only played two numbers at the Singers Club that night. And dislike him MacColl did, almost to the point of obsession. Throughout the first half of the 1960s MacColl never lost an opportunity to decry Dylan. Take this quote from *Melody Maker* –

"Dylan is to me the perfect symbol of the anti-artist in our society. He is against everything – the last resort of someone who doesn't really want to change the world...I think his poetry is puerile. It's derivative and old hat..."

Here is MacColl again, this time in Irwin Silber's *Sing Out!* – Remember him?

"… 'But what of Bobby Dylan?' scream the outraged teenagers of all ages. Well, I have watched with fascination the meteoric rise of this American idol and I am still unable to see in him anything other than a youth of mediocre talent. Only a completely non-critical audience, nourished on the watery pap of pop music could have fallen for this tenth rate drivel. 'But the poetry?' What poetry? The cultivated illiteracy of his topical songs or the fourth grade schoolboy attempts at free-verse? The latter reminds me of elderly female schoolteachers clad in Greek tunics rolling hoops across lawns at weekend theatre school."   Ewan MacColl, *Sing Out!,* November 1965

I Asked For Water – She Gave Me Gasoline…

Oddly enough, until a few weeks ago I would have surmised that MacColl's hatred of Dylan stemmed from an ageing man's dislike of the Young Turk – the jackal yapping at the heels of the lion syndrome. But now it seems crystal clear to me, it must have been a word or two of forewarning from Alan Lomax, though I must admit, it's not clear to me why Lomax would have disliked him so much. Unless of course, it had something to do with his dislike of Dylan's manager, Albert Grossman. However, let's fast forward to the Newport Festival in 1965 and Dylan's unveiling of himself as the Electric Messiah… It is Saturday afternoon and the festival is cooking –

"…Grossman became a focus of hostility for a lot of the officials, including Lomax. He'd never been popular amongst these people. He'd always been seen as one of the money changers at the gate of the temple…"   Joe Boyd

About to appear were The Paul Butterfield Blues Band, soon to be managed by Grossman. Several members of the Butterfields were going to back Dylan's first electric outing the next day. For some reason there was a lot of hostility on the festival board to the inclusion of the Butterfield Band on the Saturday line-up.

"…Lomax was really against it. Against Butterfield. Against white boys doing the blues. This is doubly ironic as The Butterfield Band were mixed race – *really…Lomax was forced to introduce the Butterfield Band at the Blues workshop…"*   Joe Boyd

"…The wind was blowing dust and sand everywhere. Then Alan Lomax got up on stage and went into a five or ten minute introduction – Like, 'Used to be a time when a farmer would take a box, glue an axe handle to it, put some strings on it, sit down in the shade of a tree and play some Blues for himself and his friends. Now we've got these guys, and they need all this fancy hardware to play the Blues…Let's find out if these guys can play at all…' Lomax walked off the stage and Grossman… walked up to him and said,
'What kind of fucking introduction was that?' and Lomax said, 'What do you know about Blues?' and Albert said,
'I don't have to know anything about the Blues to know that that was a terrible introduction,' and Lomax said,
'Oh, yeah? What are you gonna do about it?' and before anyone knew what was happening there were these two giants – both physically and in the business – wrestling around in the dust!"   Von Schmidt & Rooney[1]

Historically we know the reception Dylan got on the Sunday night. It was to be the same at Forest Hills a few nights later. Members of the backing band baled out. Dylan released his most upfront electric album *"Highway 61 Revisited"* within a few weeks of Newport. The gauntlet was firmly thrown down at the feet of Traditionalism. A US tour would follow and then a backbreaking schedule of gigging, writing and recording that would culminate in the Nashville sessions for *"Blonde On Blonde"* and the world tour of 1966. Are we ready for the trip? Because what a long strange trip it was...

All Aboard The Good Ship Chaos!

The journey from Newport across America, then to Australia, Europe and finally Great Britain, was a learning curve for all those involved. Firstly, a core of backing musicians had to be settled on. People came and went, some because of conflicting commitments, others because the stress caused by the booing of the Traditionalists was too much to take. The essential nucleus would be provided by The Hawks, a Canadian combo that had until recently provided the backing for Rock 'n' Roll singer Ronnie Hawkins. But even their drummer Levon Helm found the going too tough –

"... It was a ridiculous way to make a living: flying to concerts in Bob's thirteen seat Lodestar, jumping in and out of limousines, and then getting booed... We'd never been booed in our lives... I can take getting booed here: this is my own country. But I can't see taking it to Europe and hearing this shit."

Finally Texan Mickey Jones, late of Trini Lopez and Johnny Rivers, came on board as the drummer for the world tour that began in April 1966. As it turned out, he was an inspired choice, his particular brand of *howitzer* style percussion perfectly suited for the noisy receptions they would receive from audiences and providing the basic underpinning needed by the band.

From the off, Dylan had trouble with people accepting his *new sound*. The press in Honolulu declared the second – electric – half of the concert, *"a big let-down."* The albatross followed them to Australia where walkouts and booing marred the Melbourne concert. Dylan reportedly had trouble adjusting to the demands of a full scale PA, *"eating the mike,"* and being upbraided by manager Albert Grossman for overcompensating because of the electric instruments. It's hardly surprising when you take into account the very *newness* of staging electric performances in anything other than a Beat club. When you listen to line recordings taken from the tour it is simply astonishing how tight the outfit sound, given the circumstances. The other major problem is that the venues chosen for the tour, old concert halls, boxing stadiums and the like, were never designed for amplified music. The sound would more often than not, bounce off the back wall and come straight back at the stage. Add to that, a mid-sixties audience's unfamiliarity with anything of that volume and you have a major perceptual headache, disregarding any qualms people may have had as regards Dylan's new-sounding music. Quite simply, they had never heard anything like it. That was certainly the situation when the outfit arrived in the UK to begin the final leg of the tour.

"Just Another Beat Group Singer..."

Dylan and his unholy crew's journey round the world had been erratic in terms of audience reaction, starting off with Sydney's polite, bordering on enthusiastic, response,

Melbourne's booing, then again, polite but mystified receptions in Scandinavia. Now it was time to go into the lion's den, the British Isles.

After a short stopover in London, Dylan travelled to Ireland and played at the Adelphi Cinema. The Traditionalist Beast was rampant that night –

"Dylan assumed the role of a slightly down-at-heel paperback edition of Mick Jagger, and with the exception of the powerful 'Like a Rolling Stone' and 'One Too Many Mornings,' what came out of the amplifiers was nothing more than watered down R&B... inferior Rolling Stones. It was unbelievable to see Dylan trying to look and sound like Jagger, and to realise after a stunning first few minutes that it wasn't a 'take-off.' Someone shouted 'Traitor!' Someone else 'Leave it to The Beatles!'"
Dublin Evening Herald

They shouted other things too – *"Lower the mike!,"* *"Positively BORE street!,"* and, more bizarrely, *"Stuffed golliwog!"* The litany of infamy followed Dylan back over the Irish Sea and installed itself in the seats of Bristol's Colston Hall. Letters followed a scathing review of the concert in the *Bristol Evening Post* from attendees. Marilyn Johnson was so outraged by Dylan's electric performance that she wrote –

"I was seated in the front row of Bristol's Colston Hall, watching in anticipation as Bob Dylan arrived on stage. The lights faded and he broke the silence with his opening song. Dylan's performance until the interval did him great credit... – Intermission – *At last the stage door opened but unexpectedly a group with electric instruments walked on stage followed by Mr Dylan, who also carried an electric guitar. My heart sank as they proceeded to produce the most dreadful din I have ever experienced. It was the new commercial Bob Dylan, the cheap and ruined Bob Dylan. I was horrified at his performance. He did one of his latest efforts appropriately called 'Like a Rolling Stone.' This is indeed an apt title, describing perfectly his performance during the latter half of the concert. I endured about ten jangled up, deafening and ruined versions of previously good compositions with great disappointment and growing anger. A few people shouted objections and I found it especially encouraging to see some of his old admirers simply stand up and walk out on him. Just as I decided to do the same, the concert abruptly ended..."*

Jenny Leigh from Bristol wrote to *Melody Maker* –

"I have just attended a funeral at Bristol's Colston Hall. They buried Bob Dylan, the Folksinger, in a grave of electric guitars, enormous loudspeakers and deafening drums. It was a sad end to one of the most phenomenal influences in music. My only consolation is that Woody Guthrie wasn't there to witness it."

And so it continued across the UK, catcalls, booing, slow-handclapping, shouting, anger, resentment, grief and vitriol. Each night was an emotional roller-coaster ride with Dylan at the wrong end of a shooting gallery and The Hawks as clowns in the macabre Circus of Madness. Audience member Keith Butler unwittingly played the part of barrack room accuser in a blizzard of Traditionalist angst – *"Judas!"* – and the most famous heckler in Rock history gets immortalised forever in the ghostly tapes of oblivion. But really, I mean really, after all this time, what was it all about?

Electric Black Night Crash

What had so riled so many people that they felt it necessary to register their displeasure by vocally protesting, or walking out on Dylan? I've already outlined the Stalinistic practices of the Ewan MacColl-led Singers Club members. These autocratic dictates were reflected in the rules official and unofficial of dozens of other Folk clubs that existed in the cities, towns and campuses of Great Britain. Inevitably, a substantial proportion of the members of these clubs were of a Left-leaning persuasion. Dylan had, for better or for worse, appeared as a champion of the causes of the day. The phrase *"Protest Singer/Protest Song"* had been coined as a way of describing Dylan's early output. True, it was not a name-tag that he himself used or even favoured, but rightly or wrongly, that is how he was perceived by a significant group of his admirers. MacColl, and others, had for years preached that the contemporary Folk singer/songwriter, should harness their talents towards social change and the eradication of injustice. This was, in effect, elevating them into a kind of prestigious position where they were expected to behave in a certain monk-like manner. Kind of like puritan balladeers, there were certain rules to follow. These included a complete and total disavowal of anything to do with *"commerciality,"* or *"selling out."* The Pop charts were for mindless teenagers, being duped out of what little they earned by unscrupulous capitalists. Any artist who associated with this kind of thing was a traitor to the purity of *"the people's music."* That's why he was a *"traitor,"* a *"Judas!"* He had sold out the sanctity of Folk for his thirty pieces of silver.

Let's momentarily go back to the letter of eighteen year old Marilyn Johnson from Bristol, who wrote – *"At last the stage door opened but unexpectedly a group with electric instruments walked out."* – As with the Manchester Free Trade Hall concert which I attended, if the drum kit, amplifiers, piano and organ that had been on stage since before the audience entered hadn't given here a clue, I don't know what would have done. Plus the fact that it had been reported in all the music papers that Dylan was appearing in the second half with a backing band. Perhaps she didn't read the music papers; not everybody did. But back to her letter – *"He did one of his latest efforts appropriately called 'Like a Rolling Stone'."* – This had come out nine months previously and had been followed by *'Positively Fourth Street,'* *'Can You Please Crawl Out Your Window,'* and *'One Of Us Must Know (Sooner Or Later).'* *'Subterranean Homesick Blues,'* and *'Maggie's Farm,'* plus the electric album *"Highway 61 Revisited"* and the *half* electric album, *"Bringing It All Back Home,"* had preceded it. Marilyn and all the other people who took umbrage at Dylan's *new direction* MUST have known what was going on.

Perhaps a lot of them did, but kind of hoped it would all go away. There are some interesting stories about groups of people from Folk clubs and societies – with some Communist Party involvement, though none of it Party policy – debating furiously into the night as to how best they could register their displeasure at Dylan's errant ways. Some, like Manchester University's Folk club, voted unanimously to boycott the concert. It is not recorded if Dylan was aware of this when he played. It has been said that the Scottish party members voted to attend but boo if he played electric, and then argued furiously as to which point in the concert they should stage a walkout if Dylan persisted in the error of his ways.

...Back Home

What we have now after all those years is a collection of recordings that clearly demonstrate an artist on the peak of an intellectual and creative tsunami of a wave. Each concert has its own power and energy. The musicianship is formidable and often spine-tingling. The audience confrontations can be amusing from the perspective of hindsight, yet also deeply disturbing. I'm hard pressed to think of many other artists who have had to suffer that kind of humiliation night after night. That Dylan and the Hawks could put up with it and carry on is a remarkable testimony to the vision of Dylan. Mickey Jones has said how he often thought when listening to recordings of the night's show, *"Is it possible that we really are bad and we just don't know it?"* Yet the playback would only serve to reconfirm his gut feeling and instinct that they were absolutely right.

A final word – the protestors were not the majority, but they were certainly the most vocal. To all of you who were there and didn't boo, or walkout – well done, you're part of history too.

1 Von Schmidt & Rooney, *Baby Let Me Follow You Down*, Anchor Press

Commissioned for inclusion in *ISIS: A Bob Dylan Anthology.*

Kemper

Bucky Baxter

'95

Bob Dylan

Tony Garnier

César Díaz '02

GE
SMITH

John Jackson

MICKEY JONES

Interview with Mickey Jones
Interview conducted by Ian Woodward

Mickey Jones was the drummer on Dylan's 1966 world tour. What follows is an edit of Mickey's talk, which took place at Sachas Hotel, Manchester, England, on Saturday, May 23, 1998.

IW: Your first contact with Bob was long before you played with him, so let's start with that first point in time.

MJ: That's a question that I've been asked a lot, how did this whole association with Bob happen. I was a Bob Dylan fan long before I met Bob Dylan. I loved his folk music. I loved the statement that he was makin' in his poetry, because truly, I think that he will go down as one of the great poets of all time, not just our time, but all time.

I was with Johnny Rivers for three years and I would have stayed with Johnny Rivers had not Bob Dylan come along. We worked a club in Los Angeles called The Whiskey A Go Go. I was actually dating one of the waitresses at the club. I think it's a rule, I think you have to date a waitress at the club. And she walked by and she said, *"Bob Dylan's here,"* and then about five minutes later she came and she said, *"Bob Dylan wants to meet you, wants to talk to you."* I said*, "Yeah, right."* She said *"If ever I told you the truth, I'm tellin' you the truth now. You go over there on your break because he wants to meet you."* So I kinda walked over nonchalant; I didn't want to be too big about oh, you're Bob Dylan, you know. As soon as I walked over and got close to Dylan, he said, *"Mickey, I need to speak to you."* I walked over and said well, *"How you doin'?"* I sat down in the corner of the booth where he was sitting. He said something to me and it meant so much to me. He said, *"You're my very favourite rock and roll drummer in the world."* I was kinda shocked, I was taken aback. I said *"Wow!"* He said, *"Yeah, I've listened to your records and I love the way you play and I would love for you to record with me."* I said, *"I would love to do that, let's do it."* He said, *"Well, we're goin' to have a party tonight up in the Hills; would you like to come over and let's really talk about this."* And I said, *"Sure."*

So I went to this Hollywood party and after about two hours I didn't even speak to Bob. So finally, I said, I'm out of here, I'm going to be getting out. I walked over to Bob Dylan and I said, *"Hey Bob, it's really good meeting you but I'm goin' to split now."* He said, *"Well wait, we need to talk!"* And I said, *"Well, I've been here two hours man; you've been tied up with everybody 'cos it's like this Hollywood thing,"* and he said, *"No, we need to speak."* So we went into the kitchen of this house with Bob Neuwirth and we must have talked for the next three hours. We talked until the sun came up, and he must have said five or six times that I was his favourite drummer and that he wanted to work with me. So I gave him my telephone number and how to get a hold of me. It would be a year later before I got the call to play with Bob.

I was working a club in Detroit called Gay Haven. I'd gone out in the afternoon, gone to the movies or whatever and when I came back there were like four or five 'phone messages to call Albert Grossman in New York. I didn't know who Albert Grossman was so I just threw them away. I went out to dinner and when I came back to get ready for work there were about four more 'phone calls from Albert Grossman and they said operator call back six. I thought oh, he's payin' for the call, OK I'll call him and find out who this guy is. So I called up and the lady answered the 'phone and said *"Grossman Management,"* and I said, *"Hi, I'm returning a 'phone call from Albert Grossman."* She said, *"And your name?"* and I said, *"Mickey Jones."* She said, *"Oh my God, we've been looking for you for two weeks! Hold the 'phone for Mr Grossman."* So Albert got on the 'phone, he said, *"Mickey, Albert Grossman,"* and I said, *"Hi Al, who are you?"* (laughs).He said, *"I'm Bob Dylan's manager and Bob wants you to be his drummer."* I said, *"Like in a recording session, or what?"* He said, *"No, Bob has decided that he wants to put a band together, and he wants you to be his drummer."* I said, *"Really, like all the time?"* He said, *"Yeah, full time drummer."*

I was a little hesitant because I was makin' at the time, in 1966, pretty good money with Johnny Rivers. I was a musician bringing in $500 a week, which by today's standards was a lot of money. I flew first class, all my hotel bills were paid, and all my meals were paid. So I asked him what the deal was, *"Like how much am I gonna get?"* He said, *"Well, Bob's got all the details for that."* I said *"I'll be home Sunday about two o'clock."* He said, *"I'll have Bob Dylan call you at three o'clock."*

Sure enough at three o'clock on the button the 'phone rang and it's Bob Dylan. He said, *"Mickey, it's Bob Dylan, Albert told me to call you."* I said, *"Yeah, well he told me that you wanted me to play drums, you were putting a group together, but he didn't give me any of the details. He said that would be up to you."* He said, *"You mean how much money?"* And I said *"Yeah."* So, he said, *"Well, I'll start you out on $750 a week."* And I was like stumped, I didn't know what to say. I went, *"Err, can you hold the 'phone just for one minute?"* I looked over to my wife and I said, *"He wants to give me $750 a week."* She said, *"You know what, it's what you want to do, you should do it."* So, I got back on the 'phone and I said – timid voice – *"Oh, OK."* (laughs). Then he said, *"I'll pay all your travel, and you'll pay for your hotel and your meals."* I got to thinkin', I have to reconsider this. I said, *"I'm flyin' first class now and I have all my hotels paid and all my meals paid. If I have to start payin' for my hotels this is goin' to offset the raise in salary, so I just don't think I could do it for that."*

The 'phone went dead for a few seconds and he came back and he said, *"I'll tell you what I'll do. I'll pay for all of your hotels, if you pay for your own meals?"* I got to thinking, I could eat at McDonalds! (laughs) So I said, *"OK that's cool, that'll work."* His next line was, *"You have to be very, very silent about our arrangement! Because Robbie and Garth and Rick and Richard are all payin' for their own hotels."* So now I look back, God I was doin' better than Robbie, that was pretty cool! (laughs) The next day he sent me a telegram to the effect of our deal, and he gave me a guarantee of two years.

He came to Los Angeles and we rehearsed – I would say that we rehearsed for a couple of weeks. At the first rehearsal was the drummer that had been with the Hawks just before me; that was Sandy Konikoff. He was at the first two rehearsals playing percussion; he was playing guedra, tambourine and bells and stuff like that. I don't know if he left because he didn't like the idea that he was playing percussion and not drums, or if Bob Dylan actually let him go; that I don't have an answer to.

We got to rehearsal about eight o'clock at night, and we would sometimes rehearse until the sun came up; I mean we would rehearse all night long. Bob was on *Columbia* Records, so the *Columbia* Recording Studios on Sunset Boulevard in Hollywood is where we did all of our rehearsals.

There was a local guy in LA that had a TV show, name of Loyd Thaxton. Dean – of Jan and Dean – and I had been guests on the show. A couple of times we rode our motorcycles right in on the show live. We did that one afternoon and his guest that day was Otis Redding. Loyd Thaxton introduced me as the drummer with Bob Dylan. And Otis said, *"Oh man, I would give anything to meet Bob Dylan."* He said, *"I'm openin' at The Whiskey A Go Go tonight so if there's any chance that you could be down there I would do anything to meet him."* I said, *"Well, you know, I'll run it by him."*

So that night at the rehearsals at about ten o'clock we took our first break and we went back into this little area with the vending machines. Bob's drinking his coffee and I'm having my Coke, that's er, Coca Cola (laughs) I said to Bob, *"Hey man, you won't believe who I met today,"* and he said, *"Who?"* I said, *"I met Otis Redding."* Bob looked at me and he said, *"Oh man, I would give anything to meet Otis Redding!"* (laughs). I said, *"I could arrange that"* (laughs). He said, *"Seriously?"*

We saw the midnight show of Otis Redding and after we all went upstairs. Here I was in the middle – and I'm real proud of this – I said, *"Bob I'd like you to met Otis Redding. Otis this is Bob Dylan."* And Bob picked up a guitar and he said, *"I got a great song for you. This song is perfect for you,"* – and he played *'Just Like a Woman.'* Otis sat there mesmerised and he said, *"Oh man, I wanna cut that. I wanna record it."* He was killed shortly after that so he never recorded it, but I tell people if you look on the *"Otis Redding Live At The Whiskey A Go Go"* album, in the liner notes it will say about the night that Bob Dylan came in to see him. So, anyway, is that a good enough answer to the first question? (laughs).

I was never a fancy drummer, I didn't play drum solos, but I had a right foot like a 105 howitzer, and I played hard and I played loud. That's another thing: today they mix everything in the monitors and they wear earpieces and everything is a perfect mix of everything. We didn't have that. All we heard in the monitor was Bob Dylan's voice and I'm listening to everybody else through their amplifiers.

The only changes that I made from the style that I would have played, was that Bob Dylan had a real thing about eight notes, building eight notes – there was a lot of that. That was something Bob liked, it turned him on, you know. And I mean that was my job, to turn him on. I'll tell you this, the first half of those concerts he was absolutely bored to tears. He would come back to the dressing room, and put that acoustic guitar down and he would put that black Telecaster on and you could see the adrenaline runnin' through his veins. He would be running around, dancing, jumpin' up and down and he's still in the dressin' room! When he plugged in, nobody had any more more fun than Bob Dylan.

I can honestly say those boos really didn't bother us, because we were doin' this for us; it was for our entertainment. In fact we kinda laughed at the boos. Every time somebody would yell something out we'd kinda look at each other, smile, and say, why don't we really give it to em.

IW: Did he socialise with you guys outside of rehearsals?

MJ: I saw Bob a few times outside of rehearsals. He didn't associate with the guys too much. I don't want to sound negative, but we called Robbie *"Barnacle Man,"* because he was attached to Bob Dylan at the shoulder! I don't know, I just wasn't into bein' a hanger around all the time.

IW: I think you're going to start on the tour now, aren't you?

MJ: Sure. So we fly to Honolulu. We were two nights, I'm sure we were two nights, because Garth and I did sightseeing the morning of the concert. Unlike most of the tour the venue there was huge; it was a huge stage. I mean we were dwarfs on the stage in Honolulu. There was some booing. I mean I didn't think it terrible, but I could tell that there were some people that were upset with the electric part of the show. I don't think they were upset with the sound, as much as they were upset with what he was doing, you know, but it was small, just a sliver, but it did happen there. I guess it was a precursor of things to come because it seemed to generate. I don't know if people in the next places got word what was goin' on, but it did escalate and escalate until Judas.

Sydney was the biggest venue that we played, it was huge. It was an old boxing arena and the stage would rotate, it would turn. The stage was very small, about the size of a boxing ring. I mean it was very small for all the equipment that we had. We had to set up in a different format because the stage would rotate. Somebody said to me that on one of the tours they thought that Bob did the whole concert with his back to the audience. And it may well have been that concert because it was a 360-degree audience.

IW: As far as the band are concerned is it the same set list every night? I mean are you playing exactly the same list?

MJ: Exactly. In fact the little thing that Bob did when the crowds would get unruly, and he'd go – Mickey then performs the famous Dylan muttering game, finishing with the words, *"I wish you just wouldn't."* Well, he did that on a lot of occasions. He didn't end with the same thing; he'd say something different. But he would do that on a lot of occasions because that really got their attention. Our set was the same though. I mean the arrangements didn't change. Robbie could change a solo, but the number of bars that he's gonna play is gonna be the same. So, pretty much the same arrangement and set every night. And I'd like to believe that set got better and better each time.

We were recording most of those shows on audio, but unfortunately that same tape would be used again, we would re-record over that the next night. We would go back to the rooms and we'd listen to the concert, and we were pretty happy with the tapes. Mostly we listened to the tapes to hear the audience and we'd kinda laugh amongst ourselves. I feel that at that time they just didn't understand what we were doin'. They just didn't get it. Because his music at that time took a U-turn and went in totally another direction, and a lot of people didn't want to do that. I can look back now this many years later and I can understand why there was the booing and why they didn't like it. I don't think it was because it was too loud. I think it was truly because people thought that Bob Dylan who was this incredible poet and speaker for society, had turned his boat around and gone commercial. I think they thought he was a sell-out. It offended us to a point that all we wanted to do was say, well let's make it a little louder, we'll get even with them, but it didn't hurt our feelings.

I've heard people say that he did it for the money. The reality is he made less money on that tour than any tour he'd ever done, because to take that many people and all that equipment and all that air freight. If he had done the tour alone he would have tripled the money he made, so obviously he did not do it for the money. He did it because his musical tastes were changin'. You can only eat the same food every day for so long, you have to have a change, and I think that's exactly what this was about.

IW: Was there any difference between the audience in Australia and the audience in Europe?

MJ: I can't really say. To my recollection, I do remember that there was discontent at just about every concert, but not so much at the Albert Hall as people say.

We stayed at the Mayfair Hotel in London, and it wasn't the Albert Hall period, so we must have had some spare time in between... I was goin' out to get a cab one day and as I was goin' to get in, out steps Johnny Cash. I knew Johnny Cash from recording in Nashville... He said, *"What are you doin' here?"* I said, *"Well, I'm with Bob Dylan and we're like on tour."* I said, *"We're having a get together tonight you should come along,"* So I had him come along.

IW: This is in London, you say?

MJ: London, yeah the Mayfair, that whole deal from *Eat The Document*...

IW: Right, because somebody put in a lot of effort and time into trying to track Johnny Cash's meet with Dylan down.

MJ: Yeah, there's no question, no question about that. But he eats pills like popcorn. He was wasted.

IW: I think as time is ticking on we should move to Paris.

MJ: Paris. L'Olympia Theatre, it's a great place if you didn't have to put up with the people. French people do not like Americans, I don't know why that is. We saved their country. (laughs) Sort of. Anyway, we got to the L'Olympia Theatre and I'm convinced that it was Bob Dylan's idea to put up this flag. Because I didn't know it was there. I don't remember it being there at the sound check. I just don't remember the flag until we walked out to do the show. Was it there in the first half, do you know?

IW: Yes, as far as I understand.

MJ: Must have bin. But I don't remember it at the sound check. Anyway, there was this giant flag, it was huge. We stirred them up with that.

The Albert Hall was very special, just when you walked on that stage and you see this incredible structure it took your breath away. I don't remember the booing being all that severe at the Albert Hall.

The rest of the guys flew home and Garth and I took a ship. I was getting ready to come back to New York from LA to rehearse for Shea Stadium; we were going to do Shea Stadium, with Peter, Paul and Mary doin' the first act and Bob Dylan electric doin' the second act. Bob was not goin' to play acoustic on that show at all. And then we were goin' to Moscow to do a concert and I was all excited about that. Then about two days before I was due to get on a plane to go to New York to rehearse I got a call from Bob Dylan: he was in the hospital and basically he said: *"I'm in traction. I crashed my motorcycle. I broke my neck. We're not doin' Shea Stadium. We're cancelling everything until you hear from me."* Basically he paid me the rest of my salary for over a year. So I have nothin' but admiration and respect for Bob Dylan, because he's a man of his word. He is a man of integrity.

Tell you one more thing about Bob Dylan that you'll find interesting. My son-in-law is a professional fighter. He is the heavy weight champion of the world in full contact professional kickboxing. I was at one of his fights and as I turned to leave I here a voice, *"Mickey,"* and I turned around and it's Bob Dylan. I said, *"What are you doin' hear?"* And he had the definitive Bob Dylan answer. He said, *"I don't know. They bring me and I come!"* (laughs)

Published in issue #79. July 1998.

NOBODY
SINGS
DYLAN
LIKE DYLAN

AUSTRALIAN RECORD COMPANY LIMITED

Revolutions Per Minute
by Peter Cox & Patricia Jungwirth

A previously unknown live recording from Bob Dylan's 1966 Australian tour has emerged. Our correspondents in Australia have heard it. Here they review this remarkable audio document and explore the background to Dylan's first Australian concert.

The Sydney recording

On Wednesday April 13, 1966, 11,000 people packed into the Sydney Stadium to see Bob Dylan's first Australian concert. Today each eyewitness remembers it differently. Some speak of the crowd being hostile and Dylan being upset. Others recall a comical Dylan, bemused by the revolving stage in the middle of this huge boxing arena. Now a remarkable tape has come along to shed a little light on these conflicting reports. Recently discovered in an archive collection in Australia, the recording's original source is unclear. It is on two 10" reels of tape and according to the label on the box, it was recorded on April 13, 1966. It contains the complete concert, except for most of the first verse of the first song *'She Belongs To Me.'*

The Sydney tape, the existence of which until now was only rumoured adds significantly to our understanding of how the 1966 world tour developed. The only previously known recording from the Australian leg is an incomplete Melbourne Festival Hall show of April 19 or 20, which surfaced in the seventies and has since been widely circulated amongst collectors.

We can only guess why a recording was made of the Sydney show. Perhaps Dylan had it taped to hear how the band was shaping up. Drummer Mickey Jones remembers that most of the shows were recorded on audio but the same tape would be used to re-record the next concert – ISIS #79. Terry Darmody, who sat at ringside for both of the Sydney concerts, remembers: *"At least one guy running around on stage with a camera."* With a gap at the start of *'She Belongs To Me,'* one wonders if the same sound engineer was responsible for this mishap on both the Melbourne and Sydney recordings.

The vocal – and, consequently, the harmonica – is way up front in the mix, while the audience sounds far away. Perhaps everything was recorded through Dylan's microphone. There are frequent audible pops and hisses, especially on the 'p' and 's' vocal sounds. These are accentuated by Dylan's confident, committed delivery. This is consistent with Craig McGregor's recollection of complaining to Albert Grossman in Dylan's dressing room during this show's interval *"there's a popping, hissing sound in the mike when Bob's up close."* One is reminded of Jules Siegel's story of Grossman running on stage at North American venues to tell Dylan to stop eating the microphone, which was adding to the sound problems.

Despite this problem, it is a fine vocal performance. Overall, the sound is very good for the first half and reasonably good for the electric half. It goes without saying that the performances are incandescent and riveting. While the overall quality of the recording is nowhere near as good as the stunning, officially released *"Live 1966,"* it does provide the only other example we have – so far! – of a complete line recording of a 1966 show and as such represents something of a Holy Grail for Dylan fans. As Paul Williams writes in his *Performing Artist, Vol 1*: *"The time machine has not yet made its last trip."* The discovery of this gem makes one wonder what other delights might be sitting on dusty shelves around the world, waiting to be unearthed.

The audience

In Melbourne, Dylan taunted the folk purists in the audience by explaining that the reason his borrowed acoustic guitar kept going out of tune was that it was a *"folk music guitar."* When he took the stage with the band for the second half of his concert, some of the folkies booed and walked out, deliberately exiting towards the front and past the stage in a blatant show of disgust. The Melbourne recording reveals some of the same theatre of confrontation apparent in the UK shows.

Eyewitnesses remember people booing and walking out in Sydney too. David Pepperell, who saw Dylan perform in Sydney and in Melbourne, recalls that – *"In the second half they went mad in Sydney, booing, catcalling and screaming. But it was the best concert I had ever seen. I don't think anything was ever that good again."* Another concert-goer, Sjann Morrow remembers that the show did not meet her expectations – *"The music he played at the concert bore little resemblance to the songs I knew. I guess I was there to hear faithful renditions of 'Blowin' In The Wind' and 'Like a Rolling Stone'."*

One reviewer noted that 1000 or so people in the audience shifted restlessly and a few walked out. But one of the surprises of the Sydney recording is that it displays much less of the antagonism and confrontation that can be heard in the Manchester *"Judas"* concert. It is hard to hear what is going on in the crowd, but the repeated shouts of *'Hard Rain,'* and Dylan's muttered responses seem to suggest a kind of comic tension rather than outright hostility.

Lex Marinos, who saw the concert, remembered that Dylan was, *"comically disoriented by the revolving stage... He would lurch to the side as the stage revolved and then wait for it to stop before resuming his position in front of the next section of the audience."* Between songs the stage was rotated manually a quarter of a revolution and there are slight delays as Dylan waits for the stage to finish moving. The tape also reveals a bemused Dylan cracking jokes about the moving stage. After singing *'Fourth Time Around'* he replies to a comment from the audience with – *"Tell me when I get there."* After another 45-degree turn he greets the *"brand new people"* in front of him.

The performance

The acoustic set is very well received and the first lines of *'Mr Tambourine Man'* and *'...Baby Blue'* are greeted with warm applause. The perfect beauty and almost crushing, naked vulnerability Dylan achieved with his solo performances in 1966 remain astonishing at each hearing. Dylan has no problems keeping his guitar in tune and there is little evidence of the cough that plagued the Melbourne concert six days later. Performing solo sounds much less of an effort than it became at Melbourne and in the UK. He seems to have a younger voice, less stoned, more *up*. *'Visions Of Johanna'* is still a few days from becoming *'Mother Revisited.'*

Listening to the *"harmonica which penetrated the vastness of that old barn"* – as another witness, Lex Marinos, has attested – reveals that Craig McGregor was right – Dylan did play the harp that night *"like a virtuoso."* But there is now solid reason to doubt McGregor's recollection, always problematic, of Dylan playing *'The Times They Are a-Changin''* at the first Sydney concert!

After the acoustic set Dylan says, *"See you in fifteen minutes"* and, remarkably, that fifteen-minute interval is on the tape! You can hear the murmur of the crowd and the cry of the Stadium's lolly boys – *"Ice cream, Drinks."*

Interestingly, the two minutes or so at the start of the electric portion of the tape, preceding the first song, allow us to hear the audience reaction to the appearance of these unknown musicians taking the stage with Dylan. They must have wondered who this guitarist was in the blue velvet suit, and why the piano player was wearing maroon. As the band members appear and begin to tune their instruments, the audience applauds. No evidence here of the hostile shouts which greeted their appearance on stage in later concerts, when the very sight of the electric guitars and amplifiers seemed to provoke the audience's discontent.

In the electric set Dylan screams and spits out his lyrics with passion. It was reported that the band was loud and that the volume of sound swamped the sense of the lyrics, but on this tape the vocals dominate. The singing is in the foreground and the words are clear. The upfront vocals are somewhat startling, particularly in the opening song of the electric set. *'Tell Me Momma'* is just as forthright in its punk attitude, but this performance has more of the quality of a cocky garage band, than the cacophonous majesty we are more familiar with from Melbourne and the UK. Its lyrics vary significantly from the UK version, with Dylan singing clearly of *"cemetery grips"* and *"your babydoll chest."* The clarity of the vocal on this tape emphasises the vaguely menacing lasciviousness of the lyrics. What a jolt this opening volley of the electric set was for the unsuspecting audience!

Given that the April 13 Sydney concert was Mickey Jones' second gig with Dylan – Honolulu being the first – the band is tight, but perhaps not yet at the peak it reached a few weeks later in the UK. Dylan sets the tempo for most songs with his rhythm guitar, which is slightly louder than on the *"Live 1966"* CD, or by stamping his feet. His familiar spoken introduction to *'I Don't Believe You'* – *"It used to go like that, now it goes like this"* – is heard once again at Sydney. In *'Baby Let Me Follow You Down'* we are treated to the *"Velvet shirt/gun that squirts"* rhyme we all know and love from the Melbourne tape. Garth Hudson's organ punctuates the lyrics with witty flourishes. *'Just Like Tom Thumb's Blues'* is preceded by a quite lengthy spoken introduction, a variation on the *"Mexican painter"* monologue also used at other shows, most notably Melbourne – *"This is called... this is, uh... this, uh, story takes place in, uh, outside of Mexico City. Well, it begins outside of Mexico City and it ends really in uh, Des Moines, Iowa* (laughs)...*"*

Throughout the Sydney electric set Richard Manuel's piano is audible, a welcome improvement on most other 1966 concert recordings. His blues licks and strong left hand gives *'Leopard Skin Pill-Box Hat'* a slightly different flavour; it becomes almost a New Orleans stroll. After a somewhat lengthy pause, with audible though indecipherable talking from both the band and the audience, *'One Too Many Mornings'* is another highlight. The strength and confidence of Dylan's vocal phrasing accords perfectly with the emphatic drumming of Mickey Jones – Paul Williams has said he believes that Jones' drumming may have made all the difference between the shows on the world tour and the ones that came earlier. He describes Dylan as *"facing the drums and singing to them"* – musically if not literally. and this song is a beautiful example of that centring of the performance on the voice and the beat.

The civilized savagery of *'Ballad Of a Thin Man'* is as thrilling here as on other documents we have of its 1966 performances. Garth Hudson's swirling organ envelops the sneering, aggressive vocal and Dylan's pounding piano chords underscore the verbal menace. The set list here is the same as Manchester except for the final number, which on this night is not *'Like a Rolling Stone.'*

Frequently in the electric set and again before the final song, somebody yells *'Hard Rain!'* The repeated calls for the song eliciting laughter from both audience and performer. Dylan responds, finally, by half mumbling, half singing the words – *"Hard rain, I wish I saw some hard rain last night. Hard rain, hard rain, feel no pain. I'll be coming back tomorrow again... Is that alright?"*

Then, amazingly, the merry circus-like organ swirls which begin the last song signal an unexpected and delightful finale to this show. *'Positively Fourth Street'* closes the electric set, disproving the notion that it was not played on this world tour after March 26 – another revelation. Dylan dramatically elongates the vowels and adds verbal flourishes to show us how much fun he's having. He sings it with venom, as if he means it. This vituperative song, performed with an ecstatic glee, is a fitting end to the concert.

What is perhaps just as surprising is the audience reaction – at least as much as we can hear on this tape – no jeers, no booing or catcalls, just enthusiastic applause and calls for *"More! More!"* Dylan responds with a somewhat more sincere than usual *"Thank you very much. You're very kind. Thank you. Thank you very much."* The applause dies down then is rekindled a few moments later. Perhaps after walking the aisle to make his exit from the boxing arena the champ turned to salute his supporters in the audience once more.

But here lies the mystery. Eyewitness testimony seems to contradict the audio evidence. From the back of the bleachers, David Pepperell saw it this way – *"When Dylan came off the stage he had to walk back through the crowd. Somebody tried to shake his hand and he pushed it away. He was absolutely furious."* A backstage eye-witness to Dylan's state as he came offstage at the Manchester concert might give us a clue. He described Dylan as looking *"traumatized – like someone who'd just been in a car accident."* Was he simply drained, physically, by the ferocious creativity of these extraordinary performances? Perhaps the truth lies in the middle. Many members of the audience loved and applauded the electric music Dylan was creating, while the less open-minded fans were left puzzled, disappointed or angry.

The Sydney recording reveals Dylan, at the height of his fame, forging a musical path into unchartered territory and taking most of his audience along with him. It is a fascinating document, which sheds light on the creative path that led to Melbourne, Manchester, the July motorcycle accident and Dylan's subsequent prolonged abandonment of concert tours.

Dylan in Australia, first time around

These words which Bob Dylan bellowed from the stage each night on his first world tour in 1966 could just as easily have been describing the folklore of half-truths and exaggerations which surround these concerts. The tour was to be recognized as a watershed in the development of rock music, the interface where folk met rock 'n' roll met r 'n' b met surrealistic poetry, where a pop concert became a piece of performance art and the audience unwittingly helped perpetrate acts of dada absurdity. Inevitably, with a hungry, uncomprehending media in attendance and an audience unprepared for the alchemy being practised onstage, controversy, confrontation and misinformation ruled. In the 33 years since that tour, the legend has grown rather than faded.

As we all know, in 1998 *Sony* released *"Live 1966,"* a 2-CD recording from that 1966 tour. Known as the *Royal Albert Hall* concert – although actually recorded at Manchester Free Trade Hall on May 17 – it contains the famous confrontation with an angry fan whose cry of *"Judas"* articulated a sense of betrayal felt by fans that wanted Dylan to remain a folk protest singer. The official fanfare surrounding the release of *"Live 1966"* was perhaps only surpassed by the outpouring of praise and attention it received from critics and fans worldwide. Much bootlegged since the tape began to circulate in the late 1960s, the *Sony* release was welcomed not only for its sonic superiority, but also for the fact that at last the world would be able to hear what Dylan aficionados had known all along.

In a remarkable twist of fate, alerted by the publicity surrounding the official release of the Manchester recording, the man who cried *"Judas!"* all those years ago belatedly recognized his notorious role in the mythic events of that night and came forward to tell his story. Amid a plethora of commentary in magazines, radio, TV and on the Internet, the confrontational aspects of the tour were highlighted. This was not only the *"Greatest Rock Tour in History,"* but also an iconoclastic artist in conflict with an audience unprepared for the challenge of change in his art. Comparisons were made with the debut performance of Stravinsky's Rite of Spring in 1913, when an audience of outraged Parisians was alleged to have rioted.

The beginnings of the 1966 tour were less dramatic, and certainly less fabled. What do we hear of the twenty-plus concerts in February and March in the US, beginning in Louisville, Kentucky, criss-crossing the country, with excursions to Canada. In comparison to the later European dates, very damn little, as Kinky Friedman might say. Only that *"the sound is horrendous"* in Vancouver, or that Dylan was *"apparently well received"* in Lincoln, Nebraska. A show in Vancouver on March 26 was the last of the North American dates. Dylan and the band flew to Hawaii, where a concert in Honolulu marked the beginning of Dylan's first world tour. But Hawaii was still in the USA. Embarking on April 10 from Honolulu, after crossing the International Date Line, Dylan and his entourage landed in Sydney, Australia, on 12 April. They definitely weren't in Kansas anymore.

Dylan and the Australian media

From that first day, at a press conference at Sydney's airport, the Australian media were to reveal in their dealings with Bob Dylan, with few exceptions, a staggering degree of incomprehension, stupidity and downright viciousness. In a climate of national anxiety over the *"generation gap"* and the rising tide of protest at Australia's rapidly escalating involvement in the Vietnam War and a general mood of anti-authoritarianism among *"the young people,"* Dylan was perhaps a target tailor-made for the representatives of a parochial, conservative press. For reasons unknown, he chose to make himself available to the media and conducted numerous press conferences. Reporters arrived with a set agenda that ran like this. Dylan was a protest singer, he made a lot of money, and therefore he must be a phoney. In addition, he was American and he was *"funny-*

looking." This seemed to be the sum total of knowledge about Dylan that most journalists brought to their meetings with him. Some of the questions at Sydney that day:

> *"How does it feel to be a popular hero?"*
> *"Are you a professional beatnik?"*
> *"Why do you wear those outlandish clothes?"*
> *"Does it take a lot of trouble to get your hair like that?"*
> *"Why have you gone commercial?"*

Of course, pop stars were supposed to react with a sort of bright, boyish naivety to the probes of the *sophisticated* journalists. The Beatles had made themselves very popular in Australia in 1964 with their boyish charm and scouse wit. Their press conferences were a happy conjunction of a curious but supportive media and a band of cheerful, cheeky, if somewhat sardonic, Englishmen. They weren't *Royals* but they were from the *old country* and they were nice lads, weren't they, in their suits and ties?

Dylan's relationship with the press was vastly different. He was just one man, with the attentions of an openly hostile media focussed on him alone. The atmosphere was aptly described in an article in the Adelaide University magazine *On Dit* titled *"Dylan And The Press Gang"*:

> *"My impressions of Dylan were formed in the space of half an hour, from his handling of the Press, his tone of voice, general attitude and appearance, and can perhaps best be conveyed through quoting a series of comments he made to different members of radio and television staff:"*

> PRESS: *"What made you decide on this sort of music for your career?"*
> DYLAN: *"It's all I can do. I can't do anything else."*
> PRESS: *"We've heard a lot about you protesting about this, that and the other. Naturally you're entitled to say you're not protesting, but your lyrics suggest that there's an air of protest..."*
> DYLAN: *"Well, if they do... they do. If you wanna think they are, I'm not gonna argue."*
> PRESS: *"Deep down, you must have convictions about..."*
> DYLAN: *"Nah! Deep down, there's nothin' but guts, intestines."*

The reporter had approached Dylan with an air of superiority and proceeded to attempt to rubbish the man by pretending that Dylan could not understand his questions. However, on this occasion, as on all others, Dylan was in a position of power and knew it. He was the master in charge. Thus, faced with the opportunity to play with the Press and their inane little questions, he did just that...

He searched for ambiguity in the questions asked him and deliberately misinterpreted them. He feigned ignorance, necessitating the repetition and rephrasing of many questions. He picked up sentences and threw them back at his interviewers, often achieving satisfying results.

On some occasions, when someone stumbled across something that interested him, he would perhaps take the matter seriously, as when he was asked as to how, precisely, did he write his poetry? Dylan said, *"I write the same way I drink a glass of water. You know, if you're thirsty, you drink a glass of water. If you're hungry, you eat. That's how I write."*

Across the nation, newspapers peddled the line that Dylan was an insincere protest singer. He was continually being asked to justify the sort of *"finger pointing"* songs he had stopped writing in late 1963. The press failed to grasp that he had moved on. Had they not heard his last three albums?

A few days later in Stockholm when Dylan was asked by Klas Burling about protest songs, specifically *'The Times They Are a-Changin','* he seemed to bristle: *"Let's not sit here and talk about myself as a protest singer or anything like that... I'm not trying to be a bad fellow or anything but I'd just be a liar or a fool to go along with all this business. I mean, I just can't help it if you're a year behind."*

The Australian magazine *The Bulletin* was more like two years and a thousand miles behind. On April 16 *The Bulletin* ran a 1964 photo of Dylan on its cover with a story headed – *"Folk: The Times, Are They A-Changin'?"* The article, a nasty piece by Charles Higham, questioned Dylan's sincerity. Obsessed with how much money he made, Higham argued that folk music was now in the deadly grip of PR, with songs that stem *"from the feverish brains of the agent-manager-recording company complex."* Higham detested Dylan – *"The voice is a monotonous drone, like the sounds a man makes after sea-sickness. The songs go on and on, as inexorably and tunelessly as water dribbling down a drain."* The Bulletin may have been aiming for a sophisticated, irreverent tone, but what comes across today is a shallow cynicism born of ignorance.

On the day of Dylan's arrival in Sydney, the afternoon tabloid *The Daily Mirror* cranked up the contempt, describing, *"America's singing poet au-go-go"* as sulky and truculent.

DYLAN: *"Don't talk to me about a message, man. I don't have any message...*Time Magazine, Newsweek, Look, Life *and the* Ladies Home Journal *call me a protest singer. But I'm no protest singer."*
REPORTER: *"How do you describe yourself?"*
DYLAN: *"I don't . How do you describe yourself?"*
REPORTER: *"I have no idea but I don't have to sell your talent."*
DYLAN : *"Neither do I."*

Questioned about the civil rights movement, he replied, *"I'm not pro-Negro, I'm not anti-Negro. I have no feelings I'd care to discuss with you."* Dylan later told *The Sun-Herald* – *"It's very fashionable to participate in the civil rights movement... I don't want to hear no more about Negroes."*

Bewildered, the man from *The Daily Mirror* asked if there was a general theme behind his songs. *"Yes, they're all about the Second Coming."* When did he expect the Second Coming? *"When people don't wear clothes any more."*

The following day *The Daily Mirror's* Ron Saw published a Dylan interview in his *Sydney* column, sarcastically labelling Dylan a *"genius."* Ron Saw had read somewhere that Dylan was a man of many moods – anger, loneliness, despair, consolation and fury. Dylan replied – *"I don't have any of those moods. Terror is my constant emotion."* Terror of what? *"Well, that's like asking a happy man what he's happy about. I just deal in terror. I buy it, sell it and make a profit."*

RON SAW: *"Would you describe yourself as a folksinger?"*
DYLAN: *"I wish that I could come under some classification. But I don't have to, so I don't. I try to fall in line. I try not to be noticed. But somehow it doesn't work. Who wants to be an oddball? I am a singer whose songs are about joyful subjects. Joyful prehistoric subjects... I don't sing songs with a message. A message is an insulting way of trying to put your paranoia across. Everybody asks me about messages. In England they asked me about messages. I'm here in Australia to sing songs and they ask me about messages. I don't think they know too well what I do... I don't think they know too much at all about me in this country."*

In *The Sun*, another Sydney afternoon tabloid, Uli Schmetzer could make no sense of Dylan's behaviour, appearance or songs –

"Pygmy-sized, pallid-faced, with long fluffy hair, Bob Dylan is the latest and strangest of the new breed of mop-haired, anti-socialite, non-conformist, pseudo-beatnik comedians to invade Sydney. Asked what he did before he scribbled songs and sung them, he said 'I was a thief – cars, antennas, radios, you know'. Ever caught? 'Yes, once by a priest – he converted me and I became a folksinger'."

Dylan was ridiculed on TV as well as in the press. He agreed to appear in an interview on *Channel 9's Tonight Show* with Don Lane, which one viewer has described as an *"embarrassment."* *"Dylan was pretty contemptuous of the whole thing,"* recalls another viewer. What followed on the same show two nights later was a disgrace – Brian Henderson, the terminally square TV host of Australia's *Bandstand*, and Don Lane, the lanky American compere of the show wearing a curly wig – engaging in a monosyllabic send-up of Bob Dylan which, according to an angry letter to *The Sun*, *"was just a disgusting display of bad manners"* and a *"cruel treatment of other people's feelings."*

Asked about the pacifist flavour of his songs, Dylan insisted he was neither anti-war nor a supporter of anti-war movements. The Melbourne press also tried to get Dylan to comment on the Vietnam War. When he refused, they attacked him for his apparent indifference to social/political issues. Dylan said to Alan Trengove, who asked, *"Don't you really care?"* –

"I can't really tell you how I care. I just can't. They never ask me these questions in America. They tried to make a clown of me for three years and now I won't give interviews. I have been writing for fifteen years myself. I know reporters have to eat, but I won't let them use me... Sure I have a feeling about war, about Vietnam. My thoughts lie in the futility of war, not the morality of it."

To the Brisbane media, Dylan gave in and conceded that his songs had a message, but he couldn't say what it is for fear of offending people!

The Adelaide press labelled Dylan a *"folksy millionaire."* The insults culminated in this remarkable exchange at an Adelaide press conference:

REPORTER: *"Do you make money a yardstick? Or doesn't it matter to you at all, money?"*
DYLAN: *"Make money a yardstick?"*
REPORTER: *"In life. Do you think having a lot of money is a good thing, or doesn't it worry you at all... I mean you must have a lot of money by singing the songs you do. Do you sing songs because you can make some money out of this, or do you sing just because you like to sing the songs and money doesn't mean anything at all?"*
DYLAN: *"I consider that an insult, sir."*

By the time he got to Perth for his final Australian concert, no wonder Dylan was getting tetchy. After the concert, Dylan and his entourage – *"They're all friends of my grandmother"* – were stranded in Perth for a couple of days, apparently because the Australian government had commandeered commercial aircraft to fly its troops to Vietnam. At a Perth press conference he was again asked, *"What do you think of the Vietnam War?"* *"Nothing,"* he replied. *"It's Australia's war."* *'But Americans are there.'* *"They're just helping the Australians."*

After escaping Perth, the tour which Dylan later described to Mary Travers as *"ferocious"* rolled on to Sweden, Denmark, Ireland, England, Wales, Scotland, France and on to the Royal Albert Hall.

The Sydney Stadium

In his 1998 book *Like the Night: Bob Dylan and the Road to the Manchester Free Trade Hall,* C.P Lee reveals that during the American leg of the 1966 tour, Dylan debated with his manager Albert Grossman whether he should play in theatres or large arenas in Australia. Grossman persuaded him that Australia, being *"underdeveloped,"* did not have enough concert halls, so arenas it had to be. Although he had been warned about our primitive facilities, nothing could have prepared Dylan for Sydney's bizarre Stadium.

Officially a boxing arena, it looked more like a huge shed. Constructed in 1908 as a *"temporary"* structure for a world title fight, its design was basic.

The Stadium, which housed boxing matches for the next sixty years, had a roof added in 1911. When the flamboyant promoter Lee Gordon began touring American rock 'n' roll stars in the mid fifties, he turned the Stadium into Sydney's prime entertainment venue. The *old barn* had one only virtue – it could seat 11,000 people – some say 12,000. Whatever the exact capacity, it was more than any other venue in the city.

The interior was cavernous and stark. Bob Hope described it as *"Texas with a roof,"* a statement curiously echoed in Dylan's reply when Craig McGregor asked him how he found Sydney. Performing there *"makes me feel right at home, man. Just like Texas."* Performers had to walk or run down an aisle to reach the stage. The floor was concrete, the walls galvanised iron. The ambience was of gladiatorial combat and the dressing room stank of liniment from boxer rub-downs.

Seating was on ascending plank bleachers surrounding the boxing ring in the centre. Lee Gordon replaced the ring with a small revolving stage, thus giving everyone an equally poor view. Within the square stage was a disc that rotated. According to Johnny O'Keefe's guitarist Lou Casch, who performed there many times, an operator controlled the revolving stage manually. At the Dylan concerts the stage was turned 45 degrees between each song.

Performers were faced with a constantly changing audience, *"brand new people"* as Dylan quipped. In 1954 Johnnie Ray found it most disconcerting, since no one bothered to tell him he'd be working in the round. Some acts nearly fell over, as the motion was anything but smooth. On one occasion, Guy Mitchell was standing with his guitar when he placed one foot on the outer, non-revolving perimeter, causing him to do the splits involuntarily. The turning stage also caused Dusty Springfield to become caught up in her microphone cord. In 1973, the Stadium was demolished to make way for a new train line to Bondi.

The Sydney concert reviews

Given the hostility and misunderstanding of the press, reviews of Dylan's first Australian concert were predictably mixed. The next day *The Sun* published a cartoon depicting Dylan as a strange visitor from another planet. Beneath the cartoon appeared a review with the headlines *"Sydney's wackiest concert"* and *"Kook or genius?"* Opting for cheap shots, the reviewer made fun of the lyrics to *'Desolation Row'* and tried to make Dylan's audience appear as idiots by quoting a ringside fan: *"You don't have to know the precise meanings. Dylan makes a person think even if that person doesn't know what he is thinking about."*

Curiously, the same edition of the same paper carried a more favourable review by Joe Cizzio, who described the 13 April concert as *"a rare blend of integrity, artistry and intellectualism:"*

"Dressed like a Pickwick character in a suit of black and brown houndstooth pattern, he looked somewhat angelic with his long curly hair and pallid complexion, but there was an unmistakeable virility about him... On the first half of the program Dylan was withdrawn, unresponsive, even monotonous, and appeared to have a great weariness for one so young – yet there was a magic about him."

Cizzio reported that the second half was marred because *"the volume of sound swamped the sense of his lyrics."* Certainly, the volume came as a shock to many.

Edgar Waters in *The Australian* also disliked the volume and was less bewitched than bewildered: *"It was an ugly factory noise set to a factory rhythm, and Dylan's voice took on a new quality as though he were shouting – though I suppose he was not actually shouting – above this mechanical din... The total effect on me was rather like that of listening to an hysterical woman screaming at the top of her voice..."*

Craig McGregor's balancing review appeared in *The Sydney Morning Herald*:

"At Sydney Stadium last night Bob Dylan confirmed, as his records had already made clear, that so far he is the only singer who has been able to perform his songs and retain that abrasive, uncomfortable directness which disappears as soon as others – pace Peter, Paul and Mary – attempt them."

McGregor wrote of Dylan's *"life-enhancing"* quality, his *"virtuoso harmonica blowing"* and the *"joyousness"* of his performance with the band. The Sydney recording allows us to partake of this joy for ourselves.

Postscript

For years, there has been some confusion about how many shows Dylan played in Sydney. Most of the evidence indicates that he performed at the Sydney Stadium on Wednesday April 13 and Saturday April 16, with a Brisbane date – April 15 – in between. Craig McGregor's piece about the Sydney concerts, written in the early 1970s and published as an introduction to his groundbreaking anthology *Bob Dylan: A Retrospective*, mentions hearing Dylan in concert in Sydney on two successive nights. This has fuelled speculation of an additional show on April 14. Similarly, Mickey Jones is adamant that they played on consecutive nights, April 13 and 14. He remembers that: *"The first night was sold out and there was an overflow of people"* (ISIS #79). To add to the confusion, the Dylan expert Glen Dundas lists April 13 and 14, while Michael Krogsgaard lists April 13 and 16. Adverts for the concerts in the newspapers and the weight of anecdotal evidence suggest that Krogsgaard is correct.

Published in ISIS # 87, November 1999

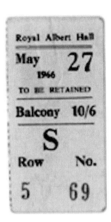

Some Great Live Performances – Royal Albert Hall
May, 27 1966
Three Eyewitness Accounts, Reconstructed

After many years of speculation and investigation we now know that the infamous *"Judas"* shout actually came from the concert at Manchester's Free Trade Hall on May 17, 1966, and that for the past thirty years the proliferation of bootleg recordings that have been circulated as *"The Royal Albert Hall"* were in fact the second half of the Manchester concert. Therefore, only the first acoustic section of the May 27, 1966 Royal Albert Hall concert circulates on tape, and then, amongst collectors only.

Below is a reconstruction of the night of May 27, 1966 complied from three eye-witness accounts and numerous contemporary reports. The body of this piece is from an article published in ISIS #66 written by C.D Smith. Additional material is from an article published in ISIS #20 by Derek Davies, and from a previously unpublished piece by Peter Smith. Together these three accounts help to recreate one of the great confrontational performances of the twentieth century.

It must have been a Thursday and I was either not working or had taken a day off! It must have been a Thursday because back then that's when the *Melody Maker* came out – unless you were in central London where you could pick it up on a Wednesday afternoon. So, I had called in at the newsagent's and picked up a copy, then made my way to the Kwela Coffee Bar – all split cane, African masks and Demerara sugar in wooden bowls – and sat down with a frothy coffee. I was just about to close the *MM* when an ad for Dylan's tour caught my eye. The Albert Hall concert had sold out even before the tour had been announced in the press! However, underneath this *"SOLD OUT"* ad was a new block of type: *"EXTRA PERFORMANCE Fri. May 27-7.30 PM."* I had been thinking about hitching up to Birmingham to try and see Dylan there; and that was a much longer journey than it is now! Maybe now I could get tickets for this extra show. I just had to. This was IT!

Should I telephone first to see if they still have tickets? Would they reserve them for me if I explained I was just about to catch the train up there? Do I have enough money for the train fare and the tickets? Then someone said – *"Why don't you go to the travel agency? They probably do theatre bookings for a small commission.*" This was a whole new concept to me; after all a travel agency was still a bit of a novelty in the town at that time. No harm in trying though. At the travel agency the man calls me Sir, and how may he help. I explain what I'm there for – *"Not the usual sort of concert that we get requests for at the Albert Hall, but I'm sure there will be no problems, Sir."* He 'phones the Albert Hall, gives the agency number and YES! *"They have tickets left at 10/6d, 7/6d and 3/6d."* "*Er, um, I've got just over £3. How many at 10/6d can I get?*"

"*The Booking fee is 1/6d per ticket Sir, so five is exactly £3.*" Meanwhile he is showing me a plan of the Albert Hall calling me *"Sir"* again and pointing out the 10/6d seats, on the first tier to the right of the stage and *"quite near the front."*

"*Yes I'll take five, thank you. Oh, you write out the tickets here, I don't have to wait for them through the post, Great!*"

The day finally arrived, but the car is not running properly and it won't get us to London. We set off for John's house. It now looks like a race against time but luckily John knows someone who could lend us a car, but he has no insurance and the last train guaranteed to get us there on time leaves in three minutes! It's seems Chris can drive it on his insurance so we pile into this big old Vauxhall and we are off. The A40 into London at this time of night is fairly quiet. Chris puts his foot down, we pick up speed and there's a clanging and banging from beneath the vehicle. *"What's that?"* he shouts, as the noise moves to the rear of the car and then dies away. Reg glances out of the back window and says, laconically, *"Well, it's not very big, so it can't be important. Keep driving."* We do, and soon we are outside the Albert Hall screeching for a parking space. Only a couple of minutes to show-time; there don't seem to be many people about. Oh God, they must all he inside. We race into the hall, show the tickets. It is now just after half seven and we hear a burst of applause from inside the hall and I hear the usher say – *"He'll still be just tuning up. If you're quick you can go in now."* We slip into our seats and are settled just as Dylan finishes tuning up. Phew! Made it. Now, YES! THIS IS IT![1]

The house lights went down; the audience went perfectly quiet, a single spot light was focused centre stage and without any introduction Dylan came out with his guitar strapped around him and his harmonica already in its harness.[2]

The first thing that strikes me is that Dylan is much smaller and more frail looking than I had imagined. He is wearing a brown and black tweedy hounds-tooth suit, Cuban heeled boots and a dark shirt. I just have time to note the two stools to the left of the stage, i.e. on Dylan's right; one with a glass and jug of water, the other with a selection of harmonicas and presumably a song list. Then he steps up to the microphones and the spotlight picks out a mass of tousled locks that appear almost red under the single stage light. The audience bursts into another round of applause and with his knees slightly bent Dylan begins a long guitar introduction to the first song. Putting a name to the tune is hovering at the edge of my mind, but then he seems to be playing something different, and then returns to the original melody. What is it? He starts singing and instantly I recognise it as '*She Belongs To Me.*' At just over a year old, this is still quite a *new* song and one of my favourites from his first *Electric* album. I am completely stunned by his rendition of the song live! I realised I had never really understood what was meant by *charisma* until I saw Dylan live; I couldn't take my eyes off him, and I had to keep reminding myself to breathe! As he leans in and out of the mike the song seems to take on whole new perspectives of form and content. Dylan's voice is also so much richer than that of his records. It seems paradoxically, contradictorily and somehow appropriately to be richer and warmer, yet more full of longing and unstated sorrow. The washy echo of the Albert Hall acoustics aids this effect. Sometimes, during the harp solos especially, you can notice the echoes bouncing back.

In his book *Like the Night*, CP Lee says: *"'She Belongs To Me' is magical and mystical. Paul Williams has described it as an 'invocation' and he is correct...This, then, is no ordinary love song...What we get is a version of a man under the spell of an enchantress – Sara? Its lyrical sophistication is light years ahead of any of the contemporary tunes that smeared their way round the pop charts at the time, or for a long time afterwards."*[3]

He finishes to thunderous applause but retreats to his stools to begin retuning without so much as a thank you. There was in fact an awful lot of returning between numbers throughout both halves of the concert. So except where relevant I'll not say much about it again, though I would like to note that during the acoustic half the audience was mostly silent while this went on, while during the electric half it provided an opportunity for the anti-brigade to vent their anger and so fuel the confrontation.

Dylan steps back up to the mike. WHAT! This is a new song! Though later we would know it as *'Fourth Time Around.'* At that time, not only had we never heard it before, we had no idea if we would ever hear it again. Proverbial pin drop time, with me on the edge of my seat. I was struck not only by the lyrics themselves, but by the very emphatic rhymes, with Dylan leaning in even closer to the mike at the end of each line, making them not just verbally emphatic but aurally as well. When he reached the line *"You better spit out your gum"* there was a suppressed but discernible ripple of laughter through the auditorium. A few people started to applaud until Dylan looked up from the mike and flashed a scowl out into the hall. Audio evidence now disproves my impression that Dylan finished the song abruptly just after that line and the look. There was however, a momentary change of atmosphere in the hall. Despite its rhymes and situations, this was obviously not one of Bob's humorous songs!

At the end of this song Bob spends even longer communing with his glass of water and his collection of harmonicas. He then moves to the mike and starts playing another intro; stops retunes some more, and then starts on the same intro again. Once more he pauses and then leans into the mike again. *"Ah, I'm not going to be playing any more concerts here, in England, and I just wanted to say that...er...that er...it's...er, it's all wrong...to er, to er...This is a typical example of probably one song that your English music newspapers here would call a drug song. Well, I don't write drug songs, you know I never have, I wouldn't know how to go about it, but you know this is NOT a drug song."* As he was saying this he was weaving and bobbing about at the microphone like a drunken sailor in a storm. There was some laughter and applause. He continued: *"I'm not saying this for any kind of DEFENSIVE reason or anything like THAT; it's just NOT a drug song. I don't, ya know...it's just vulgar to think so!"*[4]

More laughter and applause; then someone shouted something, possibly *'Mr Tambourine Man,'* to which, Dylan replied *"Yes, All right."* and then struck up the song again. Yet another new song, *'Visions Of Johanna.'* This concert was turning out to be even more spectacular and magical than I could have ever wished for. As the song progressed it was quite obvious that this was a great piece; up with *'Mr Tambourine Man'* and *'Desolation Row.'* On the subject of drugs, I was with Bob on that one. Oh sure, I'd read Kerouac and the Beat Poets so I was *hip* to the marijuana thing, but it seemed so obvious that Dylan's songs were so much deeper than that.

After such a fantastic opening salvo, the return to more familiar fare with *'It's All Over Now Baby Blue'* could have been a bit of a disappointment, but Dylan was on such splendid form that this became another sublime rendering. Another break for a retune, and Dylan approaches the mike strumming something familiar. As he nears the mike he seems to start singing, then pauses, all the while playing the intro. Then he's off and running, *"They're selling postcards of the hangin'."*...yes, it's my favourite song from his last album, the unbelievably wonderful *'Desolation Row.'* No one has been nearer to heaven without being pronounced clinically dead. Chris could go on all he wanted about how it related to Eliot's *The Wasteland* and Ezra Pound's *Cantos* – oh, and sure I'd dipped into them too, just to see what the fuss was about – and how it was all about the American *oligarchy* – whatever that meant – but I was just in love with this crazy cast of characters and the sound of the words and the way they were strung together. All of these songs had received thunderous applause as they finished, but this one damn near got a standing ovation.

In his book *Performing Artist,* Paul Williams says of the last three songs from the May 27 1966 acoustic set. – These songs – *"are good enough to stand next to the best work of any twentieth century artist – performer, painter, poet, mathematician... I find it difficult to imagine anyone listening to Dylan's May 27 performances of 'Desolation Row,' 'Just Like a Woman,' and 'Mr Tambourine Man' without immediately surrendering all preconceptions and acknowledging that this is remarkable art, an exaltation of the human spirit."*[3]

Once more Dylan retreats to his stools; he selects a harp and gives an experimental blow. He then moves over to the other stool and proceeds to swirl the harmonica around in the jug of water. This is an old trick still mentioned in some harmonica instruction manuals, to take some of the *bright, reedy* edge off the sound of a new harp and make it *mellower.* This caused some amusement amongst the crowd, which in turn made Dylan grin as he stood there shaking the water out and testing it again. Then some idiot sycophants decided this was worthy of applause until Dylan cut them down with a withering look. *"Oh, don't do that,"* slowly shaking his head, *"That's terrible, terrible."* He puts the harp in its harness and gives it a blow. It's upside down – i.e. with the scale running right to left – so he takes it out and turns it round, almost having it slip out of his hands, causing more laughter. The next song is yet another new number that we will later know as *'Just Like a Woman.'* Again all I can do is sit there with bated breath, strain to catch every nuance of the lyrics and hope against hope that all of these songs will one day be available on record. Next is the stunningly superb *'Mr Tambourine Man,'* my all-time favourite song – still is – and what a superb rendition this is. Dylan seems completely absorbed in the song, the sounds and the feelings evoked. Nothing can match the absolute purity of the harp solos that really do take you disappearing through the smoke rings of your mind. I was wrong. You can get nearer to heaven, and the transport is in those *"skipping reels of rhyme."* Dylan said *"Thank you,"* took a step back, a brief bow, a wave and he was gone. Everyone in the hall was on their feet, clapping, whistling, cheering and shouting for more, more, more.

INTERMISSION

The second half was about to begin and right from the start we knew what to expect. As was the case many years later with the 1981 UK tour with its Christian overtones, we had been made aware of exactly where Dylan was at by his records and by the media. After all *"Bringing It All Back Home"* and *"Highway 61 Revisited"* had been on sale for twelve and seven months respectively, and the media had given coverage that Dylan would bring a band.[2]

True, there was speculation as to who the group would be. On their arrival in England *Melody Maker* stated a group called *"the Group"* would back Bob Dylan. In truth,

Dylan's backing band didn't have a name. After their departure from Canadian rockabilly artist Ronnie Hawkins, *"the group"* were tentatively known as *Levon and the Hawks,* but Levon Helm had left and had been replaced by Sandy Konikoff who in turn had been replaced by Mickey Jones. Therefore, *Levon and the Hawks* was hardly appropriate! The outfit with no name would not officially become known as The Band for another two years, and then, according to Helm, only to enable record stores to file their first album.[3]

The applause starts as soon as Dylan strides onto the stage. The band is right behind him and this elicits a smattering of jeers and boos. The band were all dressed in velvet suits of varying colours, purple, maroon, green, blue and beige.[3]

Dylan had a black Stratocaster, the other guitarist – Robbie Robertson – a white Telecaster. They plugged in, briefly checked their tuning, then – Dylan stamps his foot – 1,2,3,4, BANG – turn to the mike and straight into, *'Tell Me Momma,'* only I didn't know that then. All I could hear was the loudest musical cacophony I had ever experienced. It pinned me to my seat! After a while I could make out a few of the words, but only on the refrain that seemed something like *"Only you know, that I know...you mangled up my MIND."* Obviously, another new song, so I tried even harder to listen, but it was a losing battle.

Was this a song about Dylan's new friends Edie Sedgwick and Andy Warhol? Whatever, the line *"You're just gonna make everybody jump and roar"* was appropriate for tonight's concert.[3]

After the opening number Dylan stepped back for a chat and retune with the band; we were all on our feet and cheering like mad. As the cheering died down there were shouts of *"Turn it down, you're too loud,"* which I had some sympathy with. It was too loud, and the acoustics weren't helping. It was however, still the most gloriously ragged, driving music that I'd ever heard – Still is! As Dylan returned to the mike the boos and cheers started up again and I noticed a number of people making very obvious exits, a few throwing insults towards the stage as they did so. However, I didn't notice that many people leaving, for Dylan's magnetic presence drew my eyes back to the stage. Afterwards I felt that press reports of *"hundreds"* or up to *"a quarter of the audience"* walking out were vastly exaggerated. Certainly, the place still seemed pretty crowded even at the end of the concert. Dylan stood at the mike and looked over the audience. Whereas before, when only he had been on stage he had been hunched and vulnerable, he now moved with a sinister grace, tense yet fluid and aware. As ready to caress as to rip to shreds, depending on the situation, playing with the lead of his guitar like a whip, leaning a little into the mike he said, *"I get accused of dismissing my old songs. Well, that's not true. I LOVE my old songs... I like all my old songs... I never said I didn't like my old songs. It's just that things change all the time, everybody knows that! I never said they were RUBBISH. That word is not in my vocabulary. I wouldn't use the word rubbish if it was laying in the street and I could pick it up. This music you are going to hear...if anyone has any suggestions on how it can be played better, or how the words can be improved..."* This delivered in much the same stoned slur as before, but with a sharper, more sneering edge to it.

Then it was, *'I Don't Believe You – She Acts Like We Never Have Met,'* though it took me a while to work that out. At the end of the song we were on our feet, stamping and cheering once again and so it seemed was the rest of the hall. As we sat down again during the inevitable tuning, the booing started up. The anti brigade then started into a slow hand clap, but by then Dylan and the band were ready to launch into *'Baby, Let Me Follow You Down.'* By now they had either improved the sound in the hall marginally, or my ears were becoming more attuned. It was still damn loud though.

The song ends and we go through the same routine; stand, clap and cheer, sit down and the fractious element starts again. This time the slow handclap starts sooner, and as Dylan and the band start to tune up, seemingly oblivious to it all, it starts to spread. The slow handclap is getting louder but Dylan and the band just carry on tuning. Is Dylan deliberately ignoring this – or is he manipulating it? Dylan turns to the mike; *"Shut up you idiots, I can't hear what he's saying."* The clapping dies down and Dylan's voice comes through *"... and you've given your money to them, and now they are going to give all that money to me anyway. So if you don't like it, why don't you just go home or read a book, or something."*[5]

Laughter, applause, and then the band strike up *'One Too Many Mornings.'*[6] They must have improved he sound; I'm with this one from the first line. It's still ragged and loose, but glorious and quite marvellous by my reckoning. The spell between songs is much the same as before, except this time someone on the other side of the hall shouts out, *"Woody Guthrie would turn in his grave."* My mate John is instantly on his feet bawling out *"He's not F*****G dead yet, you ignorant C**T!"* Dylan's reply is more succinct: *"Come up here and say that,"* he sneers.[7]

By now they have finished tuning up and Dylan is stepping up to the mike – *"This song is called 'I See You've Got You're Brand New Leopard-Skin Pill Box Hat',"* and they are away with a rollicking, rolling, Chicago type blues. Later I would like this song for its humorous lyrics as much as anything. Right then all I knew was it moved!

There is more cheering and jeering. The anti brigade is getting more vociferous. Also more of the pro-crowd are shouting back at the antis. This could get really confrontational. Then Bob is back at the mike:

"This music you are going to hear we've been playing this since we were ten years old. Folk music was just an interruption. If you don't like it that's fine. This is not English music you're listening to. You haven't really heard American music before. I want to say now that what you're hearing is just songs. You're not hearing anything else but words. You can take it or leave it. If there's something that you disagree with that's just great. I'm sick of people asking what does it all mean, it means nothing."

Then they were off into an ecstatic reading of *'Just Like Tom Thumb's Blues,'* all crashing cymbals and wailing harmonica, with Bob dancing around half the time, not playing his harp anywhere near the mike. The song stumbled to a close and the whole audience leapt to their feet shouting out either their approval or approbation. What a row we were now making, disorganised and confused. Someone called out to Dylan to do some of his *protest songs. "Oh, come on, these are all protest songs,"* he said, un strapping his guitar. *"Aw, it's the same stuff as always – can't you HEAR?"*[8] Then he turned and walked away. What's this? Is he walking out? Has he had enough? Oh, thank God, he's sitting down at the piano. The opening chords are instantly recognisable as *'Ballad Of a Thin Man;'* a kind of communal electric shiver goes through the audience. This is back to proverbial pin drop time. One of the odd things about this concert, probably all of them, was that despite all the barracking and booing between numbers, there was none while they were actually playing. Part of the rules of the game, I suppose. After all, the press reports said that Dylan was booed after he played electric, not during! The silence that greeted this song was palpable and the performance was spine tingling. I was thinking – *"That's showing 'em, Bob. This will shut them up."* I was wrong of course. At the end of this number the house was in an uproar yet again. Now both factions seemed to be making as much noise as possible, though whether to get their point across, or to try and drown out the other side was hard to tell.

'Like a Rolling Stone' was the most exhilarating thing I'd ever heard, and the most vicious. Dylan's vocal soared and swooped between sadistic put-downs and the wail of a soul in torment, then it was over. Once again the whole audience was on its feet, but this time with only one voice and all of them shouting *"MORE, MORE, MORE."* It was not to be. Dylan had said his, *"Thank you"* and having taken a bow, he and the group were hurrying to make their exit stage right. A gaggle of girlies, some with the obligatory long straight blonde hair, were rushing to the front of the stage stretching out their arms and crying out for *"Bobby, Bobby;"* Dylan half turned and then waved to them. Then he paused, took his harmonica and holder from around his neck and dropped it into the middle of the melée, and then he was gone.

The turbulent, chaotic and punishing 1966 world tour was over. Bob Dylan has rocked and shocked us with some of the greatest performances that we had ever witnessed and are ever likely to witness. He redefined musical boundaries with performances that changed the face of rock 'n' roll music forever and not for the last time placed himself light years ahead of his audience.[3]

Postscript

Derek Davis tells ISIS about his afternoon – May 27 1966 – on Carnaby Street. The afternoon before the concert I had gone to Carnaby Street and, as I walked its length, a large black limousine, parked at the end, caught my eye. I reached the shop – *John Stephens* if my memory serves me right – and there inside stood Bob Dylan, trying on a dark blue, or black shirt with white spots. I was too nervous, young and naïve to go in, so I stood for ten minutes or so, watching as Dylan wandered around the shop looking at clothes until he suddenly left the shop with two men either side him. He walked past me, got into the limo and was gone, but the memory of hair, white face and sunglasses remained with me.[2]

Sources

1 Another source states that Dylan started the concert about twenty minutes late. As is still the case today Dylan often started his concerts late. Owing to technical problems the Birmingham Town Hall concert was delayed by 45 minutes and the concert, at the Gaumont in Sheffield suffered a similar delay due to a bomb scare. At the other 1966 UK concerts Dylan had been between five and twenty minutes late.

2 Derek Davies

3 Peter Smith

4 The impression I, and many others got was that Dylan was referring to May 27 as being the last concert he was playing on this tour and not that he would not be retuning to play any more concerts in England. It was only the press that took his comment that way, but why let context get in the way of a good story!

5 I couldn't find any references to this speech except for a very brief paraphrase of part of it a *Melody Maker* review June 4 1966, but I remember it quite clearly, partly because Gerry – of Gerry and the Pacemakers – used it almost verbatim to put down hecklers at a concert at the Saville Theatre about a year later and I wondered then if he had been at the same Dylan concert.

6 This song is usually placed as the sixth song in the set between *'Tom Thumb's Blues'* and *'Leopard-Skin Pill-Box Hat.'* However, I remember it as coming before the new material. Also, in *Rain Unravelled Tales*, Heylin prints a programme page on which the

owner had written down the songs as performed. The programme is said to come from May 26 and shows *'One Too Many Mornings'* as the fourth song. Therefore, if it was changed for one night, why not the next, and if one change why not two?

7 Heylin attributes this cat-call to Liverpool, and Dylan's response to the May 27 later revised to May 26, though he does not say what Dylan is responding to. I know I heard it at the Royal Albert Hall on the 27th because of John's response. This raises a couple of points. The inherent problems of trying to identify concerts by matching what was heard with what has been reported elsewhere is compounded by sloppy journalism and the copycat factor. I have come across three reports from different concerts of someone shouting *"Traitor,"* and who is to say that Dylan can't repeat a good line if he wants to?

8 Compiled from a number of sources.

Texts consulted in preparing this piece:

The 1966 Acetates. Bob Dylan, Columbia Reference Recording.
Paul Cable, *Bob Dylan: His Unreleased Recordings*, Darkstar
Robert Shelton, *No Direction Home*, Beech Tree Books
Clinton Heylin, *Rain Unravelled Tales*, Ashes and Sand Pub.
Ian Woodward, *Occasionally* – pilot issue,
Contemporary newspaper reports some of which can be found in ISIS 16/17 & 44
C.P Lee, *Like the Night,* Helter Skelter Publishing
Paul Williams, *Performing Artist*, Xanadu

The body of this piece is from an article written by C.D Smith and published in ISIS #66, May 1996. Additional material is from an article by Derek Davies published in ISIS #20, April 1988, and from a previously unpublished piece by Peter Smith.

The Woodstock papers of Al Aronowitz
by Al Aronowitz

"History will remember Bob Dylan as the Shakespeare of his era. There's no doubt about that in my mind. To me, Bob is one of those madman geniuses who has chiselled his niche in the common consciousness. The Shakespeare of his time? He's a cultural Alexander the Great! For me, hanging out with Bob was like being an extra in that great movie called history. Yes, I wanted to help make that movie, even if only to play a bit part in it.

Yes, I knew he was going to be one of history's giants – more than a mere pop superstar. He knew it, too. To conquer the world, you have to have the confidence to know that you've got what it takes. And what it takes is psychic power – a term Bob used often in his conversations with me. Bob knew early on that he could draw an audience, attract worshippers and manipulate them into doing his bidding.

He played with me like a cat with a mouse, but still I worshipped him. He treated me like a fool because I was a fool. Aren't we all, or at least most of us, at some time or another? Nobody's perfect, not even an Alexander the Great."

As a higher power suddenly began wringing out the dark and dirty clouds overhead, I joined Albert Grossman and Robbie Robertson in racing for shelter inside the rear of The Band's rented equipment truck, which had been parked backstage...We were on Max Yasgur's farm in rural Bethel, New York, where, almost overnight, a community of nearly half a million had encamped for what was to evolve into several days of a quasi-religious gathering that would be celebrated as one of the most significant cultural events of the times. We were at the 1969 Woodstock Festival, where the backstage area resembled a midway at a carnival, with The Band's rented truck parked as if it were another concession stall, with its tailgate facing the midway. As someone lit a joint and we passed it around, I watched The Band's then-new road manager, tall, thin, sombre-faced and blond-haired Jonathan Taplin, brave the downpour to make sure that all the unloaded instruments and equipment remained safe and secure beneath tarps or within tents. Only when Taplin was satisfied that everything would keep dry did he come in out of the rain to join us.

"He sure seems to be dedicated," I said to Grossman.

Albert just grunted. In a few weeks, I would learn just how dedicated a road manager Jonathan Taplin was.

Woodstock was also a retreat to which Bob had retired to remain shrouded in the privacy, secrecy and seclusion of the mountaintop mist for the three years following his motorcycle accident.

"That accident came like a warning!" Bob told me at the time. *"And I heed warnings!"*

From the very first day I met him, Bob Dylan struck me as having parts of both Dracula and the Wizard of Oz in his overall mix. Bob always took great care to make himself mysterious.

"Have you ever gotten a straight answer out of him about anything? Huh? Have you?"

One of the two women who were then closest to Dylan asked the other that question in *Renaldo and Clara,* the hours-long home movie Bob made of his Rolling Thunder tour.

"Have you?" the second woman answered. *"He never gives a straight answer about anything to anyone!"*

These two women weren't just kidding. They were Sara Dylan, at the time Bob's wife, and Joan Baez, who'd once been Bob's sponsor and lover. And, with all the scenes in this movie supposedly spontaneous, improvised and otherwise unrehearsed, more jest has never been uttered in truth. Bob never even would tell the musicians playing behind him on the concert stage what the next song or its key was going to be. Bob always kept everybody guessing. Nobody could pile it as high as Bob and keep getting away with it. You never knew when he was putting you on. He started out telling people he was born in claptrap Oklahoma poverty. He even started talking with an Oklahoma twang. Once, he told me he'd served time in Redwing Reformatory. He used to try to enhance his self-image with apocrypha the way a girl inflates her breasts with falsies. But is the art of the storyteller in the telling or in the story? I adored Dylan too much to see him through critical eyes. I was too impressed with his hipness and too humbled by his artistry. He handled words with an economy that put me to shame and he aimed those words with the precision of a laser. I felt honoured to be able to hang out with this mumbling twenty-two-year-old kid, skinny as a scarecrow and wound-up as a telephone cord.

He'd sit and talk, smoking an unfiltered cigarette with his legs crossed and his free-swinging foot endlessly kicking a steady, nervous cadence, and I found him fascinating. To me, he was bigger than life and yet I had to laugh because Bob sometimes had all the flash of a 1968 Studebaker. Once, when he was already earning almost a half-million a year, I drove him to JFK and saw him off to Europe for a week or two with only an eight-pound zippered bag as his luggage. Bob Neuwirth, Dylan's chief sidekick at the time, has credited personal manager Albert Grossman with having invented Bob, but it was Dylan who had to invent himself first. Otherwise, a lot of Albert did in fact turn up in Bob. If I never got a straight answer out of Bob, I never got one out of Albert, either. Bob and Albert weren't cut from the same cloth but from the same stonewall. For instance, when I asked Albert how he happened to team up with Dylan, he told me:

"We were both waiting for the same bus."

Albert and Bob were both shifty and manipulative, but which one of them coached whom? They both used even their closest cronies as pawns in their pettiest ego games. Once Bob telephoned me from Woodstock and threatened to kill himself if I didn't immediately make the drive all the way from my house in Berkeley Heights, New Jersey, to come see him. When I finally reached Woodstock, I found him calmly writing a tune in a room over Bernard Paturel's Cafe Espresso in the centre of town. Bob seemed surprised to see me. He acted as if he had never called me at all.

By the time of his motorcycle accident, Bob had succeeded in transfiguring the art of writing pop tunes. As *Rolling Stone* was to comment some twenty-five years later, Dylan had *"single-handedly reinvented pop's known rules of language and meaning and revealed that rock and roll's familiar structures could accommodate new, unfamiliar themes, that a pop song could be about any subject a writer was smart or daring enough to tackle."* Breaking all the spoon-moon rules of traditional lyrics, Bob had shown that a pop tune could talk about politics, that it could be an anthem of love or protest, a message of hope or anger.

Just as the Beatles had freed the sound of pop music, Bob had liberated its lyrics. Pop music had become the art form at the cutting edge of contemporary culture. No other means of expression could be so searching, so outspoken, so redemptive, so rewarding, so unshackled and so true...Even John Lennon told me:

"I'm in awe of Bob Dylan."

Bob claimed he broke his neck in the motorcycle accident. Afterwards, he also broke with manager Albert. Bob was typically vague with me about both ruptures. He always seemed to have something to hide. I've heard varying versions of his motorcycle accident. In one, he'd become a junkie and Albert, taking advantage of a clause in their contract, used the occasion to make Bob detox at his doctor's house. But I was seeing Bob at the time, and I never detected any signs of him high on junk. In another version, the motorcycle accident was nothing but a spill in Bob's Byrdcliffe driveway.

My first hint of bad blood boiling between Albert and Bob came when Bob started sneering at the very mention of Albert's name, muttering angry words about a mysterious incident concerning somebody's wife. Whose wife? Albert's wife? Bob's wife? My wife? If the truth were known, all three wives were in love with Bob. Each loved Bob maybe a little too much. Bob's wife was Sara. She came from Delaware, where her father, a scrap metals dealer, had been shot to death in a hold-up. She'd been married to and divorced from Victor Lownds, a big-time fashion photographer, and she had a beautiful daughter, Maria. Soon after Bob met Sara, he'd told me he was going to marry her, *"She's strong!"* he'd said.

From the first, Sara was always one of the most queenly women. She ruled with regal radiance and with the power to calm troubled waters. She'd never lose her cheerful cool or pull a scene but, when she was really pushed to it, she knew how to do an icy slow burn.

My wife and I and our kids had started visiting Bob in Woodstock even before Sara came on the scene. We'd started going to Woodstock in 1963, when Bob first moved there to live in Albert's rebuilt colonial farmhouse, situated on a woodsy estate that Albert had just purchased from John Streibel, an artist then famous for drawing the hit comic strip, *Dixie Dugan*. The house had been transformed into a comfortable mansion with many rooms, all furnished with antiques. The house also included its primitive original kitchen, which had been left where it was when a new kitchen had been installed. The new kitchen became the main room in Albert's house, with the rare and most expensive gourmet delicacies stocked in its cupboard. Albert's life revolved around haute cuisine. In the end, he paid more attention to building gourmet restaurants than to building hit acts. I'm sure I'm not the only one to contend that Albert eventually ate himself to death.

After Sara and Bob moved into Byrdcliffe, situated where the mountaintop sticks its head into the clouds, my wife and I and our children continued visiting them, often spending the night. I would bring film cans full of the latest Hollywood hits, obtained from a friendly New York movie mogul. During this period, Bob and Sara grew to be one of the tightest twosomes I've ever known.

Bob hadn't been easy to tame. On the one hand, he was a genius, but on the other hand, he was an unpredictable, uncivil and unkempt kid who had waited too long to learn how to clean his fingernails and brush his teeth. He drugged and he drank and he stayed up all night. He was the new star and all the girls had the hots for him. They chased him wherever he went. He was the hip new James Dean. They also compared him to Billy the Kid. Once, as we were on our way out for the night, Bob looked at himself in the full-length mirror of his suite in the Gramercy Park Hotel, broke into a grin and asked:

"Well? Do I look like Billy the Kid?"

If Bob wasn't Billy the Kid, he was Bob the Kid. Everybody always falls for a guy that's nicknamed The Kid. In his chamois jacket and in his skinny stretch jeans, which he habitually kept pulling down over his boot tops, Bob defined that type. Not only does everybody always fall for The Kid, but they fall at first sight. You can't help liking The Kid as soon as your eyes are drawn to him, because he's always very boyishly good-looking. He's always smallish and slim and everybody always wants to baby him, please him, look after him and score him for a pal. Everybody always wants to play big brother or big sister or mama or papa or aunt or uncle or grandparent to The Kid. The Kid always looks like the most endearing kind of guy. He's got a certain impish quality to him but he also looks like a Billy Budd type. The Kid was born with a halo. He beams with innocence. He can do no wrong. He can tell any kind of lie and everybody will always believe him. Nobody ever wants to suspect anything ill of The Kid. He can get away with all sorts of cons and he usually does. He can be the worst kind of scoundrel but he will always be thought of as a hero, a young David who can slay Goliath. The Kid is forever young. He is forever The Kid. Even after his hair turns white, he is still The Kid.

I found him to be one of the most beguiling men I'd ever known. Beguiling, enchanting, bewitching and magnetic. To be with Bob was always magical. Every word out of his mouth impressed me as a gem. Every glance into his eyes turned out to be another surprise for me. Though calm and clear and placid, his eyes always seemed wounded, tinged with a glint of hurt. The universe I'd see in Bob's eyes never stopped jolting me. Bob's eyes also were always very persuasive. Sometimes his eyes would darken and they would command with a stern glare. Isn't it true that blue-eyed people rule the earth? Bob's eyes were blue, deep and unfathomable. They revealed everything while at the same time telling me nothing. The ability to keep a poker face is one of The Kid's attributes. The Kid is an outlaw whose nature is to be secretive, private, mysterious and deceptive. Bob wasn't famous for spilling his guts or wearing his heart on his sleeve. He kept his emotions to himself because he didn't want to show weakness. Even after Bob and Sara started having babies, Robbie Robertson, found it necessary to comment:

"I never see him itchy-kitchy-kooing his kids."

Bob ran hot and cold and he was a succession of either Jekylls and Hydes or heckles and jives, but I've never seen him treat another human as civilly, as respectfully, as lovingly and as humanly as he treated Sara. In the years following his motorcycle accident, Bob acted like a romantic cornball when he was with her. More and more, he depended on her advice as if she were his astrologer, his oracle, his seer and his psychic guide. He would rely on her to tell him the best hour and the best day to travel. For me, they were the ideal loving couple. They flirted with each other constantly. She was always just as hip as he was. Bob and Sara put on an impressive show for me, a drama full of romance and wisecracks and everyday common sense.

After the accident, rumours began to pile up like wreaths on a grave. They said he was dead. They said he was disfigured. They said he had lost his voice, his hair, his mind. I spent a lot of time chauffeuring them around in my station wagon, especially when they would come down from Woodstock to visit Manhattan. They'd stay for days at a time in the apartment of Naomi Saltzman, the woman who replaced Albert as manager of Bob's business. Naomi lived in a luxury high-rise in the Village near NYU and I often visited Bob and Sara there. I remember that once I showed up at Naomi's after Bob and Sara had gone to a Manhattan store called the Pottery Barn to shop for dinnerware. By this time, Bob had come in contact with Woodstock's arts and crafts community and he was doing a lot of painting. He also was thinking about doing some handcrafting. We were sitting at Naomi's dinner table and I innocently asked Sara what happened during the shopping trip to the Pottery Barn.

"Oh," she answered, *"we walked around and we looked at some of the pottery and do you know what he said?"*

"He probably said, 'I can make better pottery than that!'" I answered.

"How did you know?" Sara gasped.

It was after his motorcycle accident that Bob got into painting. Woodstock was, after all, an artists' colony and, living in a Woodstock that teemed with painters, Bob was bound to end up finding a buddy who would get him interested in oils. Bob's canvases were colourful and abstract, such as the one on his *"Self-Portrait"* album cover, which came out of this period. To me, Bob's canvases showed another dimension of his artistic soul.

In Woodstock, Bob's lifestyle became very country squireish. In addition to painting, writing songs, working on a book – *Tarantula* – and editing his tour films, he would sometimes drop into the drug store for toothpaste, go to a movie in one of the nearby towns, visit with neighbours or attend antique auctions with Sara. As Bob and Sara kept having more babies, Bob kept trying to add a dog to his family. But he kept having to get rid of one dog after another for one reason or another, such as in the case of a monster named Buster. As I recall, Buster was an immense Great Dane who kept biting people. Bob eventually had to send Buster to obedience school but still Buster kept biting people. Once, Buster bit a little girl, a neighbour's daughter. Buster even bit me once, too, attacking when I was defenceless. I was walking down the steps to the front door of Byrdcliffe with my arms full of film cans when Buster tore at my leg.

Built in Woodstock's own woodsy style of Rough-Hewn Modern, Byrdcliffe was a handsome house with a commanding view that somehow made me feel like I was visiting someone's version of the Hanging Gardens of Babylon. In the front, off the driveway, a small outbuilding that once might have been a garage housed a pool table, with Bob acting as the resident shark. He certainly shot a much better game of pool than I did. By this time, The Band and Big Pink had come into the picture and its members were frequent players in Dylan's tiny pool hall. The most frequent was Robbie Robertson, who had supplanted Bobby Neuwirth as Bob's Number One crony.

Dylan's post-accident period became a time occupied not only by the Big Pink basement sessions but also by many kitchen jams, which sometimes included not only The Band but also other visiting musicians. They would pass the guitar around, taking turns at singing tunes. In the same way that comedians get together and tell one another jokes. Each joke would remind one of the other comedians of another joke, and among the musicians each song would suggest another song. But too smoothly for anyone to detect a game of Can-You-Top-This. As the chain of songs grew, the musicians keep passing the guitar around far into the night. The Band's drummer, Levon Helm, usually topped everyone, playing either the mandolin or the acoustic guitar and coming up with one surprise after another, usually a long-forgotten country, folk or pop tune. I used to wonder how these musicians had enough room in their brains to remember all the words to all those tunes. I wished I had a memory like that.

Bob tried to keep himself shrouded in mystery from the time I'd first met him, but he became weirder yet after the motorcycle accident. He told me that, as he hurtled through the air when he was thrown from the motorcycle to the side of the road, he thought sure he was going to be killed.

"I saw my whole life pass in front of me," he said.

The nation's pop music stations interrupted their programs to broadcast the news as a bulletin. In London, a group of hippie fans printed a memorial poster with a space left blank for the time and place of the funeral services. At Fordham University, a Jesuit priest prepared a lecture entitled, '*The Ontology of Bob Dylan.*' I never really believed the story about Bob breaking a vertebra his neck. Later on, he claimed that was just an expression that his brother used at the time. I always felt a strange twinge of guilt about the spill Bob took because I was the one who had driven him to pick up his new Triumph bike in the first place. I remembered an ominous foreboding as I followed him while he rode the motorcycle home. But I never told him about this feeling. He wouldn't have heeded my warning, anyway.

By the year of the motorcycle accident, Bob had become America's counter-cultural idol and inspiration. Even among hip black musicians, the only thing Jimi Hendrix ever really wanted from me was for me to introduce him to Bob Dylan. By 1966, each new Dylan album had become a pop scene event. Dylan had single-handedly reinvented contemporary music, but how was he going to top himself? What was he going to do next? Poised for the rush to fill his footprint, the imitators on Bob's heels waited breathlessly for Bob's next step. But, in mid-stride, Dylan had done a Garbo. He'd pulled a vanishing act. By the time of the Woodstock Festival, Dylan's next footfall was still in a state of suspension.

The state of suspension was interrupted briefly by appearances of Dylan's other persona. Bob's participation in a 1968 Carnegie Hall tribute to Woody Guthrie seemed stiff and rusty and solemn. It was as if he dressed his show in its Sunday best because this was a formal occasion, a memorial. In 1968 also, Bob released his *"John Wesley Harding"* album. It was as if he tried to slip it in unnoticed. In renegotiating his recording contract with *Columbia*, he had demanded a clause prohibiting any advance publicity for the album. When he drove into New York two months before the release of *"John Wesley Harding,"* I took a walk with Bob through Greenwich Village. He had grown a scraggly beard and he was wearing and an Australian Gaucho hat and nobody noticed him. We even walked right past – one of the biggest names in the Village – an early admirer who had turned into one of Bob's most bitter critics.

"He didn't recognize you!" I gasped.

"He never recognized me before," Bob answered. *"Why should he recognize me now?"*

Dylan's very presence had turned Woodstock into Mecca to which the faithful had to make their pilgrimages. Soon, that tiny but burgeoning hamlet was turning into a music capital as well as an art colony. When Mike Lang and John Roberts cooked up the idea of promoting a three-day music fair in the summer of 1969, their choice of Woodstock as the site was in itself a tribute to Bob Dylan. Sticking the festival in Dylan's back yard was like shoving it in his face. The whole point of the show might have been to get Dylan to headline it. In essence, the Woodstock Festival was nothing but a call to Bob to come out and play. Years later, pilgrims still show up in Woodstock in the mistaken belief that Woodstock is where the Woodstock Festival actually was held.

With my wife and kids, I had joined Bob and Sara and their kids for a picnic in their back yard at Byrdcliffe. We were eating roast beef sandwiches and there was potato salad and other goodies piled on the wooden picnic table behind the Dylans' house. It was a sunny afternoon. It was Sunday, August 11th, and the Woodstock Festival was scheduled to start the following Friday. Earlier that day, I had visited the festival site and now I reported to Bob that whereas rain had turned Yasgur's farm into a muddy quagmire the day before, the sun now had succeeded in drying the mud so thoroughly that promoters Lang and Roberts had been talking about renting a water truck to spray the road to keep the dust down.

"I wish they'd send the truck my way," Bob said. *"The motor from my pump broke down and I haven't had any runnin' water for three days. I'm ready to sell this whole place to the land developers. My children need water. We buy a lot of food in this town and we pay a lot of taxes. We expect better service than this."*

Sara's chief complaint about living in Woodstock was always that the water dried up in August. Near the picnic table was a trampoline, which Dylan had just put together for his kids and they were playing on it. Bob knew I was going to write a story for the New York *Post* and he was choosing his words with impish delight.

We both knew that he was booked to sail for England in a few days and that he had absolutely no intention of making a surprise appearance at the Woodstock Festival. He just didn't want me to say so in print. When I told him that Lang and Roberts had just spent $16,000 to fly some 100 members of the Hog Farm from Santa Fe, New Mexico, to the festival site to install showers and portable toilets, Bob said he didn't think he'd need to spend that kind of money to do the job over at his place.

"Still, it's been three days since I heard from the repairman," he complained.

Bob said –

"I met Michael Lang once but I can't remember anythin' about him. My opinion of that festival is not any different from anyone else's. I think everyone is probably goin' t'have a good time, but I wouldn't blame 'em if they didn't. Why do they have to call it the Woodstock Festival? We like that name – Woodstock. It has a familiar ring to it. That's one of the reasons we moved up here. There's quite a few towns with that name. There's Woodstock, Kentucky. There's Woodstock, New Hampshire. There's Woodstock, Ohio. There's Woodstock, Maryland. There's Woodstock, Arkansas. There's Woodstock, Oklahoma. There's Woodstock, Wisconsin. And there's Woodstock, Hawaii. There are more every minute, but if it's all the same, we may move on to another one."

He walked past the trampoline toward the swimming pool. He couldn't use the swimming pool, either. There was too much algae in it.

"I've had it!" he laughed. *"We need some water and nobody understands!"*

The Woodstock Festival emerged as a milestone, a marker, and a signpost to show the changing directions of America. It signified the coming of age of an underground youth culture which not only had grown up to flex its muscles but which was splitting its seams and bursting out of its clothes like the Incredible Hulk.

Dylan, of course, missed the show.

Maybe it was his contrary nature. Maybe it was his insistence on being difficult and disagreeable. Maybe he wanted to be perverse or he wanted to stay mysterious. Maybe he enjoyed his reputation for unpredictability, dissonance, counterpoise.

"Y'gotta be different!" he'd once told me.

Bob always seemed to try to do the unexpected. He liked to swim against the tide. Not only did he not go to Woodstock, but he created his own Woodstock. For his first big concert reappearance since he had disappeared into the mountaintop mist, Dylan signed on to be the headliner at a festival which, the year before, had consisted of little more than an audience of 10,000 watching some rock bands perform on nothing but the back of a flatbed trailer. For America, the site of Dylan's Woodstock would be even more inaccessible than Max Yasgur's alfalfa field after the traffic jam choked the roads. The site of Dylan's big comeback would be across the Solent, that seven-mile-wide appendage of the North Atlantic that reaches between England and the crumbling chalk cliffs of the Isle of Wight.

Published in issue #95. March 2001.

1969 – Isle of Wight, UK © Dennis Grice

The Isle of Wight papers of Al Aronowitz
by Al Aronowitz

When Bob asked me to come along with him to the Isle of Wight as his road manager, I felt honoured. Also going were Bob's wife, Sara, plus The Band, which was booked to play on its own before reappearing as Bob's backup musicians. Bob's and Sara's luggage was my responsibility. There were seven pieces of luggage travelling with them and one of my jobs was to make sure that all seven pieces got where they were going.

The Dylans' luggage had been thrown together with The Band's luggage for the trip from Heathrow south to Portsmouth, where we boarded a Hovercraft, which took us over the Solent to Ryde, the port on the Isle of Wight's northern coast, where a parade of hired taxis awaited our entourage. Bob and Sara and I were going to Forelands Farm at Bembridge, a Sixteenth Century stone cottage within a walled compound that included gardens, a swimming pool, a house trailer, tennis courts, a barn, a twenty-four-hour guard and a proper English hostess, the niece of the late Sir Stafford Cripps. She was an almost matronly woman in her early fifties who went around asking for autographs while wearing a badge that read, *"Help Bob Dylan Sink The Isle Of Wight."*

It wasn't until 1997 that I got to know her better. That's when I wrote to surrealist poet David Gascoyne inviting him to the Allen Ginsberg Memorial in Manhattan's Central Park Bandshell in June of that year and got a reply from – of all people – her.

"Your letter to David yesterday brought so many memories back to me! When we were all staying at Forelands Farm at Bembridge with Bob Dylan?! I had been 'chosen' to look after Bob n Sara n his friends. It was a memorable week to me..."

The proper English hostess then named Judy Lewis, has eventually turned out to be Judy Gascoyne, wife of the noted Isle of Wight poet, who, at 83, can now hardly walk because of a broken pelvis suffered in a fall.

In her letter, Judy also wrote me:

"...I wasn't a very good cook, but the Fiery Creations Ron and Ray Foulk wanted me to look after Bob's children".

The plan had been for the kids to arrive with their parents. Bob had specified to the Foulk brothers that he was bringing them and he didn't want to stay with his family in a hotel.

"...When it was decided not to bring them, I was put in charge of looking after you all...Quite a task really, as I had no help and very little food in a strange house, and ten

of you all to feed! Bob would insist that I took supper with you all, and the menu was mostly vegetarian because of George Harrison. Breakfast started at midday and was that much easier, since George had convinced us that porridge was better for us than bacon and eggs.

However, the morning of the big pop festival concert, I decided to buy a juicy steak – to sustain Bob! – It cost 15 shillings – 75p in today's money – 50 cents U.S. It put a hole in the 7 pound; 5d a week I had been given for food.

Anyway, while Bob was eating his steak, you had popped in for breakfast and you said, 'Is that good, Bob?' And you looked at it longingly! So he immediately cut the steak in half and shared it with you. Those were generous, happy times and I've written about it in Jewels and Binoculars 1993, which came out about three years ago. So you can imagine what a surprise it was to see your letter to David!

Dylan often asked me about the Isle of Wight, Tennyson and poetry," Judy wrote. *"I suggested he go to Quarr Abbey to hear the monks chanting. He and Sara enjoyed that. They didn't go swimming in the outdoor pool because they thought it was too cold."*

Judy described Bob as *"restless and nervous and very polite,"* and she remembered him having *"green eyes"* (sic). She said she was unable to cook more than one meal a day and recalled that Bob *"didn't like women giving him food."* He ate mostly sandwiches, she said.

She always had plenty of visitors in the kitchen. Early in the morning, both Bob and George would come for cups of tea to bring to their wives, she said. And George, she added, would always insist on helping her with the *"washing up."*

"I was a sort of mother figure," she also said. *"All the time they were here, they didn't take drugs or drink alcohol..."*

Little did she know.

Judy said there were ten of us. Also with us was Albert's partner, Bert Block, who brought his wife and daughter. Then I asked Number Two Beatles road manager Malcolm Evans to accompany George so he could assist me. And there was Judy.

As for the members of The Band, they had accommodations at the Halland Hotel, a rambling old seafront hostelry rescued by this occasion from being boarded up.

My first problem was that no one had told The Band's road manager that Bob, Sara and I were going to one place and that The Band was going to another. When I hurried to start loading Bob's and Sara's luggage onto the taxi going to Forelands Farm, I found that The Band's road manager had beat me to the luggage. He already had started loading Bob's and Sara's luggage together with The Band's luggage onto a taxi going to the Halland Hotel. When I tried to tell him he was making a mistake, he refused to pay any attention at all to me. When I tried to retrieve their luggage from the boot of the wrong taxi, he gave me an argument, grabbing one end of a suitcase while I grabbed the other end until we were involved in a tug-o-war. What did I know? I was just an amateur. I was just there for the ride. On the other hand, he was a pro! I thought he was going to challenge me to a fistfight. That's how dedicated a road manager Jonathan Taplin was.

The Isle of Wight Festival was scheduled for August 29 and 30, Saturday and Sunday, with Dylan's triumphant return to the concert stage scheduled on the Sunday night. Booked to headline on the Saturday night was The Who, also one of the headliners at the Woodstock Festival.

At the Isle of Wight Festival, Dylan was the only monster on the bill capable of attracting a monster of an audience. In refusing to play the Woodstock Festival and in then letting himself be talked into playing the Isle of Wight, Dylan in effect was telling England's counterculture:

"C'mon. Let's hold our own Woodstock."

And so, on the Isle of Wight, a dot of land that certainly wasn't the easiest place in the world to get to, Dylan almost single-handedly proved an enticing enough attraction to collect an audience sometimes estimated to be as few as a 125,000 and sometimes as many as 250,000.

A few days before the festival, I watched the thousands arriving to take up residence in a growing tent city, pitched on a sixty-acre hillside at the north end of the Island. For the first time in the memory of humankind, the ferries from Portsmouth to Ryde ran all night.

Once, I went with Band drummer Levon Helm in the three a.m. darkness to watch the kids coming off the ferries at the Ryde terminal, where they debarked with a silence that seemed to show a well-mannered reluctance to break the still of the night. And yet, although they should have been burnt out from the trip, they looked bright-eyed and determined, with their rucksacks and their bedrolls piled on their backs. Some of the guys had crew cuts and some had tangled tresses down past their asses, but they were all die-hard Dylan fans, England's Woodstock Generation, all sharing the same agenda and following the same leader.

The local residents had expected the worst from this monster and the island's 130-man police force cancelled all leaves and put itself on alert, assigning plain-clothesmen to mingle with the audience. Although the monster was clearly smoking pot and treating itself to an exotic salad of other controlled substances, the authorities afterwards said they were pleased by the monster's comportment.

There were gatecrashers and the walls eventually came tumbling down and some anarchist and biker types had been reportedly looking for trouble. But this Isle of Wight crowd struck me as much more docile than Woodstock's benign beast. These kids were so mannerly that they even lined up politely to get gypped at the food shops, which had stayed open to accommodate them. At the cash registers, each kid would sweetly give his or her thanks with a *"Ta!"* even though the prices had been jacked up outrageously for the occasion.

Levon and I had hired a taxi for the ride into Ryde in our own hunt for a food shop and we couldn't help but stop to gawk at this crowd. We were on an expedition to rustle up some candies, snacks and other goodies to bring back to the rest of The Band, trapped at the Halland Hotel without room service in the middle of the night. At the Ryde Esplanade, Levon and I watched the ferries disgorging the kids, who then still had a five-mile walk to the festival site at Woodside Bay, where another encampment was already growing in a wheat field overlooked by the stage and bounded by Wootton Creek. On our way back to the hotel, Levon and I rode along the road on which this throng walked. The line was endless, reminding me of the lines that march through the epic silent films of pioneer moviemaker Sergei Eisenstein. Levon, famous for his Arkansas outfielder's ability to keep a straight face, rolled down the window to get a better look at the kids in this line. Then he broke into an overpowering smile as he said:

"Look at how beautiful they are!"

At the same time, with a few jerky motions, he grabbed the care package we had bought for the rest of The Band, reached into it and he started handing out its contents to the kids through the taxi window.

The promoters who were amateur enough to think that four portable toilet trailers were going to satisfy the needs of a crowd of 250,000 were Ricky Farr and three brothers, Ron, Ray and Bob Foulk. They also had managed to cadge the facade of a Roman temple from the old Cleopatra movie set at Pinewoods Studio so they could use it as a frame for the Isle of Wight Festival stage, which, they boasted, was the biggest ever built in Britain. Describing the promoters as *"three small-time operators,"* Variety, the show business Bible, spoke for almost all the media by expressing mystification at how the Foulk brothers managed to persuade Dylan to make his triumphant return to the concert stage on a remote dot of land off the southern coast of England. And for only an estimated $50,000 guarantee! Especially after Dylan had turned down far more lucrative and more prestigious offers – such as the Woodstock Festival, held in his own back yard.

The Brothers Foulk had campaigned for months to sign Dylan as their main attraction, starting with a tactic no more imaginative than simple foot-in-the-door salesmanship. As expected, Dylan at first told them to get lost, but by that time their foot was far enough in the door for them to be able to hand Bob a brochure extolling the Isle of Wight as a vacation spot. It was a one-of-a-kind brochure, which they had written and printed themselves. When that caught Bob's attention, they next put together a home movie for use as a travelogue. Naturally, Sara also had a say in Bob's decision to make his triumphant return to the concert stage on the Isle of Wight. When he got there, Dylan said that he had agreed to do the show because it would give him an opportunity to have the honeymoon he and Sara hadn't had time for. The poker-faced Bob told a reporter:

"I wanted to see the home of Alfred Lord Tennyson."

On his very first morning on the Isle of Wight, Bob went with Sara to visit Osborne House, where Queen Victoria had spent her summers with her eleven children. Bob was into having a big family at that time. Originally, Bob and Sara had planned a trans-Atlantic crossing aboard the QE2 with their two elder children, Maria and Jesse. It was eighteen days before the concert when they boarded the ship, and already 40,000 tickets had been sold. My wife and I had driven the Dylans to the ship to see them off and we were in their stateroom when, 30 minutes before the ship sailed, four-year-old Jesse went into convulsions. We rushed Jesse to our doctor, who met us in the emergency room of Lenox Hill Hospital, where, taking no chances, the doctor decided to admit Jesse for a day or two. Naturally, the QE2 sailed without the Dylans and the British Press wasted no time in gleefully reporting that Bob wasn't coming. Twelve days later, when Bob and Sara did in fact arrive at London's Heathrow Airport, they learned that since they'd carried Jesse off the QE2, not another ticket had been sold. When they reached the Isle of Wight, the first news they got was that the roof of the stage had collapsed because the crew had hung too much lighting from the overhead pipes. Then a reporter showed up to warn Dylan:

"You won't get another line in the papers unless you give me an interview!"

That's the kind of skirmishing that went on between Bob and the press. The media continually complained about Bob's aloofness, his inaccessibility, his uncooperative behaviour and his camera-shyness. For his part, Bob fed the antagonism, making it clear that he wasn't a trained monkey doing tricks on command to please the press. His attitude was that he wanted the world to judge him on his songs, his music and his performances alone and not on his ability to butter up to the media...The promoters, hungry for as much publicity as possible for their festival, kept pleading with Bob to hold a press conference. On the Wednesday before the show, I had to help arrange one.

It was held at the Halland. Mal Evans came down from his home outside of London to help me set it up. Mal, was the Beatles' gentle giant road manager and he came in response to my SOS. He was, after all, a little more experienced at road managing than I...When the press asked its usual dumb questions, Bob responded with his usual put-ons, what one newspaper later described as *"a few mumbled non-committal statements."* At press conferences, Bob always did his best to sound as if he were mumbling *"noncommittal statements."* At the Halland, the questions certainly were irrelevant. When he was asked why he no longer sang with the raw whine that had distinguished his singing before his motorcycle accident, he explained that a man with kids learns how to sing more sweetly. Immediately, another reporter wanted to know if that meant Bob had turned square. That night, Bob could be seen on the evening news, looking straight-faced out from the telly as he soberly put off yet another reporter by saying:

"I don't understand your question!"

Back at Forelands Farm, Judy looked extremely dignified, like a sorority den mother, and she all too soon began acting like one. She came from an aristocratic family and her title of hostess was in face-saving mitigation of the fact that she was hired to do the cooking and housekeeping. She started out as Mrs. Super-efficiency and, although she was instant fun, her titillated toadying and her super-servile style soon started getting on everybody's nerves. Worst of all, she started behaving like an overawed teenage bubblegum groupie gone gaga, starry-eyed and over the top from being in close proximity to such larger-than-life heroes as Bob Dylan and George Harrison.

When I'd called to ask Mal to come, I'd also called George, whom I'd also asked to please bring some smoke. George arrived a day after Mal, driving all the way to Portsmouth with his wife, Patti, in his blue Italian sports car, which, he joked, had cost as much as a house. Of course, he ferried the car across the Solent. George felt safer making the trip by auto because he was mauling Ringo's marijuana stash for delivery as a care package for Bob, The Band and me. This was the care package we were all jonesing for. We were all hooked on both tobacco and pot and none of us had enjoyed a toke of marijuana since we'd gotten to England. That's how big a part of our lives smoke was in those days. George also brought along a dub of the Beatles' *"Abbey Road"* album, which he played over one of the amps in the rehearsal shed. The audience included Robbie Robertson and The Band as well as Dylan and myself and, although I can confess that my own mind was blown by the album, I don't remember Bob and the boys lifting George on their shoulders to tell him how much they loved *"Abbey Road."*

Mal, George and Patti joined our Forelands Farm family to stay with us until Bob's Sunday night performance, still five days away. But as soon as George and Bob and anybody else would get together in a conversation, Judy would make sure to stick her nose into the huddle. Ultimately, she touched off a wave of paranoia and she was soon suspected of being on the payroll of the tabloids. Bob told the promoters to fire her after George discovered she was not only eavesdropping but she was also doing something that I should have been doing. She was taking notes.

Charlie Watts of the Rolling Stones was lucky I happened to be in the courtyard when he showed up to say hello. He was at the Forelands Farm gate with a retinue of friends. I had to rescue him from being turned away by the guards, who thought he was just another fan. After I ran into the cottage and got Bob to come out and greet him, Charlie joked:

"It's harder to get in to see you than it is to get in to see the President of the United States!"

We were told that Paul McCartney would have come, too, but his wife, Linda, had just given birth to their first child. There were rumours that Ringo and Maureen were going to bring Elizabeth Taylor but when they dropped in it was with John Lennon and Yoko Ono. And they really did literally *"drop in,"* arriving on the afternoon of the night performance aboard a helicopter that landed in the Forelands Farm garden. Yoko still hadn't fully recuperated from the back injuries she'd suffered in an auto accident. She'd come with John and a well-equipped video cameraman, who'd been brought to make a videotape record of everything John and Yoko did. The Lennons in addition had gone to the expense of printing thousands of peace leaflets to flutter down on the festival crowd from the helicopter. When the pilot nixed that idea, they decided to rain down balloons instead. At Apple Records, the staff was given the rush job of blowing up several hundred balloons until somebody realized that several hundred blown-up balloons would never fit into the helicopter.

With the video cameraman's tape rolling, Bob then invited the Beatles to a game of tennis on the Forelands Farm courts.

"I'll play on the condition that nobody really knows how," John quipped and, as Bob and John teamed up against Ringo and George, Patti Harrison giggled:

"This is the most exclusive game of doubles in the world!"

Tennis was too demanding a sport for a group of cigarette-smoking musicians, and, one by one, they were soon conscripting supernumeraries like Mal Evans and me to spell them in the game. I, who'd never before played tennis, didn't last long, either. Meanwhile, some citizens of Bembridge, had been attracted by the helicopter dropping in out of the sky and showed up to enjoy the game, too. Soon, there was a crowd peering through the cyclone fence, the foliage and the slatted wooden baffles that surrounded the property.

Ultimately, the game ended and, at 5:30, Dylan piled into a white van along with Sara, Ringo, Maureen and me for the five-mile drive to the festival site. We joked all the way. A year or so later, the Apple Records press agent who had arranged with me for John and Ringo to land in the Forelands Farm garden sent me the bill for the helicopter. He expected that I would give the bill to Bob for payment because, after all, the presence of John and Ringo had helped promote Bob's show. The bill amounted to a few hundred dollars, but Bob wasn't talking to me at the time and so I got stuck with paying the bill out of my own pocket.

At Wootton Creek, the growing crowd had been camped in the chill for several days and nights while trying to warm itself by trading rumours that Dylan would sing for three hours, that he would jam with the Beatles, with the Rolling Stones, with Blind Faith and that he would still be onstage with the Monday morning light.

No one without proper credentials was supposed to be allowed inside the press enclosure, a heavily guarded area roped-off directly in front of the stage. The press enclosure offered the best possible view of the stage and should have been able to accommodate a couple of hundred reporters and photographers. By the time Dylan got to the festival site, more than a thousand persons had managed to sneak into the enclosure and they were packed as tight as asparagus tips in a can. The promoters had placed seats at the front of the enclosure for special guests like George and Patti, Ringo and Maureen and John and Yoko, who braved the crush despite the fact that Yoko was in the first hopeful months of a frail pregnancy. In the press enclosure behind the special guests, the standees were packed too close together to be able to sit down and they were blocking the view of the rest of the audience, who complained with shouts and curses. When the shouts and curses didn't work, the audience at first began to spit at the standees and then started throwing bottles and beer cans and rocks at them. Soon, there were calls for a doctor. The crush in the press enclosure was so strong that people were fainting on their feet without any room for them to slump to the ground. By now, the integrity of the whitewashed plywood fences, although patrolled by security men with dogs, had broken down completely and gate crashers were stampeding into the arena, which already was holding the largest paying audience in the history of British rock.

(Richie) Havens' spellbinding performance ended with a powerful and exciting *'Strawberry Fields Forever.'* Next on the bill was a set by The Band, who were supposed to go on stage at eight-thirty. But when the clock struck ten, The Band still hadn't made an appearance. The MC was cursing and screaming from the battery of microphones in an attempt to clear the press enclosure of anyone without proper credentials, but that *wasn't* the reason why The Band finally went on stage an hour and a half late. The *real* reason was that there was something wrong with the Foulk Brothers' vaunted sound system, which, the Brothers Foulk had insisted, was loud enough to be heard for miles.

Afterwards, I would remember how, when Band pianist Richard Manuel began singing Dylan's *'I Shall Be Released,'* large portions of the crowd jumped to their feet, calling for Bob himself to come on stage. Afterwards, I would remember the deafening and throaty roar that went up when a deadpan Bob, armed with the guitar that George Harrison had lent him, finally did walk out to face the audience. The roar was as loud as any I'd ever heard from any crowd.

In all, he sang 17 songs. The audience responded with the kind of oooohs and ahhhhs you'd hear at fireworks displays. Afterwards, I would remember Sara unable to take her eyes off Bob. She glowed as she watched his performance from the wings. Afterwards, some newspapers would report that the audience jeered with complaints because the show was too short. Afterwards, *Variety*, claiming that Dylan ended up with some $84,000 for the appearance, would report that the audience received Bob's songs only coolly and then lit bonfires to protest his quick exit from the stage. *Variety* also would quote one of the Foulk brothers as saying:

"We were staggered when he walked off so soon. We paid him in advance and expected at least two hours!"

London's *Daily Sketch* devoted its entire next day's front page to a headline that said: *"DYLAN WALKS OUT AFTER A MIDNIGHT FLOP"*

But afterwards, I, for one, would remember only the monster's loud, throaty, exultant and cheering roar of approval. Afterwards, I would remember only the loud, roar of the crowd calling Dylan back.

As amateur promoters, the Brothers Foulk not only were assholes enough to think that four portable toilet trailers could serve the needs of a monster with a quarter-million assholes, but they also were short-sighted enough to think that a dressing room without a toilet would serve the needs of their star, their main attraction, the man whose very name had materialized this monster in the first place. Just as the Foulk brothers had hired special trailers for use as portable toilets, they'd also rented a trailer to serve as Bob's dressing room. They'd outfitted it with a mirror, a dressing table and a few chairs but not a hell of a lot else. The dressing room especially did not have its own bathroom.

The truth is that I'd wanted a toilet in Bob's dressing room for myself as much as for Bob and I'd made a federal case out of demanding one at a meeting that I'd held with the Foulk brothers soon after my arrival on the Isle of Wight. The Foulk brothers had assured me that Bob's dressing trailer would indeed come equipped with a bathroom. When I arrived at the trailer with Bob and Sara on the night of the show to discover that they had lied to me, I immediately exploded.

"I told them to make sure the dressing room had a bathroom!" I said. Yes, I was enraged but my rage was tempered by paranoia. Not only had the Foulk brothers thought they could get away with lying to me, but I expected a needling from Bob.

The first thing I wanted to do about the lack of a toilet was to take it up with the UN. But Bob told me to forget about it. He said it was no big thing. Bob had a habit of pooh-poohing my ideas. He always seemed to decide to do the opposite. It seemed difficult for Bob ever to give me or anybody else much credit for anything.

Ultimately, I was the first to have to take a pee. When I stepped out of Bob's dressing trailer and asked for directions to the nearest loo, some one told me there was only one bathroom in the whole backstage area. I had to keep asking directions as I made my way through the maze of tents and trailers in the backstage area, but I suppose I could have simply followed my nose. The toilet trailer certainly wasn't the sweetest smelling place on earth. Nor was it the most inviting. I didn't think Bob would enjoy a visit to this place.

In his dressing trailer, Bob, readying himself for the show, sat tuning George Harrison's favourite acoustic guitar. Otherwise, there was little else for Bob and Sara and me to do in the dressing trailer but sit around and wait. For what seemed like hours, Bob stayed quiet and stone-faced as he tried to be patient. Sometimes he'd get up and pace. As 8:30 approached, he looked at me with annoyance and said:

"I don't hear The Band on yet. Ain't The Band on yet?"

He said it as if it were my fault. He said it as if he wanted me to do something about it. Instead of busting my balls about the lack of a toilet in the dressing room, he was busting my balls because The Band wasn't on stage yet.

"Shit!" he said suddenly. *"It's past eight-thirty! Why ain't The Band playin' yet? What time is The Band s'posed t'be on? I thought they were s'posed to go on at eight-thirty!"*

"Yeah," I agreed. *"They were supposed to go on at eight-thirty."*

"Well, it's PAST eight-thirty!" Bob exploded. *"Go find out why th' Band ain't onstage yet? Go out there an' find out!"*

In the wings, I searched out Robbie Robertson, whom I found with his guitar already on his shoulder.

"What's the hangup?" I asked. *"You were supposed to go on at eight-thirty."*

"Oh," he said, *"There's something wrong with the sound system. Jon says it's not ready yet. He's working on it."*

He motioned toward Jon Taplin, who was engrossed with checking the microphone connections on the stage...As The Band's road manager, Taplin had the responsibility of making sure that the sound system worked properly. Taplin fancied himself an artist when it came to ensuring that the sound system made The Band sound as good as The Band was capable of sounding and when it came to music The Band were perfectionists...I had been trying to avoid Jon since our tug-o'-war over Bob's luggage when we'd first landed on the island but now I approached him.

"What's wrong with the sound system?" I asked.

"I'm trying to find out," he answered curtly.

"But the sound system seemed to be working all right when Tom Paxton and Richie Havens were on" I said. *"What happened to it since then? How can you tell there's something wrong with it?"*

He looked at me with contempt and disbelief. Was I really asking that question? Without another word, he turned back to what he was doing.

Back in the dressing trailer, Bob demanded to know what was wrong with the sound system. I didn't have the first clue. He had to be satisfied with chopping the head off the messenger.

I'd walked the fifth batter! Whatever kind of hot water I was in, Sara played lifeguard. Sara always went out of her way to be kind to me. She treated me as if I was a close relative. Whatever predicament we happened to be in, she always knew what to say to turn it into a joke. Before long, she and Bob were flirting with each other. I worshipped Sara as a goddess who not only could calm the storm but who also could turn Bob into a human being. Bob was never a nicer guy than when he was with Sara. On the Isle of Wight, they acted like a pair of lovebirds. At Forelands Farm, they'd hold hands or put their arms around each other and go for long walks along the chalk cliffs. When Sara glowed, she glowed like a summer's day. With her eyes bright, with her lashes dark, with her cheeks lightly rouged and with her face embellished with her Mona Lisa smile, part of her sad-eyed-lady-of-the-lowlands look, she now sat with us in the dressing room, kidding with Bob. Otherwise, we had little to say, like passengers in a New York City subway car, impatient to get to our stop so we could get the hell out of there. Living in Byrdcliffe, Bob had gotten into the habit of going to sleep early and it didn't surprise me when he started to yawn.

"It sure is takin' a long time to fix the fuckin' sound system!" Bob said, yawning again. Then he turned to me and commanded: *"Go back out there an' see if you can get 'em to hurry it up! Go ahead! Get 'em to hurry it up!"*

On the big stage, Jon was still sorting out cables, testing microphones and plugging in connections. He was on his haunches and he didn't want to be interrupted.

"Bob's getting VERY impatient," I said. *"He wants The Band to get on and do its show and get it over with so he can get on and do his show."*

"You know The Band can't get started till the sound system's working!" Jon said icily.

"But, Bob's getting mad!" I said.

Back in Bob's dressing trailer, I told Bob that Jon was still working on the sound system.

"Shit!" Bob said, sleepily. *"I start yawning at nine o'clock these days!"*

Soon, Bob was pacing again. While Sara sat and I stood, Bob kept walking around the dressing room. A few minutes later, he groaned:

"Now, I gotta pee! Shit! Why ain't there no fuckin' toilet in this fuckin' trailer? Shit! I don't want to have to go outside t'look for someplace to pee! How come you didn't get 'em to get me a dressing room with a toilet?"

I offered to escort Bob to the communal toilet.

"Naw, naw!" he shook his head.

Outside, he would have to mingle with the other performers and with the crew. They were his fans, too.

"C'mon, I'll lead you there," I said again.

"Shit!" he said. *"I don't want to go there!"*

"Why don't you pee out the window?" I suggested.

If my memory serves me right, this was one time Bob ended up doing what I suggested, even though he didn't think it was a good idea. He was getting grumpy. Soon, Bob had worked himself into a real grouchy mood. Finally, he exploded, turning toward me and commanding:

"Go out there and get them to hurry the fuck up!"

Back on stage, Jon was still too busy to listen to anything I had to say. What could I do? I trudged back to the dressing trailer. It was getting close to 9:30.

"What kind of shit is this?" Bob exploded. *"They was s'posed t'be on that stage an hour ago! I should be on that stage RIGHT NOW! Go back out there and make them get a move on! Go ahead! Go out there and make them get started!"*

"Bob's getting mad!" I told Taplin. *"He says The Band's gotta go on right away."*

Jon simply ignored me. It was as if I was having another tug-o'-war with Taplin.

"C'mon, Jon, tell me how much longer you're gonna be...Bob's blowing his stack back there!"

"Another few minutes," he said.

Back in the dressing room, Bob greeted me with an angry *"Well?"*

"Another few minutes," I said.

"Another few minutes!" he erupted. *"I want The Band to go on now! Right now!"*

He flew into a tantrum. He was like a kid stamping his feet. What was I going to do about this? How could he go out there and put on a great show after he'd worked himself into this kind of rage? Like a teacher calming a hysterical kid, Sara put out the fire. After a while, Bob started yawning again.

"It's almost ten," he complained. *"If I don't go on soon, I'm gonna fall asleep!"*

The audience was getting tired, too. Both Bob and I knew that the crowd must be feeling drained and worn out. Bob started pacing again.

"I wanted to catch the crowd when it was still at the peak of its psychic energy," Bob said grimly…*"This is spoilin' ever'thin'! This is ruinin' ever'thin' that I came here t' do, ever'thin' I wanted t'accomplish!"*

"Well, what did you wanna accomplish?" I asked. *"Why did you come t'the Isle of Wight? What do you wanna to get out of it?"*

Bob turned toward me with a look of surprise. Didn't I already know? Did I really have to ask?

"I want to feel exalted!" he said.

Soon, not even Sara could think of any more pleasant small talk with which to pacify Bob. As we waited and waited, there were long periods of silence. Bob was boiling and he soon boiled over.

"I don't care if the sound system works or not!" Bob stormed. *"Fuck their fuckin' sound system! Tell 'em t'go on without a sound system! You go out there an' tell th'Band to start playin' an' get it over with! Go out there and tell th'Band to go on right now! Go ahead! Go out there an' tell 'em!"*

I went up to Robbie Robertson.

"Bob wants you to start playing right now whether the sound system works or not." I told him.

Robbie looked at me like I must be crazy.

"Bob's having a shitfit," I explained. *"He says it's gettin' too late for him. He says you've got to start playin' now, no matter if the sound system works or not!"*

Robbie laughed at me. Nothing was as important to Robbie as The Band's sound. It would be years later, after hearing the capacity for betrayal in the accusations hurled at each other by Robbie and Levon, that the idea would enter my head that someone for some reason might have been trying to deliberately sabotage Bob's performance!

I went after Taplin but Jon got mean and elbowed me away. *"Not now!"* he muttered over his shoulder. *"Not now!"* *"But Bob's back there raising hell!"* I shrieked. *"The Band's not gonna play until the sound system's right!"* Jon said flatly.

Back in his dressing room, I told Bob that The Band refused to get started until Jon had the system fixed. This defiance threw Bob into another fury.

"You go right back out there and you get them to start right now" he ordered. *"You do it! Tell them I said that they should start right now or I'm not gonna go on at all!"*

On stage, the MC was still cursing at the crowd as he tried to sort out who belonged in the press enclosure and who didn't. The MC was Rikki Farr, son of 1930s British Heavyweight Boxing Champion Tommy Farr. I called Rikki aside.

"Look," I said, *"Bob's backstage having a shitfit because The Band is so late getting started and he still has to go on after The Band. It's getting too late for him. If things get any worse, he might refuse to do the show…He's gotta get started soon."*

"Well, wot d'ya wan' me t'do?" Rikki asked.

"Go tell Robbie Robertson that The Band's got to get started," I said. *"Insist on it!"*

Rikki went over and huddled with Robbie and then wandered away. I had to chase after Rikki to corner him.

"Well, what did he say?" I asked.

"'E says they won't start playin' till the road manager tells 'em to!"

"Look," I said. *"You were just talking on the mike to the crowd and they heard you,*

didn't they? You had amplification. The sound system works well enough.

I watched Rikki approach Taplin. He returned in a moment.

"'E says 'e can't le' th'Band play until th'sound's fixed."

I was running out of ideas. Suddenly, the words blurted out of my mouth.

"I know how you can make them go on stage and get them started!" I told Rikki. *"Just get up there and introduce them. Just get up there and announce, 'Ladies and gentlemen, The Band!' That'll force them to get on stage and start playing."*

"Naaww!" Rikki said, shaking his head and walking away. *"Naaww, that'll never work. I can't do tha'!"*

Since the Isle of Wight Festival, Jonathan Taplin has made quite a name for himself. By 1972, he was not only working for The Band but he was also working for Bob as well. George Harrison awarded him the production credit for the Concert for Bangladesh, and by 1973 he had teamed up with director Martin Scorsese and actor Robert De Niro to become the producer of *Mean Streets*, which won awards at both the Cannes and New York Film Festivals. Taplin also was later honoured at Cannes as the producer of *The Last Waltz* and *Carny*. As far as I'm concerned, however, Jonathan Taplin's performance as The Band's road manager at the Isle of Wight Festival represented his finest hour.

It was well past ten before Jon got the sound system fixed and The Band went on stage. To me, that made Jonathan Taplin one of the unsung heroes of his time. He held his position, accomplished his mission, refusing to retreat while under heavy fire. The Isle of Wight is where I learned that once Jonathan Taplin is faced with a problem, he won't let anyone stop him from getting that problem solved. One thing I never did learn, though, is exactly what was wrong with the sound system!

Published in issue #96. May 2001

Apathy For The Devil
Jacques Levy, Desire, Joseph Conrad and 'Black Diamond Bay'
by Derek Barker

Introduction

As the overly long subtitle suggests the following piece looks at Jacques Levy's collaboration with Bob Dylan on his 1975 album *"Desire."* The main object of this piece, however, is to delve into the complex and *much* neglected classic Dylan/Levy song *'Black Diamond Bay.'* En route we will also take a peek into the life and work of Joseph Conrad, before ending with an exclusive ISIS interview with Jacques Levy.

Jacques Levy

Born in New York City in 1937, Jacques Levy was responsible not only for co-writing the *"Desire"* album with Dylan, but also for directing what is regarded by many as Dylan's finest tour, the Rolling Thunder Revue.

Levy was educated at Michigan State University where he trained as a clinical psychologist, gaining a PhD in psychology. After leaving University he went to work at the Meninger Foundation in Topeka, Kansas, where as a hobby he tried his hand at directing in local community theatre. Then in 1965 Jacques made a dramatic career change, giving up his job in psychology at Meninger to return to New York in the hope of pursuing a new career as a stage director.

Levy's aspirations soon came to fruition and for the past 30-years he has been a professional theatre director in New York City where he is currently Head of Theatre Program at Colgate University. His credits include the Broadway production of *Doonesbury, the Musical,* and *Oh! Calcutta!* for which he commissioned, amongst others, John Lennon, Samuel Beckett and Sam Shepard as writers.

His Off-Broadway productions include *Scuba Duba, Red Cross,* and *Geography of a Horse Dreamer,* the latter two being written by award-winning playwright Sam Shepard.

Levy also wrote the lyrics for *Fame – the Musical,* a highly successful production that has played the major cities of Europe, including a year in London.

Levy, who is also a noted lyricist, has worked with Roger McGuinn and The Byrds and his lyrics have been recorded by amongst others, Joe Cocker, Carly Simon and Jerry Lee Lewis. His collaboration with McGuinn would eventually lead to his meeting Bob Dylan.

"Desire"

Roger McGuinn: *"I had told Bob how much fun it was to write with Jacques, how constructive he was as a psychologist. He puts me in line and keeps my concentration on one subject until I get it right...it was not surprising to me that they collaborated. I thought it was good chemistry on both parts. I knew it was going to be a good combination."*

It was the spring of 1974 and Dylan had recently finished his *comeback* tour with the Band. He had been staying with friends in Marin County, near San Francisco, but arrived in New York, on April 24 to discuss the forthcoming album of the tour. While in New York, he ran into Jacques Levy in the Village.

Levy – *"I was just walking out of the house right here on Bleecker Street and he (Dylan) was coming this way. I said 'Hey, hi!' and he didn't know who I was, but he was familiar with my work with Roger. We started talking and spent the evening together."*[1]

Although the two had several chance meetings over the next year, it was July 1975 before they were again able to talk at any length.

"I bumped into him again on Bleecker Street, and again we came up here – Levy's loft in La Guardia Place *– He had no specific plans at the time to do anything, and he said something like, 'I really like the stuff you do with Roger. How about if you and I do something together?' Which was slightly strange, right? Because he knew I did lyrics and I knew he did lyrics. But I said, 'Sure, let's give it a shot'."*[1]

The first song that they worked on together was *'Isis.'*

"We were just having a great time laughing and coming up with one verse after another and we kept on going until five in the morning and we finished the song. And both of us thought it was great. We were just knocked out by it."[1]

The next song to be completed was *'Joey.'*

Dylan: *"I was with Jacques. I was leaving town and Jacques says he was going up to some place to have supper and I was invited to come up if I felt like it and I was hungry. So I went with him and it was up to Marty and Jerry Orbach's place, and as soon as I walked in the door Marty was talking about Joey. She was a good friend of Joey's. They were real tight. I just listened for a few hours. At the time, I wasn't involved in anything that he was involved in, but he left a certain impression on me. I never considered him a gangster. I always thought of him as some kind of hero in some kind of way. An underdog fighting against the elements. He retained a certain amount of his freedom and he went out the way he had to. But she laid all these facts out and it was like listening to a story about Billy the Kid. So we went ahead and wrote that up one night."*[1]

Joey Gallo was gunned down on April 7, 1972, as he celebrated his forty-third birthday at Umberto's Clam House in Little Italy, NYC. *"Bob became very interested in it all. We were telling stories about Joey and when we left their house –* Marty and Jerry Orbach *– we came back here and started to work on the song."*[1]

Levy: *"What happened with 'Durango' was that he had a kind of Mexican melody and we were talking about Durango but the first thing that came was an image I had from a postcard that was once sent to me by Jack Gelber, the playwright. He sent me a postcard with a picture of a Mexican hacienda or something, some Mexican shack not a hacienda, a shack with a bunch of chilli peppers on the roof in the sun. So the first line was 'Hot chilli peppers in the sun,' and I remember saying, 'No – blistering sun,' so we got the first line."*

"Bob said 'Wow! That's terrific. What a great opening line!" Bob had a very keen sense of opening lines and how they meant so much. The first thing that hits him is very, very important."[2]

"Bob had been fooling with 'Sara' for a long time. He'd got the choruses down but the verses were actually written out at East Hampton. He and Sara had stayed there...out there are the dunes and the beach and all that stuff mentioned in the song. He would try things out on me, but it was a very personal song for him to write."[1]

Joseph Conrad

Like many writers in English, Joseph Conrad was not born in Britain. He was born Józef Teodor Konrad Nalecz Korzeniowski, in Berdichev, Poland, on December 3, 1857, one year after the defeat of Russia in the Crimean War, a defeat that once again raised hopes of Polish independence.

His father, a writer/poet and Polish revolutionary patriot, was arrested by the Russian authorities and imprisoned for conspiracy as a political activist in 1862. The family was exiled to Vologda in northern Russia where on April 18, 1865 Conrad's mother Evelina died of tuberculosis, aged 32.

Due to ill health in December 1867, Conrad's father Apollo was released from exile and the two were allowed to return to Poland, where they lived in Cracow until May 23, 1869, when Apollo, too, died of tuberculosis. His funeral turned into a patriotic demonstration with several thousand people in attendance.

Conrad became the ward of his maternal uncle, a wealthy and influential landowner. Wishing to escape the liability of serving in the Russian army he travelled to Marseilles, France, where he learned French and joined the French Merchant Marine travelling to Martinique and the West Indies.

In April 1878 he signed on as an ordinary seaman on an English steamship and two months later he arrived in Lowestoft, stepping onto English soil for the first time. He became a British subject on August 19, 1886 and eventually left the British Merchant Service to devote his time to writing. For his first published work, *Almayer's Folly,* 1895, he adopted the name Conrad.

Widely respected during his lifetime as a serious novelist, today Conrad is generally regarded as one of the greatest writers of fiction in English – his third language. It was probably the sheer quality of Conrad's writing, combined with the deep symbolism that is present in most of his work, which attracted Dylan to Conrad. We are of course informed of Conrad's influence on Dylan through the liner notes of *"Desire."* In those notes Allen Ginsberg says of *'Black Diamond Bay'* –

"...A short novel in verse, old fashioned Dylan surrealist mind-jump inventions line by line, except D. says he's reading Joseph Conrad storyteller."

Unfortunately, Ginsberg fails to tell us on which of the storyteller's two dozen novels *'Black Diamond Bay'* was based.

Joseph Conrad wrote the last word of the novel in question on May 29, 1914, that word was the novel's title, *Victory.*

Despite being considered by many as his last great work, *Victory* is also Conrad's most misunderstood and controversial novel. The tale is a deliberate compromise between his desire to write openly about homosexuality and his need to suppress the theme. This restriction only serves to exaggerate Conrad's characteristic tendency toward ambiguity and abstract symbolism.

Set in the same year that the novel was finished, 1914, *Victory* spins a complex tale of a pair of lovers, Heyst and Lena. In an attempt to isolate himself from all human entanglements, the story's main character Axel Heyst hides himself away on the remote island of Samburan on the north coast of Java in the Dutch East Indies.

Heyst battles with his internal conflict between detachment and human involvement and becomes entangled with an itinerant prostitute, Lena, whom he rescues and brings back to his island. Their idyllic world, however, begins to crumble with the arrival on the island of an evil trio that includes none other than the enigma that is the misogynistic homosexual Mr Jones. As in Dylan's song *'Ballad Of a Thin Man'* the antagonist's first name is never revealed.

In my conversation with Levy, Jacques rebuffs my suggestion that *'Black Diamond Bay'* is based on Conrad's novel, saying that little more than the title comes from Conrad, and that Dylan gave *"a tip of the cap"* to the novelist by including a photograph of Conrad on the *"Desire"* album sleeve.

Whilst it is clear from reading the book and from my lengthy conversation with Jacques that *'Black Diamond Bay'* and *Victory* are by no means parallel stories, a closer inspection of the two works would seem to reveal more than just *"a tip of the cap."*

Both tales are set on remote islands, both feature hotels with *"gambling rooms,"* both landscapes are dominated by volcanoes – in *'Black Diamond Bay'* the volcano erupts, while in Conrad's novel it constantly threatens to do so – both works feature utterly mysterious characters, and both have opaque homosexual overtones – *"The soldier and the tiny man were crouched in the corner / Thinking of forbidden love."* … *"The tiny man bit the soldier's ear / As the floor caved in and the boiler in the basement blew."* – *'Black Diamond Bay'*.

Moreover, as Jacques freely admits, the title of the Dylan/Levy song is a direct lift from Conrad's *Victory* –

"There is as every schoolboy knows in this scientific age, a very close chemical relation between coal and diamonds. It is the reason, I believe, why some people allude to coal as 'black diamonds',"[3].

A little further into Conrad's novel –

"...above the dense mass of vegetation that Samburan presents to view, he – Davidson *– saw the head of the flagstaff without a flag. Then, while steaming across the slight indentation which for a time was known officially as Black Diamond Bay, he made out with his glass the white figure on the coaling-wharf. It could be no one but Heyst."*[3]

Shortly after the composition of *'Black Diamond Bay'* and while together on the *Rolling Thunder Revue* tour, Dylan asked playwright Sam Shepard the question: *"Have you ever read Conrad?"* When Shepard answered, *"No,"* Dylan replied, *"You should read Conrad."*[4]

1 John Bauldie, The Telegraph #11, April 1983.
2 Larry Sloman, *On The Road With Bob Dylan* Bantom, 1978
3 Joseph Conrad, *Victory* published 1918.
4 Sam Shepard *Rolling Thunder Logbook*, Penguin 1978.

The Jacques Levy Interview
Derek Barker

JL: Hi, Derek. Firstly, let me say that's a great name for a magazine. (laughs).
DB: Thank you (laughs). You have said in the past that the song *'Isis'* has absolutely

nothing to do with the Egyptian goddess, Isis.

JL: No, no, no. It has nothing to do with that at all. If you can picture, we are sitting at a piano together and we are writing these verses in an old Western ballad kind of style. You know the kind of thing that he spent a couple of years doing with the Band in the Basement. Well, this is a similar kind of thing, and just as the Band wrote *'pulled in to Nazareth,'* you know, well, *'Isis'* has about as much to do with Egypt as Fanny has to do with Nazareth (laughs). The only thing it has to do with the Egyptian goddess is that we threw in the pyramids, which were a substitute for the hills of Wyoming.

When we first met, Bob had a few very basic partly-worked tunes. I guess the only reason that 'Isis' was chosen as the song to work together on was that we were at my loft apartment and Bob didn't have a guitar with him. I didn't have a guitar there either, but I had a piano, and 'Isis' was the one song that he had started to write on the piano.

Bob already had some ideas that he brought to me. Some of them were just little phrases, some were a little more developed musically and some had a certain feeling to them. I mean *'Isis'* was almost a funeral dirge when we first worked on it. It was so slow and rather stately and sad, it would have taken a whole side of an album!

That was the first song we wrote. We knew that song was important and that it really worked. We were very happy with it but we had no idea that it would have the sort of power that it wound up having on the Rolling Thunder Revue. When that song was sung on the Rolling Thunder Revue and that rock band played behind it, it had a fantastic impact and the song took on a whole new character.

There was a sense, and I'm sure that I had this sense at the time, that I'm writing with probably the best lyricist around, maybe ever. So the sense I had was that if this song doesn't come out well, then probably we wouldn't write together anymore. Not that we intended to do an album: there was only the intention to do one song and to see how it went. It was very informal. I guess we hoped that it may lead to working on some other songs but there was absolutely no intention to do an album.

We had a great time coming up with ideas though, we were laughing a lot and we were enjoying coming up with these rhymes like *"contagious"* and *"outrageous."* *'Isis'* was slightly different at that time; we had a chorus at the end that was different from the final version. Nevertheless, from this first song it was obvious that he loved the kind of narrative that we were doing together.

If you want to know what *'Isis'* is all about you only have to think about it and it's all there really. It is simply about two guys who go on an adventure together without knowing what they may find. I don't want to be too metaphoric here but I think you're getting the picture. They dig and dig and dig and they find something and they come back with it. On the other hand, maybe they find nothing. That is exactly what Bob and I were doing, searching. The song is a kind of allegory of what was going on at the time. What was happening in the song was exactly what was happening with us and it was really exciting.

Anyway, when we had finished our journey together, I typed up all the lyrics that we had written and that night we went down to a bar, The Other End. They were just about closing and Bob said to somebody sitting at the bar, *"Would you like to hear this new song?"* I was on the outside of this scene just sort of watching, so I got such a kick out of this. I mean, can you imagine Bob Dylan coming up to you in a bar a saying, *"Would you like to hear this new song?"* (laughs). We may have known one or two of these people – we both used the bar – but when he read the words to the song everyone just went; *"Oh wow!"* But you know, what else would they say? *"Err, I don't know about that, I like 'You Ain't Going Nowhere' better."* (laughs). Anyway, the reaction was good, so then it was just a question of going on and doing more.

The next thing we did was *'Hurricane.'* It was Bob's idea to write a song about

Hurricane Carter, but I said that I didn't want to write a song like *'George Jackson.' "Oh Lord they cut George Jackson down,"* or whatever. That song made you feel sad, but I wanted to say more than that. I wanted to try to take the part of an attorney almost, and tell the story to the jury. Of course that needed a lot of detail and so we had to do some research, so we couldn't finish that song and we went on to another one; I think actually the next song may have been *'Black Diamond Bay.'*

DB: Right, I've read a number of interviews that you gave in the late 70s where you talk about *'Isis,' 'Romance In Durango,' 'Hurricane,' 'Joey'* and even *'Sara,'* but there is absolutely no mention of what is possibly my favourite song on that album, *'Black Diamond Bay.'*

JL: I'm glad you feel that way, Derek, because *'Black Diamond Bay'* is certainly my favourite song on the album. In fact, it's possibly my favourite song on any album!

I don't exactly know the reasons why people haven't enquired about it, but I think that it may have something to do with the fact that it's one of the songs that Bob never does sing live. Also, it's a bit complicated, you know. (laughs)

DB: Of course, but most of the songs on that album are complicated, except for maybe *'Mozambique,'* which is lightweight by comparison to the rest of the album...

JL: As far as *'Black Diamond Bay'* is concerned, the title is from Conrad, but nothing much else is. I mean you can put your imagination into a South Sea Island, but frankly, I've never been to the South Sea Islands. What was in my mind were a number of the Caribbean Islands that I have been to, which are very similar. That sort of Haitian, or Martinique kind of seem-decadent Caribbean life, with rather mysterious characters inhabiting a Graham Greene novel: *'The Comedians'* kind of hotel. As a matter of fact *'Black Diamond Bay' is* set in that hotel.

DB: 'Black Diamond Bay' and Conrad's *Victory* are set in hotels and both are on islands with volcanoes.

JL: Yes, oh indeed, indeed. I mean there is that connection to that world for sure. Both Bob and I had read Conrad...but the narrative in the song is strictly original fiction, based on nothing else.

The song started with a kind of an off-hand comment. We were talking about the state of music at the time, about who was doing what, and so on and so forth. I made some kinda joke that instead of sympathy for the Devil, people had apathy for the Devil. The problem was not so much that people were evil, but that they were apathetic. All this was happening around them and they paid almost no attention to it. Although it has nothing to do with the Rolling Stones song, I mean, I wouldn't say that it was a response to it, but just another way of looking at things.

When the sting finally comes at the end of the song, when the listener realises that the whole thing is being seen through the eyes of someone watching TV in LA, someone who simply couldn't care less, the attitude of the guy is very cool; he hears something about a Panama hat and a pair of old Greek shoes, but he doesn't pay much attention to it. The way so many of us hear something on the television about a disaster or something and it's just another one of those things. *'I guess I'll go get another beer and carry on with my own life.'* It's interesting to me, and I guess it will be to your readers that the song started from that idea, the idea of pure apathy. I don't think that fact as ever been in print before.

There is also, of course, the very complicated rhyme scheme that runs through the song. One of the very nice things about working with Bob is that he loves rhyme, he loves to play with it and he loves the complications of it.

DB: Roger McGuinn has said that Dylan had never seen a rhyming dictionary until he worked with you in 1975. Is that correct or just another piece of Dylan fiction?

JL: No, no, I think that is correct. I'm sure that is true. He had never worked with one.

I work with a rhyming dictionary once in a while but sometimes it gets you into trouble. I mean you'll find some interesting rhymes but the content doesn't work with it, and if you try to squeeze them in it gets difficult. More importantly, though, you can't find the rhyme scheme thing in there and Bob was very interested in that. Most of his songs contain solid rhymes, but he doesn't come up with things like 'veranda' and 'and-a,' you know, in the first line. In a way it's a little old fashioned; it comes from Larry Hart and Ira Gershwin. The kind of song-writing where you will try to get a double syllable rhyme, where you'll rhyme into the next line, that kind of thing. He got a big kick out of that stuff, he really enjoyed it, and when that would come up he would not only enjoy the fact of it but also singing it. He got a great kick out of bending those things around. You see a lot of that in the other songs too; you see it in 'Hurricane.' The idea of following a scheme that you set up in one verse – I mean it's obvious if it's a simple AB, AB kind of thing, but if you set up a rather complicated scheme – I've forgotten now exactly what the scheme is for 'Black Diamond Bay.' It's AA,BB,CED, you know, something like that – then each one of the verses ends with three words rhyming with bay.

To set up a limit like that can be a worry – I don't know exactly what the aesthetic reasons for that are. I mean the same as a sonnet is fourteen lines, you know. I mean it doesn't have to, it could be fifteen, eighteen, but it is fourteen. When you set up that limit, and you have a certain kind of rhyme scheme in it, it becomes interesting to solve that puzzle. That's rather fascinating to me, and I think that Bob found it fascinating too: that you could do that and still connect to the content of the song.

That's true of a number of songs on that album. They have strong narratives, and you really feel when you listen to them that you want to know what happens next. At least that's what I was trying for, and I hope it succeeds.

Every once in a while Bob has tried to do that, like with '...Jack of Hearts,' but it's not easy for him to stick with a narrative. He's much stronger with a set of images, a series of images that are sometimes quite abstract, but little by little open up the idea that you're after. There may be many narratives in it for one or two verses, but the whole thing usually is not part of one long narrative. It is not his style, but it is a style that he likes. I guess it's a prose style, but it's also the style of movies and theatre. To go back, for example, to the opening of 'Hurricane,' it reads like stage directions: "Enter Patty Valentine," and "Pistol shots ring out." Using that present tense is the way in which you write stage directions.

DB: I believe that you started 'Black Diamond Bay' in New York and finished writing it in East Hampton. I assume that means it was a lengthy song to write?

JL: It was indeed. I think we wrote two of the verses in New York and the rest of it out there in the Hamptons. When we started out in New York we would work half the night and then get up at three in the afternoon; it was rough. Although what was coming out was good, it soon became clear that it was impossible to carry on the way we were. I suggested to Bob that if we were going to take it really seriously we should get out of town. He had this place out at East Hampton, so we got away. The style wasn't any different out there; we just kept on writing, but it was more relaxed and more conducive to work.

Believe it or not 'Black Diamond Bay' started with the phrase "from the mountain high above." I distinctly remember that. The phrase came from Bob saying that he had this little – I don't even know exactly what to call it – this little piece of music that he had. I think he picked it up in Spain. He'd recently been in Spain and had gotten this Spanish or Latin type influence; it's almost flamenco. It repeats in the song over and over, but it's not really what you would call a musical phrase, but it is, you know. It's a rhythmic phrase. It's almost a riff, but not quite. Anyway, Bob played that to me on guitar, and honestly, the words just popped into my head to fit that phrase, and those words were "from the mountain high *above."* Now I don't exactly know why those words popped into my head, I can't explain that, but they led me to start thinking about that island view. I had been in Haiti and I had been in the Dominican Republic and places like that where you get that feeling... So, there was this Latin feel mixed with this sort of gypsy violin that also had some Spanish influence with Scarlet Rivera. I mean it obviously wasn't written with that violin in mind, but when we went into the studio and it was played, it went further in that direction.

When we started to write the song there was this image of a mysterious woman on a veranda, somewhere with a Panama hat and a passport. Then there was that kind of slightly seedy hotel with a gambling room. There were a number of people whose background you really don't know, but you know that they are there for some quote, *important reason.* After that, the thing began to kind of open itself up to us. I remember the Greek from the second floor – that's the second verse, right – I think I wrote that line in The Other End bar. Bob and I went there a few times after we had finished up for the night. Originally, that character was a colonel. I was probably thinking about those Greek colonels that were taking over Greece at that time. Then I had this other thought to call him *'The Greek.'* You know if you're somewhere, a hotel for instance, and you don't really know the people and you are referring to somebody you might say – *'The Englishman on the second floor'*. Well, that was the sense of it that I wanted to try to get. You didn't really know much about him; the same as somebody else was thinking that somebody was the Soviet Ambassador. It was that sense of not really knowing who the other people around you are and yet you're sharing a kind of world with them.

There's not a sense of desperation, except that there is. One person is hanging himself, the volcano is erupting, and there's a woman who thinks that something terrible is going to happen to her. Then there's the guy who goes to the gambling room and breaks the bank, but the dealer knows that his time is over. So, I mean, there is this imminent danger going on everywhere you could imagine. When we started to work on the song the sense that I was feeling was like in the movies where they have all those jungle birds screeching loudly and you just know that there is some imminent danger. Well, there was something of that, just that movieish feel about the whole thing.

After those first couple of verses we sorta knew what we had; the scene was kind of set. One of the things about Bob's songs is that they don't take on the traditional pop song with two verses and then a bridge and then a verse. That's not the way the songs usually go. *'Mozambique'* is like that, but normally they're not. They are more based on the idea of an old ballad where the verse keeps repeating in the same form over and over for as many verses as you need it to go. Once we had a pattern established then I was able to just keep writing to that pattern.

I did almost all of that on *'Romance In Durango.'* Once we got the first thing down then I could just write the rest of that story. I mean, that's just a kind of old western movie, with a little bit of politics thrown in. Poor guy running away and he doesn't have any bread and all that. So that one tells a story, but I think that it's a little more linear than this one. *'Black Diamond Bay'* moves ahead in the story but it does so by painting a series of scenes as opposed to just telling the story of an individual. You know for a verse you don't hear about this woman and then she comes back again. You know that the Greek is found hanging from the chandelier, but you don't really know why. The desk clerk, well, he's straight out of a Sidney Greenstreet movie, and that was the sense of it, that was kinda what I was looking for. The men are dressed in these white suits, not beautiful pressed white suits, these are crumpled white suits, and it wouldn't be surprising to see Greenstreet or Peter Lorre come around the corner at any moment. That's the sense of the place for me. That is what I was trying to achieve. The hotel is probably run by Humphrey

Bogart: it is that kind of exotic setting. Once we'd got the second verse finished, I was intent on working on the song. So I would get another verse, I would feed it to Bob, and he would sing it to see if it set right with him. If he had an idea that he wanted to get in there then he would say: *"Well, how about this?"* In fact, there were a couple of things that we never did manage to get in. I remember that he wanted to get the sound of a sax in there, not playing, but he wanted to get the feel of a lonely saxophone playing. It would have worked, but it just never quite got into the mix; it's not really present. Sometimes I would give him words to sing that would have been tongue twisters for anyone else. To sing *"The boiler in the basement blew"* would have been a problem for most people.

Bob may not know the word *alliteration*, but that doesn't matter, he understands the concept very well, and when he hears a line like that he sings it with great gusto; he sorta leans into it. It's a great thrill for someone like me to write a line like that and then to hear somebody sing it like that. There are also lines like in *'Hurricane'* like *'triple muurderr.'* You can really feel that, you can feel him shifting down into second and going round that curve.

The thing with *'Black Diamond Bay'* was to keep peopling it with these characters, all of whom without knowing it at the time, were facing their doom. None of them knew that, like the rest of us (laughs), and just went about their business. Meanwhile, the volcano is waiting to erupt just around the corner. You get the signs of it, you feel the rain coming, the clouds are building up, but you don't quite believe that it's going to happen. That's the sense of it from *inside* the place, which is I'm afraid very much like life.

Then you take it and you look at it from the *outside*, which is when the shift in the song occurs. That final verse was intended right from the beginning, that was the whole apathy thing. Now I must confess that I didn't know exactly how to get there from the beginning, but I had to get that apathy.

The problem was that the more we got in to the song and the more juicy the characters and their situation became, the less sense of detachment the listener felt. Therefore I had to try and get that feeling back. To make the song work you have got to turn the corner and get into another place and look at it from another view altogether.

The question is how to do that. I hate those things where suddenly you wake up and the whole thing is just a dream. I certainly didn't want that; so, I had to try to get the picture of whoever this guy is sitting in L.A. scratching himself, watching the TV, and saying to himself, *"Oh no, it's another one of those hard luck stories. Let's go get another beer and wait for the sporting news."* (laughs) That same detachedness can also be found in *'Isis'* where you search and search and search, and you finally wind up with nothing. I think that in the end we got the twist just about right with *'Black Diamond Bay.'*

DB: As far as *'Black Diamond Bay'* is concerned, did you write most of the lyrics?

JL: Well, I guess so, yeah…I have to say that we worked together very well. We got to the point where we could just say to each other, *"I don't like this,"* or *"try this,"* or *"let's come at this from a different way,"* be it lyrical or musical. From time to time I would come up with a musical line and Bob would come up with a lyric idea, and after a while you don't exactly know who came up with what, and that's the way it should be.

People are always asking *'which came first, the music or the lyrics?'* Well, sometimes one and sometimes the other. For instance in *'…Durango'* we had established the beginning of the song, then I stayed up almost all night and I wrote the rest of the verses. The next morning we got together and I gave it to Bob. He tried to sing it, and he made this very funny comment about *'I can't leave you for a minute.'* He just wasn't used to that, but then he came up with some changes for that song, and so on.

In fact there are a couple of lines in the final version of *'…Durango'* that he either sang wrong, or didn't sing at all, and they just punched them out! There's a couple of slight pauses in there.

DB: It's fascinating to me that the greatest lyric writer of our time, a man that has almost always written alone, should choose to make an album where somebody else not only collaborates with the lyric writing, but it would seem on some tracks actually wrote the greater part of those lyrics!

JL: I have to tell you something, Derek; I have told this story before, but when we first talked about working together I said the very things to him. I said: *'but I write lyrics!'* He got a little insulted, it was kind of a funny moment; it was very charming actually. He said: *'Why? What's that matter, don't you like my music?'* or something like that. After a short while we both sorta laughed at it but it was a kind of interesting moment. I think one of the things that happened because so much of the responsibility for the lyrics fell on me, is that it freed him to concentrate more on the music. I mean, I think that album has some of the best music that he's ever written, and it also has some of the best performances he has ever done. I think that he is singing in an open way and he's really extending himself.

DB: Absolutely. Also I think that what followed were some of the best live performances that he has ever given.

JL: I know that, and as a matter of fact, I have talked with him about that. There are all these tapes and film footage from that tour and we really should have put out a proper tour album. He didn't want to do it, though. He just didn't want to do it because at the time he was so interested in *Renaldo and Clara.*

DB: When was it decided that you would record these songs for an album?

JL: At some point out in East Hampton when we had about eight or ten songs finished, Bob got on the 'phone and called CBS and said; *"I'm in town, we've got enough songs for an album, let's schedule a date."* I believe that he owed them an album, but I don't think there was any pressure from them to deliver. Certainly at the time we got together it was not to write an album of songs.

At this time, we also began to talk about a tour, the Rolling Thunder Revue. Again, there were no plans to do a tour to promote the album or anything. The whole thing was really very open ended. I must say to you, and this is a mater of fact, when Bob went into the recording studio to make that record he was not all that familiar with some of those songs.

This was a new experience for Bob: he was actually using lyric sheets to sing the songs. Although we had worked on them together in the Hamptons and he pretty much had them down, when he got into the studio he still had to have notations of chords, and he had to look at the lyric sheet for most of the songs. Now, this was a very new experience for Bob. Normally when he went into the studio the songs were his own, and naturally he knew what he was doing. So, there were some wonderful moments in the studio because he was sitting there reading the songs off of lyric sheets. Then there was Emmylou Harris, who had never heard the songs before, and there was no rehearsal, they would just start and Bob didn't tell her when to come in or when not to come in. It all comes out sounding very smooth, but there's a certain spontaneity to it that's very special, and I think that's part of what works on that album.

1 Graham Greene *The Comedians* – 1966, depicts Papa Doc Duvalier's repressive rule in Haiti.

Interview with Jacques Levy, December 12, 1999, by Derek Barker.

Published in issue #90. May 2001.

1976 – Houston Texas, USA © Watt M. Casey

The Story of the Hurricane
by Derek Barker

Since the release of the Norman Jewison directed *Universal Pictures* film *The Hurricane*, the extremely complex and controversial story of the ex-middleweight boxer Rubin Carter has again come to the fore.

Hurricane hysteria reached its peak in 1976, nine years after Carter and his alleged accomplice John Artis had been sentenced to three life terms. Bob Dylan's highly acclaimed album *"Desire"* featured an eight-and-a-half minute track that graphically portrayed Carter's plight. The song *'Hurricane'* was also released as a single complete with bleeped-out expletive for radio play. There was support for Carter from many celebrities and sportspeople including world heavyweight boxing champion Muhammad Ali. A benefit concert and TV documentary soon followed. It seemed that the whole world, excluding the Passaic County justice system, was convinced of Carter's innocence. Over the years, however, and more so since the release of the film, there has been increasing speculation as to Carter's guilt.

"Pistol Shots Ring Out In a Barroom Night"

At around 2:30 am on June 17, 1966, bartender, James Oliver, 51, was standing behind the servery of the Lafayette Bar and Grill on East Eighteenth Street, a bleak watering hole on the ground floor of a shabby three-story apartment building in Paterson, New Jersey. Oliver was counting the day's takings while two regulars, William Marins, 43 and Fred *"Bob"* Nauyaks, 61, who had been shooting pool for beers, sat two stools apart at the counter. At the shorter end of the L-shaped bar, in the corner by the front window, sat 51 year old Hazel Tanis. She had just arrived from the banqueting hall of the country club where she worked as a waitress.

Suddenly, and without warning, two black men – one with a shotgun, the other a handgun – entered the bar through the side door and immediately opened fire. James Oliver threw an empty beer bottle at the two assailants and tried to run. His bravado was repaid by a shotgun blast to the spine that killed him instantly.

The second assailant's chosen target was Fred Nauyaks who was duly dispatched with a .32 calibre bullet to the brain stem. Nauyaks was found hung over the bar in a pool of blood; beside him were a full beer and enough money to pay for another. A cigarette was still burning between his fingers when the police arrived.

Fellow pool player, William Marins, was also shot in the head; the bullet entered his left temple and exited just above his right eye, taking with it the optic nerve. By an amazingly fluke, Marins survived the shooting but has since died from unrelated causes.

The two men then turned their attentions to Hazel Tanis. Tanis screamed as the man with the handgun moved towards her. Her screams were soon silenced when the man discharged four rounds into her body at close range. The second assailant fired the shotgun – also at close range. Tanis was hit in the arm, left breast and lung, throat, stomach, lower abdomen and groin, yet somehow managed to crawl toward the barroom door and survived in hospital for a month after the shooting. At one stage Tanis was taken off the critical list but eventually died from a blood clot on her damaged lung.

"Enter Patty Valentine"

Patricia Graham – Valentine – who lived above the bar had been awakened by the shots. She looked down from her bedroom window in time to see two black men jump into a white car, which was parked a short distance from the bar. The car had out-of-state plates that were dark blue with yellow or gold letters. Valentine also noted that the car had distinctive *"butterfly"* shaped taillights. She then put on a raincoat over her pyjamas and ran downstairs to find her good friend, Hazel Tanis, lying on the floor in a pool of blood.

Tanis gradually opened her eyes and said: *"My God, Patty, I've been shot."* Having seen the devastation that surrounded her, Valentine ran back upstairs to call the police and Tanis's boyfriend. She then threw some clothes on and ran back down to the bar.

Jim Lawless was first police officer on the scene: *"The first thing I saw was Hazel. I knew her...Her stomach was hanging out – She asked me to shoot her..."*

Later that night Lawless took down Patty Valentine's written statement, after she'd been back up to her apartment to collect her teeth.

Valentine had already given verbal details of her sighting to the police and at 2:34 a.m. a police bulletin went out for a white car with two black occupants. A patrol car near the bar spotted a speeding white car but lost it. Then, after circling around, Sgt. Theodore Capter pulled over a white car at 2:40 a.m. The occupants of the car were Rubin *"Hurricane"* Carter, 29, John Artis 19 and a third man. Accounts differ as to the identity of the third man; much later, Carter said the man was John *"Bucks"* Rovster. Sgt. Capter knew Carter, a professional boxer, and so he let the three go on their way.

Carter would later tell police that he didn't know John Artis and that he was simply giving him a lift home. However, it was Artis who was driving the car with Carter lying in the back. Depending on your point of view, Carter was either hiding his famous face from the local police or, as Carter said, *"just taking a rest."* Shortly after being stopped by Sgt. Capter, Rovster got out of the car and Carter moved from the back to the front passenger seat.

"A Rap For The Cops"

Also at the murder scene was Alfred Bello, a career criminal and chronic liar, whose testimony would often change over the ensuing years. Bello and his accomplice, Arthur Dexter Bradley, had been trying to break into the factory-warehouse of a nearby sheet metal company. It seems that Bello then took advantage of the mayhem at the bar by relieving the cash register of $62.00, which he quickly took to his accomplice. He says he then returned to the scene because he was afraid he might be implicated in the shootings if he ran.

Unaware that Valentine had already made a call to the police, Bello also called the cops. When the police arrived he told them that he saw two fleeing black men carrying guns get into a white car with triangular taillights and out-of-state plates. Neither Valentine nor Bello got any part of the license plate number.

After taking statements from Valentine and Bello, police patrol vehicles were alerted that the suspect white car had *"triangular taillights"* and *"out-of-state plates."* Carter's white *rental* car, which had been stopped earlier, had both of these features, so the police raced back to look for Carter.

"They Haul Rubin In"

When the police caught up with the vehicle for a second time, they found only Carter and Artis in the car. The two men were requested to drive to the Lafayette Bar and Grill, where both Valentine and Bello identified Carter's 1966 white Dodge Polara as being *"similar"* to the getaway car. However, no one at the scene could identify Carter or Artis as the killers. Bello would not do that until October, saying he delayed because he was afraid for his safety, and because he hoped to slip away quietly to avoid being questioned about his own criminal activities.

A police search of the car turned up one live .32 calibre bullet and one live 12-gauge shotgun shell, but no weapons. Carter and Artis were taken to the hospital where a wounded and somewhat shocked Willie Marins failed to identify them. Carter and Artis were then questioned at the police station, given lie detector tests and released. After this, agreement on what happened rapidly breaks down. One of the few facts on which most are agreed, however, is that with the convictions of Carter and Artis came one of the lengthiest and bitterest legal disputes in New Jersey's history.

In the ensuing battle, almost every claim had a counterclaim. For instance, Carter's opponents say that Willie Marins was too scared to identify the boxer, and that in private he told his brother it *was* Carter and Artis who did the shooting. Carter says that he passed a lie detector test, while his opponents are adamant he failed. Over the years, Carter refused three times to take any further tests.

As with any account, what is left out can be just as important as what is reported. For instance, every anti-Carter report referred to John Artis as being *"unemployed."* He could however, just as easily have been described as, *"about to enter college on a scholarship."* Both statements would have been true. Much was made of the fact that on the night of the murders, Carter was driving a rental car and not his own Eldorado. Certainly a black Eldorado convertible with *"Rubin 'Hurricane' Carter"* stencilled on the side in silver would not have made the best of getaway cars, and although the white Dodge Polara that he drove that night could be described as a *rental,* in reality it was a lease car, which Carter used as a business tax concession. According to Carter, the reason for driving the lease car that night and not his usual Eldorado was simple: the white Dodge Polara blocked the Eldorado in his garage, so he took the Polara.

"Rubin Carter Was Falsely Tried"

On October 14, 1966, Carter was arrested and charged with the shootings at the Lafayette Bar. On November 30, Carter and Artis were indicted on three counts of murder. Six months later, on May 26, 1967, both men were found guilty on all counts. Rubin Carter received two consecutive and one concurrent life terms. John Artis received three concurrent terms. Both men steadfastly maintained their innocence and by the mid-1970s Carter had became the focus for a massive media campaign. Muhammad Ali became a major supporter of Carter's cause and became godfather to Rubin's daughter Theodora.

On March 17, 1976, the convictions of Carter and Artis were overturned after two prosecution witnesses recanted. Nevertheless, at a retrial on December 22 that same year, the convictions were reinstated. Nine years later their second conviction was also overturned, this time by a federal judge. All told, Rubin Carter served nineteen years in prison, John Artis fifteen. The prosecution could have sought a new trial to argue Mr Carter's guilt, but did not, because more than twenty years had passed and a number of the witnesses were now dead. For reasons best known to himself, Carter never filed a suit for damages.

"An Innocent Man In a Living Hell"

Carter's unwavering assertion of his innocence is just one reason his story continues, even today, to captivate. A flamboyant personality, he wore sharkskin suits – some of which were tailored wide around the chest to accommodate his holster and pistol – and drove flash cars. At the time of his arrest he was ranked the number one contender for the middleweight crown.

An uncompromising voice for civil rights, he was also, by his own account, an arrogant and angry man. His rage sustained him during his years in prison, where he refused to wear prison uniform or eat its food.

The Norman Jewison film, *The Hurricane,* which opened in the USA on December 29, 1999 uses *considerable* dramatic licence in recounting Carter's story. So much so, that several people have come forward, both to criticise the film and to give their own versions of events.

US federal judge H. Lee Sarokin said: *"From the thousands of pages of testimony spanning two trials and numerous hearings, the parties have reconstructed two drastically different versions of the events that tragic night."* There might indeed be two versions of what happened in Paterson, New Jersey, thirty four years ago. However, only one is true. I will let you draw your own conclusions.

The film, like the three books and the Dylan song before them, portrays a cut-and-dried case of racial harassment; all are pro Carter.

"In Paterson that's just the way things go. If you're black, you might as well not show up on the street. 'Less you wanna draw the heat" Sang Dylan in 1975.

Many people believed that it was a simple scenario of a black man framed by the police and convicted by *"an all white jury."*

"All of Rubin's cards were marked in advance. The trial was a pig-circus, he never had a chance."

Rubin Carter was born May 6, 1937, in the Passaic County town of Delawanna, New Jersey. His father, Lloyd, one of thirteen brothers, grew up on a cotton farm in Georgia and moved to the State of New Jersey after a run-in with the Ku Klux Klan. Lloyd had done well for himself in Jersey and now owned a bike rental shop, a window-wash business, and an icehouse. From an early age Rubin had learned about the persecution of black people in the Southern States. Lloyd told his children many tales of *crackers* in the South hunting down black men and hanging them, and how his own family armed with fifteen guns had held the Klan at bay. Rubin was taught that black people had to fight for their rights and fight he did.

Although Lloyd may have taught his son about the injustice that blacks suffered in the US at that time, he never condoned violence, except maybe in self-defence. Rubin, however, soon became wayward and by the age of nine had become the leader of a local gang called the Apaches. The neighbourhood gang was responsible for a great deal of vandalism and parking meters were their favourite target. On one occasion, the Apaches ran through a downtown market place stealing clothing and whatever else they could snatch from the open-fronted stalls. When Lloyd found the clothes, he beat his son with a leather strap before calling the police. This, the first of many encounters with the police, earned Rubin two years' probation.

Rubin's problems continued and by age fourteen he was sent to Jamesburg State Home for Boys, but escaped from the reformatory two years later. Carter had been convicted of attacking a man with a bottle. He told police that the man was a child molester and that he had been menacing his young friend at a swimming hole. However, after breaking a bottle over the man's head, Carter stole his wristwatch and $55.00.

In 1954, after his escape from the reformatory Carter joined the army, which is where he learned to box. Upon returning to Paterson in 1956, he was picked up by police and compelled to serve out the remaining ten months of his sentence at the state home.

Less than five weeks after he was released from Annandale Reformatory and after a heavy drinking session, Carter went on the rampage. He snatched a woman's purse; a block later, he punched a man for no apparent reason and then went on to rob another man of his wallet. All three victims were black. Carter was arrested the next day and after pleading guilty, he was again incarcerated, spending time in both Rahway and Trenton State Prisons. On August 30, 1960, prison psychologist Henri Yarker wrote of Carter –

"He continues to be an assaultive, aggressive, hostile, negativistic, hedonistic, sadistic, unproductive and useless member of society who will live from society by mugging and who thinks he is superior. He has grandiose paranoid delusions about himself. The individual is as dangerous to society now as the day he was incarcerated and he will not be long in the streets before he will be back in this, or some other institution."

It was while serving time in prison that Carter decided to make constructive use of his best attribute, his fists. He reasoned that if he could get into the fight game he could earn respect and enough money to keep him off the streets.

Carter was released from prison in early September 1961 and by the 22nd of the month he had his first professional fight in which he beat Pike Reed over four rounds. In fact, Carter won ten of his first eleven fights, with eight of those wins coming inside the first three rounds. The storm-force fists – he was said to be capable of throwing 80 plus punches a minute – soon earned him the nickname *"Hurricane,"* and by December 1964 he was fighting Joey Giardello for the world middleweight crown, a fight he lost on points over fifteen rounds.

Carter had a very promising start to his career and for a while he looked as though he might just make it to the very top. However, after his title defeat by Joey Giardello he won just six of his next fourteen fights and in truth ended up with a relatively unspectacular career record. Although Carter remained dry while in training, he was a heavy drinker. Vodka was his drink of choice, 100 per cent proof Smirnoff. At the time few knew of his drink problem, but those that did believed he was an alcoholic.

Unfortunately, Carter's celebrity status as a sportsman failed to prevent him from getting into numerous bar room brawls and he faced assault charges on at least two further occasions. The boxer's temper was notorious and many tales circulated the bars and clubs of Paterson. One such tale was regarding Carter's table at a club called the Nite Spot. The story goes that one night Carter arrived to find a man sitting at *his* table. The boxer requested that the man move, but when he was slow to do so, Carter knocked him out with a single punch.

"And Ride a Horse Along a Trail"

As the line in the Dylan song suggests, Rubin Carter owned a horse. Before Carter bought the horse, it had been turned out and had become almost wild. On one occasion as Carter was trying to break the mare, the horse bit him on his left side. Carter told *Saturday Evening Post* writer Milton Gross: *"Before that horse could turn around I whomped her on the side of the head."* As he spoke, he pulled his hand from his side and swung a vicious looking left hook at the air. *"She went down,"* said Carter. *"Bite me again, you bitch, go ahead! Bite me!...That horse never snapped at me any more. I tell you that. If she even tried, I'd kill her with my hands."* He named his horse *Bitch*.

Carter attended the March on Washington in 1963, but soon grew weary of the mainstream civil rights approach of passive resistance. He believed that blacks should use all means at their disposal, including violence, to protect themselves. His new-found position in the public eye gave him the opportunity to speak out and there is no doubt that he was viewed as a threat by many of the white authority figures in Paterson.

The evening of Thursday June 16 started much like most nights for the Hurricane. His wife, Mae Thelma, would cook him dinner before he headed out for another night on the town. Tonight he would wear shiny black trousers with a razor crease, white dress shirt, black tie and waistcoat, black patent-leather shoes, ivory sports jacket, a splash of Charlie cologne and a smear of Vaseline on his shaven head.

During the evening news, of a shooting would circulate around the Paterson clubs. Earlier that evening a white man, Frank Conforti, had gunned down Roy Holloway, the black owner of the Waltz Inn and talk of revenge was in the air.

It was now two am and the Nite Spot was about to close. Carter, however, intended to go on to an after-hours drinking club and says that on the way out of the Nite Spot he met John Artis and offered him a lift home. Thirty minutes later, two black men in a white car murdered the bar tender and three white patrons of the Lafayette.

"Bello and Bradley and They Both Badly Lied"

The testimony of Al Bello was instrumental in convicting Carter and Artis of the murders. The descriptions that Bello gave to the police directly after the shootings, however, did not fit that of Carter and Artis and after seventeen hours of questioning and a lie-detector test, the two men were released. The police stated that Carter and Artis were not suspects and shortly after Carter was allowed to leave the USA to fight in Argentina, a country that had no extradition agreement with the USA. Only four months later, when again brought in for questioning, did the two crooks identify Carter and Artis as the murderers. At the first trial in 1967, Bello kept to this story, testifying that he was on his way in to buy cigarettes when he heard shots coming from the bar. Shortly after the shots were fired, he saw Carter and Artis leave the bar. His partner in crime, Arthur Dexter Bradley, confirmed Bello's testimony. However, away from the courtroom Bello would later say that he only identified Carter and Artis because police had told him he stood to collect the reward money.

In September 1974, Bello and Bradley recanted their testimony, explaining they had lied in exchange for rewards of $10,500 offered by the police and promises of leniency for robbery charges. Bello informed *The New York Times* –

"There's no doubt Carter was framed...I lied to save myself...The cops told me I'd be doing justice for the families of the white victims – It would be an eye for an eye... They told me to help your own people, and I went for it."

However, when Bello took the stand at the second trial in 1976, he recanted his recantation! The reason given this time was that he only said that Carter was innocent because: *"He had been promised $27,000 by Carter's defence team"* to do so.

This new bizarre version of events had Bello inside the bar at the time of the shootings. Strange, then, that everyone in the bar that night was shot apart from Bello! According to Bello the reason for this was simple. He had used Hazel Tanis as a shield. This version of events was so far-fetched that by the 1976 retrial, he had reverted to his original 1967 story of being outside the bar. After the second trial Bello made a statement to the press stating, he *"simply couldn't remember."*

It beggars belief that he couldn't remember if he was simply on his way to buy a packet of cigarettes, or if he was inside a bar using a woman as a shield while being fired at by two gunmen, one of whom had a 12-gauge double-barrelled shotgun! That sure is some loss of memory!

On May 26, 1967, Carter and Artis were found guilty of the murders. Later, much would be made of the fact that the jury that convicted the two men was all white. The jury that would convict Carter for a second time in 1976 contained two blacks.

The two men were taken to Trenton State Prison in separate unmarked cars. Carter, still dressed in a smart suit that his wife had delivered to him for the trial, cut an imposing figure, with his shaved head – twenty-five years before it became a fashion statement – moustache and goatee beard. Upon his arrival in Trenton, Carter refused to strip and don the State Prison uniform. The guard called for a sergeant; a further refusal brought the chief deputy, whom Carter informed-

"...I'm not working for you, I'm not eating your food, I'm not wearing your clothes, and I'm not shaving my goatee...The one thing I will not tolerate at all is for anybody to ever put their hands on me. Because if anyone does, you're going to have to kill me. Because if you don't, I'm gonna kill you."

Needless to say, Carter's first night in Trenton was spent in the hole. However, none of the guards ever handled him and he went to the hole still wearing his shark-skin suit, black patent-leather shoes, a $5,000 diamond ring and a gold watch.

It appeared that Carter would be kept in the hole indefinitely. He was allowed out once every fifteen days to take a shower and his fleshly suit was now rotting on his body. During a routine medical check-up, it was discovered that he had a detached retina, probably from an old boxing injury. It was suggested that he should undergo an operation to save his right eye at an outside clinic, but the prison warden would not permit him to leave Trenton. Carter was admitted instead to the prison hospital where the operation was botched; the doctor blamed the lack of facilities at the prison for the failure. Regardless of the reasons, the result was that Rubin Carter was blind in one eye and any chance of resuming his boxing career was ended.

By 1971, officials at Trenton had had their fill of problem inmate #45472 and without being given any reason, Carter was moved to Rahway prison – remember *'Tweeter and The Monkey Man'?* However, Rahway soon tired of Carter and he was transferred back to Trenton. This time, however, Carter was not taken to the main prison building but to a wing of the psychiatric hospital known as the Vroom Readjustment Unit.

Carter spent ninety-two days in this home for the criminally insane before Districted Court Judge Clarkson S. Fisher ordered that he be moved on the grounds that his rights had been violated. Carter was moved back to Treton's main prison building; he had come full circle.

In the spring of 1975 the *Hurricane Carter Trust Fund* was started; the idea was to raise money for legal expenses for a campaign to get Rubin Carter a retrial. Supporters of the fund included Burt Reynolds, Norman Mailer, Roberta Flack, Harry Belafonte, Stevie Wonder, Johnny Cash and the Reverend Jesse Jackson. Also on board the Carter bandwagon were top fight promoter Don King and world heavyweight boxing champion Muhammad Ali. On October 17, 1975, Ali led a march through Trenton in support of Carter. Sixteen hundred supporters attended the rally.

That same spring, one of the fund organisers, Richard Solomon, spoke to Carter about trying to get Bob Dylan on board the campaign wagon. Carter was not a fan of Dylan's music but was aware of his previous support for civil rights. Solomon, who was a Dylan fan, believed he could convince Dylan of Carter's cause and in April 1975 he wrote a letter to Dylan's New York office explaining Carter's plight. Several weeks later the 'phone rang in Solomon's apartment and Dylan's voice asked –

"What do you want from me?"

Solomon explained the situation and asked Dylan if he would meet Carter. Dylan replied: *"Yeah, maybe."*

After being told that Carter was in a maximum-security prison, Dylan asked: *"Is it Dangerous?"*

When he was told *"no,"* Dylan said that he would *"Give it some thought."*

Dylan was due to fly to Sainte-Maries de-la-mer in the south of France for an extended holiday so any further thoughts of meeting Carter were quickly put to one side. However, when Dylan arrived home in the middle of June from his six weeks' break, a copy of Rubin Carter's autobiography, *The Sixteenth Round,* awaited him. Dylan read the book and almost immediately went to visit Carter in prison. Although the two men had little in common they immediately felt an affinity towards each other. Dylan told Carter that he had been in France because he *"just had to get away. People just suck my soul, just suck me dry."*

Dylan also told Carter he felt this was the first time that he had really talked to anyone in ages and that he would like to come back. Dylan later said of their meeting –

"The first time I saw him, I left knowing one thing ... I realized that the man's philosophy and my philosophy were running down the same road, and you don't meet too many people like that."

A few weeks later a chance meeting with Jacques Levy resulted in the two men starting to work on the songs that would become *"Desire."*

Dylan spent two weeks and five sessions in July in New York's *Columbia* Studio One recording the songs for the album and at least three of those sessions contained takes of *'Hurricane.'* Recording for the album was concluded on July 31, 1975.

Later, however, it was discovered that some of the details in the song were incorrect. Dylan and Levy had confused Bello and Bradley, placing Bradley at the crime scene, not Bello. The song also had Bradley robbing the victims' bodies and Dylan was informed this statement was libellous. Levy called up with a re-write of the offending lines, inside five minutes.

These lyric changes were not enough to keep Dylan out of court. After the song's release Valentine filed a defamation and invasion of privacy suit. Valentine lost the suit in 1983 when the judge ruled that for the purposes of this crime, she was a public figure.

After a long day in the rehearsal studio Dylan took the scribbled corrections and his band across town to Studio One where on October 24 they began the arduous task of re-recording the eight-and-a-half minute song. The session was due to start at 10.30pm but technical problems delayed the start until nearly midnight. The first take of *'Hurricane'* was going well until Dylan's harp fell out of his neck rack and from that point on things only got worse. In a couple of other takes Dylan stumbled over the lyrics, again managing to put Bradley at the murder scene instead of Bello. Five hours and eleven takes later Dylan left the studio.

As Dylan was putting on his jacket Don Devito asked: *"Do you want to hear it?"* to which Dylan replied: *"Man, I don't know. You mix it. You let me know which one you pick out."*

After listening to the tape on which there was only four complete takes, Devito decided that his only choice would be to edit together two of the takes.

Dylan would soon tour to promote his new album and while on the road he would be in a position to further Rubin's cause, by informing his public of the injustice that Dylan believed Hurricane had suffered. At the end of his 1975 Rolling Thunder Revue Tour, Dylan played two concerts directly connected with the boxer's cause. The first on December 7 was a concert in front of Carter at the Correctional Institution For Women in Clinton, New Jersey – just for the record, the prison now took men and women. The next night Dylan would hold a benefit concert for Carter at Madison Square Garden, New York. The concert became known as *The Night Of The Hurricane.* Dylan would stage another such concert in Houston, Texas, on January 25, 1976, by which time Carter had been released from prison on bail.

It transpires that it was not only men and horses that Rubin could take out with just one punch. Carolyn Kelley, now 63, from Newark, New Jersey, was working as a bail bondswoman back in 1975 when Muhammad Ali asked her to get involved in the campaign to win a new trial for Carter. Kelley agreed, and as national director of the Carter defence fund, spent more than a year raising funds for the boxer's cause. That effort was successful, Carter's appeal was upheld and Kelley was overjoyed when, on March 17, 1976, Carter was released on bail to await a retrial. Muhammad Ali posted much of the cash bail -$20,000 for Carter and $15,000 for Artis.

Six weeks after his release the middleweight boxer showed his gratitude by punching Carolyn Kelley to the floor and kicking her. She was left lying unconscious in Carter's hotel room.

Prompted by the release of the film *The Hurricane,* Kelley has revealed the story behind her beating to reporter Paul Mulshine.

From her initial conversation with Carter in prison, Kelley was convinced of his innocence. He described in some detail how he had been framed by a racist criminal justice system, saying that the police had run his main alibi, a boxer named Wild Bill Hardney, out of town so he could not testify on his behalf. The truth was that Hardney had fled the State of New Jersey to avoid making paternity payments.

After his release, Kelley says that Carter's heavy drinking disturbed her. She states that Carter drank large amounts of vodka and became abusive. However, Kelley's biggest surprise came when just before the Ali-Jimmy Young fight in Landover, Md., someone called for Carter's attention. The man was *Wild Bill* Hardney. To Kelley's great surprise, instead of showing delight at finding the cast iron alibi he had been looking for, Carter's expression changed to one of annoyance. Later, when Kelley questioned Carter about his strange behaviour he allegedly attacked her.

Over the years, Carter has given several versions of what happened that night. In one version he used his staple excuse: He *"was framed."* Kelley apparently faked the beating that put her in traction because he had broken off an affair with her. Alternatively, there's the version he told to WNEW-TV's Marvin Scott in June 1976, which has Kelley faking it because she wanted to blackmail him out of $250,000. In the book *Lazarus and The Hurricane* the story remains the same, just the amount has changed: the blackmail attempt is now downsized to $100,000.

Passaic County Judge William Marchese held hearings on the incident in July 1976 and after determining that the assault had occurred he changed the terms of Carter's bail.

It was around this time that Carter began losing many of his key allies. Dylan seemed to lose interest, or maybe he just felt that he had done all he could for Carter's cause. Carter dismissed Solomon from his defence team over an argument regarding Dylan and *'The Night Of The Hurricane'* concert and by the end of 1976, financial contributions started to dry up. Dylan's concert at the Garden had generated $217,000 in revenue. All of the musicians gave their time free that evening, yet after paying other bills only $104,000 remained. Most of the money raised from the concert went on expenses such as massive hotel bills. Muhammad Ali and his entourage ran up a $3,000 bill.

Support still came in the form of a group of people known simply as *The Canadians*. The community, which lived near Toronto as a sort of modern-day commune, had supported Carter's cause since 1980 and would continue to do so even after his release.

Rumours that Dylan would attend the 1976 retrial came to nothing. After the trial, Dylan told one of Carter's team: *"Tell Rubin I'll be down there in the spring time of my life."* Carter's hopes took a massive knock when just before the trial his defence team learned that Bello had renounced his recantation. Bello would again testify that it was Carter and Artis that he saw running from the bar that night.

At his first trial, Carter produced witness after witness who testified he was somewhere else at the time of the killings. However, in 1976 four of the alibi witnesses from the first trial took the stand and admitted they lied. *"There were a lot of lies at the last trial,"* testified ex-alibi witness Catherine McGuire.

Judge Leopizzi said that hearing these witnesses, all black, recant their original testimony made the most powerful moments of the entire trial.

At the first trial Carter had admitted owning several guns, one being a 12-gauge shotgun, but said that all the guns had *"gone missing,"* from his training camp a year earlier and were believed stolen. Detective Emil DiRobbio testified at the first trial that at 3.45 am, 75-minutes after the murders and while searching Carter's car in a police garage, he found a .32-calibre bullet beneath the passenger seat and a 12-gauge shotgun cartridge in the trunk. Although the two rounds found in Carter's car were of the same calibre as those used in the shootings, they were not identical. The .32-calibre bullets used in the murders were copper-coated; the bullet found in Carter's car was lead cased. The 12-gauge shotgun shell found in the trunk under some boxing equipment was also slightly different from the shells used in the murders. Carter's team insisted that police could have planted these bullets and it should be noted that the police had already made a brief search of the car, including the trunk, when Carter and Artis were pulled over on the night of the murders. Nevertheless, local newspaper reporter Paul Alberta, testified that he witnessed the recovery of the bullets at the police garage, though mysteriously he never wrote about this event in any of his stories about Carter. The defence also noted Alberta had a strong relationship with the local police, and that he was particularly close to the officer who said he found the bullets.

A front-page article in *The New York Times* noted that in 1974 there were irregularities in how the bullets were recorded at the police station. The police said they found them 75 minutes after the murders, yet they were not logged with the property clerk until five days later!

At the retrial the prosecution's main argument was one of revenge. Their argument was that Leroy Holloway had been murdered just a few blocks away that same evening. However, the murder of Holloway at the Waltz seemed to be an argument over money, and had nothing to do with race. Unfortunately, Carter himself added fuel to the race theory by informing the jury: *"It was all around that there was going to be some shaking* – slang for retaliation – *going on."*

Carter and Artis were again found guilty on three charges of first-degree murder and received the same sentences as before. After nine months of freedom, Rubin Carter was back in Trenton State Prison. John Artis, a model prisoner, served five more years in prison before being released on December 22, 1981. He had spent a total of fifteen years behind bars.

After numerous appeals, on November 7, 1985, Carter was finally successful. In a seventy-page summing-up, Federal Judge H. Lee Sarokin found that the State had *"Violated the constitutional rights of Carter and Artis on two separate grounds."* Firstly, that the State failed to disclose the results of the lie detector test given by the State's only eyewitness, Alfred Bello, and that the State, in claiming the killings were motivated by racial revenge *"Violated the Equal Protection and Due Process rights by improperly appealing to racial prejudice."*

Carter's opponents would argue he was never judged innocent by a judge or jury and that his second conviction was overturned only on technicalities. The State appealed all the way to the Supreme Court, which ruled there was insufficient reason to hear the case. The 1966 indictments against Mr Carter and Mr Artis were formally dismissed in 1988.

Dylan and Carter met for the last time in July 1986 when Carter and The Canadians went to see Dylan in concert at Madison Square Garden. Carter attended the July 17 concert, the last show of a three-night residency at the Garden. Just before playing *'House Of The Risin' Sun'* Dylan said: *"I also wanna say hello to my friend Rubin 'Hurricane' Carter who's out there tonight..."* After the concert, Carter went to Dylan's dressing room where he found Dylan holding court. Carter remained in the doorway while Dylan sipped his Jack Daniel's and talked to the ensemble. Suddenly Dylan turned and met Carter's eyes; the two men embraced and their conversation lasted for about thirty minutes, during which Dylan asked Carter if he would like to join him on tour. Carter explained that he was still fighting his case with the prosecutors' office so Dylan, who was spending another day in New York before going on to Philadelphia, asked Carter if he would drop by his hotel room the next day as he had something to show him.

When Carter arrived at Dylan's hotel suite overlooking Central Park, Dylan displayed two pairs of boxing gloves that Carter had once given him. Dylan pulled on the gloves and he and Carter shadowboxed. Suddenly The Hurricane unleashed one of his famous left-right combinations and before realizing that the punches had not connected Dylan let out a shout. The two men touched gloves and burst into laughter. *"You're safe with me, brother,"* Carter told him.

Epilogue –

Rubin Carter, now 63 resides in Toronto, Canada, where he heads the Association in Defence of the Wrongly Convicted. In a recent interview, Carter said he now finds boxing *"barbaric,"* though he readily accepted an honorary championship title belt from the World Boxing Council in 1993.

John Artis was arrested for possession of cocaine in 1985 and returned to prison. Now a social worker, he works with troubled youth in Virginia.

The last time anything was heard of Alfred Bello, he was living in New Mexico under an assumed name.

Patricia Valentine, 57 this year, still fears for her safety. She has moved to an undisclosed address in Florida and no longer goes by the name of Valentine.

Hazel Tanis survived for almost a month after being shot. She gave police a description for a sketch of the suspect who shot her four times. The police believed the man in the sketch to be John Artis. After her death, the sketch was not admissible in court.

William *"Willie"* Marins, the only long-term survivor, was wounded in his left eye and partially blinded. He later said he fell to the floor and played dead. Marins died in 1973, from unrelated causes.

Sources used in the preparation of this text are too numerous to list. Nevertheless I would like to mention:

James S. Hirsch, *Hurricane: The Life Of Rubin Carter – Fighter.* Published by *Fourth Estate.*
Cal Deal Web Site. www.graphicwitness.com/carter
Paul Mulshine for the Carolyn Kelly interview
Jacques Levy for his interview with ISIS Magazine
Lyrics 1962-1985 published by Jonathan Cape

Published in issue #91 July 2000

Robert Johnson and Street Legal
by Nick Train

"I hear many echoes of Robert Johnson... especially on 'Is Your Love In Vain'."
Robert Shelton: *No Direction Home*

"What records do I listen to? New records? I don't know, just the old records really.
Robert Johnson. I still listen to those records I listened to when I was growing up –
they really changed my life." – Bob Dylan

Despite handing down a legacy of only twenty-nine recorded songs, the influence of
Robert Johnson on successive performers of both blues and rock is profound. That
influence is apparent directly and by allusion in much of Dylan's work, a fact regularly
attested to by Dylan himself; see the dedication in the 1972 edition of *Writings And
Drawings*. Dylan has traded in Johnson's metaphors and phrasing from *'Corrina
Corrina,'* built upon Johnson's *'Stones In My Passway,'* through *'I Threw It All Away'*
with its echoes of *'When You Got a Good Friend,'* to *'Drifting Too Far'* and *'Got My
Mind Made Up,'* with their characteristically Johnsonian linkage of womankind with
unwelcome financial expense. Admittedly, much of this borrowing derives from the
broad blues/folk heritage. However, with *"Street Legal"* we are in wholly new territory.
We find here a systematic reference to Johnson's work, an acceptance by Dylan of many
of the principles that drove the bluesman and a recognition of deep emotional and
spiritual parallels between the two.

The young Bob Dylan performed Johnson's numbers and concocted a myth about his
early life in many respects similar to that which survives about the earlier Robert. In
1960, Bob Dylan probably wanted to be Robert Johnson, via a romantic, adolescent
transference. The Bob Dylan of *"Street Legal"* has passed beyond the requirement to
role model. Johnson had already been dead for almost a decade by the age at which
Dylan composed *"Street Legal, "* poisoned by a jealous cuckold before he reached
thirty. So Bob Dylan in 1978 cannot be Robert Johnson, a fact wryly acknowledged in
the musical accompaniment for *"Street Legal"* which, glitzy and complex, sounds as
little like the extraordinary, primitive virtuosity of *"King Of The Delta Blues Singers
Parts I and II"* as possibly imaginable. *"Street Legal"* is not bluesy musically, even

'New Pony' owing more to The Rolling Stones than Blind Lemon Jefferson. Dylan brings his own poetry to Johnson's themes and a broad range of musical styles and technology but underneath, *"Street Legal"* is steeped in Johnson. Dylan's failure to even attempt to imitate Johnson's recorded effects is partly a regretful admission that times have passed on for him and is one of the sad charms of the album.

I shall analyse the Johnson/*"Street Legal"* relationship by moving from the particular to the general. First the direct song references, through to the underlying thematic ideas of which the references are themselves just clues and pointers. The title of the album itself is an indication of Dylan's intention to investigate Johnson myth and mythology. *"Street Legal"* is a phrase used by bikers to assert the roadworthiness and regular tax and insurance status of their vehicles. It intimates a willingness and readiness to set out on the road. Dylan nervously gazing from a stairway to a thoroughfare on the album cover announces that he too has *'Crossroad Blues'* and *'Rambling On My Mind.'* Both *"Street Legal"* and Johnson's songs are shot through with images of travel, trains and the search for home. The *"endless road"* of *'Changing Of The Guards'* maps the psyches of the two performers.

The songs featured on the album are drenched with Johnsonia. From the top, *'Changing Of The Guards'* features Dylan's *"last deal gone down"* from Johnson's *'Last Fair Deal Gone Down.'* The latter song's mysterious *"captain"* also appears there. *"Falling leaves"* appear in *'Hellhound On My Trail.'* *'New Pony'* is a reworking and amplification of Johnson's *'Milkcow Calf Blues'* where the woman is crudely – in all senses – equated to an animal. Johnson wants to suck his beast; Dylan to mount his – the intention is the same. *'New Pony's'* *"Miss X"* probably matches the equally faceless *"Miss So-And-So"* of *'Rambling On My Mind.'* The voodoo, witchcraft and devil presence alluded to in *'New Pony'* are perennial Johnson themes. *'No Time To Think'* is free from direct reference, although in its frustration with modernity and *'isms'* it is reminiscent of Johnson's *'Terraplane Blues'* and *'Phonograph Blues'* where things both mechanical and emotional have broken down irreparably. *'Hellhound On My Trail'* has the same desperate sense of threat and anger at the passage of time that informs *'No Time To Think.'* *'Baby Stop Crying'* is pure Johnson. It reminds us most strongly of *'Stop Breaking Down,'* but with its archetypal symbols of pistols, rivers and doctors, relates to a number of Johnson's songs, e.g. *'32-20.'* *'Is Your Love In Vain?'* as Shelton notes, echoes, *'Love In Vain,'* though the content of the songs is very different. *'Is Your Love In Vain'* in fact is far more reminiscent of *'If I Had Possession Over Judgement Day,'* where Johnson like Dylan has been to the *"mountain."* *'Is Your Love In Vain'* has a hymnal tone, as Mellors suggests. The religious connotation of *'If I Had Possession'* is also clear and both singers use the language of religious love to elevate and decorate a secular erotic love. *'Senor'* is poetically far removed from Johnson's blues vocabulary, but the song itself describes an obsessive relationship with a metaphysical entity very similar to Johnson's *'Me And The Devil Blues.'* Johnson affected to believe that his musical inspiration derived directly from the devil, which, he relates, he met one day standing at a crossroads – scarily Johnson may even have believed this. In *'Senor,'* Dylan is clearly examining his own pact with his muse/persecutor within, with the same repelled fascination. *'True Love Tends To Forget'* and *'We Better Talk This Over'* both concern erotic relationships and have more than a flash of Johnson. Dylan's *"Mexico and Tibet"* rejoices in the same use of exotic place names as Johnson's *"Ethiopia"* of *'Dust My Broom.'* The emotional confusion of the narrator of *'We Better Talk This Over'* replicates the ambivalence toward a partner of Johnson's *'Kind Hearted Woman Blues'* where an evil female will not let him be, although it is equally clear that the singer could not begin to function without her. Finally, in *'Where Are You Tonight?'* we run the full range of Johnson references. The *"long distance train"* is probably the same one leaving the station in *'Love In Vain.'* The final verse alludes to four different Johnson songs in successive lines. Dylan's *"Killing me by degrees"* is derived from Johnson's song *'Preaching Blues;'* *"blues that like consumption are killing me by degrees."* *"Nickels And dimes"* appear in *'Last Fair Deal Gone Down.'* *"Green money"* is the objective of Johnson's relationship with *'Little Queen Of Spades.'* In addition, notoriously, *"the juice running down my leg"* is the result of Johnson's request of his woman to squeeze his lemon in *'Travelling Riverside Blues.'* The pain experienced by Dylan in the composition of this song and evidently in its recording reminds us of the *"shaking chill"* and *"aching heart"* of *"Preaching Blues."* *"If you ain't had them, I hope you never will"* Johnson genially wishes us in that song, with the same ironic tone that Dylan uses in offering to show us his scars.

Lack of a lyric sheet for *"King Of The Delta Blues"* makes it difficult to list comprehensive Dylan borrowings, although more probably exist. Nevertheless, the case has already been established beyond contention that *"Street Legal"* defers to Johnson both heavily and wittily. Dylan, however, is not simply engaging us in a game of *spot the allusion*. A mature Dylan has recognised the key concerns in Johnson's work and found them profoundly relevant to him in 1978. Dylan develops those themes and the result is his own statement – what we gain in poetic complexity we lose in primitive power. The concerns of the album, while ambitious, are traditional to Dylan – the relationship of men and women, and the possibility of redemption. On *"Street Legal,"* Dylan has explored these through the perspective of the bluesman.

This perspective is most immediately obvious, and to some critics painful, in Dylan's *new* treatment of women on this album. The reactionary aspect of this will not come as a shock to devotees of Johnson who stands at the heart of the macho blues ethic. One suspects that the sound beating promised to the female in *'Me And The Devil Blues'* would await any woman who did not 'cook and sew, make flowers grow' for Johnson. Dylan's psychic threats seem only slightly less extreme. Those flowers in *'Is Your Love In Vain?'* reappear in *'Changing Of The Guard'* and *'Where Are You Tonight?'* always associated with the feminine principle, as are the welcome flowers in Johnson's *'Malted Milk.'* This suggests a fixed and perhaps stereotypical poetic image of woman. Moreover, I don't think Dylan is joking on *'Is Your Love In Vain?'* as Shelton guesses. In his defensive quizzing of a potential mate, he is much closer to the Johnson of *'Honeymoon Blues'* who is seeking *"a little girl who will do anything I say."* Dylan is arguably a touch critical in his willingness to apportion blame to the female in *'True Love'* and *'Talk This Over'* – *"you've been two-faced, you've been double dealing."* Here is the traditional blues presumption that the female is a sinful vessel. Johnson also objected to his women going off with *"every downtown man she meet,"* although his own behaviour both in and outside song suggest that he enjoyed strenuous and persistent extramarital activity. In *'New Pony'* and *'Baby Stop Crying,'* Dylan dismisses woman as sex object or terminal neurotic. Yet, for both Dylan and Johnson life without woman would be intolerable. A yearning search for the status of a perfect partnership is at the heart of many of their songs. That partnership is urgently required to complete a spiritual whole, not just to darn socks. What Dylan is suggesting in *"Street Legal"* is that the passionate urgency of the quest for love and the manifold disappointments endured en route can conspire to devalue the object of the quest itself. The woman becomes a commodity – to be weighed in money terms. In *'Changing Of The Guards'* love must be *"repaid."* It is interesting to note Johnson's desire in *'Little Queen Of Spades'* to *"get me a gambling woman,"* because the last thing a man wants is a woman who takes all his money. Compare this to *'Gonna Change My Way Of Thinking,'* where much indeed has changed since the previous album and Dylan wants to get a *"God-fearing woman, one I can easily afford."* The glad acceptance here of even the implied financial burden of partnership would look out of place in *'New Pony'* and be unthinkable for Johnson. The bluesman seems never to have progressed beyond regarding women as conspirators with the devil, indeed as *"treacherous young witches"* as Dylan puts it. *'Changing Of The Guards'* contains Dylan's pessimistic judgement of the state of reciprocity between the sexes in 1978 – *"desperate men, desperate women, divided."* For better or worse, the rest of *"Street Legal"* examines this very Johnsonian perception.

Listening to *"King Of The Delta Blues"* is a painful but redemptive experience. Johnson's performance is consistently agonised and one feels that an exorcism is being waged on the self. He has a clear sense of his own guilt: that his suffering is in large measure due to his own sins – *"sin was the cause of it all"* he admits in *'Drunken Hearted Man.'* Moreover, this state of imperfection and lack of grace is unrelieved – Johnson's journeying and search seem endless. We guess that before his conversion Dylan could empathise powerfully and painfully with this mood. Pain and cynicism run through *"Street Legal."* Dylan knows what it's like to be *"stripped of all virtue,"* to have a *"heart as hard as leather,"* to *"have been down this way before,"* to ask repeatedly *"How much longer?"*

However, *"Street Legal"* does not depress and nor does Johnson. Dylan has understood and used the confrontational and redemptive quality of the blues. Johnson sings of his pain in order to relieve his pain and by living his pain publicly, helps relieve the pain of others. This is the traditional social function of the bluesman. Johnson and Dylan are both self-pitying individuals, but their impact is not negative, because in common with other soulful artists they can transmute the sharing of pain into a healing experience. In performance, they both assume the cares of their audiences and momentarily lift them from them. *'Like a Rolling Stone'* is Dylan's ultimate statement of transcendence through pain. *"Street Legal,"* perhaps in a more consciously artistic way, contains its own promise of temporary redemption of pain in a way that both acknowledges the achievement of Johnson by its continued reference to him, but also seeks to create its own healing effect. Dylan tells us straight that *"sacrifice was the code of the road,"* the road both he and Johnson travel. Dylan's scars are a memorial to the terrible price paid for the balanced equanimity achieved at the close of *'Where Are You Tonight?'* Dylan's performance warns us that the scarring is inevitable. Yet confronting this truth and the anguish with which it is expressed can reconcile both the performer and his audience to their lot. In *'No Time To Think'* Dylan states that *"You can give, but you cannot receive."* This perhaps defines the bluesman's predicament, the crucified Christ's sacrifice and Dylan's own state of tempered despair at the composition of this set of songs. He was shortly to find what appeared an escape into certitude. It is not recorded whether Johnson found any mercy in his bone-filled grave.

Published in issue #29 February 1990

GEN. ADM.

SEC   ROW   SEAT

9253

ADMIT ONE   THIS DATE

* * *
ROLLING
THUNDER
REVUE
* * *

TAX INCLUDED

PRICE

$8.75

SEC   ROW   SEAT

9253

GEN. ADM.

EARLS COURT, LONDON
(Opposite Warwick Road Exit, Earls Court Tube Station)

Harvey Goldsmith Entertainments proudly present

BOB DYLAN 6

in concert

Tuesday, 20th June
at 8.00 p.m. Doors open 6.30 p.m.

No cameras, tape recorders or bottles allowed in Auditorium
WARNING: Official souvenirs are on sale within the auditorium only

For Conditions of Sale see over

ROLLING THUNDER REVUE

STARRING

BOB DYLAN
JOAN BAEZ · JACK ELLIOTT
BOB NEUWIRTH

PRESENTS:

Night of the Hurricane II

BENEFIT CONCERT FOR
RUBIN "HURRICANE" CARTER

JANUARY 25, 1976

HOUSTON ASTRODOME
HOUSTON, TEXAS

The New America Filmmakers

WED., DEC. 6 through WED.
The First Extended Showing i

SCANDINAVIUM
Gøteborg
Tirsdag 11. juli kl. 2

International Concert Organisation A/S
proudly presents

* * * * * * * * *
70'ERNES KONCERT
* * * * * * * *

Bob Dylan

EKSTRA KONCERT
Onsdag 12. juli kl. 20

SÆRTOG AFGÅR FRA KØBENHAVNS
HOVEDBANEGÅRD 11. og 12. JULI
KL. 12.50 - TOG/FÆRGEBILLET
KR. 175.- RETUR

Resterende billetter til tirsdag 11. juli
samt EKSTRA-koncerten og særtogene:
KNABRO BILLETBUREAU
Knabrostræde 24 - (01) 12 41 00.

Eat The Document

(54 min.)

In full Quadraphonic sound and colour.

Artificial Eye are pleased to announce the opening date

RENALD & CLAR

Written & Directed
By Bob Dylan

Openi
Thursda
Septem
at th
Camden

311 Camden High

THE BOB DYLAN FIL

Bob
DYLAN
Joan
BAEZ

in
Renaldo & Clara

Written and Directed by Bob Dylan   Produced by Lombard Street Films, Inc.
Distributed Worldwide by Circuit Films   Metrocolor R

HEAR BOB DYLAN ON ✿ COLUMBIA RECORDS & TAPES

The Distant Ship of Liberty
by James Joughin

In 1977, I was living in St Vincent in the Caribbean and had occasion to visit the small Grenadine island of Bequia, at that time well off the beaten tourist track. As I remember it, there were some rumours that Bob Dylan was having a boat built there, although this seemed highly unlikely considering the isolated nature of the place. Then, one day while walking the beach, I came across a more or less deserted boatyard, where a half-built wooden hull was up on bamboo supports. I asked a guy who was sitting under the proverbial coconut tree about the hull, and he said the boat belonged to Bob Dylan.

Now, you have to remember how times have changed. In St Vincent at that time, there was no email or fax, not even direct telephone dialling. You had to book the telephone a day in advance and as I recall, I made only two or three calls in two years. There was no newspaper and my *NME* from home came by sea and took a month. I took in this story about Dylan's boat with a certain amount of bemusement, and after a while, I half forgot about it.

Anyway, this year I finally got around to going back to Bequia. To be honest, with the passing of the years, I wasn't clear in my mind how much I'd remembered and whether the story might have become embroidered in some way. I simply couldn't be sure.

However, and now to get to the point I was in the island's only bookshop, checking for postcards, when amongst a gorgeous set of paintings of island life – the Arrival of the Mailboat, the Blessing of the Whaleboats, the Quay, and the Seafront, etc. – there was one that reminded me almost exactly of the scene as I remembered it in the boatyard all those years before. So, imagine my surprise when I flipped it over and discovered that indeed that was exactly what the painting was: *the launching of Dylan's boat,* a painting by long-time Bequia habitué, Sam McDowell. In November 1979, at least two years after I had seen it half-finished on the ramp.

A couple of days later, I saw a photograph on the wall of a seafront bar: *the Water Pearl Under Sail.* It was framed and under glass. No one in the bar knew the genesis of the photograph. I did talk to the owner of the bookshop about all this and she remembered the launching. It was clearly a big occasion although Dylan did not attend. She said, though, that he had come several other times in connection with his boat and that he was very gracious and unassuming, *"not like that horrible Mick Jagger who was always picking fights with everyone."* She was also under the impression that Water Pearl, one of the last traditional boats to be built on the island, had sunk somewhere but she didn't know where.

Published in issue #87, November 1999.

Dave Kelly Interview
Interview conducted by Chris Cooper,
September 23,1987

Dave Kelly was Dylan's personal assistant for most of the *"Religious"* tours. An Englishman by birth, he had lived in America until 1986 and had returned to the UK to help set up a promotions/record company.

CC: How did you come to meet Dylan?

DK: Actually, how I came to meet him was that I was involved in that same church, that is the Vineyard Fellowship with Pastor Ken Gulliksen. We had common friends that had gone through that whole experience with him. He wanted somebody that would go on the road that understood the kind of thing he was going through, 'cos he was surrounded by people who were kind of antagonistic to that kind of thing. So, he wanted some buddies that could come out with him and a friend of mine suggested me, and amazingly, he had already heard of me. When I went out to visit him, he actually had one of my records on the record player. Can you believe that? This man must listen to EVERYTHING for him to have my record.

CC: Can you remember when this was?

DK: I think it was three or four months. There were three or four months of rehearsals.

CC: The gigs started in November 1979 so...

DK: It was somewhere like end of July or August. There was an intensive period of rehearsals beforehand.

CC: Was this the band that went on the road?

DK: There was more than the band then. Some got lost along the way. They started with a five, or four-piece horn section as well: Tim Horn, a well-known horn player, and some of the more famous L.A. session men. They where supposed to go with the horns on one side and the girls on the other. He had percussionists: Russ Baboo the Jamaican guy, that plays a lot of records, like David Lindley, Jackson Browne's guitarist. He did all sorts of weird things. Playing saucepan lids and things. He's a real percussionist. Things like that were in the rehearsals. It was about a week before we went on the road.

He actually sat down on a sofa like this. He quite shocked me and said, *'What do you think, the horns or the girls?'* I was totally flabbergasted! He said, *'We can't really have both, financially it's just ridiculous.'* It was like an extra ten people. I didn't know what to say except that I thought the girls were adding, where the horns were not doing a lot. Now, the next day I came in and there were no horn players. I don't think he did it because of what I said, but it was terrifying. I thought I had better watch what I say. I mean he does listen to what people say, but he does have to think it first. All through the tour he did it with me and lots of other people, just bounce the idea off you that he's already got, and if you confirm what he thinks, then he does it!

CC: The *"Slow Train"* LP had been recorded in May 1979.

DK: Yeah, that was already down; they were still rehearsing the songs to get them better. He was also writing and rehearsing the new ones for *"Saved."*

CC: Can you recall them rehearsing songs that were not gospel influenced?

DK: Only jokingly, going into old songs at the end of the day. Not his stuff. Things like Chuck Berry, stuff like that. But he did write an awful lot of stuff and he did try them out. There must have been twenty songs that he pulled from to do the tour, and they probably had like, forty. It was like nearly every day he'd come up with two or three new songs, he was so prolific. It staggered me. He'd go into his little room and come back out with a new song.

CC: Can you recall where all this took place?

DK: Oh yeah, in Santa Monica. He has a rehearsal studio, right next to Muhammed Ali's training camp. Not in Santa Monica Boulevard, which is in LA, but in the Santa Monica district, by the coast. He has a large complex, with an office, and a room with his records all around the wall. I have never heard of anyone else, except Stevie Wonder, who listens to everything. He's constantly listening, soaking up ideas from the most obscure places.

CC: In the last few years he's played a lot of blues material on the road that's not his own.

DK: A lot more than he lets on I'm sure. I mean he gets all the new stuff; they just give it to him. How it affects him, I don't know. I think he just needs to be aware of it, that's all.

CC: In '78 there were lots of rehearsals done somewhere in Santa Monica referred to as Rundown Studios.

DK: I don't know if it had an official name; you can't see from outside that it's that, though you could stand in the street and hear him play.

CC: There's a picture on the cover of *'Street Legal'* that might be that place?

DK: I saw that, yeah it certainly looks like that. That would be the side door though, the main door is actually... it goes into a hall with a foyer and they have cameras and stuff...

CC: This may be before your arrival but in an interview for *Buzz,* Ken Gulliksen claims that Dylan went on to spend three and a half months in Malibu, at a school of discipleship.

DK: He did, I was with him then. Just like a study really. That was about the time I met him when he started that course...He was very quiet the first time I went in to meet him. It was my first day on the job. I didn't know what I was supposed to do. I was just told that he needed someone he could talk and relate to. So I had to do a few odd things, but that was really for his management, they wanted to know what they were paying me for. The first day he took me into the kitchen area, up from the rehearsal stage, and he just shook my hand; it was like he really wasn't there! Very odd! We walked to the kitchen and there are all these Rastafarian guys there. He was having a problem talking to them, and he says *'Talk to them, tell them what I want,'* and he sits down to listen to me!

CC: Around the end of the 1979 tour there were rumours that Dylan was going to get married again and the person who was suggested was Mona Lisa Young.

DK: No, it wasn't her. In fact, you've probably noticed that halfway through the tour one of the girls disappears; she's the one. At the end of the first tour, they had a big row and he told her to leave. They were pretty close…

CC: The only name I can see that left after a tour was Helena Springs.

DK: Yeah, maybe it was her. She was definitely single. It was only a rumour until the big split up, when it became pretty obvious.

CC: A couple of songs have turned up that were not used on the album, one as a single, *'Trouble In Mind'* and another which we know as *'Ye Shall Be Changed'* can you remember any others?

DK: You mean the titles? Oh boy! I was just kicking myself, you know, because there always used to be sheets of lyrics on the floor. I would pick them up but was told that if they were on the floor then he had discarded them. There were several humorous songs written in conversational manner. You know, *'Moses said to God'* that sort of thing, real tongue in cheek. I wonder what happened to them.

CC: Rehearsals were obviously with the tour and album in mind.

DK: Yeah, the *"Saved"* stuff was. The producer was there all the time, Jerry Wexler. He'd pop in and work on the songs. Tell the guitarist what to play. He spent a lot of time getting the riff right on *'Solid Rock'* so they were killing two birds with one stone, I guess.

CC: The tour was meant to start in October; there were shows booked in Texas. Then for some reason they got cancelled. He did *Saturday Night Live* and the tour started proper at the beginning of November. Can you recall that happening?

DK: They weren't ready, and I think the reason was Jerry Wexler telling them they weren't ready. He really said that the *"Saved"* material wasn't ready to play to the public. It did change radically. They tried lots of different things. Bob was really in charge of that; he'd get them to change the tempo, the style. He's not really a good guitarist but he was able to show the others what he wanted. He was even telling the girls how to sing, which is phenomenal.

CC: Were you there for *Saturday Night Live*?

DK: Not in the studio, no…He hated it. All I heard for a week was how bad it was, and how terrible the people were there…I saw it: he had videos of it. I think the real problem was that his personality clashed with them…There was much contempt and derision. I really don't know why he went. I think his management pushed him into doing it, Jerry Weintraub. His words to me about him was *'This man is a unique kind of species.'* Like he didn't like him but there were contractual obligations. CBS were really messing him around also at that time. So there were pressures to promote it on and beyond touring.

CC: I can certainly see why CBS might be concerned with the change in direction, especially with *"Saved."*

DK: I think Bob himself was unhappy with that album. He certainly tried to stop its release. I don't know how he planned to achieve that though.

CC: How about the residency at the Fox-Warfield?

DK: He was staying not too far away, in a small hotel. There was something else going on in San Francisco at the time, and it was the only one where he could get a whole floor, though a floor only meant about eight rooms! Amazingly when we got to the hotel, someone had the room next to him! He was an old Englishman in his fifties. He was there for a week everywhere with us. Everybody thought he was a friend of somebody else! It turned out he was part of a fact finding...He would talk to us trying to find out what Bob was planning to do and to see if Dylan was a threat somehow. The minute he decided that Bob wasn't going to upset the world or start a revolution or something, he left!

CC: Presumably, when that audience walked into the first Fox Warfield gig on November 1, 1979, they were not expecting Dylan to play a totally new, religious set?

DK: Probably not. In those days there was no real awareness beforehand.

CC: Can you make some comment on the reaction that went down? Was there slow hand clapping and people walking out, as press reports suggest?

DK: Actually next morning we would go to this little restaurant next to the gig and he'd buy all the papers and we'd read the reviews, and you would not believe that these people were at the show. It was nothing like; I mean yeah, there were some people that walked out, but they were minute, small by comparison with people that were there. There were a lot of freaks there; it was the weirdest crowd I'd ever seen. Every night would be strange, but San Francisco was like that anyway. There was every kind of cult you could imagine, but they all stayed and I think they all loved it. I'm not sure if they understood. They always had the vocal so loud at these shows though; I'd never seen a live show where the vocals were so clear.

CC: Presumably by the time the first shows were over people were getting aware of what was happening.

DK: And it would all fall away, but it didn't: they were all sold out. I don't think there were ever any empty seats, and lots of people came back. They went more than once. I think they knew they were going through an historical event. The first time was a shock, the second was to take it all in.

CC: Do you think there were many religious factions turning up at the gigs?

DK: As far as Christian organisations were concerned, none. There were lots of cults. See, what happened was kind of sad. Previous to going, he had asked me to try to organise the various churches, saying, *"Can you bring some people to try to help out?"* I called up a couple of organisations and they didn't want to get involved unless they were the only ones. When I told them no, you'll have to share, none of them would do it. So there were no official ties with any concerts. But he couldn't stop the little weird cults turning up, some of whom were weirder than weird...after each concert, we'd collect all the books that were given to him.

CC: Do you think he read all that stuff?

DK: He read enough to recognise the common denominator. He'd just go through and that was one of my specialities, of having gone through all that...So, he'd ask me what they all were and some of them he would just throw over his shoulder. He did know an awful lot. There was one guy, the guy who introduced LSD. He wrote a lot of books. He would bring his down and Bob and he seemed to go back a long way. I think his name was Leary. Every show there would be at least ten celebrities backstage waiting in line. You'd come off stage from doing your job and you'd see a line of people like it was for a restaurant and each of them was a star. It was strange to see them standing there waiting to see him. It was really like visiting the king.

CC: I would think that would get rather irritating after a while.

DK: Yeah, but he knows it's part of it and he plays the game. He keeps them at it. They were all there, actors, singers, film stars.

CC: How did the band get around?

DK: Well, we flew to San Francisco. Then we stayed there and took buses elsewhere.

The funny thing is the night we booked into San Francisco, George Harrison was in that hotel. George, of course, is a Hindu. They have been the best of friends, but the minute Bob checked in, George checked out! He actually ran away! Bob could not understand it.

CC: Did you arrive the day of the first concert?

DK: No, the day before, there was a sound check the morning of the first show. Just the one and that was it.

CC: A lot has been said of his having his food prepared. Was there much evidence of that?

DK: Well, if there was I didn't see it. The promoter Bill Graham would have restaurants booked for the entourage for the tour, Greek, French, and Bob would be there eating the food. These were common restaurants. Frequently there was a little *greasy spoon* type restaurant near the hotels, and he'd go in there, sit, and talk to the locals for hours. He loved that chance for normal contact with people. He loved to meet people who were not shattered by his presence.

CC: The next shows were in Santa Monica: these were billed as *"Benefit for Cambodia."* (sic)1 Can you recall any of this?

DK: Well, if they were it must have been purely financial. I didn't see any difference except that they were big venues...Bob was never really satisfied with Fred Tackett's playing. The Fox-Warfield was really hysterical, 'cos after the concert there would be another concert for three hours downstairs, 'cos the Warfield is an old theatre that has a whole downstairs section that's a duplicate of upstairs. So they'd come down and they'd all be so up that they'd do a whole other show of other things! And the girls were usually the instigators of that and it would sometimes go on for hours.

CC: From the tapes, it's obvious that he does a lot of talking in Arizona, Tempe, more than usual.

DK: He really did gradually open up more and more. In Arizona, he had to talk. I don't think they were walking out but they were definitely heckling. They were insisting on the old songs. I think it was answering the hecklers more than anything. At the first one, I thought he was going to put his guitar down and leave, but he stayed and talked to them...

CC: He seldom played shows on Sundays. Was there a reason for that do you think?

DK: Well, he used to visit churches. The girls took him to a black church one time that they say he really loved. He got up and was dancing and clapping, getting as excited as everyone else. This was during the Warfield shows. The Pastor would visit; Larry Myers, was on tour with him anyway.

CC: The tour ended in December; presumably, you didn't see him after until the January 1980 tour started?

DK: Well, there were rehearsals, and there were things going on all the time. The girls were often coming up with new outfits that he would check up on. Some would be too revealing and he might get mad. He took a lot of care in what they all were doing.

...There were a number of people coming and going during that [lull] between the tours. There was a lot of business going on, him disappearing and turning up at his mother's place. His mother is a big influence on his life, a major influence. At the time I guess what I remember more than the business people coming and going were the Rabbis, and the pressures his mother was putting on him to submit to these very high Rabbis from the orthodox Judaic tradition. It was like a war going on. They were trying to get him to go away and do some other training. But CBS, Bill Graham and everyone, was pushing on to him. It was ridiculous. He was realising that the community was closing in on him, especially when the Christian community were not always supportive of him. One record distributor that was responsible for putting records in about 2,000

Christian record stores refused to put Dylan's records in for a couple of years.

CC: According to *Rolling Stone,* whilst in Seattle for the gigs, he went out and bought a $25,000 engagement ring from Friedlander and Sons?

DK: I can't imagine there would be anyone then, except Helena. I had heard that they had made up again but I never saw her after December 1979. It might have been to appease her. I remember her throwing things around the room and Bob standing there. But it didn't work out. There were certainly no other girls.

CC: Can you recall much of that tour?

DK: Death threats. There was a lot of that, but one time I remember. Don Devito was representing his manager on the road. Now Don is the classic Mafioso type. He's got connections. One day when we came back to one of the hotels, he was with this tough guy. *"I've just been on the 'phone,"* he said, and someone had threatened to blow up the stage that night. Everyone was on edge that night, except Bob. I guess it's something he has learnt to live with. I mean if they wanted to kill him when he's up there on stage, how could he stop them? The police were concerned. In fact they did actually catch someone; I think it was probably in Denver.

CC: That tour ended in February so that Bob could cut the tracks they had been playing throughout. Were you in the studio too?

DK: No. I wish I was; I heard lots about it though. They were all dissatisfied with the album. He wanted to redo it but there was no time. CBS wanted it out quick, as the tours were all going on. I did suggest that maybe he should produce his own albums and you should have seen the look he gave me.

CC: Did you know he co-produced his next album, *"Shot of Love"*?

DK: Wow! No, I had no idea he did! That's amazing.

CC: The next tour, which started in April 1980, was the last wholly religious tour. According to the reports, some were recorded and filmed?

DK: Yes, he was contemplating issuing a live record. The problem was from the beginning that *"Saved"* should have been a live album. It occurred to him to record the shows, but the record company were not interested; they wouldn't put any money into it. I think it was a good idea but it was too late. I do recall there were cameras at some shows but I don't know whose.

CC: You were around for one more tour; the return shows at the Warfield in November 1980.

DK: Actually, I left in the middle of that. I am probably one of the few who left like that. I left to do an album. He said, *'If you ever want to come back, you got a job still,'* and from what I've heard he always fires people. I never took him up on that.

CC: From the first gig, he started playing some of the old songs again.

DK: I think he had realised that songs like *'Blowin In The Wind'* were still saying the things he meant. I remember him saying at one gig: *"I told you once that the answer is blowin' in the wind, and it is. I said the times were a changin', and they are. Now I'm saying you 'Gotta Serve Somebody,' and you do."* I think that's why he started the old things again; he could relate to it, see the value.

CC: *"Biograph"* came out in December 1985. Were you aware of a boxed set being talked about earlier than that?

DK: Sure, all through this period. Maybe that was why he was reviewing his old songs. I was sure he was planning it much earlier than that...One of his problems, I think, is that he is not aware of what will sell, and throws out lots of songs that are great.

CC: Do you think that in many cases these are songs that he has decided are too personal to be used?

DK: Sure. There was one song on *"Saved"* that he didn't use but I can't remember what it was. It was a girl's name. And he didn't put it out.

CC: Was it *'Angelina'*?

DK: That sounds right. Did he record it?

CC: There's a tape that's probably a Santa Monica rehearsal. I'll play it for you.

DK: – Listening to the song – That's the one. He probably never got the chorus finished; that's why it didn't come out.

CC: Do you think *'Precious Angel'* refers to Helena Springs? She thinks it does.

DK: I can't imagine him referring to Helena as a precious angel! I think it was about his previous girlfriend who lived on the East Coast. She was a really nice person.

1 The concerts were to aid World Vision International.

Published in issue #22, November 1988.

1986 – New York USA © John Hume

Talkin' Religion
by Scott Marshall

It was twenty years ago today when... Bob Dylan and his band were engaged in the *gospel tours*. Concert set lists and studio recordings from 1979-1981 revealed Dylan's newfound faith in an old-time religion – Christianity. Or perhaps more accurately, his newfound faith in a personal Jesus, since Dylan has traditionally cast a suspicious eye toward the larger community of organized religion.

A twenty-year-old Bob Dylan shared the following with Izzy Young in 1961 – *"Got no religion. Tried a bunch of different religions. Churches are divided. Can't make up their minds, and neither can I. Never saw a god; can't say until I see one."*[1]

Then, in 1979, he saw one and proceeded to say plenty!

However, before we look at that, let's backtrack a little. The seemingly immortal Dylan of 1965's *Don't Look Back* was well aware of the loaded nature of certain words. When asked by one reporter, *"Are you religious?"* Dylan questioned the question – *"Well, I don't know. What does it mean, 'religious'?. Does it mean you bow down to an idol or go to church every Sunday, that kind of stuff?"*[2]

After the infamous motorcycle accident and the passage of a couple of years, Dylan, according to his mother Beatrice Zimmerman, had the Bible placed in a prominent position in his Woodstock, New York home.[3] In 1968, friend John Cohen seemed surprised when he learned that Dylan was only familiar with the biblical parables – *"I don't think you're the kind who goes to a hotel, where the Gideons leave a Bible, and you pick it up."* A wonderfully Dylanesque answer followed – *"Well, you never know."*[4]

Incidentally, an answer given in the same year when countless Beatles fans listened to their respective *White Albums* and heard that Rocky Raccoon had made a certain discovery upon checking into his room.

In 1974, *'religion'* meant this to Dylan – *"Religion to me is a fleeting thing. Can't nail it down. It's in me and out of me. It does give me, on the surface, some images, but I don't know to what degree."*[5]

In 1976, when Neil Hickey asked how he imagined God, Dylan laughed and said, *"How come nobody ever asks Kris Kristofferson questions like that?"*[6]

Long before *'Not Dark Yet,'* his burden was more than he could bear. And even after a very public profession of faith in Jesus, Dylan still distrusted the term *religion*. While in Tucson, Arizona, for his December 1979 concerts, Dylan was informed by Bruce Heiman that a local chapter of the American Atheists would be picketing his shows. Heiman explained, *"Well, the atheists are against any sort of religion, be it Christianity..."* and then Dylan interrupted – *"Well, Christ is no religion. We're not talking about religion... Jesus Christ is the Way, the Truth and the Life... Religion is repressive to a certain degree. Religion is another form of bondage which man invents to get himself to God. But that's why Christ came. Christ didn't preach religion; He preached the Truth, the Way and the Life. He said He'd come to give life and life abundantly. He talked about life, not necessarily religion... A religion which says you have to do certain things to get to God -they're probably talking about that type of religion, which is a religion by works: you can enter into the Kingdom by what you do, what you wear, what you say, how many times a day you may pray, how many good deeds you may do. If that's what they mean by religion, that type of religion will not get you into the Kingdom, that's true."*[7]

Less than five months after Dylan uttered these comments, he found himself chatting to a concert audience in Buffalo, New York, on May 1, 1980. He again pointed to a personal, experiential Jesus, and warned that a mere building didn't equate to salvation: *"This is a nice place. I've been here before, Buffalo. As I was walking around today I noticed many tall steeples and big churches and stained glass windows. Let me tell you once again: God's not necessarily found in there. You can't get converted in no steeple or stained glass window. Well, Jesus is mighty to save. If He's in your heart, He'll convert you."*[8]

Two weeks later, Pittsburgh reporter Pat Crosby got Dylan's response to the rebellious reactions toward his new gospel material. Although part of the following quote appeared to cast *religion* in a favourable light, the overall context reveals the same song Dylan had been singing – that is, that Jesus, and not religion, is real and personal – *"I can understand why they feel rebellious about it because up until the time the Lord came into my life, I knew nothing about religion. I was just rebellious and didn't think much about it either way. I never did care much for preachers who just ask for donations all the time and talk about the world to come. I was always growing up with, 'It's all right here and now,' and until Jesus became real to me that way, I couldn't understand it."*[9]

As we know, eventually, in November 1980, Dylan did begin to sing his older songs as roaring crowds displayed their approval. Dylan addressed the subject with Robert Hilburn – *"This show evolved out of that last tour. It's like the songs aren't... how can I put it? Those songs* – his older songs – *weren't anti-God at all. I wasn't sure about that for a while...I love those songs."*[10]

Even six months earlier, Dylan had told Pat Crosby that he loved his older songs. Yet he did have a word of caution for those rambunctious souls who believed in salvation by way of the boogie – *"Oh yes, that's right. They want the old stuff. But the old stuff's not going to save them and I'm not going to save them. Neither is anybody else they follow. They can boogie all night, but it's not gonna work."*[11]

When the dust had, for the most part, settled after the gospel tours; Dylan still didn't place his faith in organized religion. Judaism, like Christianity, could get too confining if the symbols became idols. When asked by Martin Keller if he was looking for his roots, Dylan responded – *"I ain't looking for them in synagogues with six-pointed stars shining down from every window. I can tell you that much."* For Dylan the troubadour, it seemed, the church or synagogue just wasn't a feasible option. On-the-road experiences with his God in his heart would have to suffice.

But where does Bob Dylan stand? *"People want to know where I'm at because they don't know where they're at,"* Dylan lamented. He went on to tell Keller his thoughts on the time-honoured word, *religion* – *"You can turn anything into a religious context. Religion is a dirty word. It doesn't mean anything. Coca-Cola is a religion. Oil and steel are a religion. In the name of religion, people have been raped, killed and defiled. Today's religion is tomorrow's bondage."*[12]

Just prior to the release of *"Infidels,"* Robert Hilburn asked if any *"Slow Train Coming"* songs would be included in future tours. Dylan – *"Yeah, I'll probably do a few of those. I get letters from people who say they were touched by those shows. I don't disavow any of that."* However, his distrust for certain trigger words remained – *"First of all, 'born-again' is a hype term. It's a media term that throws people into a corner and leaves them there. Whether people realize it or not, all those political and religious labels are irrelevant... That was all part of my experience. It had to happen. When I get involved in something, I get totally involved. I don't just play around on the fringes."*[13]

Once the whole *religious* deal got started there would be no end to it. In 1984, when Kurt Loder asked Dylan if he felt the Old and New Testaments were equally valid, Dylan kept it brief: *"To me?"*[14]

Also in 1984, Mick Brown dared to ask Dylan what his current religious views were, and received, in return, a wry smile and the following rebuke – *"I mean nobody cares what Billy Joel's religious views are, right? What does it matter to people what Bob Dylan is? But it seems to, right? I'd honestly like to know why it's important to them."*[15]

Dylan had the opportunity to set the record straight with Cameron Crowe in conjunction with the 1985 career retrospective, *"Biograph."* Dylan reflected on the gospel tours – *"I was suffering from that so-called religious backlash at the time and that had a lot do with affecting people's opinions. I think people were prejudiced against it."* When discussing *'Every Grain of Sand,'* Dylan was still in the time of his confession – *"The Bible says, 'Even a fool when he keeps his mouth shut is counted wise,' but it comes from the Bible, so it can be cast off as being too quote religious. Make something religious and people don't have to deal with I;, they can say it's irrelevant. 'Repent, the Kingdom of God is at hand.' That scares the shit out of people. They'd like to avoid that. Tell that to someone and you become their enemy. There does come a time, though, when you have to face facts and the truth is true whether you wanna believe it or not. It doesn't need you to make it true... That lie about everybody having their own truth inside of them has done a lot of damage and made people crazy."*[16]

In a 1985 interview with Scott Cohen, Dylan spoke about a concept that Jesus had addressed – *"Whenever anybody does something in a big way, it's always rejected at home and accepted some place else. For instance, that could apply to Buddha. Who was Buddha? An Indian. Who are Buddhists? Chinese, Japanese, Asian people. They make up the big numbers in Buddhism. It's the same way with Jesus being a Jew. Who did he appeal to? He appeals to people who want to get into Heaven in a big way."* Dylan also commented on the self-imposed labels within Judaism and Christianity – *"Jews separate themselves...Orthodox, Conservative, Reform, as if God calls them that. Christians, too. Baptists, Assembly of God, Methodists, Calvinists. God has no respect for a person's title. He don't care what you call yourself."*[17]

Around the same time period, a narration segue into a Dylan interview for *ABC's* television program *20/20* stated the following He – Dylan – *"believes in the Resurrection,"* he says, but he also *"delves intensely into his own religious heritage, Orthodox Judaism."*[18]

In the year of *"Oh Mercy,"* Dylan's tune remained the same. When talking to Edna

Gundersen, he responded to the label of *"born-again"* – *"If that's what was laid on me, there must have been a reason for it. Whatever label is put on you, the purpose of it is to limit your accessibility to people. There had been so many labels laid on me in the past that it didn't matter any more at that point. What more could they say?"*

And as for those who would say Dylan's 1979-1981 albums were *religious,* Dylan disagreed – *"You'd never hear me saying that stuff is religious one way or the other. To me, it isn't. It's just based on my experience in daily matters, what you run up against and how you respond to things. People who work for big companies, that's their religion. That's not a word that has any holiness to it."*[19]

In late 1993, after obtaining an interview with Dylan, Guy Garcia wrote the following – *"Dylan who now prefers not to discuss his religious affiliation, maintains, 'People are lost because they can believe anything... A person without faith is like a walking corpse. And now people have to fight to get the faith back.'"*[20]

In 1995, John Dolen, when interviewing Dylan, referenced a lyric from a *"Slow Train Coming"* song not performed since 1980 – *"I remember the lines, 'You talk about Buddha, you talk about Mohammad/But you never said a word about the One who came to die for us instead.' Those were fearless words. How do you feel about those words and the songs you wrote during that period now?"*

Dylan responded – *"Just writing a song like that probably emancipated me from other kinds of illusions... I can't say that I would disagree with that line. On its own level, it was some kind of turning point for me, writing that."* Asked if he still saw a slow train coming, Dylan had this to say – *"When I look ahead now it's picked up quite a bit of speed. In fact, it's going like a freight train now."*[21]

Even Dylan's youngest son, Wallflowers lead singer Jakob Dylan, recalled his dad's conversion affair when interviewed in 1997 – *"I was aware that it mattered to him. He's never done anything half-assed. If he does anything, he goes fully underwater."*[22]

When Dylan was interviewed by Jon Pareles about the songs on *"Time Out Of Mind,"* he reflected on a phrase that was heavy on his mind – *"This one phrase was going through my head: 'Work while the day lasts, because the night of death cometh when no man can work.' I don't recall where I heard it. I like preaching, I hear a lot of preaching, and I probably just heard it somewhere. Maybe it's in the Psalms: it beats me. But it wouldn't let me go. I was, like, what does that phrase mean? But it was at the forefront of my mind, for a long period of time, and I think a lot of that is instilled into this record."* The origin of this phrase can be found in the Bible, a story told in John 9:1-7.

But what was Dylan's philosophy or *religion* in 1997? He shared this with Pareles – *"Those old songs are my lexicon and prayer book...All my beliefs come out of those old songs, literally, anything from 'Let Me Rest On That Peaceful Mountain' to 'Keep On The Sunny Side.' You can find all my philosophy in those old songs. I believe in a God of time and space, but if people ask me about that, my impulse is to point them back toward those songs. I believe in Hank Williams singing 'I Saw The Light.' I've seen the Light, too."*[23]

Onstage in 1979-1980, it seems, Dylan would've gladly offered up the identity of *"the Light"* or revealed just exactly who this *"God of time and space"* was, but, in 1997, readers of *'The New York Times'* would have to read between the lines. Perhaps Dylan paid a price to get out of going through all these things twice.

During the same time period, Dylan gave an interview to David Gates and expressed the same thought – *"Here's the thing with me and the religious thing. This is the flat-out truth: I find the religiosity and philosophy in the music. I don't find it anywhere else.*

Songs like 'Let Me Rest On a Peaceful Mountain' or 'I Saw The Light' – that's my religion. I don't adhere to rabbis, preachers, evangelists, all of that. I've learned more from the songs than I've learned from any of this kind of entity. The songs are my lexicon. I believe the songs."[24]

Dylan had previously referred to a real preacher as being one who didn't require adherence – *"The basic thing, I feel, is to get in touch with Christ yourself. He will lead you. Any preacher who is a real preacher will tell you that: 'Don't follow me, follow Christ'."*[25]

Interestingly enough, Dylan's 1998 tour included a reintroduction of a song he had laid dormant since 1991 – *'Gotta Serve Somebody,'* which he opened thirty-one shows with. This marked the first time he chose to open with the *"Slow Train Coming"* song since the 1979-1981 gospel tours – for the true obsessive, there was one exception 27/10/89.

In 1999 the surprises kept coming. In addition to belting out *'Gotta Serve Somebody'* another twenty-five times, Dylan dipped deep into the lexicon. He introduced a handful of overt songs about Jesus, choosing to open many of his shows with songs such as *'Hallelujah, I'm Ready To Go'* (11 times), *'Somebody Touched Me'* (10 times) and *'I Am The Man, Thomas'* (21 times). Other songs in the concert repertoire included Christian hymns from previous centuries! – *'Rock Of Ages'* from 1776, and *'Pass Me Not, O Gentle Savior'* from 1868. And for those waiting patiently to check off the one remaining song Dylan had not played live before from the *"Saved"* album, he treated a Philadelphia, Pennsylvania crowd to *'A Satisfied Mind.'*[26]

A recently released soundtrack for the film *Wonder Boys* features the first new song from Dylan since *"Time Out of Mind."* The song, *'Things Have Changed,'* includes the line, *"If the Bible is right, the world will explode."*[27]

Hardly a surprising line considering Dylan's history. This sentiment is right along the lines of *'The Rainbow Sign,'* the song that Dylan's female singers sang some twenty years ago during the gospel tours- and along the lines of *'God Knows,'* which Dylan wrote some ten years ago – and along the lines of a song Dylan introduced at his last show of 1999 in Newark, Delaware, *'This World Can't Stand.'*

As the writer of Ecclesiastes – perhaps King Solomon – wrote, *"What has been will be again, what has been done will be done again; there is nothing new under the sun."*[28]

Some 3,000 years later, blues singer Blind Lemon Jefferson wrote a song entitled *'See That My Grave Is Kept Clean,'* the same song Bob Dylan offered up on his debut album of 1962. A then twenty-year-old Dylan adapted the Jefferson song to include the following snarling declaration – *"Now I believe what the bible told."*

As Dylan has walked these nearly forty years of road since, it seems his lexicon resembles a perfectly drawn circle. May your song always be sung. And may the Lord have mercy on us all.

Sources Cited:

1 Young, Izzy *The Izzy Young Notebooks,* entry October 23, 1961, originally published in *"Other Scenes,"* 1968 Israel G. Young

2 Pennebaker, D.A. *Don't Look Back*, Leacock-Pennebaker, Inc, 1967

3 Thompson, Toby, *Positively Main Street*, Coward-McCann, 1971.

4 Cohen, John and Happy Traum, *Conversations with Bob Dylan, Sing Out!,* October/November 1968.

5 Shelton, Robert. *No Direction Home,* New York: Ballantine Books, 1986.

6 Hickey, Neil. *A Voice Still Blowin' in the Wind,* TV Guide, September 17-11, 1976.

7 Heiman, Bruce. Clinton Heylin's *Saved! – Part Two, The Telegraph* #29, Spring 1988, transcript of Heiman's interview with Dylan on December 7, 1979; broadcast on KMGX Radio, Tucson, Arizona.

8 Heylin, Clinton. *Saved!: The Gospel Speeches of Bob Dylan,* Madras & New York: Hanuman Books, 1990.

9 Crosby, Pat. Clinton Heylin's *Saved!,* Part Three, *The Telegraph* #30, Summer 1988, transcript of Crosby's interview with Dylan on May *15,* 1980; broadcast on *KDKA* TV, Pittsburgh, Pennsylvania.

10 Hilburn, Robert. *Dylan: I Learned That Jesus is Real and I Wanted That, Los Angeles Times,* November 23, 1980.

11 Crosby, same as 9.

12 Keller, Martin. *Times Are a Changin': In Search of the Latest Bob Dylan, Dallas Times-Herald,"* November 6, 1983. Original interview conducted by Keller in July 1983 for the *Minneapolis City Pages.*

13 Hilburn, Robert. *Bob Dylan at 42-- Rolling Down Highway 61 Again, Los Angeles Times,* October 30, 1983.

14 Loder, Kurt. *The Rolling Stone* Interview: Bob Dylan, *Rolling Stone,* June 21, 1984.

15 Brown, Mick. *Dylan: Jesus, Who's Got Time to Keep Up with the Times? Sunday Times,* July 1, 1984.

16 Crowe, Cameron. *"Biograph,"* New York: CBS Inc., 1985-Dylan's quotes are from Crowe's interviews found in the liner notes and booklet.

17 Cohen, Scott. *Don't Ask Me Nothin' About Nothin,' I Just Might Tell You The Truth, Spin,* Vol 1, No.8, December 1985.

18 Downs, Hugh. ABC's *20/20,* October 8, 198 6 – according to Bill Youngblood – on rec.music.Dylan – Downs interviewed Dylan and this particular quote, a narration segment, preceded the interview.

19 Gundersen, Edna. *USA Today,* September 21, 1989

20 Garcia, Guy. *Rock Finds Religion...Again: New Groups Groping for Eternal Values, New York Times,* January 2, 1994

21 Dolen, John. *A Recent Interview with Bob Dylan On the Tracks #,7* Spring 1996.

22 Hirshey, Gerri. *Jakob's Ladder, Rolling Stone,* June 12, 1997.

23 Pareles, Jon. *A Wiser Voice Blowin' in the Autumn Wind, New York Times,* September28, 1997

24 Gates, David. *Dylan Revisited, Newsweek,* October 6, 1997

25 Hilburn, Robert. Same as 10.

26 The various set list data – 1979-1999 – obtained from Dylan folks such as Michael Krogsgaard *Positively Bob Dylan,* Mike Wyvill & John Wraith – their annual tour booklets – Mick & Laurie McCuistion – *Series of Dreams* – and Bill Pagel who all, no doubt, had help from others.

27 King, James A. Transcription of lyrics from Dylan's song, *'Things Have Changed;'* posted January 23, 2000, on Karl Erik Andersen's web page @ www.eipectingrain.com

28 Ecclesiastes 1:9 taken from the *Holy Bible, New International Version,* copyright 1973 by the International Bible Society; published by Zondervan Bible Publishers in Grand Rapids, Michigan.

Published in issue #90, May 2000

Some Great Live Performances
November 16, 1979 Warfield Theater, San Francisco, USA
by Roger Pulman

"I've escaped death so many times/I know I'm only living by the saving grace that's over me."
Bob Dylan 1979.

Bob Dylan's acceptance of Christ may well have started in a sports arena in San Diego, California! He was on the final leg of his mammoth 1978 year-long world tour when on November 17, a rather unwell looking Dylan bent down to pick up a silver cross that had been thrown onto the stage. The very fact that Dylan retrieved an item thrown by a member of the audience was unusual; the fact that the item was a cross was even more so.

Two days later while in a hotel room in Tucson, Dylan believes that he had a visitation by Christ –

"There was a presence in the room that couldn't have been anybody but Jesus... Jesus put his hand on me... I felt my whole body tremble. The glory of the Lord knocked me down and picked me up."
Bob Dylan 1980

A few days later Dylan could be seen wearing the cross on stage. The book of poems from *'Tangled Up In Blue'* had become the Bible. Dylan had a number of reasons for wishing to undertake the gruelling 1978 world tour. His marriage to Sara Lownds – performed in secret in 1965 – had finally broken down and a painful divorce case was concluded in June 1977, after which, a long and bitter custody battle had eventually ended with Sara winning guardianship of their children.

Almost immediately the custody case ended, Dylan's film *Renaldo and Clara* premiered in New York and Los Angels. The reviews were terrible, and in part justifiably so. The film was overly personal, extremely complex, and although painstakingly structured by Dylan, the result appeared to many to lack cohesion. The film certainly didn't have any kind of linear plot. These faults were exaggerated because of the tiresome length of the film, which had been edited down – with Dylan's assistance – from 240,000 feet of film. The finished article ran for nearly four hours, making it a sure-fire candidate for commercial suicide.

Dylan had remarked that he knew it wasn't going to be a short movie, *"because we couldn't tell the story in an hour...Originally I couldn't see how we could do it in under seven or eight hours."* A business consortium would later offer Dylan a cool $2 million to allow the release of a two-hour version of the film. After his previous comments regarding the proposed length of the movie, Dylan was surely aware that a two-hour version would not work. The hacked down version of the movie consisted of little more than concert footage and previous accusations about a lack of cohesion were now truer than ever. While failing to soften the blow of rejection, two million dollars would, however, help to recoup *some* of the massive losses incurred by Dylan through *Renaldo and Clara.*

It was therefore against a background of disappointment and loss of money regarding the film, a divorce from Sara – rumoured to have cost him £36 million and a half share of the royalties from the songs written while Bob and Sara were married – and more importantly to Bob, the loss of his children, that he returned to the road for 114 shows. The concert tour grossed in excess of $20 million and was dubbed in some quarters as the *"alimony tour."* It was also against this background of disillusionment that Dylan encountered Christ.

Almost immediately following the Christ experience, Dylan began to write new songs. At sound-checks he could be heard working on a song called *'Slow Train,'* and at the final show on the tour, in Miami – December 16, 1978 – he debuted a new song, *'Do Right To Me Baby (Do Unto Others).'*

After the tour, new songs continued to flow, and he soon had an album's worth of new material. *"Slow Train Coming"* was released in August 1979 and on November 1, Dylan began a 14-night residency in downtown San Francisco at the intimate 2,200 seat Fox Warfield Theater. Originally booked for seven nights, the run at this comfortable, if slightly seedy theatre had been extended to fourteen sold out concerts.

If going electric in 1966 had alienated a large faction of his followers, it was as nothing compared to the backlash to one of America's most famous Jews turning to Christ. Unlike 1966, however, the resulting alienation of fans did not manifest itself so much in a mass exodus from concert halls, but in a decline in record sales. This fall in sales was markedly more noticeable in the USA, where his next album release, *"Saved"* – 1980 – only reached #24 in the Billboard top 200 and was therefore the first Bob Dylan album since *"Another Side Of..."* not to represented on the American top 20.

The concert was divided into three sections, the opening spot being a vehicle for three beautiful black female singers – Regina Havis, Helena Springs and MonaLisa Young – to perform six equally beautifully arranged gospel songs, accompanied by Terry Young on piano.

'If I've Got My Ticket, Lord, Can I Ride?' *'It's Gonna Rain,'* *'Lord Please Hold My Hand,'* *'Look Up And Live by Faith,'* *'Oh Freedom'* and the finally Guthrie's *'This Train (Is Bound For Glory).'*

The set is received extremely well by the audience and without a break – just a dimming of the lights – on comes Dylan with his band of incredibly talented and versatile *session* musicians.

All the musicians except Terry Young have a pedigree as long as your arm. Tim Drummond (bass) who had already played on Dylan's *"Slow Train Coming"* album had worked with the Beach Boys, John Mayall and Ronnie Hawkins, amongst others. Fred

Tackett (guitar) had worked on sessions with Cher, Little Feat, Rod Stewart and Elkie Brooks. Spooner Oldham (keyboards) had played on albums by the likes of Etta James, Aretha Franklin and the Everly Brothers, while Jim Keltner, one of the finest drummers around had worked on dozens of albums by world-class artists like John Lennon, George Harrison, Eric Clapton and Joe Cocker. Interestingly, various combinations of Dylan's road band had also worked together on albums by Neil Young, JJ Cale, Ry Cooder and Jackson Browne. Without question, this was an outfit to be reckoned with.

The second part of the concert features seven songs from the *"Slow Train Coming"* album, plus two unreleased songs, *'Ain't No Man Righteous, No Not One,'* which is an outtake from the album, and a new song called *'Covenant Woman.'*

The third section of the show, which follows a solo performance by MonaLisa Young singing *'(God Uses) Ordinary People,'* sees Dylan performing two more *"Slow Train..."* numbers, followed by five new songs from the forthcoming album *"Saved,"* plus two encores.

The first thing I noticed, was the marked difference between the songs on *"Slow Train Coming"* and the new songs destined for the next album. The *"Slow Train..."* songs appear to have been written almost as a way of converting nonbelievers. *"You either got faith or ya got unbelief and there ain't no neutral ground."* – *'Precious Angel'*. Whereas the new songs are less judgemental, less *them and us,* they seem to focus more on singing the praises of the Lord and celebrating Christ's name then preaching hellfire and damnation.

During this period in his life/career it seems evident that Dylan is totally convinced that all nonbelievers *must* be made to see the error of their ways. This attitude is entirely consistent with the single-minded approach that Dylan had taken throughout his career. It seems that *now*, as in 1966, regardless of the derision from his audience or critics, Dylan would press on with what he believed. This self-belief and unwillingness to bend to popular pressure gave the press another chance to get their collective teeth into Dylan.

Unfortunately, Joel Selvin's scathing attack on Dylan in the *San Francisco Chronicle* that read *"Bob Dylan's God-Awful Gospel!"* and went onto make reference to cat-calls, boos and people walking out of concerts, was widely syndicated. After reading the review, a furious Dylan took the extraordinary step of calling Selvin at home to rescind his right to review any further Dylan concerts!

Dressed in black leather and denim, Dylan exudes a positive approach toward the task in hand and with thirteen concerts at this venue already behind him his confidence is high.

'Gotta Serve Somebody' rocks the main segment of the show to a positive start and Dylan seems in excellent voice considering the riggers of the previous year's touring.

Of the *"Slow Train..."* songs, the best live performances are *'Gotta Serve Somebody,' 'I Believe In You,' 'When He Returns'* featuring Dylan on guitar and Oldham grand piano, and even though it lacked Mark Knopfler's wonderful guitar parts, *'Precious Angel.'* Three of these four songs are included in the opening four numbers, which present a powerfully and compelling start to the performance.

As on previous nights *'Man Gave Names To All The Animals'* allows the band to relax a little. Earlier in the Warfield residency, *'Slow Train'* seemed a little under rehearsed but tonight it is spot on.

'Covenant Woman' marks the point at which the concert really catches fire. Dylan appears to still be on a high from creating this new song and while his voice and tone are passionate, he also comes across as warm and friendly. After *'Covenant Woman'* the concert just can't get better. But it does! *'Solid Rock'* rocks with great bass and a great overall power that wins the audience over almost to a man.

'*Saving Grace*' is a pleasant laid back song: not too much of Dylan the preacher here. He then asks the plaintive question '*What Can I Do For You?*' great harp solo on this one. '*In The Garden*' is a wonderful ending to the concert; Dylan's vocal performance on this one is simply stunning. This was the longest concert of the Warfield residency, featuring a one-off performance of '*Ain't No Man Righteous.*'

Dylan returns – if returns is the right word, as he doesn't actually leave the stage – for two encores: the rather innocuous '*Blessed Be The Name Of The Lord*' and a song from the forthcoming "*Saved*" album, '*Pressing On.*' For this final song Dylan moves over to the piano. '*Pressing On*' is a simple song with beautiful words and a gorgeous piano accompaniment. This was a fitting end to an emotionally stunning concert.

For most of the evening Terry Young's piano blended superbly with Oldham's organ; Tim Drummond's bass was a little too loud on several numbers, but otherwise the rhythm section worked extremely well: Jim Keltner's stick-work was immaculate. Tonight, as most nights during this residency, Keltner was reduced to tears of emotion.

With the odd exception, as the fourteen nights at the Warfield progressed the concerts seemed to get better. A tight band got even tighter and more importantly, as Dylan grew in confidence, his performances became steadily stronger. This was the coming together of all the elements that he had been working on over the past twelve months. In fact, this climax to a unique set of concerts came a year to the day after Dylan had picked up that silver cross from the stage in San Diego.

There is no doubt that Dylan was tremendously passionate about his newfound beliefs and values and that he felt he had to share these feelings with his audience – even if some of them didn't want to listen. Consequently, with only his beliefs and this new music to shield him, Dylan stood naked before his audience. As in 1966, he stood his ground and pitched himself against the nonbelievers, in the process alienating some of them forever. Now as then, he may lost have lost a few battles, but in the final end he won the war.

Commissioned for inclusion in *ISIS: A Bob Dylan Anthology*.

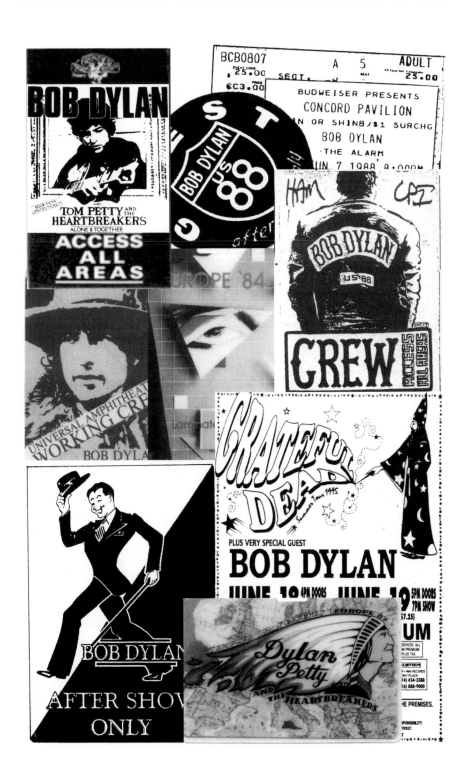

A Chat With Jerry Garcia
Interview by Michael Goldman

The following piece is a brief chat between Michael Goldman and Grateful Dead guitarist, the late Jerry Garcia. This is an extract from an interview that was conducted in San Francisco in April 1994.

I had met Jerry on several occasions and found him to be charming and extremely interesting to talk with. As usual, Jerry was responsive to my questions, but was noticeably hesitant when talking about Bob Dylan.

MG: Sixties artists seem to be the big ticket at the moment. How much of this is a nostalgia trip for concert goers?

JG: Maybe a little, but I think that we have a lot to offer, and anyway, many of the kids that come to see us weren't even around in the sixties, so it can't be nostalgia for them.

MG: What do you think the Grateful Dead, Bob Dylan and some of the others like the Rolling Stones have that has enabled them to span the decades and generations?

JG: If only I knew (laughter). It's something that can't be defined or categorised; good music endures.

MG: How long have you known Bob Dylan?

JG: I've known Bob for a number of years.

MG: How was it that you came to work together in the eighties?

JG: We asked Bob if he would like to do a couple of songs with us on that tour, simple as that. He was playing with Tom Petty at the time. We talked to him later that year and he said 'yes' to playing some shows.

MG: That's the 1987 tour from which the joint album was recorded?

JG: Yeah.

MG: How much time was spent rehearsing Dylan's songs?

JG: We worked through a lot of songs for two or three weeks before those concerts. We dug up a few songs that Bob hadn't been playing, so we had to go through those songs. It was kinda nice. It was also nice to just hang out with Bob and discuss our mutual musical influences. He wasn't writing too much then, still isn't. I think he was looking for a new direction in which to take his songs.

MG: What musical influences do you have in common?

JG: Oh, I don't know, we talked about people like Elizabeth Cotten, Mississippi Sheiks, Earl Scruggs, Bill Monroe, Gus Cannon, Hank Williams. We tried a few of those things out at rehearsal; I showed Bob some of those songs: *'Two Soldiers,' 'Jack-A-Roe' 'John Hardy'* and some others. Trouble was, Bob seemed to prefer to do those rather than to rehearse his own songs (laughs).

At a previous rehearsal we ran through one of Robert's (Hunter) songs *'Black Muddy River.'* Bob liked that song and he took two of Robert's songs for his next album. Robert had a book of songs that he'd written. We had taken a couple of them for our album, but I guess we missed *'Silvio'* (laughs). He also put a new band together 'cos things were getting a little stale for him around then.

I think Bob was looking for a change at that time. After those dates he told me that playing with the Grateful Dead had helped him rediscover some of his old songs. He found they took on a new lease of life. You need to keep the songs fresh, to create, and to go on recreating. It's all about the tension of trying to create, and expression – you have to live those songs.

MG: What was it like playing with Bob Dylan?

JG: It was great, playing and just hanging out together. Some nights we just drove around till dawn.

MG: That was here in California?

JG: San Rafael. I'd always thought what a great idea it would be to get Bob Dylan and Grateful Dead on stage together.

MG: So it was your idea to get together?

JG: Actually, the first time we got together was Bob's idea. We all enjoyed it so later on we asked Bob if he was prepared to do it again in a bigger, more organised way and he said *'yes.'*

What follows is an anecdotal piece from the lips of Robert Hunter. I, for one, had no idea how Dylan came to work with Hunter and from this it appears that their so-called *collaboration* was actually far from that!

This interview extract published in David Gans's book *Conversations With The Dead, Citadel Press*, 1991, is taken from a brief radio interview conducted, February 25, 1988, in San Rafael, CA.

The interviewer asks Robert Hunter how his collaboration with Bob Dylan came about.

R.H: You couldn't be easier to work with than Dylan. I brought the book – I think it had fifteen to seventeen songs – in to the Dead before we made *"In The Dark"* – two songs were selected. I took about three of them for the *"Liberty"* album, and Dylan took two of them for his album, set 'em, and sent me a tape. That's what I call easy to work with! He just flipped through the songbook that was sitting there at Front Street, liked these tunes, put 'em in his pocket, went off, set 'em to music, recorded 'em and... First time I met him he said – Dylan voice: *'Eh, I just recorded two of your tunes!'* And I said, *'Neat.'* (Laughs)

Q: He didn't even ask first?

R.H: Bob Dylan doesn't have to ask a lyricist if he can do his tunes! Come on, man!

I gotta just say this for the record – you got your Grammies, you got your Bammies, you got your Rock 'n' Roll Hall of Fame – as far as I'm concerned, Bob Dylan has done two of my songs, and those other things sound far away, distant and not very interesting.

Published in issue #78, May 1998

Daniel Lanois
by Derek Barker

Dylan says of Lanois – *"It's very hard to find a producer that can play. A lot of them can't even engineer. They've just got a big title and know how to spend a lot of money. It was thrilling to run into Daniel because he's a competent musician and he knows how to record with modern facilities. For me, that was lacking in the past. He managed to get my stage voice, something other people working with me never were quite able to achieve."*

In the studio – *"The meter's running all the time. The cost is unrealistic. I mean you could put up a wing of a hospital. Daniel just allowed the record to take place any old time, day or night. You don't have to walk through secretaries, pinball machines and managers and hangers-on in the lobby and parking lots and elevators and arctic temperatures. You need help to make a record, in all the directions that go into making a record. People expect me to bring in a Bob Dylan song, sing it and then they record it. Other people don't work that way; there's more feedback."*[1]

Canadian by birth and French by descent, by the time Daniel Lanois met Bob Dylan he had already gained impeccable credentials. His production work included U2, Peter Gabriel, Robbie Robertson, and The Neville Brothers record *"Yellow Moon,"* which in turn led to his involvement with Bob Dylan's album *"Oh Mercy."*

Lanois, a young looking thirty-seven, was born in French Quebec and at the age of ten moved with his family to Ontario. *"Moving to Ontario, which is an English community, I felt for the first time a sense of isolation...I suppose the language was the biggest barrier you know, I didn't like the English language, and I was forced to have to accommodate it."*[2]

These days, his recording facility *Studio On The Move,* can take him most anywhere and in the last few years as well as maintaining a flat in London, Lanois has spent a great deal of time in New Orleans, Los Angeles and Ireland. At seventeen, in partnership with brother Bob, Lanois was running his own home studio in Hamilton, Ontario, when a Toronto band called Time Twins recorded a demo there. The band later played the demo for Brian Eno who passed on the band, but loved the sound of the tape and enquired after the studio and producer. Although Brian Eno was a founder member of the seventies mega group Roxy Music and the visionary producer of among others Talking Heads,

Lanois had never heard the name.

"I was pretty isolated up there...When he called, we asked for cash up front because we didn't know anything about him, so he walked in with $1,800 in hundred dollar bills."[3]

After working together on a number of *ambient* projects, Eno and Lanois were hired by U2 as the production team for their 1984 album, *"The Unforgettable Fire."* The resulting album enjoyed worldwide sales in excess of ten million copies and Lanois was now out on his own. His first major solo production work was on Peter Gabriel's album, *"So."*

Lanois then teamed up with fellow Canadian, Robbie Robertson to help co-produce Robertson's first solo album. The presence of Lanois on the record is easily identifiable by the dark mysterious feel that runs through much of his work; Robertson's *'Somewhere Down The Crazy River,'* Gabriel's *'Red Rain,'* and latterly Dylan's *'Man In a Long Black Coat,'* all carry the unmistakable Lanois trademark.

Lanois – *"Bono had been telling me about Bob and how he thought that he was ready to make a great record, and that he figured we'd make a good team. So it was on that recommendation that we came to work together."*[2]

"Dylan then happened to be touring the south during these sessions – The Neville Brothers record *"Yellow Moon" – and he visited the makeshift studio when he played New Orleans."*[3]

"We'd had one conversation before that, so just him paying that visit was like a reassurance of the work relationship. He wanted to see how I worked, you know, like setting up the studio in a strange location, it's not a new idea but it's somewhat unorthodox."[7]

"Dylan stopped in and heard The Neville's 'With God On Our Side' and 'The Ballad Of Hollis Brown.' He just sat there and thought that 'God On Our Side' was one of the best records he'd ever heard. Aside from the fact that he wrote the song he just kept saying, 'That's a great record,' kept repeating it over and over again. From Bob that's a big compliment."[4]

Dylan arrived in New Orleans in March and took up residence in a house on Audubon Avenue, which is situated in an uptown district of the city.

"We found an empty turn of the century apartment building, a five-storey building, a fantastic place...it had a bordello-ish overtone. We essentially turned the control room into a swamp. You know, we gave it a swampish scene: we had moss all over the place and stuffed animals and alligator heads."[7]

"We hit it off. I think he understood that I provided a setting and a sound that he otherwise wouldn't be exposed to...He came in with songs completed, though three were finished off in the studio. For someone to have all their songs ready like he did is very unusual for me. I like it, it's kind of a luxury."[4]

"Bob likes to get something quickly if possible, you know, in the name of spontaneity. On this record we used both approaches. You know, some things came quick and we grabbed them that way, and then we also spent a lot of time on detail: you know some of the vocals we worked on quite a bit and the lyrics were changed and we chipped away at them. Some of the tracks went down in one take, like er 'Political World'."[7]

"We went into the studio – for seven weeks in all – with full commitment and worked real hard and put a lot of heart into the work. It shows in the record: it sounds like people playing music. Which is what it was. We just used the services of neighbourhood musicians and they came by and played and did the best versions of the songs that we could come up with, and it shows it's warm sounding. Bob is coming across real strong.

Bob Dylan is a very committed lyricist; he would walk into the studio and put his head into the pages of words that he had and not let up until it was done. It was quite fascinating to see the transformation that some of the songs made: they would begin as one story and at the end of the night they would be something else. One of my favourites is 'Man In a Long Black Coat,' which was written in the studio and recorded in one take."[2]

The cricket sounds were introduced by Lanois purely to create an atmosphere, against which Dylan could perform his lyrics. However, the effect was pleasing enough to remain for prosperity on the finished record. The song paints a picture of small town Americana, a dancehall on the outskirts of town and how a very strange individual comes in and *"Not a word of goodbye, not even a note/She's gone with the man in a long black coat."*[2]

"Bob's got this thing with phrasing that I like a lot. His ability to punctuate words is real special..."[4]

"Those are Brian Eno's – synthetic – cricket sounds. I guess I can't use them any more now that I've used them on two tracks. But that song of Bob's actually has the word crickets in the lyrics. It was just Bob and I playing a couple of guitars and Malcolm (Burn) was trying some keyboard parts and I said not to bother, just give us some 'crickets.' We were just looking to create a setting, so Brian's crickets made it onto Bob's record."[4]

"I prefer twenty-four tracks, and to use 'real' instruments, I prefer hand-played sounds and I like the presence of human beings in a track! If the track is done with machines, you get discipline and constancy, but that doesn't work for all music. I usually prefer natural sounds, especially from drums."[5]

"We put in a lot of care with the vocals and the sounds. There's not really the obvious presence of synthesizers, just straight-ahead drums and bass and guitars, yet there's this blazing strangeness around it. It's got some wonderful moments, wonderful words, and he's singing great."[3]

In summing up, Lanois says of his work on *"Oh Mercy"* – *"It's mysterious and dark, like most things that I work on. Some of the songs on this record are the best songs I've heard in a while. And his voice sounds very sensuous...He's such a fine lyricist and craftsman with words. He's staggering. The concentration that he has for lyrics has made such a strong impression on me that I decided I was very lazy in comparison."*[8]

"I will not produce records that I don't believe in, and I never write music that I don't care for. I will never cater to the demands of the marketplace, but only cater to the people I trust."[6]

After *"Oh Mercy"* Lanois took many of the same musicians back into the studio to record his own excellent début album, *"Acadie."*

1 *USA Today*, Interview with Edna Gundersen, 22-09-89.
2 *BBC Radio One "Stereo Sequence"* Interview.
3 *Request*, Musicland Record chain Magazine, *"Hoodoo Guru,"* by Don Mcleese, October 1989
4 *N.M.E. "Ambience Chaser"* by Gavin Martin, 07-10-89.
5 *The Independent, "Mix From The Sticks,"* by Andy Gill, 15-09-89
6 *The* – Hamilton – *Spectator, "Lanois Front And Centre"* by Nick Krewen, 11-08-98.
7 *Up Close* New, York Radio Interview 30-10-89
8 *Rolling Stone, "Random Notes,"* by Sheila Rogers, 21-09-89

Update: March 15, 2001.

Seven years after the release of the critically acclaimed *"Oh Mercy"* Dylan returned to the studio with Daniel Lanois in the hope of recapturing the ethereal sound of those sessions. This time Dylan was looking for a natural depth of field – the vocal out front with musicians placed behind him and others further back still – a 1950s sound.

The resulting album *"Time Out of Mind"* was, to say the least, met with a mixed reception. Uncharacteristically, the music press were solidly behind Dylan. However, Lanois' production split the Dylan community into two camps and the pro- / anti- Lanois debate continues today. The album went on to win three Grammy Awards, including Best Album.

1996 – Lollipop Fest, Sweden © Roland Hansson

2000 – Florence, Italy © Giulio Molfese

A Chat With César Díaz
Interview conducted by Derek Barker

"By the way, don't be bewildered by the Never Ending Tour chatter. There was a Never Ending Tour but it ended in '91 with the departure of guitarist G.E. Smith."
Bob Dylan, 1993.

César Díaz spent from 1988 to 1993 with Bob Dylan as Dylan's personal guitar and amp tech and as guitarist with the band. During his six months as a band member – September 1990 to March 1991 – César played a total 53 concerts, the latter ones being alongside his eventual replacement, John Jackson. After leaving the band César had an open invitation to play whenever he liked and made a further seven guest appearances with Dylan, often playing on his birthday.

Born in Old San Juan, Puerto Rico, César Carillo-Díaz came to America in 1969 with Johnny Nash before moving on to join Frijid Pink. César arrived in the USA with a Rickenbacker guitar and $20 in his pocket. *"Prejudice,"* he says, thwarted his many efforts to establish himself as a performing musician; so, he began doing repairs on instruments, amps, and for a while, pinball machines! Around 1970 César met George 'G.E.' Smith. Smith joined Díaz's band for a while and the two remained associated. Shortly after joining what was to become dubbed as Bob Dylan's *"Never Ending Tour"* band in 1988, G.E. Smith brought César on board as guitar and amp tech to himself and Dylan, and it was on the departure of G.E. that César stepped up as a replacement guitarist. César relinquished his position as band member in March 1991 to take a break from the road: *"I stayed home for nine months but they pulled me back – like Michael Corleone,"* said César.

Dylan called up and rehired César to take care of his guitars and amps for the US Fall tour of October – November 1991. César remained with Dylan until 1993, by which time a congenital liver disorder was starting to cause a rapid decline in his health.

César is best known in the biz for his work as a restorer and designer of traditional tube – or as we know them in the UK valve – powered guitar-amplifiers. While continuing to track down and lovingly restore vintage amps for the likes of Eric Clapton, Keith Richards, Jeff Beck, Neil Young and George Harrison, César began to design and hand-build his own range of *Díaz* limited-edition guitar equipment. He outfitted the as-yet-undiscovered and unsigned Stevie Ray Vaughan and the sound that César's equipment created became Stevie Ray's trademark.

César's health continued to worsen and after leaving the band he was diagnosed as having life-threatening liver problems, including congenital hepatic fibrosis and chronic Hepatitis C. On June 24, 1997 with only three weeks to live, he was admitted to hospital for an urgent liver transplant.

After corresponding with César by e-mail, he kindly agreed to give me an interview for ISIS. This first interview is the result of a telephone conversation on February 7, 1999.

DB: Let's start by talking about your illness.

CD: It's been going on for many years and you know, no one in the crew would really take it seriously; they thought that I was like having my period (laughs). Well, I don't think so. Look, I'm bleeding out of my mouth.

They took me into hospital right about the time that Bob got sick; he called me at the hospital – he was very nice and everything – he asked how much it would all cost. I told him that it was anything between $300.000 and $600.000, and he said: – imitating Dylan's voice – *"Hey, that's a lot of money...I'll pray for you."* I'm doing really quite well now, so his prayers must be pretty good, the royalties for those prayers are the ones that I want.

I had left Bob already because I was quite ill and I didn't want to die in Turkey or some other God forsaken place...but every time I told him that I couldn't come back for the next tour the ticket would show up at my front door, Fed-Ex. In the end though, I had to tell Bob *"Look it's my time to go. It's time for my boot heels to be wandering."* And it's the first time that I ever saw him open up his eyes and he said: *"Hey what am I going to do without you..."* then he said: *"Well, I wish you the best of luck, and if you ever need anything just call me."* I had left before and I came back, and I was the first person that ever did that, period. You never get re-hired.

DB: How did the transition come about, between being a crew-member and making it into the band?

CD: You know everybody was auditioning back then, they had a bunch of people, they had this guy Steve Bruton who had played with Bonnie Raitt, and a bunch of other people; he was like fairly heavyweight...I had asked for the chance to audition, but of course I was considered a roadie, so that qualified me as a moron. Anyway, on that tour they decided to book two more gigs, so I spoke to Bob and I said: *"look man, you have had all these people auditioning, and I'm really sure that you're not happy with any of them. Why don't you give me a chance? You got nothing to loose, I'm already here, I've been here for all these years, I know the songs, I know all the arrangements, I know you personally, I know the way you play, you know I can do it."* Anyway, that afternoon G.E. confirmed it; I didn't even have any stage clothes or anything. It was the last two gigs before October; it was New Mexico and some place in Arizona. – 11 September 1990 Santa Fe and 12 September, Mesa, Arizona. Anyway, G.E. comes up to me and says: *"You're on tonight."*

DB: You were working as guitar tech for the Stones when you first met Bob?

CD: This was all in the studio in Washington. I used to do a lot of studio work; I would never go on the road. He was in a bar in a place called the Twist and Shout. He had been to see the Original Sun Rhythm Band. [5, July 1986] Anyway, Bob recognised my name. He was kinda like in a nodding mood and he didn't look quite well, he looked a little blue. He was playing the next day at JFK Stadium in DC with the Grateful Dead. So, he recognised my name and he goes: – imitating Dylan's voice – *"How would you like to come over and fix my amps?"* So, I said, *"OK, fine."*

Anyway, a little while later when this whole thing started with the Never Ending Tour, G.E. got me the gig. Before Bob got G.E., he was doing lots of auditioning. Keith Mann and the Expensive Winos auditioned. After rehearsing with Bob a couple of times they just ran out the door: *"I can't take this guy. It's way out!"*

DB: Does Bob have much involvement with his equipment?

CD: Well, yeah, we would always be talking about what he wanted to sound like. He would come up with these real funny things like: *"Make me sound like Jimmy Page,"* or *"Make me sound like Jimi Hendrix."* So, we were always talking about things. When I came on to the tours, I would always bring my own guitars, even from the beginning. And he would ask me: *"What did you bring?"* And I would go, well, *"I brought my '51 Tele, and I brought this Strat, and I brought a '56 Telecaster."* I would bring two or three guitars and he would say: *"Those are the guitars that I'll be playing."* And I would go *"Fine, let's do it. Whatever you want, Bob. I'm here just to help you."*

When I came in, man, he didn't even know what type of strings he used, there were no road cases and nobody knew where any of his gear was. I thought, this guy has been on tour for thirty years: where is all his stuff? So, anyway, I had to buy everything, I had to find out how strong were his hands, what strings to use. In the beginning he broke a lot of strings because he didn't have a normal way of playing, he picked really hard. He got more sophisticated as time went on and we jammed more. I used to go into his dressing room and go: *"OK, let's practise."* and he'd go: *"I don't need to fucking practise."* But I was just that type of guy, so I would go: *"Come on let's do this, let's do that,"* and he would do it.

The above conversation took place the day before César had to fly out on family affairs from his adopted home in Pennsylvania to his birthplace in Old San Juan, Puerto Rico. This was César's first trip home in twenty-seven years and his time away from a convenient telephone would mean that it would be some time before we could recommence our chat. That was until César suggested that I might like to complete our interview by spending a week with him in Puerto Rico.

Let me think about this for a moment. Would I like to spend a week on a Caribbean island interviewing a man who recently spent five years on the road with Bob Dylan? To use the words of A.J. Weberman: *"That's like asking a strung-out junkie if he wants a fix!"*

Puerto Rico is a four-hour flight from New York City, which is where Tracy and I broke our outward journey. The island's capital San Juan marks the southeastern point of the Bermuda Triangle, the other two points being Miami and Bermuda. Puerto Rico is situated 1,000 miles southeast of Miami, the nearest US city to the island, and about 500 miles due north of Caracas, Venezuela. The same trade winds that brought Columbus to the Indies continue to push the clouds around in an unending spectacle that often brings with it rain, most of which drench the tangled slopes of the island's beautiful northeastern tropical rainforest. Some 450 billion litres, or if you prefer, 100 billion gallons of rain fall each year on the El Yunque rainforest. That's an annual rainfall of around 200 inches! The island's location, zero humidity and clear skies, make it the perfect site for the world's largest radio telescope. However, the reason for travelling 5,000 miles was not to visit a rain forest, or to view a twenty-acre radio telescope, but to continue my chat with César Díaz.

DB: When we left off our last conversation, Bob had just called you back as his tech.

CD: That's right, Bob was very unhappy with the sound: that's why even after I had told him that I couldn't come back for the next tour, the air ticket would show up. But, having been in the band and then coming back as tech, it was like *guitar tech goes to jail.*

The crew resented that I got what they thought was better treatment, when in reality, the crew stay at Hyatt Regency and Bob and the band stay at Motel Six at the side of the road away from town. That's because Bob likes to be incognito; plus he likes to see what the low life is like so he can get inspiration (laughs). It wasn't bad in Europe, but in the States, definitely, they booked themselves away from town because Bob doesn't want to be found.

…I stopped with the band, which was my worst mistake. I should have travelled with the crew. When I got my gig in the band everybody went, *"This guy's from the crew, he's a fucking roadie."* They had no respect whatsoever. Victor Maymudes told me, *"You're going to go out there and a lot of people are going to be against you, and you better watch yourself because everybody's going to try and knock you down."*

DB: When you joined the crew in 1988, Kenny Aaronson was the bass player.

CD: Kenny Aaronson, he was beautiful and he played great. Kenny was the sort of guy that would hang out with the crew. In fact, that band never hung out together and that's sad because a band should be a unit. They should eat, drink and shit together; that's how you become a nucleus. Kenny was told that he could come back into the band if he should get well. He had a tumour. Well, he got cured and came back hoping to play again, but he never got taken back.

Tony Garnier is a great bass player, but he's not a good bass player for the Dylan stuff…as far as I'm concerned, I will go to my grave saying that Tony doesn't play that stuff correctly. When Kenny Aaronson played the stuff he was correct and he had the energy, and he had the drive, and he had the inventiveness, you know. But Tony's very programmed and he doesn't really want to take any chances. With Bob you just never know what's going to happen, when he's going to throw something at you, and you have to be ready to re-invent yourself at that moment.

The drummer was Ian Wallace; he's a horrible drummer. Bob has had some horrible drummers. I liked Charlie Quintana; that period when Charlie was in the band was great. I liked Charlie as a person, but once he left the magic was gone. Chris Parker was a great drummer, but there were too many drums for Dylan; too much shit going on.

Let me tell you about Elliot Roberts and Jeff Kramer…I really don't know the exact date that Elliot went, but it was in Spain… Anyway, Bob got into this heated argument with Elliot and the next thing I know he's on his way home…and to make a point Bob makes Elliot's assistant – Jeff Kramer – his manager. So, I really believe that Bob makes the decisions and Jeff Kramer just carries out Bob's instructions and that's the reason why things are kinda nutty. Because an artist cannot self-manage. Someone with experience in a certain field has to be able to advise you. Anyway, the people around Bob were Suzi (Pullen), the one that dresses Bob like a clown. (The late John Bauldie once wrote of Suzi Pullen: *"She couldn't dress a salad."*) *'Coach'* (Ed Wynne) was *Front of House.* He had been with a few big names before Bob, the Eagles and John Mellencamp. He took it upon himself to make the band sound a certain way. He didn't reproduce what was happening on stage, he'd have his own mix and Bob would be completely out of it. Bill Thomson was the other tech; he did the bass and drums. He was a large man with a big, big heart. He was a real sweet guy, so we began calling him Sweet William. He was a lot sweeter than me (laughs). We became a duo, *Sweet and Sour,* because he was so sweet, and I was very sour (laughs).

Hanging next to the table at which César and I are seated is his winged wheel 1998 tour jacket.

DB: How did the jackets come about?

CD: The denim jackets were given to us at the Hammersmith Odeon. I'm not sure exactly how many were made but they were given to the band and the crew. The leathers are very, very few. I think there were only about six of the leather jackets. No one else wore their jackets. I don't know why; maybe they were keeping them as new or something. Also, someone said that I should not wear the jacket because Dylan wouldn't like it, 'cause he does not like to see his name around the place.

DB: Back in 1992 or 1993, in *"Guitar Player"* magazine, you talked about Bob being the *"Mother of invention"* when it came to his guitar playing.

CD: Yeah, all those double stops...

DB: You said, *"Not even Leon Redbone knows how to play that old."*(Laughs)

CD: Can you read that article to me again?

DB: Yeah, *"Well, he's not the most incredible guitarist, but only because he doesn't want to be. I call him the mother of invention – he is the most inventive guy I've ever met. He can play one of his songs many different ways in five minutes. He is just brilliant at what he does, which is reinventing everything that he's already done. It's his antidote to boredom. He's trying to come up with a whole different approach to playing the guitar. It's kind of like you're playing the guitar, but you act like you're playing the cello."*

CD: Yeah that's right. He would just go right across the whole guitar as if he were bowing the strings. He would do all these things that were like non-guitar parts.

DB: That's interesting, because that is something we had been debating in the pages of ISIS. Bob said in an interview that he used the guitar as though it were a wind instrument.

CD: Well, or a piano. But that's basically what I meant in that piece, he would just do all these things that were like non-guitar parts. He would just throw in these things that a normal guitarist would not do. Never would you think about playing that way.

I continue to read from the article:

"For instance, he chooses to play a lot of double stops where other people would play chords...He'll be playing 'Tangled Up In Blue' and start doing something like 'South of The Border' with double stops in sixths based on the major scale. You know, a flamenco 'Hey senorita' sound. You would think that it would be wrong for the song, but it would mix right in. Whoever he learned to play the guitar from must have been very old because his chording and approach to melody is so old-fashioned.

For example, he plays a first-position D-minor by fingering F on the D string, A on the G string, and D on the B string. He has this formula worked out where he plays these triadic shapes all up and down the neck."

CD: It's not really a D-minor. Well. it's a rather strange D-minor...For example *'Like a Rolling Stone'* would be a case. Instead of just doing a normal D-minor, he would do this – César demonstrates. And this is definitely the Dylan G. He almost puts a C on top of it.

I just love the tone of those Gibson guitars. Listen to the original version of *'Don't Think Twice,'* that flatpicking! He went through what I would call his Picasso period. He actually took his art so low that all he had to do to come back was just to throw out a signal that he was still alive. He became so incomprehensible within his own self, reinventing the songs. No one can blame him for that. After playing those songs for all those years, he must have got sick and tired. So, anyway, he became so alone in his art.

I would say it was about 1989; that was when it all started. That first couple of years was pretty low. But the whole time I was there it was an up and down thing. I don't think he always enjoyed playing with G.E as much as people might think. He used to spit at him constantly! That has never been written about, but they would be on stage and he would spit at him, really. Those Hammersmith 1990 shows with G.E. were just wonderful though.

...The band would sometimes get criticised for not being tight but it was usually a case of Bob going his way and the band going their way. I would always wait for Bob to make his move and then I would make my move. Some of the other guys would try to make their move before Bob and Bob would just go the other way out of spite! He would just fuck with them to prove a point, so they would realise that you can never really know what he's going to do. So, in reality the band was fairly tight. Bob was the one that would throw the whole thing into chaos.

DB: Can we talk about Bob's guitars for a moment?

CD: On tour Bob would probably have two or three acoustic guitars. There would be the Martin D18 and he used a blond Guild and a Gibson. He ended up giving me the Guild when I got my gig. There were maybe four electric, two Telecasters and two Stratocasters. G.E. would be quite excessive; he would have maybe ten guitars and I would have to re-string all those guitars before every gig.

DB: What about the sparkle Telecaster? I believe it was from the California Custom shop.

CD: All the Telecasters were made for him by a friend of mine, J Black at the Custom Shop in California.

DB: In 1998 Bob used a Gibson Les Paul for a short while. I believe that was a custom model, which was lighter than the standard Les Paul. Was that because of Bob's back problems?

CD: Yeah.

DB: Was that a factor in choosing guitars for Bob?

CD: No, because he just didn't want to use Les Pauls.

DB: You got Bob on to using tube amps. What model Diaz amp did he use?

CD: The CD-100. It was made especially for him. I think the amp I made for him was number ten. I guess he still has it somewhere collecting dust.

DB: I'm told that after you left they continued to use your amps, but that the *Dìaz* name was covered over with tape!?

CD: Yes! That's is so true – I have seen pictures. It just shows how stupid things can get!

DB: Did you see Bob during the day?

CD: No, very rarely did he show up even for sound checks. He would be in his room or hanging out at his hotel doing God knows what...I think he would draw, maybe write the odd song, who knows.

DB: How were the set lists chosen?

CD: What would happen is before a concert the bandleader would go into Bob and get the night's set list. Now, after G.E. left, Kramer told me that I was now the bandleader, so I would be the one to go in and get the set lists. The one thing that would sometimes happen right before a gig is that he would change the key depending on how good his voice was. Sometimes, but not very often, he would change an arrangement. If that happened, I would have to go straight to the rest of the band with that arrangement.

DB: When would new arrangements be worked out, always at pre-tour rehearsals or sometimes during the tour itself?

CD: Before the actual tour, there were always rehearsals.

DB: So only very rarely would there be new arrangements after a tour had started?

CD: Correct.

On our final evening on Puerto Rico we visited San Juan's Hard Rock Café, which I have to say, does not have a particular heart-stopping collection of memorabilia – only one Dylan poster in sight. On our walk back to the house, our conversation was punctuated by the sound of the island's unique singing frog. The *Coqui* is less than two inches long, it hides away by day and is almost never seen, but by night, it sure can be heard! These singing mini frogs are found nowhere else in the world, and believe me: if it were to exist elsewhere someone would have heard it by now! Conventional wisdom insists that while the *Coqui* may survive if taken off his native island, he will never again sing.

DB: OK, let's get on to that final tour.

CD: We had all these names for the tours you know. *It's a Hard Tour;* – I think that was 1988 – because he would do *'Hard Rain'* a lot on that tour. *Till The Money Runs Out Tour*; that was after GE left – Dylan called it: *The Money Never Runs Out Tour,* in the *"World Gone Wrong"* liner notes. *Where Is The Oil Tour?* was around the time of *"Oh Mercy."* We found the oil in New Orleans and then Bob bought a house there. He kept asking me where the oil was; I told him it was down there. Then there was *It's a Parody Of Himself Tour.* And one of those southern tours, maybe it was the *Southern Sympathizer Tour,* was when I was in the band and we played *'Oxford Town'* in Oxford, Mississippi. The fact that we played *'Oxford Town'* together was no mere coincidence. I do look black to most Americans from a distance until I open my mouth, then they detect my tropical accent.

DB: Bob mentions some of those tour, names in the liner notes to *"World Gone Wrong."* I thought that maybe it was one of his jokes!

CD: Well, those were names that we had for those tours. Every tour had a name. On previous tours, I had been helping with everything, but I was not to touch anything on that last tour because they already knew that I was ill and I already had broken my finger twice.

As soon as we started that tour Al Santos – production manager – was abusive toward me …The crew in general took it that I had come back begging for my job, when of course in reality it was my own decision to quit first time around and I didn't really want to come back! I only came back because Bob Dylan wanted me to and because it was going to be on my terms. Prince called me up and I had said *"No"* to Prince, and I had offers from a whole bunch of other people to go back on the road and I had said no. Then I got a personal call from Bob Dylan. Who could say no to Bob Dylan calling you? It was like Pops is calling me, so I got involved again…It was decided that I would not do John's guitars on that tour because he had been a band mate. I only came back just to do Bob's guitars. I only came back at all because Dylan was personally asking me to come back and for no other reason… But in the end, I left the crew after that tour because of the thing with Al Santos...

DB: But also your illness?

CD: Oh yeah, my illness was out of control. Every time I ate I would throw up, and I didn't realise that as the food was going down it was bursting all these veins in my chest. My liver had become so hard and crystallised by this time that it wasn't accepting any blood. But yeah, at that point I knew it was the end: I had been taken real ill a couple of times on that final tour, the last time we were in Milan – June 27, 1993 – I spent the whole day in hospital under observation. I was there the whole day not knowing what was going on. So, I broke out of hospital (laughs), Yeah, I escaped. I just got in to a cab and went back to the gig. It was the Palatrussardi, and you know what, the crew were just about taking off without me! I just thought, wow! They were never going back to the hospital to get me, and I thought man, this is a real good hit. If I fall ill somewhere these people are just going to leave my ass behind. There'll be no meeting at the *oil spot* for me! That's what we used to say after a gig. You would meet outside by the trucks, and you know when a truck has been parked up for a while there's always a spot of oil on the ground, so that would be the crew's saying: *"Meet at the oil spot."*

Hey, did you know Sara that followed the tour everywhere?

DB: The girl that changed her name to Sara Dylan! Yes, I met her once. She was always around though.

CD: No one knows what happened to her. One day she just disappeared!

DB: I heard a story about you and Bob in a lift...

CD: Oh OK, news travels. Yeah, Bob and I were in this lift and this guy gets in and he says to Bob: *"You don't know me but I know you."* And just then the lift door opens and as Bob steps out he says, *"Let's keep it that way."* But you had to be there, the timing!

DB: You take off Bob's voice so well!

CD: I got to be so good that I used to answer Bob's telephone. And Bob would go: *"Why don't you answer the telephone, you can do it better then me."* I had his voice down to the last detail and he would just stand there laughing and stuff, he would be in tears, we would just have the greatest time. I don't know if you have ever seen *Sesame Street*? They have these two old timers, they sit on the balcony at the theatre and they are always criticising everybody...

DB: Yeah, that's the *Muppets.*

CD: Yeah, the *Muppets,* that's right. Bob and I were the *Muppets.* Every concert he would come over to me and say: *"What do you think?"* You know, we had Counting Crows when they were just starting, they were like a kids bands then, and I would go: *"Well, they might get some place,"* or: *"They're shit!"* or: *"Bob, the guy from Counting Crows, he wants to be you!"* And that was before they did the *'Mr Jones'* thing, you know. And he goes: *"Yeah, look at them, what a piece of shit."* And the two of us would just bitch about everything. He would always agree as long as I was negative. He would go: *"Yeah you're right."* So, that was another reason why people got so anti, because we got close. And you know because everybody tries to get next to Bob. He decided that I was the guy that he was going to talk to, that I would be the wicked messenger. So, most of the hiring, no not the hiring, but most of the filing, was done by me. I would tell someone something and they would bitch back: *"I bet Bob didn't say that. That's you talking."* So I would just say: *"OK, you go ask Bob."* And it would be, *"Oh, err, well."* Everyone was so afraid of him.

Bob's a great guy but he's surrounded by so many assholes and there's so many people protecting him. That's what makes Bob so much of an enigma. You know in a way he kinda likes it, but in another way, he really suffers for it. He can't be human and no one allows him to get close to anyone because everybody wants to be the one that he's close to!

DB: You told me before that Larry Campbell uses one of your effect pedals. Was that coincidental?

CD: The *Tremodillo.* Oh, I didn't know that he was using one. He took me on stage and showed me. He was a friendly guy.

DB: When did you meet him?

CD: After my operation, I was supposed to sit in at a show. It was pre-arranged with Tony Gamier. I did the sound check and at the last song the tech told me I was on. The lights were down and I heard Bob saying, *"Shit"* and *"You have no right to invite..."* I thought I heard my name: *"You don't bring him up here,"* etc, so I left the stage. The amp was set up, my guitar was there, I was dressed and had been there all day. There were even nurses and doctors from the University of Pittsburgh Hospital there! The lights went on and then signs in the brightest pink that you've ever seen went up saying; *"We love César,"* but I wasn't there! A day that will forever live in infamy: the band left without even saying goodbye! That was the last time, August 12, 1997, forty-five days after my transplant.

Late into the night the chatter peters out, the tape machine is switched off and the warm Puerto Rican night is returned to the incessant cacophony of crickets and to the Island's beloved little frog. *"Ko-Kee, Ko-Kee, Ko-Kee..."*

Published over three issues #s 83, 84 and 85.March to June 1999

Postscript

In a later conversation with César Díaz we were discussing some of Bob Dylan's eccentricities…

CD: During a concert in the early nineties, Dylan called me over between numbers and asked me get his dresser Suzi Pullen to bring him some more boots. Suzi came to the side of the stage with another pair of cowboy boots and Dylan changed into them. He then passed the other pair of boots to Pullen informing her, *"These boots are jinxed. Give them to César. He will know what to do with them."*

CD: one night before a show, Dylan asked, *"Where's my bottle."* The previous night while on stage he had been putting liquid from a bottle onto his hair. I told him that I had thrown it away and that I would replace it with fresh water before tonight's show. To my amazement, Dylan informed me that the bottle did not contain water, but Ouzo! He then asked me, *"Did my hair look good last night?"* It seemed that Bob was gelling his hair before it became a trend. However, this was not gel, but Ouzo. I had to send out for a replacement bottle before show time; but the only place nearby that sold Ouzo was a bar, and they would only sell it by the shot. So, we ended up paying $150 to replace Bob's hair gel!

Some Great Live Performances
March 11, 1995 Congress Hall, Palac Kultury,
Prague, Czech Republic.
by Derek Barker

After an unusually long Christmas break, Bob Dylan's first concert of 1995 was scheduled for March 10. The only hiatus for the rest of the year would be August. The tour started with three concerts in the beautiful ancient city of Prague and I was determined to be there. Prague is a city contrasted by extremes of wealth and poverty with very little in between. Our hotel – shared by Dylan's band, but alas not Dylan – was two minutes walk via a footbridge that linked the plush hotel to the equally plush Palac Kultury. On the afternoon of March 10, I had gone to my room for a shower and a change of clothes when the telephone rang. It was Lambchop – anyone who has been to Dylan concerts in Europe will doubtless have seen Lambchop and his hat – calling from the hotel lobby: *"The show's off. Bob's ill,"* said the sombre voice. I almost said, *"You're joking,"* but somehow I stopped myself from making the ridiculous comment. There is *no way* Lambchop would be joking about this. A few minutes later and I was in the lobby, just in time to bump into Dylan's travelling companion, the late Victor Maymudes. In his usual slightly surly matter-of-fact manor, Victor explained, *"Bob had 'flu, but would be all right by tomorrow."* Those lucky enough to attend the next evening's concert – the first of 116 shows he would play that year – were unaware what a blessing this bout of 'flu would turn out to be! We could never have guessed that after an uneasy twenty four hours' wait, we would be repaid be seeing the most remarkable performance of the *"Never Ending Tour."* In fact, March 11 at the Palace of Culture was probably one of the most extraordinary concert performances since – insert your own date here.

Dylan, still visibly suffering from the effects of 'flu made worse by jet lag, arrived on stage armed with two surprises. Being confronted by a guitarless Bob Dylan was the first shock. The second surprise was the opening number, the live début of *'Crash On The Levee (Down In The Flood);'* a powerful bluesy rocker with great vocals and determined harp playing. After the audience had dusted themselves down from the shock of *'Crash On The Levee,'* they began to realise that Dylan had started to sing the second song of the night and again his guitar was no where to be seen; apart from a brief two-minute jam with John

Jackson halfway through the main set, nor would it be. The change in tempo from the raucous *'Crash On The Levee'* to the gentle melodious *'If Not For You'* was a jolt.

The opening chords to the next song were unmistakable. For the greater part of the 1990s *'All Along The Watchtower'* occupied the third slot in every Dylan set and tonight was no exception. However, while the arrangement remained the same, Dylan changed the emphasis, particularly the line endings. He sped through the song's second stanza at break neck pace and in doing so ran the end of each line into the beginning of the next.

Another familiar beginning gave way to a beautiful – if too short – harp solo. *'Just Like a Woman'* was sung with feeling and again with changes of emphasis, which drew out words like *"girl"* and *"woooman."* The song closed with a harp solo that had the crowd standing and cheering for more.

After *'Tangled Up In Blue,'* which despite some storming harmonica worked less well than most of the night's songs, Dylan told the crowd: *"Thanks. I'm sorry about last night. This is a good place to recover from 'flu."* A male voice then rang out the words: *"Bobby, I love you,"* to which Dylan gave a grin and asked: *"Do you wanna say that again?"* Not leaving room for an answer, Dylan continued: *"This is a song, my ecology song"* and he was into *'Watching The River Flow,'* during which he strapped on a guitar for the only time in the show. The resulting jam with John Jackson was quite pleasing.

A beautifully measured *'Mr Tambourine Man'* was marred only by a couple static cracks from the PA. Tonight would be the first of a number of glorious outings for this old chestnut during 1995. At several points during the night's performance Dylan sat on the drum rise to take a rest. On one occasion he was bent almost double with pain.

'It's All Over Now Baby Blue' started slowly and for most of the song Dylan's voice was accompanied by little more than a gently strummed acoustic guitar. The song closed with a harmonica break to die for; this performance was pure 1966.

Before his audience could catch their breath he moved on a quarter century to *"Oh Mercy"* and the dark, ominous, unhurried intro of *'Man In a Long Black Coat,'* an atmospheric song that visits death through Small Town Americana. In the later stages of the concert Dylan seemed to be dreadfully tired, his visits to the drum rise became more frequent and my concern for his well being increased.

After an unhurried start, *'God Knows'* moved up several gears and by the close had reached fever pitch. The band – John Jackson, guitar; Bucky Baxter, pedal steel, guitar and mandolin; Tony Garnier, bass, and Winston Watson, drums – gave it their all, while Dylan bobbed and wove to dance steps that were all his own.

'Maggie's Farm' rocked the concert to an energetic close with some spirited slide from John Jackson. At the close Dylan introduced the band ending with a strident: *"Thank you, everybody,"* dragging out that last syllable as only he can dooo.

Dylan returns for a superlative hymn-like *'Shelter From The Storm'* that brought tears to your eyes. His vocal was magnificent and the audience was again on its feet and cheering. In fact, the audience was on such an emotional high and making so much noise, when Dylan placed the harp to his lips for the final salvo of the evening, they found it difficult to raise their appreciation past its current level!

Apart from the opening number, *'Shelter From The Storm'* was the only surprise in a song selection that was predictable and unexciting. However, if there was ever a case where reading the set list on paper meant absolutely nothing, this was it. Tonight it was not the songs, but the performances that mattered. Even the bootleg recordings of the show didn't convey what went down, because March 11, 1995 was as much a visual experience as an aural one.

During the second and final encore, *'It Ain't Me Babe,'* a young German girl, Sigrid

Maria Heimdl, joined Dylan on stage. Several of Dylan's security men ran on to the stage to prevent the adoring fan from reaching her idol, who was about to sing the line, *"Go melt back into the night babe."* Dylan simply turned and told his security: *"It's all right."* Sigrid sat behind him throughout the song, picking up his harmonicas and eventually Dylan's acoustic guitar. As the girl gazed with wonder, Dylan turned and told her: *"You can play that. I'm not going to."* All too soon, Dylan played one final sublime harmonica break and he was gone.

From adversity came splendour. Without the distraction of a guitar, Dylan could concentrate fully on his vocal and in the process managed to incorporate many of the eccentricities, that are normally found in his guitar playing, into his singing. Speeding up, slowing down, changing emphasis, texture and expression. This same spirit was also to be found in his harp playing. With no need for a harmonica rack and not much else to do with his hands, Dylan played harp on nearly every song, blowing some of the sweetest sounding breaks I've ever heard.

His stance during this extraordinary show has been described as *"shadow-boxing."* For much of the time he stood, knees slightly bent, holding the microphone with his right hand while passing the cable through the fingers of his left hand. With his arm outstretched he crooned his way through the concert like a Vegas veteran, but this wasn't Bing Crosby or Frank Sinatra; this was ole blue eyes Bob Dylan, yet a vision of Dylan as never before. For the umpteenth time in his long career Dylan had again reinvented himself. Incidentally, a brief chat with the band afterwards revealed that Dylan had previously rehearsed some songs without his guitar, so maybe he had planned to play a few songs *"unstrung"* – thank you, Paul Williams – at some stage and tonight's illness merely provided the opportunity.

As for the band, it seems that several members were also suffering from varying degrees of influenza, but it certainly didn't show. During his time with Dylan, John Jackson was usually focused on his boss's erratic chord changes, but tonight, free of that constraint, he excelled.

Commissioned for inclusion in *ISIS: A Bob Dylan Anthology.*

1999 – Murcia, Spain © Andrea Orland

It's The Top Of The End
Andrew Muir

"The songs are my lexicon. I believe the songs."
Bob Dylan *Newsweek* interview, 1997.

Isn't it just sooo exciting to have a new album to discuss – OK, argue – and write about? This review will accentuate the positive, concentrating on the highs which for me are four songs that I have grown to love, that I have put on a separate tape away from those I am not so fond of. The four?

'Standing In The Doorway' / 'Trying To Get To Heaven' / 'Not Dark Yet' / 'Highlands.'

These songs have a total time of about half-a-minute more than the whole of *"Under The Red Sky,"* the last album of Dylan originals. All of the themes of the whole album are present – and best expressed – within these tracks. I say all of the major themes, and I am presuming we are all in agreement on them. The album is, as Dylan himself has said, shocking in its bluntness. In addition to the complete clarity in what Dylan is singing about there is no escaping the major concerns as they come back again and again in song after song; so I may not point out anything here that hasn't occurred to you while you have listened to it, but it may be useful to group together what I think they are –

Walking through the valley of death, the fallen world – sometimes contrasted with a Heavenly alternative, sometimes not.

Uncertainty.

Isolation from the community, from human contact.

Inefficacy of words.

Lost love(s).

Ageing, death, pointlessness of life.

Mental illness.

Not the cheeriest of pictures emerges, it must be admitted; but with my new slimmed down *"Time Out Of Mind"* I can marvel at, and be uplifted by the artistry with which these messages, impressions, sentiments and feelings are conveyed.

Just before I write about the tracks, I should ask you to note that I am presuming *the narrator* of each song to be Dylan. I am fully aware this is a large presumption and perhaps I should refer to *the persona Dylan is adopting for these tracks;* however, I am going to continue writing *Dylan*, because there is no sense of authorial distance and it is exceedingly awkward to have to write the caveat in every observation. In addition, the *Newsweek* interview makes it clear that Dylan himself is – for once – not distancing himself from the lyrics.

"*It is a spooky record,*" says Dylan, "*because I feel spooky. I don't feel in tune with anything.*" Yet he's proud of having registered his ambivalence and alienation so nakedly.

Further evidence can be found in the *New York Times* interview, a remarkably candid comment by Dylan's standards –

"*I've written some songs that I look at, and they just give me a sense of awe,*" Dylan says. "*Stuff like, 'It's Alright, Ma,' just the alliteration in that blows me away. And I can also look back and know where I was tricky and where I was really saying something that just happened to have a spark of poetry to it. But when you get beyond a certain year, after you go on for a certain number of years, you realize, hey, life is kind of short anyway. And you might as well say the way you feel.*"

'Standing In The Doorway'

The opening notes come straight from '*Can't Help Falling in Love With You.*' "*Wise men say...*" is what I hear each time it starts. This is no coincidence. All through the album musical and textual references are made to a whole slew of traditional songs; the usual Dylan touchstones are represented: Guthrie, Johnson, McTell, Elvis, The Stanley Brothers, Rev Gary Davis and Dylan himself, oh – and whoever that chap who wrote the Psalms was.

Then for the third successive opening – but for by no means the last time on this album – we find our singer walking, this time through summer nights. I like the mention of the jukebox, I can feel the summer night, imagine the scene, Elvis hasn't left my mind – so I can almost hear '*Can't Help Falling In Love With You*' coming from the jukebox. Also I just love it when Dylan makes references to music playing in his songs – "*the last radio playing*" in '*Shooting Star*' gets to me every time.

But, whatever anyone thinks of this album, surely we must agree it is extraordinarily depressing – realistically so, but still depressing. The next four lines detail a Dylan in desperate straits –

"*Yesterday everything was going too fast/Today it's moving too slow*"
"*I got no place left to turn/I got nothin' left to burn*"

It was rumoured that these songs would contain Dylan's mid-fifties meditations on the ageing process. The rumours were true. What a bleak contrast this is though to the bright fire of Dylan's youth, – think of the 1965 press conferences, for instance.

For most people, growing older is synonymous with time going too fast – the feeling that Christmas comes every two months, that when you were setting out on life's path you had aeons of time to accomplish all the things you planned to achieve, only to find out that the years have all been eaten up. What could be worse than this feeling that life is speeding by too fast? Dylan knows – he tells us it is the feeling that even this high speed career through life is too slow. What comes next, if you are in the situation he depicts throughout the album, is the feeling that you want it to hurry up and be done with. "*Nowhere to turn nothing to burn*" – bye, bye fire of youth. Is this really all that is left? It would seem so; bereft of the love or loves from the past – loves being real women, his muse, at times it seems all spirituality too – life is something he seems *condemned* to.

Part of the angst of the album is, of course, this woman – or these women – who he still yearns for even after she – they – have left him. The attraction-repulsion side of love is something that Dylan has brilliantly delineated throughout his career – *'Don't Think Twice,' 'If You See Her Say Hello,' 'She Belongs To Me,'* etc. – There are too many to quote – He sums it up perfectly in the next line –

"Don't know if I saw you/if I would kiss you or kill you"

and then, in a magnificent follow up, shows exactly where he stands in this, long-since-ended, remember, relationship –

"It probably wouldn't matter to you anyhow"

The verse ends with the line – *"I got nothin' to go back to now"* taking us back to the previous stanza's closing – *"I got nothin' left to burn."* He can't make it much clearer than this. This track has grown and grown on me the more times I've heard it, and by now I am in almost a hypnotic trance each time it plays; it holds me now as he sings on –

"The light in this place is so bad/
Making me sick in the head/
All the laughter is just making me sad/
The stars have turned cherry red"

As he frequently appears to be on this album, Dylan has *trouble in mind*. Mental illness and insanity are a disturbing thread through the songs. The third line reminds me very much of that painfully revealing comment he made in a interview about walking by an inn on a cold, rainy night and being attracted by the light and laughter inside. He went in to join the company but they all fell silent and stared at him when he entered. He killed the laughter just by appearing; no wonder he feels fame is a curse.

So what does he do? He strums his guitar and smokes his cigar. Cigars are an important symbol in American folk and blues songs – something Dylan has picked up on. Cruel oppressors often smoke cigars – Maggie's Pa, Davy Moore's manager – at the very least they are a symbol of wealth and status – Catfish. However they are prevalent in the folk songs of the poor too, almost always, as here, a *'cheap cigar.'* The poor white trash trying to ape his *betters* (sic), the slave showing he is a slave no more, the bum on the train trying to convince himself good times are coming: you'll find all of these *"Smokin' a cheap cigar."* This is one the many couplets I half expect to have come from some earlier song.

There is a brief gleam of hope and redemption in the lines –

"There are things I could say, but I don't/
I know the mercy of God must be near"

The first is uplifting in that Dylan feels he has things he could say – even if he won't – as much of the album expresses the pointlessness of saying or writing anything at all. – He doesn't contradict that here, but still it's nice to know there was something to say.

The second line is perhaps not surprising to the long-term Dylan listener but it is extraordinarily hopeful in the terms of this particular album as we will see in *'Not Dark Yet.'* The verse –

"I would be crazy if I took you back/
It would go up against every rule/
You left me standin' in the doorway cryin'/
Sufferin' like a fool."

is interesting in as much as the rest of the song seems to make it clear he's no chance of ever *"taking her back."* Given the *'Can't Help Falling In Love With You'* melody line, the phrase *"like a fool"* irresistibly brings the fools rushing in of that song to mind.

The following verse is my favourite of this track and one of the best on the whole album –

"When the last rays of daylight go down/Buddy, you'll roll no more/I can hear the church bells ringin' in the yard/ I wonder who they're ringin' for."

As he reflects on a life ruined by the loss of his true love, drawing to a close with him ill and unhappy, he hears the church bells and wonders for whom they toll. If it is not for him this time, the song is telling us they will be soon. It hints too at the uncertainty of redemption – a strong theme elsewhere, though much mollified on this track by the earlier line about God's mercy being near) while gently enforcing the stark fact of mortality and the inevitability of death. The *"buddy"* in line two is thus Dylan himself, the individual listener, the person the church bells are now ringing for and all of us – all at one and the same time.

The phrase is bleakly humorous too, in that one who is dead most certainly cannot *"roll"* any more. A dip into the great folk and blues heritage that Dylan carries inside him reveals this phrase occurring in a number of settings: the train hopper who meets his end and will not *"roll"* on the next train pulling out of the station; the gambler who has thrown his last dice; the itinerant lover who has had his last roll in the hay. Perhaps it is, in fact, another direct quote. I do not know, and only partly care; this verse breaks my heart.

We are then back to Dylan with a temporary companion who only reinforces the fact that the one he wants – needs – is not there – now where have you heard that before! – before we get the evocative – *"In the dark land of the sun"*

At first glance a striking enough phrase that fits well with the anti-life mood; the sun, that symbol of light and life bringing only darkness to the singer's world. Perhaps, like me, you thought of *"Darkness at the break of noon"* when you first heard it. However, later in the album Dylan makes a blatant pun on sun/Son as in the Son of God, a traditional double meaning and one Dylan himself has used before but never quite so forcibly as in *'Highlands.'* This means that the next time you hear this line – which is very soon afterwards on my continuously playing four-track album – you cannot help but hear the same Sun/Son pun. This immediately brings *'Dark Eyes'* to my mind, where Dylan sings of the emptiness of life if religious certainty gives way to doubt – an emptiness starkly realized in these tracks.

'Dark Eyes' would fit well on this album as would *'Shooting Star,' 'Lone Pilgrim'* and *'Rank Strangers To Me.'* It's an album replete with the themes, images and influences of so many of Dylan's album closers.

The next stanza opens with a quote of another song that would sit well on *"Time Out*

Of Mind," namely *'Moonshiner.'*

> *"I eat when I'm hungry, drink when I'm dry"*

Then there is a line remarkable both for its alliteration and to use Dylan's word again *"bluntness"* –

> *"And even if the flesh falls off of my face"*

The alliteration is not just a fancy flash of Dylan's ability with no other motive than to dazzle; there is a gruesome onomatopoetic effect at play that leaves unsettling questions as to who the someone is who will be *"there to care."* We are still pondering this as he slyly sings *"Even the softest touch:"* I mean, the softest touches are often the most tender anyway, and therefore these are what he would be wanting at this time – would he not? So why *"even"*?

Suddenly we are back to a bald statement on the inefficacy of words –

> *"I see nothing to be gained by any explanation/*
> *There are no words that need to be said"*

and we leave our singer, where he has been all through the song, where he is staying until the last rays of daylight go down –

> *"...standin' in the doorway cryin'*
> *Blues wrapped around my head."*

Indeed they are, and he plucks phrases, images and melodies from great blues songs – including some of his own, which he seems to regard and treat as songs from someone else – in the other tracks too. In fact in the next song of my selection I think every line may be a direct quote from some previous lyric – oh but what a quilt Dylan makes of this in *'Trying To Get To Heaven.'*

Before you start panicking that I am going to go into the same amount of detail in each song, I can tell you to relax. The same themes come round again and again. Just finish reading this and then go listen to Dylan piling on the detail!

'Trying To Get To Heaven' has, from the very first hearing, been my favourite song on the album. It is full of such great lines –

> *"When you think that you lost everything/*
> *You find out you can always lose a little more."*

and

> *"They tell me everything is gonna be all right/*
> *But I don't know what 'all right' even means."*

How splendidly Dylanesque.

> *"When I was in Missouri, they would not let me be/*
> *I had to leave there in a hurry/I only saw what they let me see."*

The first line reminds me of *'Wanted Man'* and the second forces you to wonder what in Heaven's name it was that they did not want him to see.

Oh, – and the whole of the last two verses, just perfection.

The singing too is exquisite, the way he phrases *"a-beatin"* and *"parlour"* and the lines about Miss Mary Jane.

Most of the themes I mention at the beginning of this article are to be found here; the imminence of death underscored by the yearning to get this life over with as quickly as possible is evident in the very refrain.

Note again that it is hot in the opening lines. Once again he is *"walking,"* this time *"through the middle of nowhere"* – he walks so many miles on this album, through the most desperate of places, for nary a smile. The lost love that ruined his life and the irrelevance of words – a desolate theme given Dylan's reputation – are baldly stated in the middle of the second stanza –

"You broke a heart that loved you/
Now you can seal up the book and not write anymore."

But, you know, there's something odd about all that great, Dylanesque, writing and this blunt personal honesty and that is that most – if not all – the lines in this song are direct lifts/references to songs from the past. A web of allusion has been created that may have us back in the scenario of film references in *"Empire Burlesque"* and nursery rhymes in *"Under The Red Sky."*

From the Rev Gary Davis title to the beautifully apt Guthrie – and therefore early Dylan – lines –

"Some trains don't pull no gamblers,
No midnight ramblers, like they did before."

The song is built upon the foundation of song that Dylan seems to have decided is the one thing that cannot be taken from him –

"...I find the religiosity and philosophy in the music. I don't find it anywhere else...
The songs are my lexicon. I believe the songs."

Indeed. Perfectly said. No Dylan fan au fait with the Never Ending Tour can help but think of his renditions of Elizabeth Cotten's *'Been All Around The World'* and *'Shake Sugaree'* when hearing the lines –

"I've been all around the world boys,"
"I've been to Sugartown, I shook the sugar down,"

But it is next to nothing just for Dylan to list references and us to have the fun of spotting them. What he has done here is fuse them into a new artistic whole – not just here but most particularly so – because he has, of course, *been all around the world* many, many times and we all know this and this album makes it sound like he is doing it because there is nothing else he can do until he *"gets to Heaven."* Taking our knowledge of Dylan the performer away from this, the line still resonates in its own right as it sounds on this album as if the singer has walked the circumference of the globe time after time for no apparent reason but just because there may be some point to it if he just keeps walking, walking...

As for *"I've been to Sugartown, I shook the sugar down,"* this may well be a direct allusion to *'Shake Sugaree'* but that is only one of many potential references. This line, brilliantly delivered, is positively teeming with possibilities relating to other blues songs, to sugar as *candy*, sugar as *drugs*, sugar as sexual slang, sugar as the sweetness of – usually hedonistic – life, and Bob Dylan did not just go to Sugar Town he damn well shook the sugar down. Yeah, good on you Bob but that was then, and this is now, when he is simply *"trying to get to heaven, before they close the door."* Before that wonderful climax, there are the lovely lines about Miss Mary Jane –

"I was riding in a buggy with Miss Mary-Jane/
Miss Mary Jane got a house in Baltimore."

This triggered a memory or two for me and Seth Kulick provided the context from that most likely of sources, *"The Folk Songs of North America"* compiled by Alan Lomax. Dig out your ol' folk anthologies and find the song beginning –

"Ridin' in the buggy, Miss Mary Jane/
Miss Mary Jane, Miss Mary Jane/
Ridin' in the buggy, Miss Mary Jane/
I'm a long way from home."

You may be intrigued to find verses as –

"Sally got a house in Baltimo'/
Baltimo', Baltimo'/
Sally got a house in Baltimo'/
And it's three stories high/
Sally got a house in Baltimo'/
Baltimo' Baltimo'/
Sally got a house in Baltimo'/
An' it's full of chicken pie."

So what does it all mean? The above reminds me of nothing so much as a lewd *"Basement Tape"* piece – God, I can hear Dylan slyly singing *chicken pie* – clearly Sally ain't got a house, she got a home.

In *'Trying To Get To Heaven,'* though, the lines reek of the elegance of some by-gone time – I am referring to the voice and the music – so perhaps Dylan is not at all intimating at any link with this previous song – or, rather, as it became, stream of variants – On the other hand, why is he so specific in his reference?

More time is needed, I believe, before we'll know the answer to this question. I can feel the scurryings of Dylanologists the world over tracking down every possible quotation on the album.

'Not Dark Yet' is my third track; it is many people's favourite track and I can see why it is rated so highly. Again nearly all the album's major themes are present, the writing and singing are well ahead of most of the rest of the album. Good Lord, but it is bleak though. Just take the penultimate lines – all rhyme with *"It's not dark yet, but it's getting there"* –

"There's not even room enough to be anywhere"

"I just don't see why I should even care"
"Sometimes my burden is more than I can bear"
"Don't even hear the murmur of a prayer"

that last surely being one of the bleakest things from someone who has professed such deep religious faith. It is a question the interviewers have pursued. Jon Pareles in the *New York Times* received an expansion on the *Newsweek* answer

"Those old songs are my lexicon and my prayer book," he adds *"All my beliefs come out of those old songs, literally, anything from 'Let Me Rest On That Peaceful Mountain' to 'Keep On The Sunny Side.' You can find all my philosophy in those old songs. I believe in a God of time and space, but if people ask me about that, my impulse is to point them back toward those songs. I believe in Hank Williams singing 'I Saw The Light.' I've seen the light, too."* Dylan says he now subscribes to no organized religion.

For those of you following the references in the songs, Dylan told David Gates of *Newsweek* that he had used an old jug-band guitar line in *'Not Dark Yet,'* and Jon Pareles that he *"structured one song around a guitar line in the Memphis Jug Band's '1929 K.C. Moan'."*

The lyrics return to our by now well-documented themes. Estrangement from community –

"Well my sense of humanity has gone down the drain"

Pointlessness, lack of achievement –

"I know it looks like I'm moving, but I'm standin' still."

One thing that has baffled me about the release of *"Time Out Of Mind"* is that people seem to be taking extreme sides: you – allegedly – have to either love it or loathe it. If I mention that I love or loathe an individual track I am always presumed to be talking about the album as a whole. I don't understand why this is so, but I have noticed the same thing about the lyric writing. If you mention that you find some of it poor or sloppy – and there are many examples to cite in the tracks I have left off my four track version – you are presumed to be wanting a return to the surrealistic splendours of, say, *"Blonde On Blonde."* This is nonsense: one can admire Dylan's writing at many points of this album. Some I have already cited, good *simple* (sic) writing is as great a wonder as complex, dazzling wordplay – bad versions of either do not need to be supported in some kind of *"which side are you on?"* game.

This track evinces some of the album's tautest and finest lines –

"I've still got the scars that the sun didn't heal"

is fine as a straightforward descriptive line but it holds a strong resonance for the Dylan listener.

The *"scars"* evokes *"Street Legal's"* closing song – *'Where Are You Tonight? (Journey Through The Dark Heat)'* – the last song before the explicitly Christian albums and tours –

"If you don't believe there's a price for this sweet paradise just remind me to show

you the scars." Which in turn makes us hear – yet again – the *"Sun/Son"* pun and turns the line into –

"I've still got the scars that the Son didn't heal."

which in turn makes all the more fitting the closing couplet of –

"Don't even hear the murmur of a prayer/It's not dark yet, but it's getting there."

Other great lines include –

"I was born here and I'll die here, against my will"

One of the best on the album, I feel, and desperately hope it is a Dylan original, though I did read somewhere on the Internet a suggestion it came straight from the Talmud.

This track, uniquely for this album, has some praise for the written word – or artistic expression – It is noticeably not from Dylan himself –

"She wrote me a letter and she wrote it so kind/
She put down in writin' what was in her mind."

As for the singing, well who could resist it? The perfection of the vocal on *"gay Paree"* is one of the reasons we all get so excited by new Dylan material, why we read fanzines such as ISIS.

Of all Dylan's many apocalyptic album closers this one stands as the most final of *finishing ends* and would have been a magnificent choice as last track on the album – that is, if Dylan had not blessed us with the present of a sixteen-and-a-half-minute tour de force of a talking blues end-piece.

A lot of people seem to dislike *'Highlands,'* or dismiss it as a trifle; I cannot agree with them in the slightest. Apart from its summation of the album as a whole, its wit, the consummate artistry of its ending and it's gorgeous delivery – how can one fail to be moved by its humour?

There is humour elsewhere on the album too, but it is generally of a rather grim type. Even here, in the track with the *lightest* moments, there is heavy gravitas behind most lines. Nonetheless, how can you fail to react to the hilarious – and perfectly apt – *waitress scene;* again I hear/read of people who feel this episode is an indulgence, a *"silly aside"* -we must be listening to different songs. It is funny while making a number of important points and it also continues our echoes of the past as most Dylan listeners are bound to recall the waitress in *'Tangled Up In Blue'* while hearing this.

There's the humour in the way the name Erica Jong comes to the rescue of both the narrator of the song and the lyric writer. The former, because he clearly is out of his depth with the waitress and she has deduced his ignorance of feminist thought by his conversation, actions and most particularly his attempts to draw her on the napkin – a test of his artistry he was, sensibly as it turns out, doing his best to avoid. The latter, because it is damned difficult to think of another that would give him such a felicitous rhyme that even has the *bonus* of echoing back to the lovely Neil Young verse from earlier in the song.

All of this is just one part of an exchange that amusingly, but deftly and accurately, demonstrates the character's estrangement from other people, from community itself throughout the record. The theme of art or writing's inability to bridge that gap is illuminated by this little side scene. It's great; you gotta love it – don't you?

And what about the wit and the very Dylanesque phrasing of lines like –

"If I had a conscience, well I just might blow my top/
What would I do with it anyway/
Maybe take it to the pawn shop"

– He's referring to the conscience, not his *'top'* I presume! –

All of the things I have talked about throughout this article are in the song; according to Dylan this melody comes from Charley Patton while guitarist John Perry has pointed out it has the same feel, tempo, structure, and vibe, as *'Meet Me In The Morning.'* When I first heard it I thought of J.J. Cale; those I mentioned that to were dismissive of the idea but I noted at least two other reviewers who wrote the same thing.

We have the usual suspects rounded up –

Insanity – *"Insanity is smashin' up against my soul."*

Isolation – *"Feel further away than ever before."*

No Direction Home – *"Well I'm lost somewhere, I must have made a few bad turns."*

Ageing – *"I wish someone'd come and push back the clock for me."*

and that whole verse –

"I see people in the park forgetting their troubles and woes/
They're drinking and dancing, wearing bright colored clothes/
All the young men with the young women looking so good/
Well, I'd trade places with any of them/
In a minute if I could"

which takes us back to *'Standing In The Doorway,'* *"All the laughter is just makin' me sad"* and its attendant memories of Dylan-the-legend's inability to share in such carefree laughter. Of course this is only one time this summarising song reflects on previous songs –

"You could say I was on anything but a roll"

takes me back to *"Buddy, you'll roll no more"*. And so it goes on, references within echoes within allusions.

Where does it all lead, though? All these songs built on other songs – Dylan's *lexicon:* what he *believes in* – all this walking, searching through a world he is isolated from, all this *trouble in mind*, all these tortured memories of lost loves? It leads to the Highlands.

I do not want to go into the Burns thing at great length; it struck me right away and is an element of the song but it has been written about extensively now by various people, including me. Suffice to say that it is particularly apt that Burns' verses are based on traditional songs and depict an idealized place of the imagination. The Highlands in Dylan's song starts off by being that same idealized place and reappears in various guises to offset the pointless, confused reality of the fallen world that the singer is – seemingly- endlessly walking through. Images of dream lands, of idealized historical, romantic, country settings build up to a specifically heaven-like image of a place Dylan believes he will get to –

"There's a way to get there, and I'll figure it out somehow"

though the ending of the song is very delicately poised and balances finely between the earlier

"I Know the mercy of God must be near and *Don't even hear the murmur of a prayer."*

Indeed, the last two verses of this remarkable song strike me as being amongst the best written on the album. The sun/Son pun becomes explicit and, therefore, affects our hearing of *'Trying To Get To Heaven'* and *'Not Dark Yet.'* The reason for his distance from everyday life becomes apparent; there is an upbeat ending tempered, however, by the gorgeous nursery rhyme/fairy story distancing of *"over the hills and far away."* This is a quite beautifully apt way of describing the location of his Highlands Never-Never Land of black swans, honeysuckle, horses and hounds, bluebells, etc. He does not have a clue when he will get to the Highlands nor even how to get there or where it is. He can visualize it – *"I got new eyes"* – in his mind, however and believes he'll get there one day. I wish him the best of luck on his journey.

"The sun is beginning to shine on me/
But it's not like the sun that used to be/
The party's over, and there's less and less to say/
I got new eyes/
Everything looks far away.

Well, my heart's in The Highlands at the break of day/
Over the hills and far away/
There's a way to get there, and I'll figure it out somehow/
But I'm already there in my mind/
And that's good enough for now."

Published in issue #76, December, 1997

Old Friends Bob Dylan and Paul Simon
by Derek Barker

*"We have been great fans of each other for years
and are really looking forward to touring together."*

That was the official joint statement made by a spokesman on behalf of the artists on the eve of the Dylan/Simon 1999 US tour.

The following piece sets out to examine what contact, if any, occurred between these two artists as they struggled to achieve stardom via the same streets and folk clubs of New York's Greenwich Village. The various Dylan biographies provide only scant insight into any contact between the two.

Soon after the birth of Paul Frederic Simon on October 13, 1941 in Newark, New Jersey, his family moved to a smart two-storey house in Forest Hills in the New York suburb of Queens. The music coming in his ears – *'Baby Driver'* – would almost certainly have been courtesy of his father, Louis Simon, a professional bass player with a radio dance band.

Paul Simon and Arthur Garfunkel lived just three blocks apart in Forest Hills and had met at grade school. The two shared a love of music and soon began hanging out. With adolescence came an interest in rock 'n' roll, and in October 1955, convinced of his seriousness about music, Simon's father bought him his first guitar. The *Stadium* guitar costing $25 was given to Paul on the occasion of his fourteenth birthday.

A year later the duo were to spend eighteen months knocking the many doors at the Brill Building on Broadway and visiting numerous record companies, but the recording contract that they so badly sought continued to elude them. Eventually, a record producer named Sid Prosen gave them a break and they released a single, *'Hey, Schoolgirl,'* on Prosen's new label, *Big Records*. At the time they were using the name Tom & Jerry. For the record, Art was Tom (Graph) and Paul was Jerry (Landis). According to Paul Williams in *Crawdaddy*, Art chose *Graph* after the graph paper that he used to plot the progress of the hit records of the time, while Paul's choice of *Landis*, was taken from the name of his then girlfriend, Sue Landis. Unbelievably, the single made it half way up the Billboard Top 100 and remained in the chart for nine weeks!

The two sixteen year olds sold over one hundred thousand copies of the record and for a while became local heroes.

Prosen quickly got Tom and Jerry to cut more singles but the success of *'Hey, Schoolgirl'* was not to be repeated. By the winter of 1958 their careers were put on hold while the two would-be musicians were packed off to college.

By the beginning of 1963 Simon had started to become interested in the folk music that was filtering out of the coffee houses of Greenwich Village. He again teamed up with Art, and they began to get bookings at some of the smaller venues around the Village. It was therefore only a matter of time before Simon's path would cross that of Bob Dylan. In actual fact, while Simon and Dylan saw each other perform on a number of occasions, the two men were not officially introduced until March 1964!

Having recently been signed to Columbia Records, after being spotted by record producer Tom Wilson, Paul Simon was in the process of finishing the songs for the duo's first album *"Wednesday Morning, 3 AM."* Simon – a painfully slow writer – decided to head for England in search of inspiration. Wilson, however, soon pulled him back, insisting that the album, already six months in the making, had to be finished. It was while Simon was back in New York that the meeting took place. Robert Shelton takes up the story.

"Carla (Rotolo) *introduced Dylan to Simon, assuming they'd have a lot in common... Simon and Dylan chatted, but only guardedly. A few nights later, Dylan and I were at Folk City as Simon and Garfunkel came on. They began to sing ethereal harmonies that sounded out of place at Gerde's, home of the weather-beaten ethnic songs...At the bar, Bob and I, who had been doing quite a bit of drinking, had an advanced case of the giggles over nothing. We weren't laughing at the performance, but Simon could have thought we were.*

Certainly Simon's talent is great, and he has sold more records than Dylan. But he appeared to be uneasy for a long time about the musician that laughed at the bar in Gerde's Folk City."[1]

A few weeks after that first meeting with Dylan, and with the album now complete, Simon decided to head back to the UK where he spent a lot of time over the next couple of years. The kid from Queens just didn't seem to fit into the Greenwich Village landscape. Simon: *"I could play music there* – Britain. *There was no place in New York City. They wouldn't have me...In New York I was a kid from Queens. That was bad. In England, I was an American. That was good."*

Many people maintain that Simon stayed away from the Village for no other reason than to escape the spectre of Bob Dylan, and although the problem was far less acute in England, people would still draw comparisons. More often than not, Simon would react to such comparisons by attacking Dylan.

Al Stewart remembers Simon's aversion to Dylan: *"I had a furious argument with Paul about Bob Dylan.* "Highway 61 Revisited" *was just about to be released and I got a copy on the Wednesday, two days before its official release, and locked myself in my room for two days learning* 'Desolation Row' *...Paul wandered in while* 'Tombstone Blues' *was playing, that bit about* 'the city fathers trying to endorse the reincarnation of Paul Revere's horse!' *He said,* 'That's rubbish'. *I made him sit down and listen to* 'Desolation Row', *which to his credit he did for all eleven minutes. I said,* 'This is fantastic!' *He said* 'It's rehashed Ferlinghetti'...I snapped back, 'The day you write a song as good as that is the day you live to be four million years old!' *He didn't talk to me for a month!"*[2]

In reply to a letter printed in *Melody Maker* in September 1965, Simon wrote that

Dylan's folk-rock songs were *"old-hat"* and lacked *"real anger."* Simon went on to say that he found Dylan's poetry *"punk"* and *"just rehashed Ginsberg."* A year later, again in *Melody Maker,* Simon told Chris Welch that: *"The biggest thing that Dylan has got going for him is his mystique,"* and that he thought it was *"stupid to grow your hair long because it's cool."*

As late as May 1969, Simon told *Seventeen: "...I don't believe the kind of obscurity Bob Dylan practices is good. I think it is more of a hoax."* He went on to brand the type of music that Dylan and others such as The Animals, and wait for it, Herman's Hermits! played as a *"hoax or pap or a copy of something somebody else should be doing."* It should however, be noted that *"Wednesday Morning, 3 AM."* had included a cover of Dylan's *'The Times They Are A-Changin'.'*

While in England Simon recorded a solo album, *"The Paul Simon Songbook"* – CBS 1965 – containing the song *'A Simple Desultory Philippic.'* He would subsequently update the song a year later for inclusion on the third Simon and Garfunkel album, *"Parsley, Sage, Rosemary And Thyme."* The original version has been described, probably justifiably so, as an affectionate satire. It concerns a man who has not heard of Bob Dylan, only Dylan Thomas, and as such the singer feels that the man lacks culture. The song also includes the spoken line: *"It's all right Ma, it's something I learned over in England,"* taken from Dylan's own *'I Shall Be Free No 10.'* At the close of Simon's 1966 re-write, however, you can hear a clatter, followed by the singer, complete with whining voice, saying: *"I've lost my harmonica, Albert."* Make of it what you will, but clearly this updated version is by a man with a growing paranoia of living in the shadow of Bob Dylan.

Rumours were rife in early 1969 that Simon's new classic song *'The Boxer'* was written about Dylan's life. For instance the whores on Seventh Avenue were believed to portray Dylan's record company *CBS.* Admittedly, there *were* some parallels with Dylan, but the song could be interpreted to fit any number of people, including Simon who also recorded for CBS Records.

Patrick Humphries – *"Upon the release of 'The Boxer' there was much speculation that the song was nothing more than a veiled attack on Bob Dylan – his contemporaries in the Village compared the young Dylan to a boxer – and the chorus – lie la lie – referred to Dylan's concealment of his real Robert Zimmerman persona".*[2]

Simon made much of the fact that Dylan had denied his Jewish roots by changing his name from Zimmerman. Simon and Garfunkel were of course both Jewish. Simon – *"Our name is honest. I always felt it was a big shock to people when Bob Dylan's name turned out to be Bobby Zimmerman. It was so important that he should be true."*[2]

However, the *"Li Li Li"* referred to in *'The Boxer'* turned out not to have been written about Dylan at all. As Simon later admitted, the song was written about himself and his own uncertainties and inadequacies. Dylan recorded his own version of *'The Boxer'* for his *"Self Portrait"* album and in the process laid down two vocal tracks, one for Paul Simon's part, the other for that of Art Garfunkel.

For Dylan's part he never seemed to have a problem with Paul Simon, and why should he? Dylan never saw Simon as any kind of threat. After returning from his last stint in England Simon had taken up an apartment on New York's East Side, which meant that the two now crossed paths more frequently. On one of these occasions Dylan invited Simon back to his home, and on another – toward the end of 1969 – he dropped into Columbia Studios to witness the recording of the album *"Bridge Over Troubled Water."* Art Garfunkel remembers – *"We were recording 'Why Don't You Write Me?' and when we came out of the booth...there he was."*

Melissa Manchester was a student at a song-writing workshop held at New York University during the summer of 1971. Simon undertook some of the workshops and Manchester recalls Simon talking about visiting Dylan. *"He said he went over to his house all excited and the place was a total mess, with junk all over and wrinkled old scraps of paper covering the floor. Dylan kept walking around the room talking and thinking aloud. Paul followed, picking up every loose scrap of paper he could find – anything with words on it – and stuffed them in his pockets. He said, 'I wanted to know if he was doing it like I was doing it. But I couldn't even find out what it was he did'."*[3]

In private, Simon had confided in Art that he could not understand how Dylan could write so well, so quickly. To Simon song-writing was a chore, albeit one he mostly enjoyed. To Bob Dylan, it was almost as natural as breathing. Dylan has nearly always worked fast and almost never revised or revisited any of his previous work and his studio technique, or some may say lack of it, is renowned. In contrast, Simon would spend months writing a song and would revisit partly finished songs time and time again. Simon is also known for his obsessive attention to detail in the studio. *"Bridge Over Troubled Water"* is reputed to have taken more than eight hundred hours to complete! By contrast, Dylan spent just ninety days in the studio recording his *entire* studio catalogue up to and including *"Desire."* To put the above into context: if Dylan worked a nine hour day, he would have recorded his first *fifteen* studio albums – two of which were doubles – in the same time that it took Simon and Garfunkel to record *"Bridge Over Troubled Water."* By the time they split in 1970, Simon and Garfunkel had made just *six* albums.

Following their Grammy award winning album *"Bridge Over Troubled Water,"* the duo broke up, choosing to pursue their own musical interests. For Paul Simon, this would mean achieving global success in the 1970s with songs such as *'Me and Julio Down By The Schoolyard,' 'Fifty Ways To Leave Your Lover,' 'Still Crazy After All These Years'* and *'Kodachrome.'*

During the 1980s Paul Simon's popularity faded and because, as Simon himself put it, *"nobody was paying attention to me,"* he was able to pursue his admiration for South African music. Collaborations with prominent South African musicians, notably Ladysmith Black Mambazo, produced the Grammy Award winning Album of the Year, *"Graceland."* In 1990, Simon released the Brazilian-flavoured album *"Rhythm Of The Saints,"* featuring percussion and melodies from South America. While still working on this album Simon began the process of creating a Broadway musical based on the crime, imprisonment and eventual rehabilitation of Salvador Agron, *"The Capeman."* Told in the language of doo-wop and salsa, the show opened on the Great White Way in January 1998, and while it achieved rave reviews for its haunting score and vivid sets, serious problems of production and storytelling led to its downfall. The musical closed on March 28, 1998 – just two months after opening – and is rumoured to have lost its entire budget of $11 million.

Simon hadn't toured since 1992, and has never toured on a double bill with anyone. Why then did Simon decide to tour with his old adversary Bob Dylan? As was the case with Dylan after the commercial failure of *Renaldo And Clara,* Simon may just have wanted to get back to music, a case of, *Do what you do do well.* Also, with a reported guarantee of $250,000 per artist, per concert, the tour would prove a way of recouping some of the huge losses made by *The Capeman.* But whose idea had it been for the two to get together?

"I think it was one of those industry powwow things," said a Paul Simon publicist, who asked not to be identified! She said the idea of the *"PaulBob"* tour came from one

of the artists' managers. *"It's really grass roots. Somebody woke up one day and said this would make a great pair and made all the right calls."* Dylan rehearsed his rearranged line-up during the first week of June and sometime during that week Simon and Dylan also got together. Having played his own *warm-up* concert on June 1st in Philadelphia at the Theatre of the Living Arts, Simon joined Dylan four days later, June 5, for the Dylan band *warm-up* in front of an audience of 3,600 at Denver's Fillmore Auditorium. The two artists duetted together on *'The Sounds Of Silence,' 'I Walk The Line,' 'Blue Moon Of Kentucky'* and *'Forever Young.'* Previously, the only time the two had been on the same stage was in January 1985, and that was in the company of forty-three other artists gathered together for the making of the *USA for Africa* video *We Are The World.*

Simon was supposedly set to join Dylan in July 1985 for the *Live Aid* concert but, if there ever was a real chance of that liaison, it fell through well before the event itself. When this possibility was mentioned to Simon he retorted by saying – *"I can sing harmony with most people."*

After his track record of adverse comments about Bob Dylan the above cheap shot should not have come as much of a surprise. However, it came at a time when it looked as though Simon may have finally put his Dylan phobia behind him.

During a 1984 *Playboy* interview Paul Simon, possibly for the first time, had something complimentary to say about Dylan! *"To me, the person who wrote the most moving lyrics was Bob Dylan, in the early days. 'Boots Of Spanish Leather,' 'Girl From The North Country,' 'Don't Think Twice, It's All Right.' 'Blowin' In The Wind.' It's funny to hear myself saying that. It may be the first generous thing I've ever said about Bob Dylan. In the early days, I was always too angry about being compared with him. And then, he's hard to be generous to, because he's so ungenerous himself. I never felt comfortable with him. He didn't come at you straight. It's a big error to think that because you like somebody's work, you're going to like him."*[4]

Since that 1984 *Playboy* interview, and even more so since the success of *"Graceland,"* Simon has become rather more gracious toward Dylan. Maybe the joint tour and those duets will be the final element required to exorcise the Dylan spectre from Paul Simon's memory. If so, then maybe the two artists can now become the *old friends* that never were?

1 Robert Shelton, *No Direction Home.*
2 Patrick Humphries, *The Boy In The Bubble.*
3 Victoria Kingston, *The Definitive Biography.*
4 Tony Schwartz, *Playboy* Magazine, 1984.

Other texts consulted –

Old Friends Joseph Morella & Patricia Barey, plus the Paul Simon web-site *Lasers In The Jungle.*

Published in issue #86, September 1999

Things A-Changing
UK Tour, September 2000
by Paddy Ladd

This article, which was not initially intended for publication, is culled from the private diary of Paddy Ladd. I felt the piece was so interesting and wonderfully perceptive that I persuaded Paddy to let me reprint an edited version of his piece in ISIS. My editing, however, has reduced the piece to half its original size.

The 2000 tours saw another resurgence in the quality of Dylan's concert performances and the following review could be from almost any one of a dozen superb shows.

"Ring them bells for the blind and the deaf..."

It's been hard to begin this year's tour report, and harder still to work out why. Nevertheless, I think I've nailed it. In the past, the focus of show going was clear – Bob-watching and trying to have a damn good time. Now, getting older, I seem to have crossed a watershed and my focus has become divided – between Bob and myself. Strange, or is it?

One reason for my anxiety is that since last seeing Bob in the UK in 1998, my hearing has got steadily worse. Therefore, the struggle with doing all that it now takes to enjoy a show as much as I once did, has taken on comic proportions.

For starters, I use a regular old hearing aid that has now become special, i.e. it isn't made any more. Seems it was just too popular with folks for the boffins' good.

"The one we've got now is much better," says the woman in the white coat.

"Oh yeah?" says I. *"Your saying that me in my forty-four years of using these contraptions, doesn't know more about this than someone who's never missed hearing a note of music in their life?!"*

"Oh this one has a greater range," Big Nurse insists.

"And I'm telling you that not only is my old wreck here the best thing for hearing music that's ever come along, but there's nothing even in the same class."

"Well yes, it's true that our patients say they prefer it," admitteth she!

Consider, dear reader, as I must now myself consider and accept, the absurd sight of moi, a few feet ahead of you, near the front, next to that tall guy with the Grateful Dead shirt.

What is he doing? He seems to be trying to juggle a balloon and two sets of lyric books. A torch, a notebook and pen, pair of glasses and maybe some other stuff I can't even see! When he's not doing that, he's hassling the guy next to him for the song titles.

Yep, the Ladd – Dylan ritual... Not very different from the Ladd Springsteen ritual, truth be told. Or the... well you get the picture.

First, there's the business of getting close enough to said artiste to ensure maximum lip-readability. Getting close-in tickets isn't a luxury – it's a necessity, and one not easily achieved.

Every show requires a separate tuning in of the wee antique to the sound of the first songs. Treble setting? Bass setting? Hmm, out with the 'ol screwdriver, on with the torch. Place torch between teeth so my hands are free to use screwdriver. Apologise to the person next to me for flashing the light in eyes. In so doing, open mouth and drop torch to the floor. Bend down to find it amid dancing feet. Resolve once again to stop apologising my way through life...

Retrieve torch and begin process again. Select setting, if you can get screwdriver into the tiny slot. Whoops, damn, now for the first time ever, I need my glasses to carry out the adjustment. Put on glasses and fiddle till little sod finally clicks across. Adjust volume and extra treble switches. Thumb slips onto controls with all the dexterity of Tommy. Music gets louder now with the vocals. Quick, slide the thing back before the result blows your ears apart. Quieter now, hmm... Adjust treble setting to locate guitars. There they are, nestling together like a family of gazelles by the waterhole. Very nice. Oh shit, the vocals have come in again. Quick, slide that damn thing before Bob sets your ears to ringing like bells! OK, let's run with that for now. Right, what song is this? Look up to lip-read Bob. There's a fog all around him – how weird. Damn, I still have my glasses on. Slip them back into handy pouch. On the other hand, maybe the waistcoat pocket would be easier. Take an age, and then decide. Bob emerges from fog unscathed. He sings the last word of the verse. I wait for the next verse to come round... Whoops, song's ended...

Be careful man; don't draw attention to yourself. Remember Manchester 1995, when the heavy hand of the security descended to throw you out for taping with a hearing aid! Not once, but twice. Since when has a hearing aid looked like a D5 recorder?

Next song begins. Place balloon between my thighs and try not to wiggle like a bowl of soup, lest it spurts out onto the person in front. Make like it's an everyday occurrence that people stand around with balloons between their legs. Notice person next to me staring. I begin to explain, but voice is too deaf to be controlled bawls out across the music just as the music drops to near-silence. *"IT'S A BALLOON. IT'S FOR MY EARS."* No... That's not what I mean...

I recognise song, but don't know all the words. Damn. OK, out with the lyric book. No, first, insert torch into mouth; or should that be second? Compromise. Insert torch, but don't switch it on. Hmm, balloon has slipped out and gone between that lady's legs. Shall I retrieve it? Think better of it for now, maybe later.

It's time to re-adjust hearing aid controls for the electric set. Notice ears starting to ring from neglecting thumb-slide action. Clearly failed to get through my heat in the Deaf Olympics tonight.

No, I can't pretend any more that I'm just a normal Bob-watcher, digging a concert nice and regular just like everybody else – cue impassive face, arms folded and *'show me'* body language – I can't pretend to have the cultivated thick skin of the ageing hippie, flying his freak flag high for being eccentric. It's time to accept that my freak flag is a wee minority nation of one here. It's time to face up to what's happening to my life and me. My back already told me that after last night's show, but I wasn't listening then. Don't know what I'd do if I had to stand through a support act. Thanks Bob, for dropping all that bullshit!

The challenge now, is how to set my mind so it can overcome all of the limitations I've just described. Yet still there's a constantly recurring toothache voice that reminds me of how beautiful music once sounded compared to now.

That's not quite the end of it, because the hours queuing cannot be savoured as before – the degree of hearing loss now means I can't converse with the other Bobcats. The edge of a conversation – the loneliest place in the world.

But now, let's flash forwards to a moment in time. It's the second Portsmouth show – September 25, 2000 – Dylan has come out fighting after the previous night lethargy or tiredness.

They've been in the groove all night. The guitars chime in, delivering an assured and stately set of cross-rhythms that are, or seem to be double, or almost quadruple-timed. Together they sound, not for the first time this tour, modern and yet old at the same time and are able to build in and on the *"Time Out Of Mind"* sounds with something brighter and newer. It sounds like the best indie band you've ever heard, but with its roots unashamedly in the R and B, the country and the rockabilly of those earlier eras. To utilise that much-overused phrase, it's that wild mercury sound, but a different one than we have become used to.

There is sweet beauty. Then there is menace, the edge that Bob's best work must always possess, the dark reverb of the soul.

As the music hangs in the air, Bob leans into the microphone with the supreme confidence of someone who is *on*, and intones *"She's got everything she needs, she's an artist, she don't look back."* The audience draws a collective breath at this new creation, which it now realises, is going to unfold before its eyes for the first time. This is not the slow ballad form we saw from 1995 onwards, poignant though that was. It's another creature of shimmering beauty. Writing this now, it occurs to me it would make a jewel of a setting for *'Visions Of Johanna.'* But we'll get to that later too.

As each verse proceeds, the mood grows and intensifies. Garnier's five string bass adds so much warmth and mood to the midrange; Kemper's drumming throws in sparse fills, rapped out more loudly, that make the heart jump and tingle. Bob's delivery stays inside the mood for once, not changing sounds for the sake of sound, but changing nuances for the sake of serving the song – because in the end Bob, to be up there after all these years, you've realised that you gotta serve somebody, and right now you've decided to serve the Muse. Just as at the same time, as it happens, you're singing about Her...

The break begins with Larry Campbell at lap-steel taking the solo and then Bob leads the others toe to toe with him, stretching and twisting the rhythm onwards and upwards, inside and out, without losing the plot. It builds to a powerful, understated, controlled climax before dropping into that trademark pause of silence, and then – *"Bow down to her on Sundays"* in that uniquely authoritative way. The end jam continues to develop to the point where it almost seems he will repeat the first verse, and then, another pause and it drops back into the well from when the song spiralled, curling down into the last few bars and silence.

As I watch this, I am caught on that beautiful high wire of ascent; that clear headedness; that lucidity and calm that comes of being at one with such amazing controlled power, calm and artistry. Embracing its menace like an old friend; acknowledging the darkness within, at the heart of Bob's feelings and visions, yet being uplifted by the sweetness and compassion that is also somehow present, both in his vocals and one of the guitars.

Here instead, it's pain and pleasure mingled. And there is indeed a place at the heart of some music's, where the sheer *exactness* of what is conveyed carries in itself its own power that whips your breath away and catches you in its magical moments. So far on this tour, Dylan and band have manifested numerous examples of this exactness, maybe more than I can recall from past years. Then that's maybe because without tapes I forget how often he can do it. At any rate, in such moments as this tonight, in a song I didn't especially want to hear, it feels like, as Phil Lesh quoted – *'The wire is Life. All else is waiting around.'*

There's also the relief that comes from hearing the whole thing just well enough to be able to get lost in the three dimensional work of art that just filled every space in the room. Every ear, every body too, as it vibrates us through the wooden floor and is absorbed into and takes over every molecule of this tiny *village hall*, filling it and creating a shimmering pool in which we swim. It's both sonic and visual. To be completely in the moment, becoming as one with Bob, myself, and the others around me. I look up smiling as the faces upstairs rise to their feet for the first time that night with their own huge grins.

No doubt for each of you, there were several moments like this on the tour. This one was of course mine – where expressive and receptive powers and abilities came together for a little bit of Heaven.

However, we haven't seen the back of the split-focus issue yet. You don't think a monster like that would be shifted by a single song performance, no matter how glorious, do you?

There is also the mythological dimension to contend with. My recent visits to shows by the post-Grateful Dead creature have set me to serious thinking about mythology and what role this has had in my show-going. I found myself increasingly forced to admit that, no matter what the considerable merits of the Other Ones or Phil Lesh and Friends amount to, I attended those shows for something that is more than music. For Deadheads, that means the scene itself. We assert that there is unquestionably a spiritual and philosophical/political link between what we have come to believe and how we behave, and the nature of the music and attitudes manifested in and around the band itself. We know that we cheer numerous song lines because they are the points at which our two souls – theirs and ours – commune, as it were, where those links are made manifest.

We know this has all become part of a mythology that we have created ourselves: a set of values to live by. This summer, interestingly enough, even when the music was good and those values were still visible amongst us, I had to face up to something else, some other level of the mythology that I, or we, don't want to confront. And that is in the realms of having some kind of continuation of the Family spirit up there onstage. I thought I had got past the whining about Jerry not being there, and had prepared for the Siddhartha-like lesson that in the end it is not the passing show which counts, but the intangible core – the simple quality of the music, stripped of all trappings and pretensions, which matters; not who is actually playing it.

I thought I managed to grow past this last year; but it seems I haven't. Why was that important? Why is it shameful to have to admit it? Moreover, where to, now that the singer is gone – what must I do for the song?

All this has come with me to the Bob gigs. There wont be any Dylan splinter bands, that's for sure. I can't imagine a band of Winston *'Animal'* Watson, Tom Petty, Garth

Hudson and Kenny Aronson going around trying to recreate Dylan-ness. But to what extent, I am forced to ask, is all this observation, this Bob-watching, this desire to see him create stupendously jammed shows, contributing to some myth I have been building up in my own head? Just another soap opera? Maybe the Clintons and Grays are right, that Bob sucks nowadays, and I and others like me are, for our sins, simply scrabbling after breadcrumbs?

Imagine if you will, someone up there performing as well as Bob and this band is. They are singing in exactly the same way – if that were possible! – so that in theory we could get off on it as music qua music. It's just that the guy doing the singing did not write any of the songs...

It doesn't work, does it? In fact, it all comes crashing down. The music is still good, so why then does it have to be Bob that sings it?

I bet that any answer you give will end up being couched in mythological terms. We want the real thing up there, because...?

Because we are, like it or not, Bob-watching. We are watching someone who is the absolute iconic epitome of certain attitudes and beliefs for our generation. Watching him struggle with ageing, with the later-life crises and the temptation to *"get as far away from myself as I can."* Watching for clues about how we might carry ourselves, how the attitudes we think we see, that we imagine still exist within Bob, and for which we study every sung line and facial movement, can somehow continue to inspire us and be our crutch. What does Bob mean therefore, if not something, which evokes mythology?

So, as *'She Belongs To Me'* comes to an end; it's with more relief than I can express here in lines, to know, absolutely and for certain, that there is still substance to the core of the myth. That doesn't let me off the hook. Some serious rethinking still lies ahead; but at least the delusional part is resolved!

One change in how I've caught myself in the myth is this article. I don't want, perhaps because I can't any more, to document a show from song to song, describing which breaks worked, which ones blew our heads off, which stumbled and fell, and what pattern this all created each night; instead, its reflection time.

However, in one hour's time, another dimension to this mythology will take a twist and emerge from years of hiding in the darkness and become known before our eyes. Stay tuned...

A village hall, I said. Well words don't do justice to what it felt like to be in that building; So grand on the outside, so shabby and plain inside. This is what it must have been like in those little civic halls up and down the land in 1966, drab and seedy, but not a bad seat in the house, and a tiny, tiny floor to die for.

I can't say if it was coincidence, but two songs into the show, in this hall the night before, the sounds of *those* chords signalled a long awaited moment in history. Yes, the first *'Visions Of Johanna'* in the UK since 1966.

As if that was not enough – and there wasn't much else to stir the heart at this first show – two songs into the encores and their usual dreaded clichéd predictability, the acoustic strumming produces:

"When she said, 'Don't waste your words, they're just lies,' I said she was deaf"... Yes, only the return of the other and final song from that year not to be played here since...the Royal Albert Hall, 1966.

"And you, you took me in, You loved me then, You didnt waste time. And I, I never took much, I never asked for your crutch, Now don't ask for mine." For once, I wished I had been further back to experience whatever amazement was flooding the hall. Surely, Bob realises what he is just done? It was already obvious that these Portsmouth shows

were of a particular kind. Bob wanted two nights in a small hall on the South Coast of England for some reason best known to him. Everyone knew these were going to be special shows, including Bob. But special in what way? What lay inside that special-ness, in our minds or his?

So, in getting these two elusive songs in one starry night, surely the core of the answer to that question lies herein. Now, is that or is that not – noting the lines of the song – simultaneously part of the mythology, and the mythological denying of that mythology? But now with a newer dimension, as we will see at the end of the next night, of a kind of acceptance of the myth from Bob's side, a drawing attention to it as something that he and we can smile upon, since it marks our collective journeying down all the years. Moreover, in accepting that myth, he has simply begun to create an extra new dimension to it.

We discussed this afterwards, and just laughed about what it might mean. *"If it means anything"* said Chris. *"He'll open with 'She Belongs to Me' tomorrow.' Just as he did back then in 1966. Then we'll know."*

Well he didn't. But the song happened anyway – in the electric set. It used to go like that, and now it goes like this...

Rewind the tape to my first night of the tour, in Cardiff, with a teeming and steaming full house. It's Saturday night in the capital of Wales, with the energy of many younger folk helping to create an atmosphere that's already electric.

Fifty-five minutes after Bob has come out, we are one song from the end of the main set and as far as I am concerned, I could leave now and be not only satisfied, but *'Dead and gone to heaven.'* This has to have been the longest hour of music in my life! Bob has indeed stopped time...

Normally, a great experience at a show finds you checking the watch and saying, *"Wow, is that really the time? How come it went by so fast?"* This show didn't do that. It was a case of *"How the fuck did I go so many places, so intensely, in so short a time?"*

At the risk of overloading this article with an excess of froth, I have to tell you that it was not only my best Bob experience of the nineties, just edging out the last night of Hammersmith 1990. It was up there at the pinnacle of any musical experience. And therefore by definition, any Life experience...

I cannot tell you how staggering it was! I couldn't say this if I hadn't gone back over set lists and shows I had seen before and asked myself serious questions about what the difference was.

I think the answer is somewhere in between. I have been lucky enough to see some great shows in the nineties – of that there is no question. Spring 1995 was in some ways good enough to be semi-legendary. Liverpool 1996 was powerful, and autumn 1997 became so too. When I look back over my old notes I find things like, *"This was the best 'Rolling Stone' I ever saw"* etc, so maybe my words can be taken with a pinch of salt. At the same time, the tapes do reveal that there have indeed been performances of individual songs, sometimes several in a show, that have had people coming out with similar raves.

On the other hand, Summer 1998 came in short for me, and of course there have been the lows of 1991 and the *'nothing much specials'* of 1993. Therefore, I do have some sense of perspective. I guess this time it was just one of those nights where everything came together. A whole confluence of factors. It is when you have a show that is firing on all these factors, that you can feel inspired enough to try and identify the ingredients of each, which makes this whole business of writing about Dylan a much more useful exercise.

How did Bob achieve this, then? Let's see.

There's the *"Bob being in a committed mood"* factor. There's the *"Bob having enough energy to deliver what he wants to be committed to"* factor. There's the *"band being in the groove"* factor. There's the *"Bob not being tempted to hide behind vocal noise-makings, but to feel the emotions in the words"* factor. Along with its cousin, the *"Bob not being so on that he overbalances through sheer enthusiasm into afore-said vocal noising"* factor. There's the *"Bob being on enough to remember the words well enough to deliver the feeling in them"* factor. There's the *"Bob being in touch with his emotions enough to allow them to come through strongly"* factor. And there's the *"Bob as bandleader succeeding with his own playing more often than failing"* factor.

Well... Consider all the above basically being hit on the nail for starters, with perhaps the only question mark coming against the *'emotions'* one and for that I have perhaps set my standards too high, using spring 1995 as the benchmark.

Sometimes it was vocal delivery that stood out. Sometimes it was the musical sparks flying. Sometimes it was an actual musical theatre of experience successfully created by the total sound. Sometimes it was tiny flashes exchanged between him and us, expressed in a look to the audience and a few chords struck sharply and another piercing, humorous look as if to say *"Didya notice that? That's for you over there, right now."* But it was always one or the other of these from start to finish. The show was all about the sound of jaws dropping steadily for 105 minutes. I can't recall any other show I've been at where I've reached the point where at the start of the next song, I have simply covered my face with my hands and said *"Enough Bob. No more. I simply can't cope."*

With my usual hyperbole afterwards, I blathered, *"He can retire now. Tonight. No need for any more shows! Surely he can never take me higher than that ever again?"* Of course that won't stop me going to more concerts, but what a thing of joy to be able to even use such words, to be even close to such concepts.

And so, just when I swore I'd never do another song-by-song review, I feel I must, simply to see if it brings out deeper levels of thought than simply stopping at a generalised rave.

The first thing I noticed was that he had come to sing *words* to us tonight. Lyrics. For once, it was not simply that they were one essential part in a musical whole. They were that too. But, he wanted to *talk* to us tonight. That seems to be one way this structure of acoustic openers has opened us to a potentially new dimension. Instead of pounding us with six rocking electric songs, he's created a space in which it is possible to have a conversation with him.

In the acoustic sets of 1966 and before, the fun and the magic were in the singing. But he was most often singing to himself somehow. He was inside himself, expressing the rage, sorrow, humour, whatever, that he was feeling and letting it pour from his throat up to us to catch in flight, singing to some higher power maybe. That is of course musical genius, itself. Yes, when singers are lost inside themselves, caught up in the spirit, and we listen and are ourselves transported.

That wasn't what happened tonight. Bob was confessing to us, directly. It was in the tone of voice, that quality, which no scientist will ever be able to identify, the way we know that, someone is talking to me and not to you or the person next to me. Believe me, it was for real.

The first two songs were a warm-up in a sense. However, the choice for the second told its own tale: *'My Back Pages,'* with all that those lyrics represent... To open a show with something, whose mood is normally suited to the closing valediction, is to give it a whole other set of meanings. I haven't got to the bottom of that one yet, so I won't dwell here. But the superficial point was clear. There were a *lot* of lyrics and he was keen to carefully remember them all. *Clarity*, that's the key word. He was just so clear and so *there*.

He hadn't quite arrived at *the* musical place yet. But once they began the lengthy ominous introduction to the next song, it hit me that these past three years, of gradually growing into an acoustic *band* once Kemper had arrived, had paid off to create something totally new. No *electric* instruments, and yet an absolute electric sound, with more real menace than Mettallica will ever deliver. We seemed set for a show that would gradually ascend, but where there was complete congruence between both acoustic and electric sets that they would in effect be one. It would not be a case of *"light hearted acoustic"* and *"heavy electrical metal."* Already there was potential for a great new artistic show-structure.

However, there is also another level going down. The final circle-closing, nail in the coffin of the whole Dylan goes electric scandal of yes, 1966. That year where one, folk-left, tradition seemed to end and, as we now know, a new one was born, one which has liberated all of us and showed us that there was nothing in literature, in theatre, in poetry, that could not now be captured and encompassed in song. That we *could* have songs to accompany our every thought, feeling, idea, our internal debates and musings. To lead or journey with us in our attempts to make sense of Western Twentieth Century fake-life and to strive to create our own beliefs – myths? – To find ways to carry us through the struggle that entails from not leading *normal* straight lives, and to learn to understand ourselves and what we must do at each stage of life. All in order to have lived as fully and as honourably as, upon laying on our deathbeds, we would have wished.

By bringing poetry, if you like, to popular music, Bob Dylan opened the door for all the rest. In effect, he did it single-handedly. You know I don't exaggerate. By going electric, he created a space that a new generation of people could walk into, inhabit, and live by. As even the *NME* conceded on his fiftieth birthday – *"No Bob Dylan – no rock music."*

So at this point in the show, then, yes, it would make perfect sense for the band now to emerge out of the ominous intro and for Bob to lean into the mike and sing *"They're selling postcards of the hanging."* A song full of words and more words. The one everybody on the fringe, when they want to give a clichéd image of Dylan, would highlight. And of course a song on the very cusp of 1966, coming from the very heart of that transforming moment in time, and also perhaps the one song which encapsulates the hippie movement's entire vision of the straight late-capitalist world that surrounds them.

Of course, that could all add up to nothing. This could be a crap version with a few throwaway verses. But, as Don Was is fond of saying: *"Bob knows."* When I say he leaned into the words with vengeance, I mean just that. He physically leaned and his whole body began to enlarge itself somehow, as he began to perform that indirect speech that he so uniquely captures, with the Cinderella, Romeo and *"someone says"* characters.

He's not performing in a numb acknowledgement of what the song means to us. But it's clear that he's aware of what we might call the more literary section of his audience. And tonight with this clear-eyed gaze, he is singing on three levels.

One, *"Yes I know what this song means to you"* and two, *"I'm comfortable with that. I can now find meaning in it again too,"* and three, *"I'm gonna celebrate and have fun with it and you."*

Well, that's what Bob is like tonight and he can sing. Boy can he sing! – If we may allow ourselves that word here, when he is indeed closer to talking than he used to be – I cannot begin to tell you what it was like to watch that second verse in particular, but also some of the others too. The way the crowd were transfixed by his own certainty, his growing conviction that he was himself spot on, cool, calm, collected, yet with exuberance creeping in, becoming a grin as the crowd burst into applause at the ends of certain verses simply because of how he had delivered them. And that positive appreciation – which is, I will never tire of saying, our necessary contribution that makes this a *conversation*, not a lecture – then in turn fuelling him to go for even more *there* spaces in the next verse.

All of us know this factor of Bob-shows, of course. The video of *'Tangled Up In Blue'* from 1984 – the audio too – reveals how clearly the audience can hear the words, so that they can hear almost every changed line and verse in that version, and how they show that they do. That example is a kind of touchstone for this factor. So whilst I rave here, I have nevertheless been following a timeworn path.

I think I am about ready to swear to you that I haven't heard him be quite so – *exact?* – so utterly *there* as he is now. And the thing is, and why this is important, is that the more *there* he is, the more that somehow releases another power of its own. A space where quantity is no longer a yardstick for getting to the high place that one desires for catharsis. Music usually needs a length of time to build up and bowl you away, like Bruce, the Dead, Indian ragas, African drums. But the more Robert Allen Zimmerman is present on any one night, accepting and playing Bobby Dylan, and having the two interact with each other, then the more something else takes place. From this clarity, this exactissement, comes an incredible intensity all of its own. And this intensity stops time.

You have this ominousness then, from these acoustic instruments. But you also now have – fun. Fun, a naked laugh in the face of death and time from a man who wants us to experience these words right now, and who can sing them, knowing that what we love most is actually centred in the humour of those words and – if you like – the whole play-power worldview that they have been created from. It's a grim place, *'Desolation Row.'* But it's also funny as hell. Yet no-one ever cares to point that out. It's the same old litcrit, same old cage. That's *not* what brings many of us back here, year after year. We come for the fun of it, the fun of all the twists Bob builds into the delivery of these words, teasing our expectations and darting away again, left hand drawing back as right hand advances.

Often our experience of this has been in just one or two songs a night. Tonight, however, something else is being opened up to us. He is beginning to get on a roll – and so are we. We've established that Bob is here to talk to us, but what is he talking about? He's telling us that he clearly remembers and understands what made his whole vision of that *'mad parade'* and that he too can now savour and enjoy it and share that with us. On that musical base as it were, he can build and dance his rhythmic guitar and vocal delivery, rather than just attempt that because that is what is expected of him.

I guess part of the reason I raved about shows in recent years, is because somehow I sensed this quality coming back. And loved it each time the percentages grew, thus each time raved anew. Except I didn't know what it was that I was referring to. Now that *it* has finally arrived, it has at last taken a form I can at least partially capture in words.

So, what does he want to talk to us about? Again it's clear; he wants to focus on the fun, the humour of these words and the political surrealism of his 1966 visions. If we had any doubts, the next song completely wiped the floor of them. "*Frankie Lee and Judas Priest, they were the best of friends*"! The first acoustic treatment of the song in Europe, an idea developed only about three months ago, thirty-three years after being written. So utterly perfect, too, for this band. And so full of *words*. There have been years, decades, even, where he would never dare to sing this many words because he had no chance of remembering them. Yet, somehow his memory has got better!

Once again, these words are so full of – fun. This is one of his all-time funniest songs and his awesome ability to master indirect speech and narrative means that he can deliver this sucker in ways the record version could only dream about. The first two verses are utterly breathtaking. The man next to me, his head was exploding, and more than a tear came to his eye at this point. Then alas, Bob stumbles on the next lines – oh no – the Hammersmith 1990 *'Fourth Street'* disaster looms. But no, he manages to right himself and then just takes off with each verse becoming more deliriously awesome, until of course, "*The moral of this story...*" The words finish, whilst the music continues. But there is a huge roar. Everybody in here *knows*, you know.

That was it, really. You could have gone home there and then. My friend Jake managed to convey through his delirium that this was like the *"Blood On The Tracks"* outtakes voice being transposed to a different era's material and a different sentiment. And of course the music has also been taken from another dimension, so that somehow we had a Bob who was not only clear about the present, but also about each stage of his musical past.

Bob at his best is celebrating something in life through the Chaplinesque absurdities with which he can deliver a tale, from his talking blues onwards. What was back then a form of celebrating our youthfulness, has, in this new manifestation, become a laugh in the face of death. He lost his humour for the most part after the Christian era, so that the best of the later songs had an awesome, almost pagan power. However, the world was no longer capable of being a funny place for him. Yet now, once again, it has.

Having reached such a peak of intensity, we were able to cruise through the next two songs, one tangled full of words again, and the other a nod to that folk tradition we spoke of earlier, with the *'Soldier's Grave,'* which could be as ancient as *'Jack-A-Roe'* but in fact is not. We could cruise through the *'Country Pie,'* a delightful *throwaway,* which is actually deceptive, because it contains so much sheer *playing*. This band is now beginning to show their own special merits, now we have moved to the electric section of the set and they can use colour and sustain. The whiplash twang of Sexton's guitar is really something. For contrast, listen to the last part of the song, where each has to play fast *'chicken-scratch'* notes like a two bar solo and Larry instead of playing eight notes, simply plays one long drawinnnng sound across those bars.

Now the country mood darkens to something else entirely, as the electric bouzouki heralds the very special rare treat of *'Blind Willie McTell.'* This is a tough one to get right. Somehow the groove is one of the hardest to find. However, once they hit the instrumental break, they soar, and the whole thing rears up and comes crashing down to silence, as Bob just leeeeans into *"God's in his heaven. And we all want what's his."* Everybody's transfixed. Oooh... No way even a deaf boy can miss how he's got this so utterly in the moment. Such clarity, such tricky words, yet clearly singing, making sure the right words hit home with the power that we once only dreamed would be possible again. Tonight he's conversing with us, where once the post-1979 lyrics would talk *at* us.

There's barely pause for awe before we are lifted up and smashed onto rocks at the other extreme. An amazing *groove* arises – what is it, rockabilly meets rock 'n' roll? It's utterly on, that's for sure, it's up at the running speed needed for take off. And the vocals deliver exactly that flight. *'Tombstone Blues'*! A rarity again really, a song few people think much about, except those lucky enough to catch one. But here it's turned into a centrepiece, a showstopper. Since this is a new arrangement, Bob has to sing the whole thing differently.

It is of course it's another one of *those* songs. Yes, it's full of words. It's from 1966. And it's surrealistic fun to the max, more than all the rest of the canon even? He is totally on top of the three verses we get. Again, this is indirect speech to die for. Listen to the second verse and how the doctor slopes into the room and talks to the bride. Oh, this is a celebration by a man with conscious knowledge of the essence of his art.

It doesn't stop here either, because at the first musical break Sexton is let loose and the roof just lifts off, not with volume but with the intensity which they create. Jaw-dropping continues. You don't want this music to end. This is an absolute shock to the system, and yet, tonight – just another one.

The music now shifts back to the other extreme, a quietness that also contains moments of absolute silence, and we are treated to a new song, *'Trying To Get To Heaven.'* In general, placement of new songs in this ballad slot is a strategy that we haven't seen much of over the years. It's certainly the step up we were hoping for once *'Make You Feel My Love'* moved in here, because the prominence of this slot sends its own message. This is where we are intended to concentrate the hardest in a show. So to have the confidence in the new songs to place them here, telling their own unique tale, that could not be less rock and roll, of a man waiting for Death to take him, this is perhaps the height of encouragement for those judging Bob by how much he delivers from the present, not the past.

And of course, it's not some persona that's being acted out in this song – it's Bob's own core feeling – and he knows we know.

Perhaps it's for that reason that he doesn't deliver it with the same emotion as on the record – when life feels as good as it does tonight for him, why should he? Then there's the very fact of it being played, and in a new arrangement again – already!

How can he be in such command of so many different moods? He doesn't quite get the words right near the end, and it feels a bit too subdued for me to easily get into. But hell, he is showing that, unbelievably he still has more to say. And this band are the ones responsible for this music, since no-one before them has played it live.

The emotional contrast too, where one could not get a more painful switch, from fun and celebration to the realities of dying, the almost whispered pleading for mercy. *"Pass me not, oh gentle saviour. Rock of ages, cleft for me, let me hide myself in thee."* I've spent the time since *"Time Out Of Mind"* puzzling how such absolutely final songs could coexist with the fun onstage, the dancing, the audience-relating thing, and here's the perfect example right in front of me. And I still cannot explain, except to say that if someone can be so clear headed about their death, then they can also become this clear headed about where their life has been, accepting the high points and the glory days without regretting them. Thus becoming unafraid to sing as if one was still young and in that space somehow, as well as confessing to us – that concept again – from the dark places of recent times.

Maybe that's the thing that keeps him going, the striving to finally arrive onstage and being able to be truly present with all his life held in an organic whole. Like the quote from show at Madison Square Garden in 1998 where he said *"I've played here many times. But this the first time I've been here."* The last few years have all built towards this opening up of the emotional channels. Somehow, it now seems, it was necessary to have *"Time Out Of Mind"* in order to make this all happen.

It seems the urge to write those songs has helped Dylan to make sense of himself and what he was feeling. Having achieved this, he was then able to turn back to the shows and invest them with that final amount of X factor, which enabled him to really live out the older songs more fully and to trace a line between all the thens and now.

As if our minds were not already blown, the mood takes a sideways shift and the ominous feeling that was quietly underneath the last song now becomes feedback and space, before the overt menace of *'Cold Irons Bound'* just rises up and breathes fire all over us. It's an incredible version and it works soooo much better down at this end of the show. Again lots more words; but this time they encompasses themes that are both linked to the last song and yet which also lace together the many years between, from 1974 till now. The performance and delivery are so gigantic, there's nothing more I can say here. As the ending builds into a crescendo, I know in one sense that this truly is it. I could go home now and so could Bob. Game over.

And yet the show is only halfway through...

Sit back and bop to the completely incongruous *'Leopard-Skin Pill-Box Hat.'* I guess it serves as a point to introduce the band, but there's absolutely no need for another song in the set anyway – it's an anti-climax. But it's also full of words, you know. Full of fun, surrealism and 1966.

Then there's this other new piece of theatre at show's end. The taking of bows! Let's hold that one for now, except to say it's one of the most hilarious things I ever saw, and it needs rapping about. It's as much part of the spectacle/show/relationship as anything else tonight. True performance art. How long can Bob stare impassively out at the smiles and joy and cheers without moving a muscle? He is coming more and more to resemble a lizard! The next sixty seconds could be like an eternity indeed...

The intensity doesn't ease up when they return either, because we get a superb version of a superb song – which also happens to be hot spanking new. *'Things Have Changed'* indeed. When was the last time we had a single that even got featured, never mind focused in such a concert slot? When was the last time we had a song quite this brilliant in the up tempo mode? *'Dignity,'* I guess. So if there's anything in what I've been saying so far, then that song will surely be cropping up in a show very soon...

As Jake pointed out, this one now is perfectly in tune with the Millennium. The ultimate single word summary of Bob's life, and almost his greatest achievement too. Change and change again, and yet to do so this successfully. How many of us can boast of a life of so many changes which have borne so much fruit?

This is a song that on its own would make you proud to be a Dylan fan, with thirty-eight years of history packed into it and with new sub-themes pouring off of every page. Indeed this whole article could now spill across page after page relating these lyrics and how they are at one with everything we are experiencing so far. As Jake says, *'It feels like he's saying, "I used to worry about all this external shit, but now I don't need to any more – I just accept it."* To accept the ennui and pain of the *"Time Out Of Mind"* emotions, the bullshit of the circus, and the problem of having to be the *"sad man my friend that's living in his own skin and can't stand the company,"* as Bruce has it.

Yet in so doing, I don't deny the pain that keeps coming along. I acknowledge there are times I slip back, and so I can express both states of being in the one song.

Again – He's full of words for the first time in years. And I want to put them to you and see what you make of them. I want to be funny one line and deadly sad the very next. He wants to tell you, finally, standing here naked before you, that *"I hurt easy behind this Bob Dylan mask. I just don't show it. You out there, you do exist for me. You can hurt me and you'll never know."* I'm not quite ready to admit that you actually make me happy. Maybe someday...

Whew. The day this song becomes a ballad, is the day we'll all realise just what he's offering up to us here...

The over-familiarity of *'Like a Rolling Stone'* now comes as an actual relief. But I should mention that it's of course one of those nights when even the oldest clichéd songs seem reborn. Not so much in the jamming, but just in finding a new pattern of delivery that almost bluesily fits the old rhythms.

Likewise, *'Don't Think Twice.'* Except that at the end the song goes down to silence and then a solo harp just rises out of the ashes and builds, until the music comes back in and then it all just liiiiiifts off and flies. More jaw-dropping. Give me a rest pleeeease Mrs Henry. I'm down on ma knees, and I can't take any more.

But there still no respite. *'Watching The Rover Flow'* has now become an ultra-rare encore and is again different from the last few years – not bluegrass now, but country rock, almost like the Band/Grateful Dead way again. The groove is still monstrously there and by the second verse and break, it can be found up in the rafters, swinging from beam to beam. By the last verse he is utterly on top of the lyrics – lots more words again – so that he grins hugely between each pause. Although he cannot see his face, Tony Garnier grins likewise, so palpable is there something happening in the vocal. If you note the words, you'll notice they're confessional again, yet now somehow revisited, as if he can remember both what it was like to feel that way back in 1971, and can find it funny and also find a present day meaning for it all. The human mind can only take so much *nowness*, Bob. And half this amount normally would serve us for weeks to come.

No letting up, though. After the quiet intro to the next song, the words come through the silence like I've never heard them sung before – a feeling that takes your breath away – a simple, quiet, *"May God bless and keep you always."* I've always had problems with this song live since 1978, but this is IT, this is the real feeling deal...

Then it's *'Highway 61'* and *'Blowin' In The Wind,'* done well. More fun 1966 wordiness contrasted with a simple summing up of all the thirty-eight years in between and the one truth that has remained constant. That the answer to all our human frailties and fuck-ups and oppression, our *'What Good Am I?'s'* to our *'Dirges.'* or *'Masters Of War'* to our *'You're a Big Girl Now's,'* that answer is still blowing in the wind of our all too human endeavours. And yet in the final end, that is all we still have in life on this world. Yes, the whole show remains remarkable right to the very end, as he even manages to have fun with little guitar phrases and volume strums and picks that amuse and yet do not jar with the song. Because tonight he is so utterly there that anything can just be dropped in and will work.

To see and feel and hear a human being performing at the very peak of their human potential somehow has a life enhancing effect on us. An athlete, dancer, actor, may also be in *the zone* as it were, and thus lift us up. But they aren't really in dialogue with us as this has been tonight. This was a true dialogue, conversation, between him and us about *life* and now and then and all the days and years between.

Or is this simply still more Mythology? I'm too close to tell right now. All I can do is to try and be as faithful to the moment, and as detailed as I can in reporting what seemed to take place. The other amazing thing about being human is that all these thoughts, observations and feelings that have taken so many pages to write down, happened in split seconds. You know that you knew. But until writing it all down, you don't know just how much it was that you knew! They were just so deep and so complex that they required all this pouring off of pages, certainly written in my soul, just to put them into words so that we can begin to share our own experiences with others.

At the time anyway, we didn't need all those words. We could just look at each other with popping eyes and go *"Yeahhhhh,"* and know that we all were feeling our own versions of the exact same things. It's a truly high life-point.

Whew... It's time to cool all this down somewhat and just try to reassure you that my sanity does still operate. The best way I can do this is to roll the tape forwards to the end of the next night, the first Portsmouth show.

A night where both *'Visions'* and *'Fourth Time'* are played for the first time since

1966, Where a magnificent *'Can't Wait,'* a superb *'Wicked Messenger'* and a remarkably placed encore – *'I'll Be Your Baby Tonight'* – also happened.

And a night where I was left profoundly unmoved.

Now I'm not saying this wasn't a good or great show; that's for others to tell. But it didn't happen for me, no matter how much I might have wanted it to. Maybe the factors involved shed some more light on the art of Bob? OK, so what were they?

Average performances of songs like *'Ramona,' 'Mama,' 'If Not For You,' 'Lovesick,'* for one. In a word, song-choices. Related to that, hearing numbers you are so not into that you are literally stopped cold, where it's left to the rest of the show to build up momentum again, like the *'Gotta Serve Somebody,'* which ironically was in response to a bannered request. Credit to both parties, but why couldn't it have read *'Up To Me,'* or something a little more unusual!

In this vein, I would say that we have some clues as to how the transportation occurs. The second song needs to speak deeply to us, so that the third song in each night is ready as a kind of apex of menace, musically – *'Desolation Row,' 'Alright Ma,'* and now *'Visions'* – This sets the rumbling off, and it then depends whether the fourth song can build on that. If it can't, as *'Mama'* didn't, and whilst *'Soldier's Grave'* is a fixture, then we haven't hit lift-off by the halfway point.

This leaves the second half needing to do the mind-blowing. After *'Can't Wait,'* the potential was there to make the leap, but then the next two songs – the other was *'If Not for You'* – pulled it back down, so it didn't explode by the fifty-five-minute mark. And without that, the encores are not designed to blow your mind and of themselves – they can only finish it off.

Another factor is that Bob was clearly tired tonight. He also seemed a little overawed by how close we were in that hall, not least because the lighting rig, being designed for big venues, lit the whole fucking place. You could see one third of the way back into the balcony almost the whole night. This all seemed to serve to make him retreat into himself – I was not the only one who saw and felt this – certainly he barely smiled at all tonight before the encores.

A related factor was that of course he could therefore see the balcony crowd just sat like puddings. It came over to me like, *"Entertain us, Bob. We don't have to give anything back to you."* I can't help but feel he was painfully aware of the flat atmosphere they helped to maintain, if not create. This could all be unfair. After all, the *'Fourth Time Around'* choice could hardly happen if they had pissed him off? Maybe it was at that moment that he twigged the 1966 connection of passivity/ negativity, and aimed both to placate the audience and spit at them at the same time?

Another factor – I was right at the front, and maybe too much was too visible? Maybe one needs a little more smoke and mirrors, especially if it's not a happening show? My companion Rob felt the same.

Then there's the sad train-spotter dilemma – song choice, and how much individual enjoyment of a show is reflected in such a mundane thing. Certainly, that was true for me also, but then it's cancelled out somewhat as a defining factor by the rarities above.

It was only a greedy boy – a picky Deadhead? – who would want more really, because the music created is generally so impressive that one is happy just to hear different songs each night come forth in their new forms, and to observe how well the structure works according to which types of songs are chosen. Just one closing note: At the end of the show, Tony appeared to mouth *"Baaaaaa"* at the audience. If he did, I know what he meant.

So to the last night here at Pompey once more. There are several themes to thread together here. The first is to briefly run through what happened. There was no doubt from his demeanour that he had come to play tonight. For the first time he got a grip on the opener, so that when he was singing *"Hallelujah, I'm ready to go,"* he came over like *"I'm ready to take off tonight"* – no kidding. Then we got a now-rare *'Tambourine Man'* in the second slot, played differently yet again, with a semi-up-tempo arrangement. Laudable, though he tried to fit the vocals to the music and ended up not very near the emotions of the song. But it was very interesting nonetheless. Then a debut for the ominous slot, one that could not be more so – *'Hard Rain,'* which maybe was designed as a comment on the weather outside. It was impressive and the end jam was something else – it really took off and the rhythms almost leapt beyond the one a la the best *'Masters Of War.'*

'Frankie Lee' just exploded vocally. There were no mistakes this time, so the momentum could just build. Way more dynamics and enunciation in the vocals, to the point where he almost went over the top and ended up in sound-making; but it was breathtaking stuff. So we reached the break as it were well up, even with the mangled penultimate *'Tangled'* verse, where he sounded like he forgot the words but was trying to make up new ones on the spot rather than just making sounds. This one had more than the previous two – even though it is finally time to rest it – and *'Country Pie'* was the best yet also. These musicians are really the business! This of course is the point where the *'She Belongs To Me'* appeared and used the show's momentum to take full flight.

Now undoubtedly some felt that the repeats from hereon in, *'Tombstone,' 'Trying To Get To Heaven,' 'River Flow'* etc, stopped them from getting off; but it didn't work that way for me. What was coming over was a real sense of the cogs and gears behind what makes up a working band. Oftentimes this would distract and detract from the experience, being most noticeable in shows that aren't working. But on a great night, sometimes you can be flying anyway – and this is where it helps to have already been *"Dead and gone to heaven"* so that one is relaxed, because having already achieved transportation, the rest is gravy, and you can somehow be inside and outside the experience at the same time – So they may have been repeats, but it felt like they were selected again so soon because Bob knew how well they had worked at Cardiff and wanted to make sure he knocked this audience out, rather than risk slipping down from this peak. And since they were delivered quite blisteringly, I'd say he achieved his aim.

The *working band* approach also enables Bob to reduce the classics to mere mortal songs, and from there, perform them well enough to make them into great works once more.

Now, the show's nearly over, so this is a good moment to turn to the band. Over the past few years, the question of how good the band are, how appropriate they are, individually and collectively, has been a major factor for me at Bob-shows. Most Bobcats seem uninterested in this, and since I've already explored the reasons for my feelings, in relation to jamming and band members therefore staying onboard long enough to become able to do this well, I won't say any more now. I was very happy to have Kemper come aboard for his pedigree in the jamming arena, and Campbell too for the tonal qualities and colour he brought to the sound that Jackson, much as I liked him, didn't seem to reach for. But what I found fascinating was to read my 1998 piece and find the following:

"Mind you, the tension between "Time Out Of Mind" and the country may yet prove too wide a gap to be bridged comfortably. Much may depend on whether Bucky can shift across to eerie menace and feel happy with it. Or how much Bob will let Larry's sound-skills converge with his essentially a melodic approach."

Then Bucky Baxter left! Which kind of set me up to think about the new music. Replacing him with a guitarist immediately suggested a loss of the washes of sound, and a question mark over how Sexton would replace that, and since he is famous in his own right, I wasn't sure how long he would stay.

What I found this time, which excited me so much was that somehow, this new sound *does* bridge the *"Time Out Of Mind"* – eerie and the country. The sound-washes have indeed gone, or rather, are partly replaced by someone else playing more on a newfound boundary between those two sounds/styles. I think its Campbell doing this, whilst Sexton holds down the rhythm. But he too showed that he has some amazing sounds at his own command and maybe he is also adding tonal colouring and some sustain. Somehow this pairing is creating a total effect that moves between sparse and sustained much more easily than pedal steel could or would do. Tony has gone back to the five string bass, which is sonically such a fantastic instrument and also one which allows him to spread his skills out more. The mid-range tone is the big gain – he can inhabit that for effect without getting in the way sonically of the guitars – indeed at such moments he augments and amplifies what they are doing – and can shift back to the regular bass sound in a split second.

All in all, the music for the most part sounds quite different – some have pegged it as country, but there's much more happening than that. Somehow the guitar sound on, say *'Tombstone Blues,'* doesn't feel that far now from the *"Time Out Of Mind"* songs, and somehow not that far from *'Country Pie.'* It's your job to figure this out, folks – my ears are past that now!

At any rate, the excitement comes from finding it all so much more of a seamless whole somehow. The new sound of *'Messenger/Drifter/Crash'* seems to straddle these two extremes in a way that is truly new. The funny thing was that somehow even in the acoustic set, the sounds of those guitars on the third song at least, had a tone that connected to the electric sets.

My feeling overall is that – at last – Bob has finally got rid of the *bar band* feel, laudable though that was, and now has a fully-fledged regular band to withstand any carpings from the pondlife section of the media.

The final piece of the jigsaw is to situate Bob's own playing in the picture. The first thing to note is that the three guitarists have a contrasting blend that seems often to really work. The second is that Bob on a good night is now very audible. Maybe the prominence he has in the acoustic set has allowed him to face up to his more leading role in the electric part. But for sure, at times – e.g. the second Portsmouth show – he is leading from the front and forms if you like, the audio apex of a three pointed spearhead. This is different from the three note weedles, which are still there, and which still seem to have the role of upping the jams to a take off point. This is somehow like – he is the lead instrument, even if it is just rhythm guitar – which it isn't – it's something more – and the others filling the sound out behind that. At any rate, something rather good is happening.

All this is reinforced by a subtle development in Bob's own attitude to the band. The new willingness to wing it is great, but before, Bob would just go off and do it, and they'd have to figure it out. Now he cares, enough either about them or the *music* or both, to ensure they're all in on it together. Several times, the word *professional* popped up in my mind. There is much more a sense of Bob actually leading a band – he seems, simply, more *caring*.

So to that total picture then, namely the jamming mission – well this is interesting. They are still there in that space, very obviously in the acoustic set, since Bob can wander free, playing off the other two in a realm of his own, But right now it feels like it actually doesn't matter whether they can 'make it' with the jams. Sometimes they will find the mood and room to go for it, and sometimes they won't. There's neither a sense of the 1996 compulsion to jam, nor the 1998 feeling of receding back to simple music breaks. What happens, happens, and that's fine for now. Maybe it will feel different in a few years – if we are blessed with those.

All of which brings the tape to that moment, when all the years combined, where the myths and the man came together and we had the perfect ending, were there to be no more Bob-shows.

'Highway 61' came out smoking, back up at the level of 1997/8. And then... Somewhere early on in the song, it was clear Bob was fired up in a particular way. He started to look upstairs more until he was virtually looking there the whole song, in between looking at me and others near the front. This was noticeable to more people than just me; so we were able to look at him and then at the balcony front centre, and then watch back and forth at what was happening.

Now understand that this section was the hard-core Bobcat block. Having Lambchop in the middle of it might have been a clue. Or maybe Bob had his own ways of finding them out. Regardless, it became clear to me that he was playing for *them*, at them, and to them. But mainly *for* them. They seemed to take a while to catch on, funnily enough. But once they did, the magic just redoubled. Instead of being confronted with rows of suet puddings, he had some live humans, engaged for once in exchanging energy with him. The hardcore, arms folded, impress me Bob, crew, actually remembering what a rock concert is supposed to be about. And once he found he had them, oh boy, did he then let loose! He started to stand in different ways, play little bursts of notes at them and convey a sense of, *"How did you like that? That's for you."* Over and over again, stretching the song till he was sure that he had them thoroughly hooked. Tres amusement!

This continued even into the supposedly downbeat *'Blowin' In The Wind,'* becoming more hilarious each time and yet not ruining the mood of that song, somehow.

So there I was, watching and laughing, but also deeply moved at the same time. For those he was speaking to now were those who had kept the flag flying all these years. Who kept the UK interest up at the current level. Who created the texts and arts so essential to Bobdom – who in effect conversed with him indirectly in-between shows.

Laughing too, because these of course include the very people who have a *magazine* dripping with naughtiness. Reviews of illegal tapes fill the inside along with illegal videos and illegal CDs, and articles discussing the implications of all of these. Thoroughly naughty, as I say.

And yet, in some way, accepted by him, no matter how the role of the goons appears to contradict it.

It gave me a lump in my throat. And when at the end, they had figured it out enough to react so that Bob could see that in turn, it felt like our Dylan-lives had reached their perfect climax, here in this tiny hall, reeking of 1966, with a circle finally closing between him and us.

And at that very instant, while the song was ending, he spoke: *"Alright, thank you all you people up there."* Some of you wouldn't have noticed it if you didn't lip-read it, maybe, because the music was still going.

And there you have it. He's already there in his mind. And that's good enough for now.

It seems an anti-climax to have to continue from the above, but I guess this is the point where I am allowed to link the final theme to myself. Earlier in the electric set, the over powerful lights formed freak diagonal waves which regularly lit up sections of the floor quite far back. One of them had that Chaplinesque man, juggling his balloon and his back pages and God knows what else, directly in its path... Except he has given up trying to be inconspicuous and is engaged on a Deaf coming-out; signing the songs known well enough, joyfully to himself and to Bob.

There are a few glimpses where I think to myself. *"He seems to have noticed me. No, that's bullshit. And anyway it doesn't matter a damn."* Curiosity gets the better of me and I pay more attention. Until, a few more songs of this later, and I can't deny it, even to myself.

Understand, it is not *me*, neither Paddy Ladd, nor Deaf person, that he's in contact with. And I doubt it has anything to do with the signing. But he's looking for reactions out there. The front rows are packed to tight to dance, and so his eye is roving, trying to spot those who *are* dancing, and to work off them. I attempt to check this by watching the people around me in that light. Sure enough, none are really dancing. Aha, so that confirms it for me in a very personal way. His conversation needs, wants, demands, our feedback in a particular way. He then starts to play *at* those people and the energy level starts to build. *"Everybody must give something back for something they get."*

By the aforesaid *'Highway 61'* the balcony looks and posings and playings are divided between them and me, and a few others dotted out across the hall in an arc. Each time this goes round – at least three times – it just gets more *out there* musically.

Look, he's a song and *dance* man, remember! How much more convincing do you need? His whole musical oeuvre is to play his own unique rhythm-lead in patterns that counterpoint the main rhythms, cross-playing that is nothing so much as *conversational* for the most part. Little statements. Some just put out there to see what comes back. Some comments, jazz-like, as if he was Miles or something – within this rockform of course. Above all, the conversation takes place in rhythmic form, not emotive notes per se. And that means yer supposed to dance to them!

I couldn't wish for a more perfect summation of my whole Bob-time than those moments here tonight, where it all made sense, and where it all got so personal for those who have made the long strange trip down the years.

Postscript

In the final end, I guess that the only way I can conclude is that Bob *has* done the business. Done whatever the best art is supposed to do. Because the only way to measure it is by whatever effect it has had on one's life.

And for me, yeah it has helped me. There are some rough things in my life these days. But now I am back to being able to walk around singing various songs aloud. Tuneless, no doubt. But at least back to a certain level of happiness or acceptance. A shot of love from the man, that seems to have helped jolt me up another level. To make the bad times more bearable, and thus to allow the human spirit to try and do its own healing based around this extended flow of happiness endorphins.

So, thank you Bob. You did the trick again. No one else could play that tune. I guess it truly was up to you.

Fuller version published in issue 93, November 2000.

"I live in another world where life and death are memorised"

'Dark Eyes' Bob Dylan 1985

The Psychosis of Dreams
by Petter Higginson

Though I cannot bear criticism that attempts to psychologise the work of a great writer and reduce it to symbols of his unconscious struggle with, say, his mother, we do Bob Dylan less than justice if we do not spend time considering his struggle with insanity. Specifically, I am interested in exploring the borderline between great art and the threat of psychosis, which engenders it. It is an old and hoary cliché that the line between genius and madness is a thin one, but Carl Jung once told James Joyce that *Finegan's Wake* differed from the thoughts of a schizophrenic in only one detail – the schizophrenic was drowning in language, and Joyce was swimming in it. The element – or contents – was the same. Only the sense of form *swimming* differed. For me, Bob Dylan's best art represents the effort to swim in the waters of psychosis. I believe Dylan is what a psychiatrist would clinically call a borderline psychotic who, through a tremendous effort of will, talent and love, strives to translate the threat of his psychosis into art. I know that most readers will immediately hate me for introducing these clinical terms. Nevertheless, I have, for twenty-five years loved Dylan's work more than that of any other artist or entertainer. Therefore, I am not here to do an academic demolition job on either him or his art. Bear with me, as I think my case kind can strengthen rather than weaken our appreciation of his struggle.

"I'm beginning to hear voices and there's no-one around," cries the character of Dylan's *'Cold Irons Bound.'* If this character had been sitting in his GP's surgery when he said this he would by now be receiving treatment for schizophrenia. Schiz (split); phrenia (mind). Schizophrenia is most strongly distinguished by the manifestation of voices which/who often wish the patient harm and can be seen as personifications of extremely deep guilt complexes. The psychiatrist R.D. Laing, however, believed that such experiences were rooted in the patient's impossibly deep grief. He interpreted the word schizophrenia as schiz (broken), phrenia (heart, or solar plexus). I believe that Dylan suffers from a contained form of this kind of schizophrenia, where the agony of a broken heart that is threatened all the time by manifestations of psychotic pain, *"Where the ways of nature will test every nerve,"* – *'Born In Time.'* Where, *"You can hear the night-watchman click his flashlight, ask himself if it's him or them that's really insane,"* *'Visions of Johanna'* Where *"It's sadder still/To feel your heart torn away"* and where

"The universe has swallowed me whole," 'Cold Irons Bound.'

The experience of schizophrenia can best be understood as dreaming whilst you are awake. Where the ordinary person snaps out of the dream-world and heads off to work, the schizophrenic continues to conceive of himself as a dream-character, perhaps as an angel, devil, or saint. Perhaps, also, as an animal, object or process. Dylan conceives of his worldly life as a dream-process: *"I live in another world/ Where Life and Death are memorised," 'Dark Eyes,'* and *"You're coming back to me in black and white/When we were made of dreams," 'Born In Time.'* His genius is his skill in translating this madness into a gorgeous-ugly form of art. But his pain is that the threat of psychosis is always very real for him, shattering him in the doubt of whether dreams are really experiences of other worlds or just manifestations of bizarre inner processes: *"Reality has always had too many heads," 'Cold Irons Bound.'* Dylan, more than any other person or artist that I know, needs his dreams to be sacred and astral *"Because my dreams are made of iron and steel/With a big bouquet of roses hanging down from the heavens to the ground" 'Never Say Goodbye.'* His terror is that they might just be illusions and distractions from the *real* games of boredom and death. *"I close my eyes,"* he writes, *"and I wonder/If everything is as hollow as it seems," 'Highlands.'* Dreams have to be transcendental for Dylan or he's dead.

"I've been double-crossed so much/I sometimes think I've almost lost my mind," wrote Dylan in 1975, *'Idiot Wind,'* and it's clear that the pressures of celebrity, nay myth, that this man experiences are so diabolical that they can drive him mad. However, it is the pressure of inner psychic experience, I think, that preys on him most greatly. Dreams are the source both of his inspiring brilliance as a writer and his debilitating fragility of self.

For a while in 1994-5, Dylan had to be wrapped in blankets and nurtured like a baby. He is notoriously fickle, moody and abusively defensive. He looks smashed by life sometimes and his voice can be withered, cracked, and seedy. This could be put down to tour pressures but I think it is better explained by the energy that is absorbed in the containment of threatening psychic pain and the floridity of latent psychosis. *"Time Out Of Mind"* contains some extremely bizarre perceptual experiences: *"The stars have turned cherry red ... up over my head clouds of blood ... waist deep in the mist, it's almost like I don't exist ... "* and the character at the centre of this maelstrom is fugitive, desperate, burnt-out like a patient in the psychiatric hospital of the world. Dylan's bravery in owning and expressing these awful states of being stirs my deep admiration. There can be great shame in admitting to being so beaten, but he slaps it all down with exceptional courage. There is not a moment of self-pity in all his horror. But there is an acknowledgement of the violence of the psychotic threat to his coherence and integrity in the straight statement that *"Insanity is smashing up against my soul," 'Highlands'.* Here, the world of his dreams is disintegrated and murderous. There is no escape to the *"other world,"* because the world of his dreams is the insanity. A psychosis is, to echo Bob, A Dream Gone Wrong.

In 1989 Dylan had been *"Thinking of a series of dreams – Where ... everything stays down where it's wounded, or comes to a permanent stop," 'Series Of Dreams.'* This, I think, expressed the frustration and terror that had dogged him since 1979 and the experience with Christ. His dreams had become dysfunctional. That is, they were no longer sweet, fluid and exotic as they had been in that glorious period from 1974-78 when his imagery was aflame with psychic energy and the dreamscapes of mysticism. For a man who, it would appear, literally *"lives"* in dreams as much as he does the empirical world, this must have been a terrifying experience. Knowing that the nightscapes of satanic capitalism held no safe places for his sweet, intelligent soul. Dylan must have felt deeply threatened when his dreams refused to include him or, worse, came to a permanent stop.

For me, image of a door being closed *'Standing In The Doorway'* is obviously religious. The peculiar image of God's children *"closing the door"* on Dylan in *'Tryin' To Get To Heaven'* represents the fear of being permanently shut out of his own dreams. The onset of psychosis can encourage this feeling because it is really an agonising assault in which the contents of the dream are so complex and constellated that the recognisable personality is swept *from* the dream in a flood, *'Down In The Flood,' "Before The Flood."* The patient can feel like they are being swept or pulled aside from their own centre, shoved into a corner of the shelf as it were, as the insanity is unleashed against the soul – the centre of life. The experience is there in that early line, *"These Visions of Johanna* (Gehenna) *have now taken my place," 'Visions Of Johanna.'* There were later indications of such an attack in 1982-3: *"It's like I'm stuck inside a painting/That's hanging in the Louvre/My throat starts to tickle and my nose itches but I know that I can't move," 'Don't Fall Apart On Me Tonight.'* It's not because Dylan is physically trapped here. Dylan is trapped by the failure of his inner world to enfold and support his coherent personality. It's a psychotic experience – a feeling of invisibility, compression, one-dimensionality of the psyche. Some psychotics report that their *self* becomes an outline with no corporeal existence. Dylan had captured the horror of this experience brilliantly in *'Shelter From The Storm'* which is a hymn of gratitude for being pulled out of a nervous breakdown. *"I came in from the wilderness,"* he writes, *"a creature void of form."* It's precision like that, which should win him the Nobel Prize. Notice how he's *"void of form,"* then try to imagine how one could experience that. It precisely echoes what Jung suggested to Joyce. To be void of form is to be psychotic.

There is no doubt in my mind that this man has walked with the gods and goddesses of his own psyche in times and places we will never hear about because they are too sacred to divulge. Dylan *travels,* I feel, in metaphysical countries: deserts, ancient cities, verdant groves and mindscapes of brilliant beauty. Nevertheless, he has always returned across the threshold of the mundane, refused settlement rights in his *other* world. His horror is that the dream-door might close behind him and imprison him forever in the wasted landscapes of post-redemptive, i.e. purely physical, hell. Importantly, this is one of the most common fears articulated by psychotics. Their dreams begin as exciting escapes and end up as damnably carnal affairs in which they become eviscerated and wasted. The horror of psychosis is that it threatens to reveal that all dreams are merely psychosomatic illusions, which *"conquer the mind."*

'Visions Of Johanna' is not just about a drug-trip but a sub-psychotic ride through Gehenna where *"The jelly-faced women all sneeze,"* and where *"My conscience explodes."* Taken out of artistic context, these are deeply and typically psychotic insights – panoramic, bizarre, and terrifying. If Dylan actually experiences such things not just as imagination but on nerve-endings worn raw with stress, then it is no wonder he clings so faithfully to the mercy of God. I think we should take him literally. I think Bob Dylan suffers from pre-psychotic breakdowns which he barely manages to contain: *"I have had some rotten nights," 'Seein' The Real You at Last.'* It must be sweet relief when his Muse flows and allows these chains of flashing images to be alchemised into art.

Bob Dylan once said that he was not a mystery to anyone who had experienced what he had. He's right, I think, and is actually quite a simple writer, but one describing very complex experience. He has a very mercurial psychic structure with an extraordinarily precocious grasp of the multi-facetedness of life. That is, he sounds like he'd lived five lives by the age of twenty-one. Daniel Lanois suggested at the Grammy ceremony in 1998 that he believes Bob has led previous lives and that this accounts for it. However, we don't have to turn to reincarnation to understand the Dylan phenomenon, attractive as the prospect is for many of us. The thing about an archetypally mercurial personality is that experience *comes,* as it were, to him. Through dreams, which are mercurial in their structural principle, all experience is available on the *grapevine* of the collective unconscious. But Dylan's psyche is peculiarly and uniquely sensitive to the mystery of certain sounds, tones, moods, feelings, the forms of wildness and the forms of tenderness of that vine. This is no time for a Jungian exposition, but I feel Dylan's soul abides by a silver pool of memory, upon which he draws and through which extraordinary experiences seek their expression in him.

There is something of *The Magician's Nephew,* by C. S. Lewis, about him. He is a kind of Silvio of the collective dream. However, tragically for him, the experience is half delightful and half poisonous. Just as Mercury or quicksilver is a delight to the eye and -more mystically – to the ear, it can be a lethal threat to the mind. It can induce the beauty, which makes us all gasp at Dylan's genius with say, phrasing, or insight; but it can also wreck the psyche of its lonely medium. Dylan pays for his talent with the mercurial poisoning of his mind by a latent psychosis. As he ages' this threat seems to be getting more pronounced. The two experiences – madness and majesty – are deeply related. Dylan is one part Mercurius, one part Dorian Gray. One part angel and one part schizophrenic. He is my favourite writer by miles because he somehow survives this bizarre fate and twists it constantly to his advantage as great art. No one else can play this tune. You know that it's up to him.

Published in issue #88 January 2000

2000 – Zurich, Switzerland © John Hume

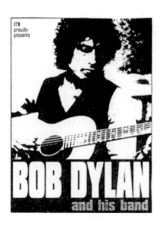

Arriving Where He Started
by Alan Davis

After reading the closing words of its final chapter, I put down my copy of Michael Gray's *Song and Dance Man III* and contemplated what I'd just read. I was left with a strong impression of a testament not so much to Bob Dylan's art as to the author's disappointment in what it has become – much the same kind of impression, in fact, as I felt after reading the updated version of Clinton Heylin's *Behind the Shades*. Both books – in their very different ways – are the result of an enormous amount of time, expertise, thought and passion for Dylan's music on the part of their authors. Both deserve great respect. But both leave me puzzled by their dismissive attitude towards Dylan's performing art of the last few years. Apart from a nod in the direction of Woodstock 1994 and one or two other isolated instances, any recognition of the great renaissance in Dylan's live performance which has occurred since 1994 is disturbingly, one might say shockingly, absent from Michael Gray's book.

I remember being no less baffled a year or so ago, when I tried an experiment on three friends, all of them committed admirers of Dylan's music of long standing. I wanted to illustrate the greatness of Dylan's recent reinterpretations of his earlier songs, and chose for an example his performance of *'It's All Over Now, Baby Blue'* from Gothenburg, Sweden, on June 10, 1998. – You can find it on the bootleg CD *"At The Globe Arena"* – At that time I considered it to be the finest performance I'd ever heard of any song by any artist, and I still regard it as an example of Dylan's performance art at its most magnificent. I expected my friends to be entirely overwhelmed. Yet these were their responses –

Friend A: *"It sounds as though Dylan's just going through the motions. This seems to me to be a routine performance."*

Friend B: *"Where's the tune? That song has a wonderful tune, and he's destroyed it!"*

Friend C: *"This is an interpretation of such out-on-the-edge genius that it teeters on the brink of absurdity."*

As you might imagine, I was nonplussed. Even allowing for their unfamiliarity with it on this occasion, I strongly suspect that friends A and B will never come to share my sense of the transcendent majesty of this particular performance of *'Baby Blue.'* So what's going on here? I freely admit that I'm overwhelmed by the many wonderful performances offered by Dylan in recent years, yet it's the opinion of people I respect that these performances are tuneless, routine, or – in Michael Gray's words – rigidified into *"deadweight classics."*

I'm inclined to think that the problem arises because of our individual expectations when we approach Dylan's music – though this is hardly an original observation, given the roller-coaster history of its reception over the last thirty-odd years. Friends A and B had both been deeply satisfied, for decades, with the original 1965 studio recording of *'Baby Blue;'* so both were disconcerted by a new version which challenged their established and much loved perceptions of the song. I, on the other hand, had no particular fondness for earlier versions and indeed felt it to be a song that deserved better treatment than I'd so far heard and therefore there were no expectations to hinder my own appreciation of the Gothenburg masterpiece.

However, Michael Gray's expectations of Dylan's music, and the reasons why today's Dylan fails to live up to them, are more difficult to come to grips with – but at least he does state them clearly. For Michael Gray, Dylan's preoccupation with his old songs in live performances of the nineties is a sign of creative bankruptcy. *"It would be infinitely healthier,"* he writes, *"for today's Bob Dylan voice to be singing today's Bob Dylan songs. That's what artists do."* And he goes on to ask: *"Why isn't he, like any other authentic artist, bound up in his new work?'"*

What I want to suggest is that actually Dylan is doing exactly that. Dylan himself has given us some strong clues about his present view of his own art. With remarkable clarity, he's explained that his *old* songs are very much alive, for him; that his recordings should be regarded not as definitive performances, but as *"blueprints,"* and that those blueprints mark the beginnings of the lives of the songs, not the end. In other words, it would be entirely wrong to regard *'It's All Over Now, Baby Blue'* as a museum item filed away in some pigeon-hole of Dylan's past, to be taken out and dusted off when required for performance so that he and we can wallow in nostalgia. No, it's still one of *today*'s Bob Dylan songs, to be explored and invested with new meaning in performance. Whether or not we approve, and whether or not we're willing to accept it, it's primarily *this*, not the recording of new songs, which is currently the essential nature of Dylan's new work.

If we must have some kind of validating artistic precedent, then consider Constable's and Turner's frequent re-working of material from their old sketchbooks when creating some of their greatest paintings, often decades later. *New work* doesn't necessarily imply *new songs* for Dylan, any more than it implied *new subjects* for Constable or Turner.

What am I saying then? That all those endlessly repeated *'Tangled Up In Blue's'* and *'Highway 61's'* are great works of reinterpretative performing art, if only we had eyes to see and ears to hear? Well, no, mostly they aren't. But my impression is that for Dylan these old war-horses form part of a necessary structure which has the potential to allow him to paint – and repaint – his – real – masterpieces. I don't understand why this is, but it certainly works. Look at the transformation that has taken place in *'Trying To Get To Heaven,'* for example. The original recorded version had the seeds of greatness in it, but the song as currently performed is so meltingly beautiful, so heartrendingly human and so achingly poignant, that it must now rank among Dylan's very finest work.

At Newcastle in September 2000, Dylan produced performances of *'Wicked Messenger,'* *'Standing In The Doorway,'* and *'Forever Young'* which, alone, were worth paying £23 and travelling 100 miles to see and hear. Of course I'd have liked to hear magnificent performances of *'Times'* and *'Tangled Up In Blue'* as well, but as things turned out they were pretty poor. Well, so what? That's the nature of his art, whether we like it or not. I can accept that, in some way I don't understand, he saw those songs as necessary to the set list – and this time they didn't come off. That doesn't affect my opinion of Dylan as an artist because I don't make an assessment of any artist from his worst work, or even from some impossible-to-define average. An artist is known to be great through his *best* work. And Dylan's best work, today, lies in his magnificent reinterpretations of his *old* songs; in finding within and through those songs important new meanings, depths, perceptions and ways of musical expression, using the insight and self-knowledge gained through a lifetime of experience. It's a road that carries risks, but then the highway always was for gamblers – Bob Dylan said that. And the particular road that Dylan is currently following does have the sanction of another great artist –

"We shall not cease from exploration
And the end of all our exploring
Will be to arrive where we started
And know the place for the first time."

T.S. Eliot said that.

Published in issue #96, May 2001

"To this day, wherever great rock music is being made, there is the shadow of Bob Dylan."
Bruce Springsteen

"Songwriting is like fishing in a stream; you put in your line and hope you catch something. And I don't think anyone downstream from Bob Dylan ever caught anything."
Arlo Guthrie

"Dylan was the single most important force in maturing our popular music."
John Peel

"Dylan was a big hero…We admired him a lot. We liked him because he was a poet, a friend of Ginsberg, on the same road as Jack Kerouac."
Paul McCartney.

"He's been called everything from the voice of his generation to the conscience of the world. He rejects both titles. He's been, and still is, a disturber of the peace, his own, as well as ours."
Jack Nicholson

"He's the man. I think the world is a better place because he's in it."
Chrissie Hynde.

"Dylan's like the Beatles or the Eiffel Tower – he's just there, his presence is so strong that you don't see him anymore."
David Gray

"Bob Dylan! It's like trying to talk about the pyramids. What do you do? You just stand back and . . . gape."
Bono

"Seems like people are always waiting for the 'new' Bob Dylan. There will never be another Bob Dylan. There is only one. The one we have is the only one we'll ever need."
Patti Smith

"Listen, God, look closely after him. He's more fragile than most people."
Joan Baez.

Appendix

Recommended Book Resources

Biographies
Down The Highway – The Life Of Bob Dylan, by Howard Sounes – *Doubleday* 2001
Bob Dylan Behind The Shades Take Two, by Clinton Heylin – *Viking* 2000
No Direction Home, by Robert Shelton – *New English Library* 1986
Bob Dylan, by Anthony Scaduto – *Abacus* 1972 / *Helter Skelter Publishing* 1996

Studies of Dylan's work
Song & Dance Man III – The Art Of Bob Dylan, by Michael Gray – *Continuum* 2000
Performing Artist 1987- 2000, by Paul Williams – *not yet published*
Performing Artist 1974-1986, by Paul Williams – *Underwood-Miller* 1992
Performing Artist 1960- 1973 by Paul Williams – *Underwood-Miller* 1990

Tour Accounts
Razor's Edge, by Andrew Muir – *Helter Skelter Publishing* 2001
Like The Night, by C.P. Lee – *Helter Skelter Publishing* 1998
The Ghost Of Electricity, by John Bauldie – 1988
On The Road, by Larry Sloman – *Bantam Books* 1978

Photographic Books
Early Dylan, by Barry Feinstein, Daniel Kramer & Jim Marshall – *Pavilion* 1999
Bob Dylan, by Daniel Kramer – *The Citadel Press* 1967

Miscellaneous
Tangled Up In Tapes 4th Edition, by Glen Dundas – *SMA Services* 1999
Just Like Bob Zimmerman's Blues, by Dave Engel – *Amherst Press* 1997
A Life In Stolen Moments – Day By Day, by Clinton Heylin 1996
Dylan – Behind Closed Doors, by Clinton Heylin – *Penguin Books* 1995/96

Books by Bob Dylan
Drawn Blank, by Bob Dylan – *Random House* 1994
Lyrics 1962-1985 – *Random House/Jonathan Cape* 1987
Tarantula, by Bob Dylan – *Macmillan* 1971

Recommended Internet Resources

Official Bob Dylan Site (General information)
http://www.bobdylan.com/

Bob Links by Bill Pagel (Tour information and links)
http://www.execpc.com/~billp61/boblink.html/

Expecting Rain by Karl Erik Anderson (Everything Dylan)
http://www.expectingrain.com/

ISIS Magazine by Tracy Barker
http://www.bobdylanisis.com
P.O. Box 1182, Bedworth, Warwickshire CV12 0ZA England

Some Great Historic Live Performances

July 25 1965, Freebody Park, Newport RI, USA

After rehearsing through the night and sound checking the following afternoon, Dylan hit the stage running and roared out a warning that he wasn't going to work on Maggie's farm no more. His backing band for the day, The Paul Butterfield Blues Band, consisted of Michael Bloomfield on guitar, Sam Lay on drums, Jerome Arnold on bass, and were supplemented by Al Kooper on organ and Barry Goldberg on piano. No one, least of all, the band, could have been aware of the mayhem that was to follow!

Other than previous night's rehearsal, it seems that little or no thought had gone into this *electric* performance. In fact, Dylan's road manager at the time, Jonathan Taplin, has stated that the thought of playing electric at Newport was *"on a whim."*

Time alters people's perceptions, and recollections are often coloured by reading the thoughts and opinions of others. Therefore, the real reason for the audience reaction to this performance will never be known for sure. However, audio evidence seems to disprove theories about the music being too loud or the set too short. There is no doubt that some of the audience dissatisfaction was due to the brevity of the set. However, it was the sight of Folk hero Bob Dylan backed by electric instruments on hallowed ground at Newport that caused the greatest irritation.

The short electric set consisted of 'Maggie's Farm,' 'Like a Rolling Stone' and 'Phantom Engineer,' a high-speed blueprint for 'It Takes a Lot To Laugh, It Takes a Train to Cry.'

After what seemed like an eternity, the massed chanting of *"We want Dylan,"* brought the desired result, although even this crowd reaction might have had a double meaning. Did *"we want Dylan,"* mean we want *more*

Dylan, or we want the *real* Dylan?

Acoustic guitar in hand Dylan returns to the stage to say farewell to the folk fraternity with a poignant rendition of *'It's All Over Now Baby Blue.'* A further delay followed before the final song *'Mr Tambourine Man.'*

There is no doubt that Dylan was wounded by the audience reaction; was it then pure coincidence that four days later he would be in the recording studio cutting the hate filled *'Positively 4th Street'*?

This rather short concert set is available as part of a number of bootleg recordings including "Live In Newport 1965," "Quest For Newport" and "Folk Rogue."

September 3, 1965, Hollywood Bowl, Los Angeles, California, USA
Reviewed in full elsewhere in this anthology.

"It had to get there – with an electric band. It had to go that way for me, because that's where I started, and eventually it just had to go back to that." – Bob Dylan, 1977.

At this point in time the raging glory that would become Bob Dylan's electric set had not fully developed and the resulting experiment sounds like a cross between an acoustic and electric performance, which, in reality is exactly what it was.

This audio document is extremely important in helping us understand Dylan's development as an artist at this time. Available as a mono PA recording on the two-CD bootleg "From Newport To The Ancient Empty Streets In LA." Note – this CD also includes most of the Newport '65 set.

April 13, 1966, Sydney Stadium, Sydney, Australia
Reviewed in full elsewhere in this anthology.

This was the first concert on the

Australian leg of Dylan's 1966 world tour and only the second concert with drummer Mickey Jones. Dylan sounds fresh and performing solo seems much less of an effort than it at this juncture, the sheer power and tension that would develop as the tour progressed is not fully in evidence.

As with the September 3, 1965 Hollywood Bowl concert, this audio document is extremely important in helping us understand Dylan's development from acoustic troubadour to rock 'n' roll performer. Tonight's set closes with the only known 1966 tour performance of 'Positively Fourth Street.'

Available as a stereo PA recording on "Live Sydney '66." Also available on the eight-CD boxed set "Genuine Live 1966."

April 20, 1966, Festival Hall, Melbourne, Australia

Most of this performance is available as a bootleg recording and from the audio evidence, 'Just Like a Woman' alone would have been worth the entrance price of 1.55 Australian dollars.

Dylan sounds extremely stoned, slightly tired and is suffering from a cough. He also seems to have real or imaginary problems in keeping his acoustic guitar in tune and decides to use this to taunt the folk purists in the audience, by informing them the guitar is only borrowed and keeps going out of tune because it's a "folk music guitar."

This concert gives us a superb insight into how Bob Dylan can create success out of extreme adversity. An incomplete mono PA recording of this concert is available on various bootleg CDs, including the eight-CD boxed set "Genuine Live 1966."

May 17, 1966, Free Trade Hall, Manchester, England

Recorded for a possible live album and mis-labelled by an engineer, the electric half of this concert circulated amongst

collators for almost twenty years as Royal Albert Hall.

Definite proof has since emerged, however, that the historic "Judas" concert is in fact from Manchester Free Trade Hall, May 17, 1966. The electric half of this concert captures an artist completely at odds with a significant section of his audience, and the vitriolic exchanges between artist and audience makes this the most memorable concerts in the history of popular music. Dylan replied to non-believers verbally and more aptly through his music, which has been described as "a vortex of sheer noise" and "like a squadron of B-52s in a cathedral." Surely, nobody has ever made a more fabulously ominous sound than Bob Dylan and the Hawks did in 1966.

After a veritable plethora of bootlegs – mainly of the electric set only – the 1966 Manchester Free Trade Hall concert is at last available in full as an official release on "The Bootleg Series, Vol 4 – Bob Dylan Live 1966 – The 'Royal Albert Hall Concert'." It seems that even Sony Music Entertainment are willing to perpetuate a myth to sell product.

Prior to the official release, these concert tapes were also available on the two-CD bootleg "Guitars Kissing & The Contemporary Fix." All circulating concert material from 1966 is now available on the stunning 24-carat gold eight-CD boxed set "Genuine Live 1966."

December 4, 1975, Montreal Forum, Montreal, Quebec.

Without doubt, the best concert of the Rolling Thunder Revue, and many would say that 1975 Rolling Thunder was the best ever Dylan tour. Tonight's twenty-three-song set provides the bulk of the live footage for Dylan's epic film Renaldo and Clara including a stunning performance of 'Isis.'

Three songs from this concert were made available on the four-track Renaldo and Clara promo EP. Two of those songs appear on *"Biograph,"* with *'Romance In Durango'* making a third appearance on the b-side of the US single *'Jokerman.'* Although an audience recording of this concert circulates amongst collectors, it is not available on a bootleg CD.

November 16, 1979 Fox Warfield Theater, San Francisco, California, USA
Reviewed in full elsewhere in this anthology,

After accepting Christ into his life, a passionate Bob Dylan felt compelled to shout about his newfound beliefs from the rooftops, or at least from the stage at the Warfield Theater in San Francisco.

The final evening of this superb run of concerts, which saw the culmination of fourteen nights of growing confidence and steadily improving performances has to rate as a landmark concert in a career that is choc full of landmarks.

Taken from an audience tape, this concert is available as a two-CD bootleg recording *"Contract With The Lord."*

January 12, 1990, Toad's Place, New Haven, Connecticut, USA

Before embarking on his 1990 winter tour Dylan chose to rehearse his tour band at a seven hundred capacity club in Connecticut. The length of this show,

plus the song selection, makes it one of the most extraordinary concerts ever given by Bob Dylan.

For their eighteen dollars fifty, the attendees were treated to a show comprising four sets and fifty songs. The evening began at 8.45pm and went on until approximately 2.20am.

The set included many cover songs including *'Walk a Mile In My Shoes,'* *'Across The Borderline,'* *'I've Paid The Price,'* *'Help Me Make It Through The Night'* and Sprinsteen's *'Dancing In The Dark.'*

Available as an audience recording on two, two-CD sets *"Toad's Place Vol 1"* and *"Toad's Place Vol 2."*

March 11, 1995, Palac Kultury, Prague, Czech Republic.
Reviewed in full elsewhere in this anthology,

Bob Dylan has reinvented himself constantly throughout a career spanning forty years and a bout of 'flu now provided an opportunity to do so again. After delaying the start of his 1995 European tour by one day, Dylan turned adversity into splendour with an extraordinary guitarless performance that must rank as one of his finest concert moments.

Taken from an audience tape, this concert is available as a two-CD bootleg recording *"Bob Dylan – 12/- A Pound."*

Selected Bootleg Recordings

The first rock music bootleg was born in the summer of 1969 when a white-labelled record in a plain white sleeve hit a hand full of record stores in Los Angeles. This untitled collection of unreleased Dylan songs, which was soon to become known as *"Great White Wonder,"* was to spawn an industry that has survived to the present day. Since sound recordings did not receive copyright protection in the USA until February 15, 1972, these products received a wide distribution and business flourished. Even so, claims that various early incarnations of *"Great White Wonder"* sold 350,000 copies are a vast exaggeration!

During a recent court case involving Dylan, an RIAA official gave evidence stating that Bob Dylan was the single most pirated (sic) (substitute pirated for bootlegged) artist in America if not the world. His evidence concluded with the statement *"I am of the opinion that Mr Dylan is probably the most bootlegged artist in the history of the music industry."* And while that statement is factually incorrect – Beatles, Led Zeppelin and possibly the Rolling Stones take that accolade; his relentless touring has, in recent years, seen new Dylan titles 30% higher than those of the Beatles and 60% higher than the Stones. Therefore the slightly dubious honour of most bootlegged artist might soon be his.

The mystic and beauty that was the vinyl bootleg record has long since given way to the compact disc, and it is a selection of titles from this digital medium that are listed here. Fifty recommended bootleg CDs might seem a little excessive. However, since the arrival of the bootleg CD in 1986/'87 almost 900 Dylan titles have emerged! These discs have been chosen for a number of reasons including historical significance, sound quality and packaging. Plus, I happen to like them!

The Dylan's Roots *Skeleton* 1CD 1961
The Bootleg *Wanted Man Music* 1CD 1961
Finjan Club *Yellow Dog* 1CD 1962
Folksingers Choice *Yellow Dog* 1CD 1962
The Freewheelin' Bob Dylan Outtakes *Vigotone* 1CD 1962
Live In New York 1963 *Black Panther* 1CD 1963
Live In New York 1964 *Black Panther* 1CD 1964
From Newport To The Ancient Empty Streets In LA *Dandelion* 2CD 1964-65
Thin Wild Mercury *Music Spank* 1CD 1965-66
Genuine Live 1966 *Scorpio* 8CD 1966
The Genuine Basement Tapes Vols 1-5 *Scorpio* 1CD each 1967
Blood On The Tapes *Columbus* 1CD 1975
Songs For Patti Valentine *Wanted Man Music* 1CD 1975
Flagging Down The Double E's *The Razor's Edge* 2CD 1975
Tell It Like It Is *Spacematic* 1CD 1975
Creatures Void Of Form *The Razors Edge* 1CD 1976
Contract With The Lord *Silver Rarities* Parts 1 & 2 1CD each 1979
Solid Rock *Wanted Man Music* 2CD 1980
You Can't Kill An Idea – Part 1 / Part 2 *Silver Rarities* 1CD each 1981
Birds Nest In Your Hair *Rattle Snake* 2CD 1981
Rough Cuts *Gold Standard* 1CD 1983
Clean Cuts *Sick Cat* 1CD 1985
Precious Memories *Three Cool Cats* 1CD 1986
The Final Night And More *Dandelion* 2CD 1987
Stuck Inside Of New York *Kiss The Stone* 2CD 1988
Golden Vanity *Wanted Man Music* 1CD 1988-92
The Deeds Of Mercy *The Razors's Edge* 1CD 1989
All The Way Down To Italy *Great Dane*

2CD 1989
Staying Here With You *Wanted Man
Music* 2CD 1990
Toads Place Vol 1 / Toads Place Vol 2
Wanted Man Music 2CD each 1990
The First Supper / The Second Supper
Wanted Man Music 2CD each 1993
Great Woods *Wild Wolf* 2CD 1993
The Pedlar Now Speaks *The Razor's
Edge* 2CD 1995
Bob Dylan – 12/- A Pound no label
2CD 1995
F*** The Playlist: Briton II *Sterling
Sounds* 2CD 1995
White Dove *Dandelion* 2CD 1997
San Jose '98 *Dandelion* 2CD 1998
Eating Caviar In a King Sized Bed
Rattle Snake 2CD 1998
Highlands Of Worcester *Wild Wolf*
1CD 1999

The Lonely Graveyard Of My Mind
Dandelion 2CD 1999
Across The Borderline *Wild Wolf* 2CD
1999
Ace Of Clubs *Scorpio* 5CD 1999
Horsens Teater *Crystal Cat* 2CD 2000
Cardiff 2000 *Crystal Cat* 2CD 2000
Portsmouth – First Evening *Crystal Cat*
2CD 2000
Portsmouth – Second Evening *Crystal
Cat* 2CD 2000
London First Evening *Crystal Cat* 2CD
2000
London Second Evening *Crystal Cat*
2CD 2000
The Genuine Bootleg Series *Scorpio*
3CD various
The Genuine Bootleg Series Take 2
Scorpio 3CD various

Discography of Bob Dylan's official releases

As of May 2000, worldwide record sales for Bob Dylan were estimated to be approaching sixty million units. From the listing below, the RIAA have certified seventeen albums as gold, eight as platinum and four as multi platinum.

These albums are listed in order of preference as selected in a year 2000 ISIS readers' poll. Number of votes listed below. Albums in *Italics* indicate live recordings.

Album title	Released	Catalogue #	RIAA certified	votes
Blood On The Tracks	Jan 20,1975	PC 33235 – CK 33235	2xP	1225
Blonde On Blonde	May 16, 1966	C2L 41 – C2K 841	P	940
Highway 61 Revisited	Aug 30, 1965	CL 2389 – CK 9189	P	550
Time Out Of Mind	Sept 30, 1997	68556 – CK 68556	P	400
Desire	Jan 16, 1975	PC 33893 – CK 33893	2xP	215
Street Legal	June 15, 1978	JC 35453 – CK 35453	G	175
Oh Mercy	Sept 22, 1989	OC 45281 – CK 45281		160
John Wesley Harding	Dec 27, 1967	CL 2804 – CK 9604	G	145
Bringing It All Back Home	March 22, 1965	CL 2328 – CK 9128	G	120
Bootleg Series Vol 4: Live 1966	Oct 13, 1998	CK 65759		105
The Freewheelin' Bob Dylan	May 27, 1963	CL 1986 – CK 8786	P	95
Slow Train Coming	Aug 18, 1979	FC 36120 – CK 36120	P	73
Infidels	Nov 1, 1983	QC 38819 – CK 38819	G	69
Hard Rain	Sept 10,1976	PC 34349 – CK 34349	G	58
Planet Waves	Jan 17, 1974	S7E 1003	G	43
Another Side Of Bob Dylan	Aug 8, 1964	CL 2193 – CK 8993	G	42
The Times They A Changin'	Jan 13, 1964	CL 2105 – CK 8905	G	38
The Basement Tapes	June 26, 1975	C2 3368 2 – C2K 33682		33
World Gone Wrong	Oct 26, 1993	CK 57590		30
Self Portrait	June 8, 1970	C2X 30050 – CK 30050	G	29
The Bootleg Series Vol 1-3	March 26, 1991	C3K 47382	G	26
Shot Of Love	Aug 12, 1981	TC 37496 – CK 37496		22
Empire Burlesque	June 8, 1985	FC 40110 – CK 40110		19
Good As I Been To You	Oct 27, 1992	CK 53200		17
At Budokan	Nov 22,1978	40AP 1100 – C2K 36067	G	11
Nashville Skyline	April 9, 1969	CKS 9825 – CK 9825	P	11
MTV Unplugged	May, 2 1995	67000 – CK 67000	G	11
Saved	June 20, 1980	FC 36533 – CK 36533		11
New Morning	Oct 21, 1970	KC 30290 – CK 30290	G	10
Bob Dylan	March 19, 1962	CL 1779 – CK 8579	G	9
Pat Garrett & Billy The Kid	July 13, 1973	KC 32460 – CK 32460	G	5
Biograph	Oct 28, 1985	C5X 38830 – C3K 38830	P	5
Under The Red Sky	Sept 11, 1990	C 46794 – CK 46794		3
Before The Flood	June 20, 1974	S 201	P	2
Bob Dylan Greatest Hits Vol 2	Nov 17, 1971	KG 31120 – C2K 31120	5xP	2
Down In The Groove	May 31, 1988	OC 40957 – CK 40957		1
Greatest Hits Vol 3	Nov 15, 1994	CK 66783	G	1
Dylan	Nov 16, 1973	PC 32747 – CK 32747	G	0
Real Live	Dec 3, 1984	FC 39944 – CK 39944		0
Knocked Out Loaded	Aug 8, 1986	OC 40439 – CK 40439		0
Dylan And The Dead	Feb 6, 1989	OC 45056 – CK 45056	G	0
Bob Dylan Greatest Hits	March 27, 1967	KCL 2663 – CK 9463	5xP	0

For the purpose of this listing, we have included only those albums that have been officially released in *"all territories,"* i.e. those that have received world-wide release. At the time this list was compiled – September 1, 2001 – Bob Dylan had officially released forty-two albums world-wide. In recent years, an increasing number of *"best of"* CDs of Dylan material have been released in selected territories only. These include *"The Best Of Bob Dylan Volume 2"* – Europe only, *"Bob Dylan Live 1961-2000"* – Japan only, and *"The Essential Bob Dylan"* – USA only, to name but a few. Therefore, the above list does not include the album *"Masterpieces,"* which was released in March, 1978 in Japan – and later that year in Australia and New Zealand – only, but does include *"At Budokan,"* which was originally released in Japan only, but later gained world-wide release. The only album that has been released in all territories, but not included here is *"Bob Dylan – 30th Anniversary Concert."* For the purpose of this, and most other listings, this 1993 live tribute album is classified as "various artists."

Bob Dylan's last release, the Grammy Award wining *"Time Out Of Mind,"* has to date sold 1,800,000 units. A new Bob Dylan album *"Love And Theft"* will be released on September 11, 2001.

Notes

"The Freewheelin' Bob Dylan" – Very few copies of this vinyl record were released in the USA containing four alternative tracks. This item, which was quickly withdrawn, is the most collectable of all of Dylan's albums.

"Bringing It All Back Home" – This album was released in the Benelux countries as *"Subterranean Homesick Blues."* As most European – Columbia/Sony – CDs are currently manufactured in Holland, the album can often be found in other European countries, including the UK with this erroneous title.

"Highway 61 Revisited" – Japanese

and early USA pressings had a different version of *'From a Buick 6.'*

"Blonde On Blonde" – Columbia records lists the album as being released on May 16 1966. However, in his Dylan biography *Behind The Shades: Take Two,* Clinton Heylin states that a final overdub on *'Fourth Time Around'* was not recorded until June. Heylin also points out that the album did not enter the US charts until July 30, 1966, which would suggest a release date somewhat later than May 16. The Japanese pressings feature some slightly different mixes and extended fades on some tracks.

The original UK and USA releases of this album on CD – April 1987 – were nothing short of a disaster! The playing time of the CD was 71:00 minutes, which was a cut of almost two-minutes from the vinyl. The harshest cut of all was *'Sad Eyed Lady Of The Lowlands,'* which lost 32-seconds. The USA was quick to make amends and two subsequent pressings corrected the problem. The UK, however, was extremely slow to rectify the cuts. The best versions of this album are one of several special gold issues.

"Bob Dylan Greatest Hits" – UK and USA releases of this title have slightly different track listings.

"Bob Dylan Greatest Hits Vol 2" – Released in the UK under the title *"More Greatest Hits."* UK and USA releases have slightly different track listings.

"Dylan" – a.k.a *"A Fool Such As I."*

"Planet Waves" – Originally released by *Asylum* in the USA / *Island Records* in the UK. Later re-released on *Columbia/CBS.* This album was available for a short time in quadraphonic.

"Before The Flood" – Originally released by *Asylum* in the USA / *Island Records* in the UK. Later re-released on *Columbia/CBS.*

"Desire" – Available for a short time in quadraphonic.

"At Budokan" – Originally released on November 22, 1978 in Japan only. World-wide release April 23, 1979.

The first nine Dylan albums plus *"Greatest Hits"* were all available in mono. Note: The mono release of the *"Bob Dylan"* album sounds far better than the stereo release. *"Nashville Skyline"* was not available as a mono release in the USA. The mono version of *"Greatest Hits"* actually features the stereo mix tracks with the left and right channels combined rather than tracks taken from the original mono mix albums

.Mail Order

All Helter Skelter, Firefly and SAF titles are available by mail order from the world famous Helter Skelter bookshop.

You can either phone or fax your order to Helter Skelter on the following numbers:

Telephone: +44 (0)20 7836 1151 or Fax: +44 (0)20 7240 9880
Office hours: Mon-Fri 10:00am – 7:00pm,
Sat: 10:00am – 6:00pm, Sun: closed.

Postage prices per book worldwide are as follows:

UK & Channel Islands	£1.50
Europe & Eire (air)	£2.95
USA, Canada (air)	£7.50
Australasia, Far East (air)	£9.00
Overseas (surface)	£2.50

You can also write enclosing a cheque, International Money Order, or registered cash. Please include postage. DO NOT send cash. DO NOT send foreign currency, or cheques drawn on an overseas bank. Send to:

Helter Skelter Bookshop,
4 Denmark Street, London, WC2H 8LL, United Kingdom.
If you are in London come and visit us, and browse the titles in person!!

Email: helter@skelter.demon.co.uk
Website: http://www.skelter.demon.co.uk